OUR SHADOWED PRESENT

By the same author:

The Dynamics of Change: the Crisis of the 1750s and English Party Systems

Revolution and Rebellion: State and Society in England in the Seventeenth and Eighteenth Centuries

The Language of Liberty 1660–1832: Political Discourse and Social Dynamics in the Anglo-American World

Samuel Johnson: Literature, Religion and English Cultural Politics from the Restoration to Romanticism

English Society 1660–1832: Religion, ideology and politics during the ancien régime

EDITED:

The Memoirs and Speeches of James, 2nd Earl Waldegrave, 1742–1763

Ideas and Politics in Modern Britain

Reflections on the Revolution in France, by Edmund Burke

Samuel Johnson in Historical Context (jointly)

OUR SHADOWED PRESENT

Modernism, Postmodernism and History

J. C. D. Clark

Atlantic Books
London

First published in Great Britain in 2003 by Atlantic Books,
an imprint of Grove Atlantic Ltd

1 2 3 4 5 6 7 8 9

A CIP catalogue record for this book is
available from the British Library.

ISBN 1 84354 122 X

Typeset by FiSH Books, London

Printed in Great Britain by CPD, Ebbw Vale, Wales

Atlantic Books
An imprint of Grove Atlantic Ltd
Ormond House
26–27 Boswell Street
London WC1N 3JZ

CONTENTS

PREFACE

Is history at risk? Mankind's historical sense has created a Protean subject, sometimes grandiose, sometimes prosaic; yet beneath all its varieties lies the noble enterprise of locating ourselves in time, of visualizing and enjoying a fair ground and a goodly heritage. Historians had always disputed over methods and results, but profound changes in popular culture and in academic fashion (say some) now challenge the very activity that they shared: all contestants alike are said to be threatened with losing control of the broad acres for which they so eagerly fought each other. This book is an attempt to understand what is at stake.

If recent changes in history's role really are surrenders to a unique threat, perhaps it is now too late to rescue this mental dimension. Perhaps the self-destructiveness of some areas of academe has fed irreversible developments in popular culture so that the historical outlook itself is being regretfully eroded or joyfully abandoned. So it seems from the writings of certain historians, who implicitly update Marx's dictum: for them, the point is not to interpret the past but to change it, to mock, to ridicule or to parody. Yet it is only a recent undertaking to saw off the historical branch on which we still sit. How did we find ourselves in such a predicament? Is this anxiety justified?

We hardly know. Historians are so preoccupied with the daily detail of work on our historical estates that we sometimes fail to notice the silent revolutions beyond our walls. This book had many starting points, but took shape in an increasingly conscious response to deep shifts in those general assumptions that give historians their cues. The first of these cues was the unheralded decline of 'modernism', that secularizing project of the late nineteenth century, identified with material progress and with the new intellectual disciplines that claimed to explain it. Modernism enclosed both Marxist and Whiggish approaches, yet their curious congruence, and substantial collapse, are now widely acknowledged. So is the waning of the influence of the modernist social sciences. In a famous article of 1976,[1] Lawrence Stone described twentieth-century historical writing as a series of phases in which history was dominated in turn by adjacent disciplines: economics, sociology, psychology, demography, anthropology. Since he wrote, their exaggerated claims had profoundly weakened: once-vainglorious social sciences had either moved closer to history, as with economics;[2] or had come to seem self-parodic, as with anthropology; or had been exposed as unverifiable, as with psycho-analysis. History would re-emerge as the master discipline if historians were able to steer among the cross-currents of that ocean which their social-scientific colleagues had so vainly commanded to recede.

Yet historians did not inherit the earth after the decay of modernism, and here was my second cue. For so preoccupied had they been with the inadequacies of modernism's positivist, functionalist or materialist-reductionist approaches that they had failed to provide against the growth in the opposite direction of an ultra-idealism. Much in postmodernism, as in modernism, should of course be taken as read by historians (as I well recall it was in Herbert Butterfield's Peterhouse, before we attended to postmodernism by name); but as a polemical project, postmodernism is quite different. This book is not a systematic history of that doctrine. Indeed, it would be too slippery a subject: since postmodernism expresses an extreme subjectivism it lacks the clear boundaries that history needs and finds expression under other labels as well, notably post-structuralism and deconstructionism. Since they all collapse into a common solipsism, these schools' claims to distinctness will be disregarded here.

This book offers some historical responses to both modernism and postmodernism. It makes, for example, the historical claim that post-modernism is only another 'stadial' theory, claiming itself to be a new stage and identified by a transition from modernism (but since historians had just dismantled the old divide between 'pre-modern' and 'modern', this was implausible). It argues that modernists and postmodernists (both having historically inadequate understandings of their own positions) are not as different as they think. The decline of Marxism, in particular, encouraged postmodernists to defend, within their now-fragmented private spheres, and behind subjectivist smokescreens, some programmatic commitments that look oddly familiar. Such beliefs are not sacrosanct.

This book takes a middle position in pursuing an historical understanding of much-debated contemporary issues. I have tried where possible to avoid focusing on individuals, since I have aspired to hate the sin while loving the sinner (and have sometimes succeeded). I also argue from the specific case. Discussions like this too often overlook the pattern on the ground, swept as it is by shadows cast by wider and cloudier attitudes and assumptions that have no names. I have preferred to locate my enquiries within this larger landscape of popular culture, and to examine national, ideological and geopolitical issues that concern us deeply as well as the abstract matters of principle that they raise.

Postmodernism is still in the ascendant, and so succeeds in having itself analysed and praised in its own terms: as rescuing historical studies from modernist philistinism, as reinstating religion, cherishing traditions to the point of reinventing them, privileging popular memory and the historical experience of everyman. This book challenges that self-praise and questions some of the results that flow from it. If modernism and postmodernism can be historically explained, the larger purpose of this book is to explore alternatives, and to offer historical analysis rather than rhetorical rebuttal. It does not argue that the barbarians are at the gates; but it claims the candour of detachment to point out that the successive worlds of the modernists and the postmodernists alike have been troubled by a wind of change that is hostile to them both: unnoticed, our weather-vanes have turned, and now point neither East nor West. Perceptive readers may therefore sense that at the intellectual centre of this book is a subject that seldom directly appears. They would not be wrong.

Callaly Castle, Northumberland
December 2002

ACKNOWLEDGEMENTS

These chapters had diverse origins: I am grateful to a number of patrons and publishers for their encouragement and, where necessary, for permissions to reprint material. I am also indebted to a wide variety of audiences and readers for their comments and advice; if I have inadvertently failed to acknowledge a debt, I offer apologies. Chapter 1 was written at the invitation of my friends and colleagues Nathan Tarcov and the late François Furet at the Committee on Social Thought in the University of Chicago, and was a contribution to their conference on 'The Meaning of Modern Revolutions': I am grateful both for their comments and for those of the late Peter Laslett. Chapter 2 originated with a conference on national identity held at the Institute of Historical Research, London, organized by Tony Claydon and Ian McBride, and was first published in the *Historical Journal*; I am grateful for the help of Jeremy Black, John Gillingham, Marjorie Morgan and John Pocock. I owe a particular debt to Patrick Wormald, who first taught me to appreciate the significance of Anglo-Saxon history. Chapter 3 was written at the invitation of Dale Van Kley for a conference on patriotisms and nationalisms at Ohio State University. Chapter 4 arose from a conference on the history of British radicalism at the University of Hull, organized by Glenn Burgess and Matthew Festenstein. It was read by Victor Bailey, Stewart Brown, James Burns, Richard W. Davis, Jacob Ellens, Gareth Stedman Jones, William Thomas and Anthony Waterman. Chapter 5 was written at the creative insistence of Niall Ferguson, and first appeared in the collection he edited, *Virtual History: Alternatives and Counterfactuals.* The *Historical Journal* first published a version of Chapter 6, and in its writing I was indebted to Margot Finn, Thomas Heilke, John Morrill, Stephen Presser, Benjamin Sax and Reba Soffer. Günther Lottes provoked me to reflect on the subject of Chapter 7, which was first delivered as a paper to the Sonderforschungsbereich Errinerungskulturen that he directed at the University of Giessen, and to the Institut für Europäische Geschichte, Mainz. For comments I am grateful to my hosts and to Richard J. Evans, Harold James, Daniel Johnson, Patrick O'Brien and Hans-Ulrich Wehler; for references I am also indebted to Carl Strikwerda, Ted Wilson and James Woelfel.

OUR SHADOWED PRESENT

INTRODUCTION

The dead hand of history

I.   THE NATURE OF THE POSTMODERNIST PROJECT

Noel Coward's *London Pride* is a song about London in the Blitz. It is set in 'our shadowed present', and that evocative phrase gives this book its title. The shadow that falls, as the rhythm of the song pauses, is on one level the shadow of the bomber: shadowed means threatened. But shadowed and its related words have other resonances in English, too. Shadowed also means followed, purposefully followed by someone with an interest in one's fate, an interest that may be benevolent or malign. It also invokes a cognate term, foreshadowed, which means to presage, to suggest or indicate something to come. People who are shadowed or foreshadowed in these senses stand in a relationship to the past and the future that is now often explicitly denied: we are invited to think that we have emancipated ourselves from our pasts.

Yet this is a novel attitude to adopt, at least in Europe in the last two millennia. Ordinarily, people have pictured each generation as part of a procession, emerging out of the past and winding into the future; and this image has been regarded as a source of strength. That is what happens in Noel Coward's song. London present, London under dire threat, is upheld by a history that is especially meaningful at a moment of crisis. It is in part a religious image, often generalized beyond the specific message of the churches, just as Charles Dickens's ghosts of Christmas past, Christmas present and Christmas yet to come in *A Christmas Carol* offer the record of happiness, express a dire present warning, and yet hold out the prospect of future redemption. It is this that has made people regard the past as 'their' past, the future as 'their' future.

To have a sense of the numinous and unextinguished quality of objects and places is a frequent and normal part of human experience; and this sense is generally held to be a reaction to the historical rootedness of things themselves. Everyday objects, institutions, buildings, or the natural world at the scene of momentous (often evil) events are commonly said to evoke such feelings. Cities too can create in their inhabitants a sense of a corporate personality with enduring characteristics, benign or malign. All this suggests the persistence of the past not in the form of 'survivals', implying anachronistic and fragmentary remains or relics, but as a vast and immanent present.[1] If this sense of immanence is often taken for granted by those who experience it, and seldom discussed, it becomes dramatically noticeable if contrasted with areas of the world like the American mid-west, sufficiently populated yet historically empty. Memory itself, and its processes, demand the sympathy of the historian.[2]

It has until recently been assumed that the roles which we act out in our lives are historical roles, and for states as for individuals a historical sense is commonly claimed. Dean Acheson expressed this assumption in 1962 when he observed that 'Great Britain has lost an empire and has not yet found a role'.[3] However correct the analysis, it is perhaps ironic that in the years since Acheson's speech, the United States itself has been influenced by a general shift of assumptions which has slowly weakened its previous sense of identity, its relation to its own past; and this is arguably part of a wider movement that is visible in Western Europe also.

In the enclosed worlds of literary scholarship and philosophy we know this fashion by the name of postmodernism,[4] but there may be far wider social changes in attitude and outlook of which postmodernism in these narrowly academic fields would then be only a part. We still lack an accurate sense of what that wider movement is, and we lack a single term to identify it. Technically we might call it de-historicization, since it involves the foreshortening and even the discarding of the historical dimension. More generally we might call it presentism, since it is a privileging of the present that provides the movement with its attractive ideal.

By whatever name it is known, the movement has made important modifications to a prior world view, whether at the high level of theory or at the low level of assumptions that seep into every intellectual exchange. It has also generated rhetorical hostility, and the denunciations against it, as well as the phenomenon itself, demand historical explanation rather than equally rhetorical endorsement or denial. Within the USA, these denunciations take a particular form. In 1997 James Ceaser, a professor of political science at the University of Virginia, published a book entitled *Reconstructing America*. It began:

> If it were acceptable in a work of modern scholarship to rise with indignation in the defense of one's country, I would begin this book with a simple call to arms: it is time to take America back. It is time to take it back from the literary critics, philosophers, and self-styled postmodern thinkers who have made the very name 'America' a symbol for that which is grotesque, obscene, monstrous, stultifying, stunted, leveling, deadening, deracinating, deforming, rootless, uncultured, and – always in quotation marks – 'free'.[5]

All these terms were quoted from the postmodern writers who had, Ceaser regretfully admitted, come to dominate US culture. Thanks to the postmodernists, he believed, his countrymen inhabit a present that is present in the fullest sense: its past is held to be irrelevant except as a source of the characteristics Ceaser listed.

In the USA, such issues are fought out as contests for the control of a 'civil religion', and they take different forms elsewhere. In general, they have in common some doctrines expressed at the level of high theory. Postmodernism is the most theoretically expressed version of a rejection of the historical. This rejection is a consequence of the way in which postmodernism has set itself against what it takes to be 'modernist' ideas of truth and objectivity, replacing what it sees as a set of grand narratives claiming objective authority with a diverse pattern of localized narratives and fluid identities. Postmodernism therefore defines itself against 'positivism', which it associates with the scientific method that is itself held to underpin 'modernism'. Positivism, materialism, production and false claims to objectivity are held to characterize modernism.[6] Consumption rather than production is at the heart of the postmodern vision, and the commercialization of culture geared (or so it is alleged) to the diverse demands of a mass consumer market. The politics of class, based on production, everywhere gives way to the politics of cultural identity, built around consumption.[7] Because 'truth' is made problematic, placed within accusatory inverted commas, history is assimilated to myth, fiction and advertising (and also, necessarily, to propaganda).[8]

Narrative (involving history) now assumes a key role. Postmodernism collapses a grand narrative into a collection of little narratives, and within those little narratives the passage of time, and the differences created by the passage of time, are hardly important. A 'performance' of *King Lear* contains within it a narrative, but it is a narrative isolated from history. Each 'performance' is free-standing, able to be realized and assessed as an isolated episode. Each 'performance' may be different, and each has the freedom to be different, to offer a different interpretation of Shakespeare's text. For these reasons it is of little importance when any particular performance of *King Lear* takes place. If Lear were a real person, it would matter greatly whether we place him in the ninth century or the nineteenth; but this significance is what postmodernism denies to chronology. Postmodernism's emancipated world becomes timeless.

Postmodernism is also an essentially secular doctrine: if its aim is to destroy the 'grand narratives', it must of necessity define itself against that grandest of narratives that purports to set out the story of man's creation, fall and redemption. Postmodernism can therefore draw support from the sociological convention of describing 'modern' societies as secularized. Religious identity was once a potent source of a sense of historical bearings: it underwrote individual identity in a way that turned history into a procession, and a procession set within a wider providential scenario. The 'long march of everyman' initially had much of the quality of a pilgrimage. Membership of a church, too, once located an individual within that denomination's account of its origins, its purposes, its self-definitions, its trajectory over time, and its cosmic destiny.[9]

Churches rivalled nation states as historical vehicles for human consciousness, and often surpassed nations in that respect. Churches acting in association with nations gave even more powerful endorsement to man's perspectives on the past. The growing separation of Church and State, formally avowed in statute and delivered in practice by the market, therefore produces a culture that is not only officially secularized, but also silently de-historicized. Within this perspective, what may be distinctive about recent decades is that the intelligentsia has finally accepted capitalism, while finally rejecting religion. The combination of economic conservatism and cultural reformism becomes the characteristic intellectual formation of the present, and it is one which, according to its critics, is deeply hostile to public morality, to civic humanism, to duty, and to the historic sense.[10] Lifelong reformers who have at last accepted the market compound for their sin by blaspheming against their ancestral gods. For them, History did not deliver Utopia and History is therefore to be abolished.

Yet reformers as well as conservatives can be found who deplore this trend: they object that a society which de-emphasizes its past is one which, paradoxically, de-emphasizes its future also. Grand schemes of social reform, previously framed by liberals or socialists and each with a clear historical genealogy, mapped out a temporally specific picture of a better society. However optimistic, these schemes were clearly located in time and had clear temporal goals. Within a postmodern idiom, reforming initiatives tend to focus merely on erasing symbols or institutions that are designated 'old'; these postmodern schemes tend to say little or nothing about the new social forms that are intended to flourish once some undergrowth of prejudice has been cleared. Debates about the desirability of outcomes are less won than avoided (or even suppressed).[11] Politics becomes much less interesting: it seems that there are no longer any real options.

Everywhere, argue its critics, we see the results of this presentism. In area after area of social life, observers complain that cultural continuity hangs by a thread. At risk, allegedly, are the complex, composite identities and institutions built up in a former era. At a level below the state, many large cooperative enterprises like churches, political parties and trade unions are in numerical decline: it is often remarked that society increasingly comes to be made up of pressure groups whose loyalties are to a single cause, and these groups demand that this characteristic be reflected in historical writing.

Politicians thus increasingly favour an ahistorical vision. In 1999, President Clinton condescendingly described the parties to the conflict in Northern Ireland as being like 'two drunks in a bar', unable to break an addiction to a conflict created by six hundred years of history. The British government chose to mark the millennium by building an exhibition hall, the Millennium Dome: instructions were given that the Dome contain no reference to the national past, or to the person whose anniversary was commemorated. The Dome accurately captured a movement.

Increasingly, complaints are being voiced that history as a subject for instruction in schools is being marginalized or redefined. In so far as students still study history, they do so in later and later time-frames: in History Departments in US universities, courses on Hitler and the Holocaust attract hundreds of students, while courses on ancient Rome, or the Reformation, attract mere handfuls. In Britain, medieval history was withdrawn from the GCSE syllabus in 1997, and a controversial attempt made to drop Anglo-Saxon history from the A level syllabus of one examining board in 1999.[12] Other countries share similar experiences. Without argument, the assumption has taken root that events and episodes are more 'relevant' to the present the closer they are to it in time. The old idea of an engagement with an historical record which was independent of the pupil but determinative of the pupil's life has been implicitly challenged by a new set of teaching terms, including 'critical skills' and 'empathy'.

Neither seems objectionable on the surface. They may be used, however, in quite new ways. It has been asked whether the purpose of inviting the uncritical and unskilled to exercise 'critical skills' is rather to give students the impression that the historical record as presented in their books is false or partial. 'Empathy' presupposes the possibility of immediate access to the real meaning of the past, without wrestling with the arcane, biased, 'constructed', 'invented' apparatus of historical writing. Such implications form the present-day version of the Reformation rejection of the authority of the priest and the intermediary role of the Church. Individuals, even individual children, are supposed to have all the faculties required to recover 'their' past, 'their' identity. In place of the Reformation idea of the priesthood of all believers, we now have everyman his own historian. Each person has a story to tell: by implication, each story is to be different.[13]

Different societies experience different symptoms of presentism. In the United States the separation of Church and State, and the sociological orthodoxy of secularization in the early twentieth century, led to an attempt to formulate a secular substitute of uplifting culture, defined by a canon of 'great texts'. This could only be effective for a time. Soon, the quasi-scriptural status of this canon attracted criticism rather than disarmed it: if the canon were sacrosanct, it became a more attractive goal to appropriate it, to delete its previous components and to insert new ones. It is now commonplace to identify the leading characteristic of these new insertions as being the expression of the self-interest of some minority group, but a second characteristic expresses an even lower common denominator: the new insertions are normally in later and later time-frames. The antiquity of the canon is as much of an affront as any other characteristic. In response, defenders of the canon establish its importance by asserting the eternal and so timeless value of its components: they, too, de-historicize what they defend.[14] Taken out of their diverse and alien historical contexts, the authors in the canon become subtly Americanized, conscripted to fight the cultural battles of the present-day United States.

Presentism in popular culture involves a reversion to a more restricted mental world: it is as if the Renaissance invention of perspective were progressively forgotten, and everyman again depicted his physical surroundings in two dimensions instead of three. A characteristic of recent American speech patterns is, appropriately, the reduction of discourse to the present tense. If a past episode is brought to mind, it is as if it were replayed in the present tense, just as some old television programme is repeated years later. Acceptance into a presentist culture makes all things present. What is disregarded by presentist culture is by definition dead. Effective disparagements within popular American discourse are now the phrases 'that's old' and 'that's history'. 'That's old' does not mean 'that originated some time ago', but 'that is vexatious'. 'That's history' does not mean 'that is important because it has made us what we are'; it means 'that is laughably irrelevant to us'. What is different is absurdly, ridiculously so, not to be spoken of except disparagingly.

This wider willingness to disparage history stands behind the characteristic tone of some recent academic writing: even some widely admired historians address their subject not in order to do justice to the past but to satirize it. It is as if present society, with its passionate new affirmations, increasingly hates past societies for being different. Moderns still want the past to be (in Whiggish fashion) the ratification of the present; when they find it otherwise, they do not ignore it, but repudiate it. The intelligentsia of the present age characteristically does not turn away from the past with indifference; it reaches back into the past to silence its message.

Academic phenomena like these may be symptoms of a wider movement. Ours is often held to be an era of cultural dissociation: social groups grow apart; old loyalties fail. New minorities are defined for whom old symbols of identity are made symbols of their predicament. The political process by which that reinterpretation of symbols is promoted draws strength from what is understood as an academic ratification. In the Whig history prevalent until the mid twentieth century, the past ratified an historically located present; in postmodern history, the past ratifies a present made new by the attempted elimination of all reference to the past. Ideological revolutions have often entailed a systematic erasure of some particular system of ideas held to be antithetical to the new order, as French Jacobinism entailed a programme of de-Christianization, and as German Nazism entailed the elimination of international Jewry; postmodernism is new in that the enemy is defined more vaguely, or more extensively, as 'the past' itself. We need to understand historically what is meant by that anti-historical project, how it has arisen, in order to predict how it may develop.

What are the characteristic approaches of the postmodernist to historical problems? Two should be noted, and they are significantly different. The first is more indebted to older objectivist explanatory schemes. Human affairs are held to be stadial, to have progressed through a series of historically demonstrable stages. They have now reached the final stage: the objective evolution of historical processes has brought history's problems to an end. History in this sense is merely a repository of problems, illegitimately surviving to trouble the living, but deserving of dismissal or debunking rather than respectful attention. The only thing needed to emancipate oneself from them is an awakening to reality: a reality in which we can abolish the grip of the past on the present by adopting a public doctrine which corresponds to 'postmodernity'. Postmodernism both describes the historical phase in which we now are, and is also emancipatory.

Emancipation is, of course, a project with much older origins. It can be traced at least to the eighteenth-century rejection of the norms imposed by patrician custom and convention. As Rousseau's *Emile* instructed its readers,

The whole sum of human wisdom consists in servile prejudices: our customs are nothing more than subjection and restraint. The member of the civil state is born, lives, and dies in slavery; at his birth he is sown up in swaddling cloaths, at his death he is nailed in a coffin; so long as he preserves the human form, he is fettered by different institutions.[15]

In recent years, Rousseau's argument has taken a different form, and one which shows that presentism is not a project of one political group alone. In an article of 1989 and a book of 1992, Francis Fukuyama classically argued that the end of the Cold War meant the triumph of a public ideology indistinguishable from that of the United States, 'an unabashed victory of economic and political liberalism'. Moreover, that ideology was no ideology, in the sense that Marxism and Fascism had been ideologies. It was a series of self-evident truths, which would be naturally and uncontentiously absorbed everywhere. Unlike other ideologies, its victory would not be clearly defined, polemically or militarily: it would be the universal and diffusive acceptance of a set of self-evident assumptions, as other and sharply defined ideologies collapsed. It would be 'the universalization of Western liberal democracy as the final form of human government'.[16]

The wide reception of this analysis suggested that the postmodern project to bring about the end of history joined hands with modernist America's complacency about its values. Fukuyama's message was so quickly and widely received and applauded within the USA because it had been well rehearsed already. Emancipation had been a major theme in history from the 1760s, and had been systematized by that figure of the 1930s, Henry Steele Commager, in his book of 1978, *The Empire of Reason: How Europe Imagined and America Realized the Enlightenment*. Yet far from being non-ideological, as Fukuyama claimed, the American project appears from the outside deeply ideological because historically conditioned. How US public doctrine escaped being analysed as an ideology is an important question.[17] But without this ancient historical foundation, postmodernism would not have enjoyed the influence it has had in American culture.

Fukuyama went further, not merely celebrating US history but implicitly undermining alternative models. For him the 1950s modernist trope of the 'end of ideology' meant, in the title of his article, 'The End of History' itself. History is depicted throughout its text in the most disparaging language. History was something that 'the vast bulk of the Third World remains very much mired in'. Unless the Soviet Union followed the path 'staked out by Western Europe forty-five years ago', it would remain 'stuck in history'. Large-scale military conflict would in future only occur between states 'still caught in the grip of history'.[18] The public doctrine of the USA was still emancipationist, but now in the widest and most vainglorious sense: its object was to emancipate mankind from history as such.

This purposefulness was revealed in Fukuyama's argument about history's stages. 'To say that history ended in 1806' with the battle of Jena, as he argued that Hegel had rightly claimed, 'meant that mankind's ideological evolution ended in the ideals of the French or American Revolutions'. He did not distinguish historically between the two. Nevertheless, his sense of the nature of 'the West' was clearly an extension of what he understood as the nature of 1776: the American Revolution, that is, as viewed through the eyes of present-day US public doctrine. He even went so far as to declare that 'the egalitarianism of modern America represents the essential achievement of the classless society envisioned by Marx'.[19] Envisioned, but not realized. For Fukuyama as for Commager, if Europe imagined the Enlightenment, the USA achieved it. History, as the archetypal modernist Henry T. Ford had put it, was 'more or less bunk'.[20] Fukuyama, like Ford, summed up his country's ideology.

The second approach of the presentists is different. They omit any rigid logic of stages, and begin from a subjectivist account of identity. They assume that the grand errors of the past were oppressive because they were unifying, and they offer a pluralized alternative. The key terms in their vocabulary are 'identity', 'self-fashioning', 'construction', 'invention', and 'performance'. Their analysis is designed to produce a particular variety of usable past. It depicts a past which is indeed different from the present, but different because it was malleable, unstable, in flux; its identities 'constructed', its traditions 'invented', its structures 'imagined', its individuals 'self-fashioned'. Identities, traditions, institutions, personal characters that the postmodern commentator happens to dislike are depicted as being built on sand. They are the result of 'mystification', the result of deceit and manipulation by (usually unspecified) ruling elites in the past. As soon as the deceit is unmasked, mankind will realize that it is in fact free already, free to adopt any and every identity, tradition, institution or personal character it wishes. Postmodernism, we might say, is the historical ideology that corresponds to the plural society.[21]

The purposiveness of this project might encourage doubts as to whether the object of pluralism is to extend genuine respect to fundamentally different cultures and value systems. It suggests instead that the covert object of pluralism is to invoke those other cultures to diminish the authority of the host culture, to undermine its claims to reverence and replication by locating it as merely one among many alternatives. Confirmation is offered by the way in which, on a personal level, postmodernism is turned to as the appropriate ideology for groups that have indeed emancipated themselves, or think that they have done so. Ours is an unusual era in this respect, in that the area of unfettered choice has extended to sexuality itself: homosexual conduct has been made emblematic of emancipation, just as heterosexual conduct has been made emblematic of the arbitrary oppression of tradition. Self-fashioning has been taken to its ultimate conclusion, for this is the age of the plastic surgeon, who allows pop stars apparently to change race, and allows the unhappy and confused apparently to change sex.

These are trivial examples, however symptomatic. There are weightier reasons for thinking that presentism is a novel ideology rather than an insight into the nature of things. We now confront serious manifestations of the breakdown of the historical manner of analysing and dealing with the world's problems.

The early and mid twentieth century was characterized by differently framed attempts to suppress ancient identities and to establish secular republics. Middle Eastern states like Turkey, great continental empires like the USSR and the USA, emergent Asian and African nations, notably in the Indian subcontinent, sought 'modernity' through a separation of the religious and the secular. Religions (historically grounded religions) were to fade away as the secular republic, premised on secular ideologies, emerged to prominence. Those ideologies were to different degrees ahistorical, but tended to become more ahistorical over time, and have ended in a set of attitudes which are openly anti-historical. Such a de-historicized political vision now confronts a world the political conflicts of which suggest that both the modernist and the postmodernist political tide is everywhere receding.

Conflicts based on historically conceived religious, ethnic and nationalist differences (these being normally related) are everywhere visible: in Northern Ireland, in Turkey, in the conflict between India – with the militant Hindu nationalism of the Bharatiya Janata Party – and Pakistan, influenced by Islamic fundamentalism.[22] In Eastern Europe, the chief agent in the fall of communism was the Roman Catholic Church, a fall that western European political scientists markedly failed to predict. In what remains of the USSR, the Russian Orthodox Church plays a central role in resurgent Russian nationalism. In the internal politics of the USA, conflicts over public morality and ethnicity are at the heart of an otherwise limited political debate.

Just as the secular republic generally failed to produce social harmony, so there is no simple relation between religious or ethnic difference and political mobilization. Nevertheless, these conflicts cannot be understood and addressed without a knowledge of the historical antecedents which preceded attempts to erase the past as inconvenient. Historians and others who play at politics in this field play with fire. National identities which are indeed invented in the postmodernists' sense, like Celtic 'nationalism', constructed in and after the nineteenth century on bogus racialist theories, lead to bloodshed. So do modern or postmodern theories that repress and deny national differences which are all too obvious, as communism did in Tito's Yugoslavia. Doctrines that deny the past will not make it go away, and, as we shall see, postmodernists have not escaped theirs.

II.   WHAT IS THE LEGITIMATE FUNCTION OF HISTORY?

It might be suggested that the historical sense is one of the distinctions between civilization and barbarism. Claude Lévi-Strauss argued that 'The characteristic feature of the savage mind is its timelessness'; the 'great civilizations of Europe and Asia', by contrast, 'have elected to explain themselves by history'. Primitive societies were based on an attempted denial of history: they sought 'to make the states of their development which they consider "prior" as permanent as possible'.[23] The savage mind has been said to inhabit an 'island of time', with no structured sense of a past before that of the individual's parent (or, at most, grandparent).

It may indeed be that the leading characteristic of barbarism is not violence or insecurity but historical amnesia, the imprisonment of mankind's ancient self within a two-dimensional present, the invention of a world without legacy and without foresight. To destroy the distinction between myth and history is to revert to that subtle, carefully structured world-view that Lévi-Strauss termed totemism. The controversies over postmodernism and over the presentism of popular culture both reveal, however, that the ahistorical vision is not confined to 'savages' in 'primitive' societies. Much evidence suggests that it is, on the contrary, a way of picturing the world which is widespread, and becoming more widespread, in more affluent societies.

Its advance also produces a present without religion as we have understood it, for Christianity did not arise spontaneously as a result of some innate and timeless religious sense. It arose from man's engagement with divine revelation, a revelation, in turn, that was made within history, and the record of which was transmitted within history. Religion as understood in Europe was not based on subjective intuition but on claims of objective command, and on the historical preservation of the record of that command. A de-historicized mental universe must also be an atheistic one.

There is another way in which presentism is no substitute for the historical sense. Everyday usage misleads us when it invites us to 'look forward' or blames us for not doing so. The future is a blank, the present a fleeting moment in which we cannot stay. We live in the past, and our only choice is between alternative pasts which might supply our mental furniture. We walk backwards into an unknowable future, and what distinguishes us is only whether we are myopic or long-sighted as we do so. What makes the future recognizable as we enter it is nothing substantive in the idea of 'the future' itself, which recedes continually beyond our grasp, but rather the continuities in ourselves and our contemporaries, continuities established by our historical sense. To look forward, to display foresight, to show prudence is not to penetrate the future, for the future is and must always remain to us a featureless silence; it is to reflect intelligently on the past, and to understand what lessons can and cannot be learned from it.

The self which makes these judgements is not born 'free' in the sense of 'timeless'. Personal identity is established largely by history, by the persistence within an individual of a set of experiences and learned ways of reacting. To lose one's memory is not emancipation but a serious mental disorder, for without memory we cannot function as ourselves. If a society loses its history it has the same effect on a larger scale: that society could now have only a disembodied existence. It would have lost all those many things which made it itself.

The formation of personal identity reminds us how history is a mediation between two activities which, in balance, are essential. On the one hand, we look to the past for practical guidance. Obviously, the problems we face are historically structured: only by knowing the story so far can we have any idea of what to do next. On the other hand, we address the past in order to escape from it. Much of our waking mental activity, and our dreams, may be concerned with our efforts to cope with unhappiness and conflict, to digest it, to forget it by achieving a correct understanding of it. Just as the individual forgets his childhood, or remains always a child; forgets distress, or is overwhelmed by cumulative grief; so societies seek to be emancipated from tragedies and unhappinesses which are more immense only by being more general. Why else do we have such a stream of books about the Western Front in the First World War, or the Holocaust in the Second?

Yet if these are two legitimate functions of history, each has its inbuilt vice. History understood as practical guidance alone is quickly self-defeating, for how do we know the right questions to put to the oracle? Only a fuller understanding allows us to shape helpful questions – an historical understanding, in other words, that has not been formed already by a utilitarian programme to interrogate the past only for helpful answers. We do indeed have a term for such a programme: we call it law. It can be conducted with intelligence, with scrupulous attention to detail, even with (in some practitioners) a desire for justice; but law is not history. Law ignores what makes the past special, what makes it different, what, in other words, creates difficulties for us as its heirs. A society which sees itself as unconstrained by the past – undisciplined by duty, by morality, by honour, by custom, by religious aspiration – will therefore be a society with many lawyers and much litigation. That is indeed the society in which we now live.

History's second function is also legitimate: not to remember the past for present advantage, but to forget it. Yet this too is perilous if carried further than custom allows. For the past is not some remote and abstract catalogue of names and dates, but the very fabric of individual identity. Talk of rejecting the past, looking to the future or living in the present can therefore never be more than rhetoric. Men are made up of past experiences: the short-term past, the medium-term past, and the long-term past. For individuals as for nations, the most formative events are not necessarily the most recent: they may come early in the life of either. We cannot be burdened with the full detail of our pasts, cursed with the gift of total recall: that would place us in the position of Borges's *Funes the Memorious*. But to go to the opposite extreme is to be in the position of Robert Musil's *The Man without Qualities*. To forget our history is not to be free, but to be mad. Far from making us free, presentism would make us unable to act, for what we did would be meaningless.

'Tradition' is now used as a synonym for collective social continuity. History indeed shows us discontinuities, but it also shows us continuities that are just as remarkable. No historical theory which systematically denied these continuities would be adequate. Nor is falling back on the identities of the subgroup sufficient, for to write about a small group alone, without integration into the wider history, tends to produce less group history than group grievance. To write the history of a state in this way is to produce a thousand myopic narratives of grievance: academic integration and political mobilization would become equally impossible. An ideology which further explains why the history of a minority can only be written by its members condemns the minority to a marginal position, and makes collective political action impossible, whether by the minority or the state itself.

History allows us better to understand phenomena in our own time, including (I shall argue) modernism and postmodernism. It shows that presentism has its historical logic too,[24] the result partly of the political failure of the Marxist reforming idiom, partly of new intellectual tropes for celebrating old goals of self-fulfilment and emancipation. As the older, wider schemes for economic reform were regretfully replaced on the shelf, the intelligentsia turned to defensive mechanisms that would both safeguard the solipsistic integrity of their 'private spheres' (a new catchphrase), and wreak an ironic revenge on their enemies. There was no risk of cutting off their noses to spite their faces if it was all a language game, after all. A powerful postmodern claim to general validity was the contention that postmodernism did not just denote an historical stage, but the system of ideas which showed the unreality of all stages; yet this is contradicted by another branch of presentism, which identifies postmodernity as the chronological era in which we now live. If true, this opens it to historical analysis. Postmodernism, to establish its credentials, must be able to demonstrate that it succeeded something else; but what, and when?

III.   WHY EVEN POSTMODERNISTS CANNOT IGNORE THE PAST

The problem with using 'modern' and 'postmodern' as historical (that is, chronologically assignable) categories is that no agreed dating of them has been established. 'Modernity' depends on an implied transition from 'pre-modernity', but this has broken down: attempts to locate the great divide in the English Civil War, the American or French Revolutions, the Industrial or Scientific Revolutions, are now often undermined by scholars of those episodes.[25] 'Postmodern' governments prove, when in office, to be as authoritarian as 'modern' ones; the historical rehabilitation of early-modern governments has flattened the alleged practical contrasts.[26] The ideological contrasts have also been flattened by the dismantling of the idea of a unified Enlightenment, committed to a project of modernity in a way that other thinkers in the eighteenth century were not: a 'conservative Enlightenment' has shown how the ideals of what we now call modernity were widely shared, and did not define an era.

If the historical revision of our ideas of 'pre-modernity' has wide implications, 'postmodernity' is equally vulnerable to historical doubts about 'modernity'. 'Postmodernity' is presented as the historical era allegedly identified by the collapse of 'modernity': modernity, that is, defined as a 'Western' project asserting the possibility of progress in human affairs, especially economic progress, and tracing this to the development of scientific and technological knowledge. Modernity allegedly rested on a 'grand narrative' of social improvement, begun in the West but adopted equally in the Third World.

Again, this has been challenged by historical studies which emphasize (for example) the early origins and wide acceptance of scientific and technical change; the pessimism of many political economists even in the classic phase of the Industrial Revolution; and the prevalence of optimistic ideas that are held to go with the continued prosperity and dynamism of the world capitalist economy in the closing years of the twentieth century. 'Progress' was never without its questioners, even in eras held now to have been most complacent.

If postmodernity consists in a challenge to the 'grand narratives' of the march of progress, our own age is one in which new grand narratives merely arise to replace old ones. If all this is so, it becomes acutely difficult to explain when postmodernity succeeded modernity. No securely grounded historical date is possible, and it is significant that the single key event cited by a standard reference work, the oil price crisis of 1974, is one that relates most closely to the biographies of a particular generation of academics in Europe and North America.[27] Where those economies recovered, and in the 1980s and 1990s entered another phase of optimism and growth, many areas of academe did not. History may indeed be able to locate postmodernism as a stage, but not in the emancipatory sense that postmodernists seek.

Postmodernism in the political arena presents itself as moderate, pragmatic and non-doctrinaire. Yet beneath this image can be concealed a far-reaching programme for political or social change which is made to seem uncontroversial only by the ideology in which it is contained. It is this programme which, examined sceptically, dates the postmodern project, places it in an historical time-frame. Since this is the case, the major premise – that postmodern politics are non-historical or non-ideological – can only be defended by the manipulation of the media. Observers have remarked on an air of menace in postmodern politics.[28] It is not merely that opponents are to be combated or unreliable elements within a party to be disciplined, but the very premises on which constructive political arguments are built are denied, indeed made unmentionable. But denying those premises does not abolish them. Do the postmodernists in fact escape from history?

They fail to escape because presentism has serious flaws of substance. Extreme relativism, after all, cannot apply to itself. If all traditions are invented, all must be equally invented, equally open to study, including their own. Yet such is clearly not the postmodernists' intention: their own traditions are to be above such scrutiny. Neither was this equality of attention the message of the modernist book which in 1983 opened this phase of presentism in England before the term 'postmodernism' had much currency, *The Invention of Tradition*. Far from being a neutral comment on its host society, driven by abstract concerns for historical method, this text was specifically, even parochially, located in its authors' antipathies. It was, in various ways, a polemical attack on what it defined as 'tradition'. Its Introduction listed, as the first three of its 'invented traditions', the 'pageantry which surrounds British monarchy in its public ceremonial manifestations'; the traditions associated with 'the colleges of ancient British universities', specifically 'the annual Festival of Nine Lessons and Carols in the chapel of King's College, Cambridge on Christmas Eve'; and 'The royal Christmas broadcast in Britain'.[29] Outside its narrow polemical setting, this might have seemed an unusual list.

Its choice of counter-examples was equally revealing, counter-examples chosen to illustrate an alleged distinction between 'custom' and 'tradition'. 'Custom' was held to be the flexible sanction which justified change as well as continuity in important practical areas of life, such as 'peasant movements' or 'the British labour movement'.[30] 'Tradition' by contrast was claimed to aim at 'invariance' by 'fixed (normally formalized) practices'. 'Tradition' was the 'formal paraphernalia and ritualized practices' which surrounded custom's 'substantial action'. Substantial action identified some justifications as 'technical rather than ideological'. Again, the example was illuminating: motorcyclists wearing crash helmets 'makes practical sense', but 'wearing a particular type of hard hat in combination with hunting pink makes an entirely different kind of sense'.[31]

It was a rhetorical rather than historical identification of the cast-list of evils responsible for the world's ills: the monarchy; Oxford and Cambridge colleges; the monarchy again; and fox-hunting. It was not a demonology to which realists like Karl Marx had devoted much attention. Poverty, disease and political oppression did not bulk large in it. Not Stalin (that hero of 'substantial action') but the Service of Nine Lessons and Carols; not Belsen, but the royal broadcast; not famine, but fox-hunting: such were its key symbols. Compared to the gross record of human misery and suffering writ large across the pages of history, there seems something a little abstracted about the symbols chosen by presentists; something formulaic; something ritualistic; something, indeed, in the present sense of the word, traditional. For the postmodernist's list of 'usual suspects' is itself an historical formation, and a recently inherited one at that. Far from being one of the solutions, it is one of the phenomena; to some eyes, one of the problems. The question for historical explanation is how substantial and honourable traditions of reform have ended in such a narrow agenda.

Without this legacy from modernism to postmodernism, it would be a paradox why institutions in Britain like the peerage and the monarchy, currently at their lowest ebb of political and economic power, should attract more and more academic attention. It is not merely that a 'declinist' scenario can most plausibly be set out by focusing exclusively on a few well-documented (or, at least, well-anecdoted) institutions which have declined, though this is part of the story.[32] It is rather that, within the postmodern world view, the barrister's wig, the don's gown and the fox-hunter's coat can be read as symbols, as a shorthand code for the whole social order that is to be condemned. If they could be read in that way, a coded critique could be framed which seemed immune to the naively empirical objection that the barrister's wig was hardly a central social institution. Champions of market capitalism may have won that argument, but their guns would be left pointing in the wrong direction if it transpired that the real point at issue all along had been not the industrial revolution but (say) fox-hunting. And here the postmodernists found key allies.[33] For the objection to the barrister's wig and fox-hunter's coat was unexpectedly congruent with the Marxist's claim that an unreformed 'superstructure' had survived and was contradicted by the realities of production in the economic 'structure'. In respect of method, Marxism and postmodernism should have been incompatible, indeed antithetical;[34] in their wider social purposes, the principle 'my enemy's enemy is my friend' made them allies.

Of course, the cast-list of historical villains did not end with the parochial roll-call of recent British symbols. Nazism and the nation state were both brought forward as allegedly linked targets, and targets on which old Marxists and new postmodernists could agree. States had indeed acquired new symbols like national anthems and national flags, and did so at known dates and as part of processes which have often been seen as the emergence of 'nationalism'.[35] For the Marxist, this newly acquired attention to symbolism was useful in implying the arbitrary, unjustified nature of superstructural developments. So useful was it to Marxist and postmodernist alike that the empirical dimension to the question is still often overlooked: can it indeed be shown that symbols like John Bull, or songs like 'God Save the King' and 'Rule, Britannia' did have a large role in creating a sense of British national identity after the Union with Scotland in 1707? Or was national identity rather a far more ancient thing, at least in England, extending back over centuries, established in ways which Hanoverian or Victorian symbolism embellished but did not fundamentally modify?[36]

If all traditions are equally invented, when they were invented would be irrelevant; yet certain authors have thought it a point scored to show that some objectionable tradition was weak because it was invented *recently*. The argument implicitly concedes that there may indeed be powerful continuities in thought and practice over long time periods, continuities obscured by a more recent preoccupation with a carefully selected list of very recent, and datable, developments.

One way of seeing presentism is as a narrow and limited project to delete certain symbols only from the repertoire of symbols we inherit from the past. Usually, the symbolic function of the chosen examples is pronounced, since they relate (like fox-hunting) to practices that are engaged in only by a tiny minority. In this sense, presentism may prove to be a passing fashion: some symbols may be suppressed, but other symbols will arise in their place. Symbols are always being slowly renewed, as trees in a forest fall and are replaced: presentism is therefore true but unimportant, although some trees are clearly more splendid than others.

Another way of conceiving presentism is more disturbing, however. If limited de-historicization is successful, it can only be by the widespread propagation and acceptance of its underlying ideology. How, then, can the effects of that ideology be confined to the few symbols on the agenda of present-day reformers? Will the same solvent not dissolve all those practices, values or institutions the authority of which involves some reference to antecedents? If so, de-historicization would not be important but untrue; it would be important because untrue. A widely accepted untruth is one of academe's most powerful levers on the world of affairs. But this wider presentism would undermine a key component of postmodernism, the idea that we are now in a happily terminal historical 'stage' marked by certain values (whether liberal democracy, capitalism, human rights or any others). Those values, and the historical rationales for them, would themselves sink beneath the waves.

The nihilistic implications of the presentist project widely conceived suggest that postmodernists are not people who dispense with the past. Like the Whig historians of old, they appeal to some elements of the past against other elements. They too construct a usable past, and in most cases a past that is, in a deeper sense, a ratification of the present. Post-modernism has been well described as 'the ideology of a specific historical epoch in the West, when reviled and humiliated groups are beginning to recover something of their history and selfhood'.[37] But the way in which the histories of these groups function as *their* histories undermines the universalizing promise of the wider parent project. Postmodernism professes to give systematic attention to the value systems of groups or minorities that have been allegedly 'excluded' both from socially dominant forms and from dominant historical writing. Whatever the value of this goal, the general project is called into question by the way in which the minorities selected for study correspond with the 'minorities' that have been organized into political pressure groups in recent decades. All those other subgroups, minorities, movements, or systems of ideas which made up the vast diversities of history are not only passed over: they are consigned to an oblivion more profound than that which the favoured minorities are alleged to have suffered. Far from a new history being written that replaces hegemonic unity with emancipated diversity, we have a picture of hegemonic diversity replaced by an alternative hegemonic picture in which a new array of groups, possibly less diverse than the old, takes centre stage.

In this sense Whig history has returned under the name of postmodernism, and with renewed moral indignation. It returns in a strengthened form, however, since it is no longer a diffuse ratification of 'the present', but a clearly focused ratification of the self-interest of certain groups. But it is not clear that postmodernism has gone far in clearly identifying the ways in which old grand narratives themselves functioned in the ways alleged, to serve sectional interests: postmodernism has, on the contrary, tended to depict highly generalized and reified enemies like 'imperialism' and 'patriarchalism', ascribing to such formations a unity and a coherence which postmodern theory itself ought to bring into question.

Postmodern theory claims to embody a refusal to privilege any one perspective on the past: all narratives are to be equal. Yet postmodern practice cannot live up to this ideal, for in its essence it heavily emphasizes certain perspectives and disparages others. How are we to judge whether such a new mix of components constitutes a 'balanced' account? Postmodern theory offers no answers, since the idea of balance belongs to older, empiricist attitudes to historical writing. Cultural difference, though real, can be overstated; whether it is or is not overstated is an historical-empirical question. Diversity, accurately reported, is not synonymous with multiculturalism. Postmodern theory ought to dissolve the coherence not only of the hegemonic groups but also of the groups or minorities which are held to have suffered exclusion. Yet these problems are seldom raised in postmodern practice. Instead, postmodern practice acts as a distorting mirror in which the ordinary, the normal and the mainstream are displaced and the peculiar, the aberrant and the exceptional are prioritized. It produces a world view in which every dog is wagged by its tail and (to borrow an image) the worms always appear to be larger than the cheese.

Postmodern theory, again, would leave us unable to judge between different stories about the past (or the present). Yet in everyday discourse we feel the need so to judge, and do so without evident difficulty. The new claim that certain groups have been excluded from the old master narratives is indeed plausible to us (when it is) because it satisfies old criteria of evidence, not new ones. Postmodernism is, to that extent, dependent upon residual empiricism or positivism. An entrenched Establishment which internalized a postmodern account of itself could shrug off postmodern criticisms as being merely truisms.

More familiar historical schools can mount defences against presentism. History can, of course, only be written from the perspective of the individual and the present: it cannot tell 'the whole truth' about the past. This does not discredit it, however. A telephone directory does not tell the whole truth about the region it covers: it contains answers to certain questions only. That does not invalidate the distinction between an accurate and an inaccurate telephone directory, or the further distinction between an inadvertently inaccurate directory and a deliberately misleading one. To seek to abolish the distinction between history and myth may only open myth to intellectual domination by history rather than vice versa.[38]

Yet a defence of academic history such as that attempted here now lags well behind deep attitudinal shifts in society at large. Many examples, trivial in themselves, could be adduced to show the new common currency of daily debate. An ideology becomes fully effective only when it is debased into the clichés of journalistic exchange, and just such a translation has occurred in Britain. Low-level rhetoric becomes a key to the assumptions people entertain about the past and their relation to it. So it is in newspaper articles by authors who revile their opponents not as class enemies, or as economic incompetents, or as imperialists, but as 'survivals' from 'an almost vanished world'. The enemy is identified not by his class (for formal class analysis has become problematic) but symbolically, by his clothes: social roles are an 'act' whose players are in 'costume'. Religion has been reduced to a marker of social identity, to be noted like a Jermyn

Street tie. British institutions, called 'the Establishment', are to be denounced for being successfully inclusive, absorbing the talented and ambitious. Their success is depicted as a sham, a show, a matter of style, paid for by others. Set out without the rhetorical postmodern trimmings, this can all seem strangely familiar. It is, indeed, the old modernist agenda of the class war in a new idiom. Postmodernism is not as subsequent to the preoccupations of 'modernity' as its exponents would like to make out.

There are weightier issues at stake, as dealers in such postmodern satire cannot but be aware. Public policy questions are invariably drawn back to historical debate. Can Britain's government be safely merged in that of a European Union? Is Europe securely democratic? Is European law impartial, European bureaucracy under effective democratic control? European integration is normally presented as a postmodern project, but such questions inevitably lead public discussion to the historical track records of Britain and continental European states. Those who wish to argue for European integration point to the fact that at many periods in the late nineteenth and early twentieth centuries the franchise in many continental countries was wider than in Britain; those who wish to argue against integration point to the ineffectiveness of wide democratic electorates in controlling continental governments at moments of crisis like 1914 or 1933. In both cases the argument is – has to be – historical.

Yet this historical argument now takes as its target the integrity of the state itself. Composite kingdoms are particularly vulnerable in an age of postmodernism: states, that is, which were assembled in a pre-modern era and which then accorded a recognition to their various component parts which 'modernism' later neglected. In such states, regional identities are not destroyed by a centralized process of homogenization: they survive and can be made the platforms for attempts to break up the union. Such attempts normally take the form of a celebration of what is depicted as a regional proletarian culture and a denigration of what is depicted as a unifying patrician one. Whether these depictions are accurate can only be an historical question. Assertions of regional identities on the part of Wales or Scotland are closely associated with flourishing historical scholarship into the pasts of those societies, and take the form of attempts to reverse the historical processes of state formation by which a unified composite monarchy was put together.

In already unified and culturally homogenized societies the effect of postmodernism is different. The similarity of the material circumstances of life across America is an obvious point, often made, but already in the early twentieth century commentators like George Santayana were remarking on how like each other US citizens were.[39] A process of acculturation had taken place, by force in the case of the expropriation of the native inhabitants or the conquest of the South in the Civil War, by intellectual coercion in the propagation of a 'civil religion'.[40] It is that civil religion more than the unity of the state that is the target of American postmodernists. They dismiss the achievement of the Founding Fathers and the present-day idolatry of the creation of the Republic as 'founderism'.

They challenge an American public myth built up around the events of the Revolution and their aftermath by voicing the claims of minority groups each to have its own 'history'. Yet this too is more historical, and less postmodern, than it looks, since each of these groups is really seeking to construct a teleological history for itself. Whig history as the ratification of the present is alive and well in the politicized programmes of America's component groups. American academe witnesses the rivalry of these different teleological histories, not the destruction of a teleological national myth by the non-teleological alternatives of the minorities. Seen from the rest of the world, there is no one as American as the militant feminist or the black activist, and that, indeed, is why they are so successful in US society. This is a predisposition that long predates postmodernism, although postmodernism gives it unprecedentedly explicit expression.

Within the British Isles the target is not a modern construct, the nation state, for political unity was achieved before the age of the nation state, but that pre-modern achievement, the dynastic union with the cumbersome title 'the United Kingdom of Great Britain and Northern Ireland'.[41] The object of postmodern critique is not usually Englishness, since such a critique would tell against Scottishness and Welshness also, but Britishness, depicted as a recent political construct. In the present devolution debate it is only the high-level, synthetic identities which are under challenge. 'Can one be British?' means 'Can one be both British and Welsh at the same time?', not 'can one be said to have a national identity at all?' Democracy can be invoked in aid of this critique, since a Scots or Welsh polity would be a more homogeneous and by suggestion a more consensual unit. Yet a double standard is employed, for not all composite identities are condemned: a united Europe is embraced at the same time as a United Kingdom is rejected. And it is not clear why de-historicization should not be equally damaging to the historically grounded identities of ancient kingdoms or principalities like Scotland and Wales themselves.

Accounts of devolution within the British Isles do not only point to a fragmented future; they point to a picture of the past in which Wales and Scotland played, allegedly, a much larger part in the historic forging of Britain than used to be generally acknowledged. A re-forging of Britain could therefore be expected to be the result of reassertions by the historically grounded ancient identities of Wales and Scotland. Not, of course, by Northern Ireland, for the historic identities of that province cut across the postmodernist project and offer a clear contradiction to its rhetoric about the malleability, the impermanence, the constructed nature of identities. Inhabitants of Northern Ireland, moreover, assert identities openly and unashamedly on the basis of denominational allegiance. They talk of political loyalties, and are even ready to die for them. Both sides in Northern Ireland use their local identities not as the basis for dissociation from some larger 'grand narrative', but in the opposite way, as a claim to membership of just such a larger, constructed identity: the Catholics in the Irish Republic, the Protestants in the United Kingdom. Postmodernists who are enthusiastic about devolution to Scotland and Wales are silent about devolution to Northern Ireland: history functions in tactical ways within political rhetoric.

Devolution campaigners, then, invoke a selected past. For them, devolution is merely a long-overdue recognition of differences in the British Isles which have, they say, always existed. 'Long overdue' is a phrase that introduces the historical teleology, and does so with a faint air of menace: to deny it is to deny the future. The past is plural, diverse, constructed, malleable, fluid; History commands you to reconstruct your polity according to a single formula. The past displays a wide variety of relationships between the British Isles and the European continent over many centuries; History supports Britain's integration into the European Union as the only solution. As with Whig historians in the twentieth century, the presentists of the twenty-first reach for historical precedents, examples and lessons where these seem to support their policy commitments. Presentists everywhere are eager to break up one particular account of the state in which they live, but revert to speaking of their fellow-citizens as 'we' and of history as 'our history' when they seek to frame an alternative version of it.

The consequences of such intellectual trends are usually identified in terms of cultural conflicts. All this has provoked various sorts of resistance, often uncoordinated. Some depict the problem as very recent where it is of long standing. Beneath the banner of postmodernism, we are asked to believe, has grown up a new idiom of intolerance as the institution of the university has been politicized.[42] 'Political correctness' is the term used to identify a yardstick, a set of values summed up as multiculturalism, by comparison with which aberrant opinions are to be excluded. Yet like most social movements, multiculturalism is most effective when operating at the level of general assumption rather than clear-cut ideology. The key mechanism is the way in which multiculturalism asserts that other subjects found their way on to the agenda for political reasons. The university, say the critics of correctness, now becomes an arena for political conflict between highly purposive programmes. Yet this problem is less original than it seems. The academic arena can be turned into a forum for present-day political programmes only because it had long ago been absorbed into a particular American democratic process.[43]

Multiculturalism, then, attempts to fragment the grand narratives of history thematically. It also fragments them chronologically. Freed from the difficult task of grappling with a past which is different, intractable, and distant from the present observer, the framers of history syllabuses in schools and colleges are now free to dip into the past for small episodes that might be made to seem antecedents of modern pluralism. For the postmodernist is, at heart, no different in one respect from his Whig ancestors. He, too, needs the reassurance of a genealogy, and if one does not exist it must be invented. The postmodernist is unlikely to have escaped his past if the past embodied in history syllabuses drawn up by postmodernists is still often some secularized and multicultural variant of 'the long march of everyman'.

These were among the weaknesses in the version of de-historicization that emphasized the impermanence of identities. There were equal weaknesses in its other variant, that stadial theory which established the present as a postmodern historical phase. The major premise of this stadial version was that history was dead, but like all great synthetic systems its major premise was its weak point. Even as Fukuyama wrote, historical research was going forward in ways that were to undermine the claims of US public culture to ahistorical self-evidence. The results of two areas of research in particular (the Enlightenment and the American Revolution) were to mean that the public doctrine that Fukuyama referred to as economic and political liberalism was to be revealed not as a set of pragmatic, neutral and timeless recipes for the smooth running of governmental machines everywhere but as a particular historical formation, indeed a unique historical formation. The public doctrine of the USA was now a problem that demanded historical analysis rather than a series of self-evident truths that provided a series of keys to practical problems and that made history (that grand repository of problems) obsolete.

James Ceaser's rhetorically strident lament in the face of the developments discussed here has been noticed already. His book was a call to return to political science as the discipline able to 'take America back' – able to provide a theory on which political action can be based:

> America's experience is bound up with political science to a degree that surpasses that of any other nation. The government was established with the assistance of political science, and America's founders can claim credit for reintroducing it as a practical force in the world for the first time since antiquity. Not modern medicine, not modern telecommunications, but the revival of modern political science has been America's greatest contribution to modern thought.[44]

In that spirit, he celebrated the ubiquity of US cultural influence around the world. In other words, Ceaser called for a rallying to a normative, modernist, pseudo-scientific project which had long characterized US academe.[45] The feasibility of this project is open to doubt. Fukuyama's proud vision may yet prove to be an hubristic boast. If even Marxism-Leninism can disintegrate as a system of ideas, the modernist or even the postmodernist public ideology of any nation must now be insecure.

IV.   SOME REASSERTIONS

The premise on which this book is written is that historical amnesia is not some independent process, an act of God or nature, a creeping disability (or a growing strength). Nor is it the outcome of a grand conspiracy; it is the result of a thousand separate, distantly related acts, the promptings of widely absorbed assumptions. Together, these unrehearsed, uncoordinated responses to a doctrine nevertheless amount to a distinct enterprise of historical disinheritance. That doctrine is, as we have seen, flawed, but it can have profound results nevertheless.

Postmodernism, seen from within the modernist experience, is the opposite of liberating; indeed it excludes the possibility of 'emancipatory knowledge',[46] and mocks mankind's attempts to grapple with objective and hostile structures of authority and action. To accept that 'there was nothing constant or continuous about the chronicle at all' would amount to 'a betrayal of the dead, along with a majority of the living'. A socialist sees the consistencies of history as residing in, chiefly, 'the stubbornly persisting realities of wretchedness and exploitation'.[47]

By claiming to emancipate the present from the past, presentism promises to abolish the future also, for the future cannot look essentially different from that which we now have. The world ceases to be a narrative of suffering and achievement, and becomes a timeless cultural shopping mall. Generations cease to relate to each other, since the termination of development makes currently dominant values seem normative. Past generations cease to relate to future generations, since past generations did not shop in the same mall. Future generations will raise no problems of difference or continuity, since, it is presumed, they will continue to shop there.

Yet modernism is not the only available vantage point from which to observe postmodernism: the historian has a position to occupy also. For the historian, it might be a truism that war, famine, disease, massacre and persecution are the normal lot of man; they lead historians who may reject the timeless validity of modernism and postmodernism alike to practise the discipline of history as the record of these things, and lead them to give professional attention to the historic achievement of stable institutions and values as the means by which such evils are averted.[48]

If history is the record of a series of difficult problems which humanity is required to answer, merely declaring history to be over is unlikely to resolve those problems. It is likely to make them more intractable. Meanwhile, however, historical studies are turning to a theme which promises an historical rehabilitation, the theme of counterfactual analysis. It is this, above all, which has freed our vision of the world from the overdetermination which underlies all stadial theories, whether modernist or postmodernist. It reminds us that all historical episodes have prehistories, but those prehistories are prehistories of the many things which might have happened as well as of the fewer, but still hugely diverse, things which did. No mere listing of 'preconditions' can reconstruct within the past a high road leading in only one direction. A prehistory is not a set of determinants that exist long before their outcome, but a set of circumstances that make a particular outcome possible.

To restore history to life means to restore to it its open future, and this entails restoring an open future for our present also. To do so is to recapture the counterfactuals which identified to men in past time the many roads into the future. But even counterfactual analysis is not enough. The recovery of the play of contingency shows us that, once the short run is absorbed into the medium term, there were not many roads to the future: there was an infinity of roads.

This book brings together a series of explorations of these themes, written under the shadow of an advancing enterprise in popular culture and academic history of which the author had, at the outset, no clear understanding. It is offered as the record of a series of responses to a generalized problem that only came into focus as my responses, and the responses of others, progressed.

Chapter 1 sums up a critique of some aspects of modernism that I had been shaping over two decades. It is, I hope, a final farewell on my part to the network of assumptions which surrounded and hampered my generation of historians in the early part of our careers: those powerful hangovers from modernism that subjected history to adjacent social sciences, and imposed on historical method a functionalist straitjacket. This chapter was written in response to the specific challenge to explain whether or not there had been a revolutionary tradition in England: whether, that is, historical development had organized itself around the existence of structural discontinuities and transformations like those that political scientists had seen in the events of 1789, 1917 and other episodes. My denial of that thesis leads out to a broader argument against the subordination of historical method to modernist social science.[49]

A general implication of chapter 1 is that 'being' does not determine 'consciousness': that how we understand and perceive things is not a simple reflex of their objective, structural or functional characteristics.

This leads on to the subject of chapter 2, for it begins to be asserted that national consciousness in Britain, the sense of 'Britishness', had been formed in response to such objective circumstances, and that the present dissolution of those circumstances would happily bring the disintegration of Britishness also.

This argument is, in other words, a familiar and indeed already old-fashioned reductionist one. But it draws its main strength not from its unemphasized reductionism but from the exploited fashions of postmodernism, first and most symbolically present in England with a volume of essays entitled *The Invention of Tradition*, published in 1983, and already noted above. The prospect of a rapid dissolution of identities was mainly the result of assumptions about the malleability of identity as such that postmodernism made plausible. It was made more plausible by historians if they could show that identities were of very recent origin, indeed that they had been made up very recently for explicable and faintly discreditable purposes.

The *reductio ad absurdum* of this argument was Hugh Trevor-Roper's contention, in the satirical manner of Lytton Strachey, that that totemic garment the Scots kilt had been the invention of an English Quaker ironmaster who sought a more practical working dress for his Scottish employees.[50] In 1983 this may have seemed amusingly irreverent; in the following decades the school of interpretation that it encouraged began to acquire a practical engagement as the UK's plans for domestic devolution and further integration into the European Union had to be assessed against relevant historical criteria. Yet however fashionable postmodern-ism had become on a low level, it was now vulnerable to the implication of the work reviewed in chapter 1. For if (as is there argued) there was no clearly demonstrable transition between pre-modernity and modernity, it began to look highly implausible that there could have been any clearly demonstrable transition from modernity to postmodernity either.

Chapter 2 offers a review of how a variety of schools of thought have been brought to bear on the question of state formation and national identity in Britain; it contends that far from being modern, secular and 'invented', collective identity in the case of England has been ancient, theologically shaped and of spontaneous growth. To advance these arguments, however, is not simplistically to argue for the earlier origin of 'nationalism', for we now see that nationalism was a new doctrine, coined in the nineteenth century, to claim a new basis for collective identities in race and language.

If English identity long preceded 'nationalism', how did it change when nationalism finally arrived? Chapter 3 embodies a second response to the postmodern critique of identity which argues that nationalism is 'false consciousness'. In chapter 3 it is argued that older forms of collective consciousness were already so well entrenched in England that 'nationalism' did not sweep them away; indeed that these much older forms of self-perception proved stronger and more durable than nationalism. 'Nationalism' was indeed devised and propagated in the nineteenth century, and with striking practical effects, but it was a phenomenon that affected Wales, Ireland and Scotland more than England.

Nationalism, then, was an ideology, not a universally applicable tool of modernist political science. Indeed the component parts of modernism increasingly yield to historical analysis in just this way. From being unchallenged categories, the building blocks of explanations, they become themselves the subjects for historical study. How far can historians go in probing the genesis of that world of discourse that we still take largely for granted? Chapter 4 had its origin in an attempt to demonstrate that the term 'radicalism' is not applicable across many centuries, but came into being as a specific and novel ideology at a particular time and place. A similar exercise could be performed for other doctrines, including liberalism, socialism and conservatism.

If this attempt to reassert historical analysis is successful, it will have an impact on the perceived shape of a country's domestic history. It will also have an effect on the relations between the histories of different countries, and the rest of this book is concerned with a sort of intellectual diplomacy, the interactions and rivalries of the historical, sociological and political science traditions of neighbouring nations.

Chapter 5 derives from my work on colonial American history. It is an attempt to question the most self-evident of those truths that, by their very self-evidence within US culture, shield the history of the USA from serious comparative study. It addresses that central component of the state's myth of origins, the inevitability of the American Revolution. States normally have such myths of origin, and there is nothing unusual about the USA's possessing one; what is at issue for the historian is merely the form it takes and the effects it has on historical study. In chapter 5 the response takes the form of counterfactual analysis, a substantive exploration of the general features of colonial American society which might plausibly have led to outcomes other than those witnessed in 1783 with the independence of the Thirteen Colonies and 1787 with their adoption of a centralizing, unifying constitution.

This was a substantive discussion, but it leads to further reflection: why is counterfactual analysis so resisted within the USA?[51] Did British and US historiography have a natural affinity, as their two countries had been presented in the twentieth century as natural allies? What were the general social and intellectual pressures tending to realign the outlook each society had on the other? Chapter 6 is an attempt to explore these questions by comparing some general points of method and substance in British and US historiography in recent years.

It comes to the conclusion that these two intellectual traditions had pulled apart. It identifies the divergence primarily in terms of the social function of the historian in the two societies, and the historical methodologies that those societies tend to prefer. But there are other pressures at work here too. Chapter 7 extends the discussion to consider the way in which history, sociology and political science can come together to create a metahistory, a version of a country's self-image. These potent intellectual constructs can then acquire a life of their own and interact almost independently of what a modern scholar might wish to say about the historical record.

Chapter 7 extends this analysis to consider not only Britain's relations with the USA, but the relations of all three with Germany. It shows the way in which counterfactuals have been obscured by the elaboration of grandiose metahistorical interpretations. As the United Kingdom enters into closer association with its European neighbours, these issues will inevitably be reopened by events. Counterfactuals cannot be historically suppressed in an age in which they are being practically explored.

1

BREAKING THE GRIP OF THE SOCIAL SCIENCES

The case of revolution

I.   THE POWER OF WORDS

The influence of the social sciences on the humanities in the twentieth century hardly needs demonstration. Yet, although the humanities were everywhere born in chains, they are becoming free: in innumerable individual instances, for countless particular but related reasons, the stranglehold of the social sciences is weakening. Even quite recently, large processes, events, or concepts in history seemed to share a common character: they were overdetermined. Every major episode or outcome was prefaced in the pages of historians by an array of causes which purported to show that it just had to happen. This chapter focuses on one case: the way in which historians organized general accounts of historical change around the category 'revolution', and how these attempts have disintegrated. Similar disengagements from 'historical inevitability' feature in chapters which follow: nationalism in chapters 2 and 3, ideology in chapter 4. Here the focus is on revolution, allegedly the locomotive of history, certainly a locomotive of much twentieth-century historiography. This chapter poses the question: was there a revolutionary tradition in the English-speaking world?

The weakening of the hold of 'revolution' went with a changing attitude to concepts, the building blocks of historical and social-scientific writing. Concepts gradually ceased to be regarded as words which simply corresponded to the shape of things in an independently existing external world; with the growing power of the history of ideas, concepts came increasingly to be seen as terms embodying an implicit doctrine, designed to rearrange men's perception of their world; indeed constituting that world itself. Concepts did not, in other words, impose themselves from outside; they were generated from within. They were indeed indispensable to human action: as one distinguished historian of ideas put it, it is now evident that 'men cannot do what they have no means of saying they have done'.[1] If 'revolution' had any meaning, men must have known it before they could act it out; without the concept, they would have been performing some other historical act for which they did have words. The historian can only understand past events if he knows how men at the time conceptualized both their intentional actions and the results of those actions (whether intended or not). This point has now been widely and implicitly accepted, so that, by contrast with the dominant historiography of the late twentieth century, many of the most successful studies of revolution have recently begun with linguistic usage. Such scholarship has, however, been carried far further in France and Germany than it has in the English-speaking world.[2] The implications of this methodological shift for the political societies of the Anglophone North Atlantic are substantial, and need to be better appreciated. First, however, I review the way in which that advance has changed historians' approaches to the subject in recent decades.

II.   IDEAL TYPES AND THEIR POLEMICAL PURPOSES

In the academic arena as in the public realm, revolution as such appeared, until quite recently, to be an actor on the historical stage. Men might come together to create 'a revolution', just as the forces of nature might come together to create 'a tornado' or 'an earthquake': the individual examples would differ, but would have a necessary inner unity and a broad functional similarity. This assumption invited a triumphalist account of the role of social science. According to Lawrence Stone, writing in 1965, 'Social scientists can supply a corrective to the antiquarian fact-grubbing to which historians are so prone; they can direct attention to problems of general relevance, and away from the sterile triviality of so much historical research.'[3] The contribution of social scientists in recent decades to the study of revolution was immensely influential, but it consisted, as it necessarily must, of typological speculation at a considerable distance from the original research that Stone vividly characterized. The attempt of social scientists to propound ideal-typical categories of revolution was at the heart of their approach: yet we can now see that the typologies which they established as dominant already contained within them implicit answers on the causes and consequences of 'revolutions', the nature of the evidence which related to the problem, and the social constituencies which might be expected to give rise to revolutionary episodes.

Social-scientific enquiries began with definitions in order to exclude phenomena which might not support the chosen typology.[4] The central aim of this sort of typological analysis was 'to distinguish between the seizure of power that leads to a major restructuring of government or society and the replacement of the former elite by a new one, and the coup d'état involving no more than a change of ruling personnel by violence or the threat of violence'.[5] The significance of the latter was to be diminished a priori.

In the 1960s this distinction was heralded as a new analytic insight and confirmed as central to historians' accounts of revolutions in early-modern Europe. Robert Forster and Jack P. Greene, invoking the theoretical writings of Eugene Kamenka, Harry Eckstein and Lawrence Stone, characteristically excluded from their vision two 'categories of events: (1) public and private palace revolutions or *coups d'état* which, though they produce a change in regime, wrought little alteration in the structure of either government or society; and (2) the many localised *jacqueries* which sought redress of immediate grievances but no change in the nature of existing social and political arrangements'.[6]

By contrast, the 'great' revolutions, which alone were allowed to be real revolutions, were defined as parts of the 'modernizing revolutionary process';[7] they were taken to be those episodes which could be analysed in social-structural terms as aspects of the changing pattern of wealth creation, or the rise or decline of different social groups. In the nineteenth and twentieth centuries the key development was supposedly the making of the working class; in the eighteenth century the totemic social constituency was the middle class or 'middling sort', and its mythic 'rise'; for early seventeenth-century England the key variable was the decline (or the rise) of the gentry.[8] Within this typological vision there was held to be an essential difference between political changes that were analogues or gauges of major social change and, by contrast, political changes that were merely superstructural and therefore trivial. Among the latter were normally placed dynastic discontinuities. Wars of religion did not feature within this modernist typology at all.

Historians were sometimes unhappy about this imposition of a modern typology on ancient phenomena, but its appropriateness was made to seem inescapable in the case of a small number of revolutions that were successfully presented as archetypal great revolutions, especially 1789 and 1917. Crane Brinton, Christopher Hill and others powerfully argued that England's civil wars of the 1640s were merely an instance of this type, the occasion when England underwent a rite of passage through which social scientists, and especially social anthropologists, held that all nations passed en route to modernity. A few historians of early-Stuart England reacted against such an interpretation by trying to rescue the 1640s from this analysis, but their defences implied at most that they considered that the validity of the typology of revolution could only be postponed: since it obviously applied in 1789 and 1917, it seemed impossible to question it.[9]

They argued, instead, only to remove the problem from their chosen period. The term 'revolution' itself, they observed, was hardly used of politics or society in the seventeenth century. Peter Laslett contended that a better understanding both of the philosophy of John Locke and of the nature of early-modern social structure depended on a re-examination of that term and the deletion of the historical reifications that had grown up in its shadow: the English Revolution, the Agricultural Revolution, the Scientific Revolution, and others. If Locke wrote most of the *Two Treatises* before 1688, as Laslett established, rather than after that event as a rationalization of what had occurred, it followed that the world before 1688 needed to be reinterpreted and detached from the teleological sequence of great national revolutions: English (i.e. 1688), American, French and Russian. In an unforgettable title, the old world, by implication the world before 1688, became *The World We Have Lost*.[10] Yet to have lost it still implied revolutionary social change at some time.

Vernon Snow examined the seventeenth-century meanings of the word 'revolution' and showed how they were dominated by scientific usages, especially the ideas of circular motion employed by Copernicus, Galileo and Newton. Seventeenth-century English dictionaries consistently gave the sole meaning of 'revolution' as circular motion; not until after the Glorious Revolution did they admit a political meaning to the term. As a result, when a political meaning was adopted, it was (as in Locke's *Two Treatises*) that of a return to origins or first principles.[11] John Pocock's work on civic humanist discourse, especially the transmission of Machiavelli through Harrington to their late seventeenth-century followers, greatly strengthened this interpretation.[12] These historians went beyond Laslett's argument of 1956 in seeking to include 1688 within the old world rather than accepting 1688 as the decisive break with it: the Glorious Revolution now became the defining use of 'revolution', a conscious return to the *status quo ante* James II. This episode, not the indecisive turbulence of the 1640s, was held up as the archetypal revolution for the English polity, constructive and decisive because it was not (in a twentieth-century sense) revolutionary at all.[13] It was still, however, a revolution as turning point.

These partial corrections seemed to be vulnerable to Christopher Hill's subsequent demonstration in 1986 that the term 'revolution' was much more commonly used in the seventeenth century than had once been thought, and that it carried meanings which seem much more modern even though they were not yet adopted into seventeenth-century dictionaries. Yet Hill's reinstatement of the term 'revolution' is open to scrutiny. Although the term 'revolution' was in widespread use in the English-speaking world throughout the seventeenth and eighteenth centuries, it was part of a quite different mental universe that is not accessible to social-structural analysis. The most general consequence of this difference of mental universes is the conclusion that the typological approach pioneered by modern social scientists and championed by historians, especially from the mid 1960s, has in reality told us nothing of value about catastrophic change that we did not already know, but has been a cheat and a delusion, deceiving mankind with a spurious expertise and persuading us that we can control our political future when we see so regularly that we cannot.

III.   HOW PAST MEANINGS DISSOLVE PRESENT POLEMIC

Christopher Hill argued that the crucial transition came, and the revolutionary tradition was established, when the term 'revolution' was subject to 'a changed application from astronomy to politics', and that this was 'a consequence of the mid seventeenth-century English Revolution'. It was this transference, he argued, that gave the term revolution 'its modern political meaning', and it was important for his purposes to date this new meaning to the 1640s, not to 1688. This changed application marked not just the extension of a metaphor, argued Hill, but a change in the meaning of that metaphor. 'Revolution' corresponded to the social upheaval of the 1640s, not the limited events of 1688.

The historical process, Hill maintained, like the motions of the heavens, had formerly been understood to be cyclical. This sense, he argued, broke down in the 1640s. It had, indeed, been eroded since the Reformation, itself a 'decisive break', but from 1640 millenarianism was widely preached, and the millennium abolishes cyclical history. By contrast, 'the modern idea of a revolution suggests a break in continuity', releasing Englishmen into a world of linear history. In that linear world, the millennium was to be expected via 'a series of revolutions – the wars of Armageddon, the defeat of Turkish power, the raging and ultimate overthrow of Antichrist'.[14]

New evidence[15] calls for an important modification of this argument. The term 'revolution' was indeed transposed from astronomy to politics, but this did not imply such an expansion of meanings in the way suggested. First, the insights of the English into historical change had been limited and fragmented, so that even before the 1640s they had seldom been able to perceive large social or divine historical processes as fully cyclical. The Second Coming itself, that paradigmatic episode of social change, would not be a simple restoration of the world before the Fall. It was not easy for men to conceive of a liberation from a cyclical to a linear world, and few did so. Even those who championed a millenarian theology did not see it as an alternative to cyclical processes. When men looked for a new Heaven and a new Earth, as they sometimes did, it was as the result of God's action, not man's self-emancipation: even the scenario of the apocalypse or the millennium was not envisioned in terms of revolution.

Second, 'revolution' had a significance not merely via astronomy: astrology linked the circular motions of the planets to an area of theological dispute concerning fortune and chance, and gave 'revolution' its primary meaning as a turn of fortune, especially in relation to the fall of great men. Since the English lived through increasingly dramatic, sudden and incomprehensible changes, they were increasingly impressed by their inability to predict the future and by their helpless dependence on fortune or on Providence: such a dependence did not encourage them to think of themselves as inhabiting a linear world in which major change could be engineered by 'revolution', conceived as purposeful, even structured, human action.

Third, this sense of revolution as a sudden, astonishing change in human affairs survived not only through the seventeenth century but to the end of the eighteenth also: such changes were understood not as superstructural analogues of structural change or as stadial evolution but as turns of Fortune's wheel or as the interpositions of Divine Providence. This meaning was even strengthened by the insistence of Enlightenment historiography that modern, professionalized history demonstrated how great events might be the products of small causes. This new historiography was a deliberate attempt to liberate mankind from Providential history, that is, from the close superintendence of Divine Providence, from predestination and from 'priestcraft';[16] but in so far as it was successful, it had the effect of leaving men in a setting in which the power of contingency had been enhanced while no general, secular schemes of historical explanation had been (or, now, could easily be) propounded to replace Providence.

The astronomical metaphor had carried a number of implicit meanings in the seventeenth century. It would not necessarily imply a renovation, since one point on a planet's course is just like another. It would, however, imply vastness, complexity, irresistibility and overwhelming force. Especially before Newton, it would imply the helplessness of man in the grip of forces beyond his ability even to understand. It would imply the essential lack of uniqueness in political turbulence: the rise and fall of governments had happened before and would happen again. But it was Fortune's wheel that was increasingly involved rather than the circling of the planets: the motions of the heavenly bodies were predictable, and, from Newton on, came to be seen as intelligible also, as proof of the rational, benign intentions of the Creator. The transference of these meanings to the political realm did not establish there the modern meaning of revolution.

The political world continued to lack a mathematical proof of rational design: it was still the realm of the inscrutable, whether described as Providence, Fate or Fortune. Fortune's wheel provided people with their definition of the malevolent uncertainty of human affairs, and from the Middle Ages it was Fortune who linked perceptions of causation not with Newtonian physics but with the mysteries of Divine Providence. The ideas of Fortune or Providence attended to the ways in which human events might seem to be (as celestial bodies could not be) thrown out of their normal course by extraordinary changes, even violent reversals. A Newtonian universe was a Whiggish one in which all was ultimately for the best; but observers did not always perceive such cosmic regularities in the human catastrophes through which they lived.

Men wished, where possible, to see themselves in a benign historical scenario, in tune with the harmony of events (a perception of the world later termed 'linear history'). They did this chiefly by examining the notion of Divine Providence, and attempting to recruit it to their cause. Royalists after 1660 and Whigs after 1688 and 1714 did this with particular conviction. But there were always substantial sections of the population who were alienated from this triumphalism, and Britain's military affairs too were often marked by uncertainty, undecided outcomes, narrow victory or sometimes defeat. The fall of the monarchy in 1649 and 1688, and the loss of the American colonies in 1783, were warnings against too complacent an appropriation of Providence, or indeed against any sense, among those well-disposed to the British state, that 'revolution' was a facilitating phenomenon, an articulating event, a catalytic process in a benign and linear history.

Events in England and the British Isles in the 1640s and 1650s were bloody, savage and destructive: they created a sense, sometimes exhilarating, of their momentous nature. In modern phraseology, they inspired and empowered individuals. Those events are not diminished in their drama, immensity and importance by the discovery that contemporaries did not picture them as a single thing, a unified process with a structure and a logic of its own. On the contrary, the English acted as they did in the 1640s and 1650s, and left so evanescent a republican legacy, partly because they had no such sense. Revolutions certainly happened in the seventeenth century, and many of them, but they necessarily conformed to seventeenth-century understandings, dominated by contingency and mysteriously overshadowed by Providence. It can no longer be argued that they happened as a result of any plan to move from 'feudalism' to 'capitalism', or of attempts to implement secular schemes of social reconstruction or redistribution, though such schemes sometimes flourished in the fertile chaos left by the collapse of governments.

The seventeenth-century sense of 'revolution' was fully consistent with revolutions as capricious topplings of rulers, as in the 1640s or 1688, or as the long-prepared and volcanic eruptions of domestic violence, as in 1776. But the events of the 1640s were not prototypical of 'modern revolutions' since, until much later, men had no idea that the episodes of disaster and catastrophe that blighted their lives might be interpreted as an evolutionary sequence. The English republic of the 1650s did not therefore export 'revolution', as the French republic of the 1790s was to do (and as, it might be suggested, the American republic began to do after 1789). Nor were the events of the 1640s and 1650s at the time reconceptualized to make life easier for Englishmen in 1688: no one in what quickly became known as 'the Revolution' of 1688 (sometimes with an adjective, usually 'happy', later 'glorious') looked back to any prior event identified as an 'English Revolution' for a model of structure or process, although, undoubtedly, the politics of the years 1640–60 made substantial and lasting differences to the politics of 1660–88. No one embarked on the events of 1642, 1688 or 1776 attempting to make, or to prevent, 'a revolution'. By the late eighteenth century, human affairs in the historical record were no longer widely seen as cyclical (if indeed they ever had been); but that did not mean that they were seen as strongly linear either. Men often spoke of revolutions all through the eighteenth century, as they had in the seventeenth; this did not imply an adoption of new meanings, still less nineteenth-century structural, stadial or evolutionary ones. What meanings did the term carry?

IV.   HOW PAST MEANINGS FIT PAST EVENTS

It is now possible to be somewhat more specific about what the prevalent political meanings of 'revolution' were in early-modern England, and how these related to European meanings. Continental sources in the sixteenth and seventeenth centuries certainly called disruptive political and social changes *révolutions* or *revoluzioni*, and Englishmen were familiar with this usage by reading Guicciardini, Montaigne and others, in the original or in translation.[17] Societies less overawed by the threat of civil war and social breakdown could still emphasize the prime meaning of 'revolution' as planetary motion, as did the French Academy's dictionary of 1694; other societies might give priority to a political meaning, like Sperander's German dictionary of 1728: 'Revolution, the upheaval, alteration or course of time, *Revolutio regni*, the change or overturning of a kingdom or of a land, if such suffers any special alteration in government and police.'[18]

In such examples political and social change was not conceived in a structural way, or as a liberating, transformative process. 'Revolution' in these sources did involve innovation; it was capable of being repeated; it did imply turbulence, a threat to the established order, even an inversion of hierarchy. Revolution was not, however, pictured as an historical process, a thing in itself, still less something that had as its subject the nation. Although its primary meaning was not a return to origins or to first principles, since few enough such episodes could be found in human affairs, the term 'revolution' could be easily and naturally used when such reversions did occur, as it was with the restoration of the monarchy in 1660. Its primary meaning, not inconsistent with 'restoration', evolved from planetary motion to a sudden, astonishing reversal of fortune in the political realm.

This conceptualization of fundamental social and political change was shared across Europe with substantial uniformity. French, German, Italian and English contained the same word, and instances of dramatic reversals of political fortune could attract Europe-wide attention, even when they lacked strategic importance, because of their clear exemplification of this explanatory trope. One archetypal episode was the revolution in Naples in 1647.[19] Contemporary accounts available in English made clear that that revolution was not something that men had consciously made. Even the individual who was most elevated by fortune, Masaniello, was the most astonished at the transformation in his circumstances from fisherman to dictator, and proved unable to hold for more than a few days the astonishing power that he had astonishingly gained.

Although contemporaries were well aware of the practical grievances of the people of Naples against Spanish rule, especially their resentment at the forms and level of taxation, it was not generally held that those grievances were a sufficient explanation of the transformation that had occurred. Providence and Fortune, not taxation or constitutional conflicts, were the key historical variables. Neither Masaniello's revolution nor many others could easily be seen as planned restorations of the former state of affairs. The events of 1660 and 1688 in England were so described, but this characterization was contested by significant numbers of men, widely divergent in their politics, who for opposite reasons regarded each in turn as a vicissitude, as an instance of the unlucky turns of events that divided happy reigns from unhappy ones.

In French discourse as in English, '*révolution*' before 1688 was rather an abstract, reflective term, not often used, and seldom displacing specific, concrete labels like *soulèvement, révolte* or *guerre civile*. These were the terms French observers tended to prefer to describe the Fronde or the English Civil War. Only 'the Revolution' of 1688 gave the term 'revolution' a wider currency, and produced, first in France but by extension in England also, a vogue for writing the history of countries as a series of revolutions. But this greater currency as a political term did not greatly modify the meanings attached to it, any more than English society after 1688 was regarded as having been transformed compared to its state before the Revolution.[20] The perceived changes were, of course, normally located in the fields of law and religion.

Since the Englishmen who lived through the bewildering and chaotic changes of 1640–60 did not regard them as a single entity with the nation as its subject, it is historically unintelligible to seek *the* meaning of those events: they had no single meaning. Such a question can more easily be asked of 1688 and 1776, since both episodes were quickly reified and held by participants to be imbued with principles; but to the question of their meaning and causes, the historian must similarly record as an answer the bitter disagreement at the time and lasting conflicts over interpretation since. Neither 1688 nor 1776 had more than a small element of prior planning (or conspiracy) in its causation, and neither revolution left a clear legacy in the English-speaking world, a model which could be acted upon in later decades. They left an inspiring example or a dreadful warning, but not a model. To put it in the most simple terms, 1688 did not copy 1642, and 1776 did not copy either.

Social transformation, of course, was a familiar enough ideal in the early-modern world: dreams of the regeneration of man, of the institution of heaven on earth, and of the thousand-year rule of the saints, were older than the Protestant Reformation. It did not need the modern revolutionary tradition to produce the disastrous conflicts which devastated substantial parts of Europe in the sixteenth and first half of the seventeenth centuries: millenarianism, heterodoxy and schism regularly had that effect. The English who embraced ideals of the regeneration of man did not think of doing so via a 'revolution': even after 1688, when the idea of a revolution was extended to include a foundational event in the political world, its significance was chiefly that of a defensive deliverance from Popery and tyranny, secondarily that of a programmatic opportunity for moral regeneration effected by the Church and the sects. 'Revolution' itself was not pictured as a moral agent, but as a moment when the wheel of Fortune turned, sometimes opening up a benign future, sometimes a malign one.

For England more than for other nations, Providence tended to override Fortuna, and by the middle of the eighteenth century, and especially by the triumphant close of the Seven Years' War, the balance had temporarily tilted in a purposive direction. Whig Providentialism had produced in increasing numbers of the English (but especially of the Whigs) a growing confidence in the outcome of Providential interventions in national affairs. The abbé Mably's *Des Droits et des Devoirs du Citoyen* (1750)[21] drew a distinction between the two nations' attitudes through a dialogue between an Englishman and a Frenchman. As Professor Ozouf has described it: 'The English gentleman paints a history of optimism and will: the good citizen can work to make revolutions "useful to the fatherland".' By contrast, the Frenchman 'sees fate at work in all history, particularly that of France'; to loosen the grip of fate would 'take nothing less than convocation of the Estates General and a call for permission to remain in permanent session; amid "the general cry of approval" aroused by this meeting, it will be easy to eliminate abuses, weaken the royal prerogative, and institutionalise the nation's rights – the revolution in a nutshell'. Even so, Mably 'still used the word "revolution" in its astronomical sense (his Frenchman believed that the monarchy had reached a point of obedience that England eventually would also achieve); he still thought of revolutions as plural and continual and of men as passively caught up in a tumultuous flood of events they could never control'.[22] Nor would it be right to use a French idealization of England as evidence of what English attitudes really were without careful qualification.

English attitudes seem rather to have been essentially similar to French ones until the 1790s. By the eighteenth century the word *révolution* was everywhere in French discussions of every aspect of human life, normally used in the plural to signify not a (singular) return to origins, by analogy with the revolution of a planet; instead, plural revolutions referred 'largely to changes of fortune, to accidental mutations in human affairs, to innovations and disorders erupting within the flow of human time. They refer, in short, to all the vicissitudes and instabilities of human existence that Machiavelli saw arising from the operation of human passions – and which he held it to be the function of political order to contain and stabilise.'[23] Professor Baker has rightly indicated three characteristics associated with this French usage: revolution, as an aspect of disorder, was essentially plural; it was a retrospective characterization of what had already happened, not a blueprint for future action; and it had 'no internal chronology or dynamic of its own'.[24]

All these characteristics apply almost equally to Anglophone usage also, throughout the seventeenth century[25] and into the 1790s. The English, too, saw revolutions everywhere (despite their own singular 'happy' or 'glorious' revolution of 1688), and conceived of them in general as turbulent changes of power embodying astonishing reversals of fortune. This is remarkable, perhaps more remarkable in the English case, since where France experienced its last major period of internal upheaval in the conflicts of the Fronde (1648–52), the British Isles and England's North American colonies acquired in the seventeenth century a Europe-wide reputation for political instability and retained it into the eighteenth. It was not France but the English-speaking world that was the melting pot of revolution in the two and a half centuries before 1789. It is particularly important, therefore, that English discourse did not reify the notion of revolution as such in that period, although it was the Anglophone world that had most examples of dramatic, violent change at hand.

Revolution was not even reified as 'restoration'. True, some of the English could point to the 'revolutions' of 1660 and 1688 as restorations of previously existing liberties and legitimacy; but these claims were disputed too often within England itself for this meaning to be easily accepted as the sole one, and far from producing the hoped-for settlement of affairs, both 1660 and 1688 only seemed to lead to fresh conflicts and new motives for destabilizing the state. It was because the English polity was continually contested, both through regular Parliamentary channels and outside them, that no episode, not even the Glorious Revolution, could seem to many or for very long a release from an older pattern of disastrous subversion into a new world of linear progress.

In a French context, it has been argued that this usage of *révolution* discloses a consistent assumption that political stability could only be secured by absolute monarchy, and that such stability was at serious risk from the disorder continually threatened by political and religious change. French authors of the eighteenth century who wrote the history of other European nations as catalogues of their *révolutions*, it has been suggested, were presenting apologias for absolute monarchy.[26] Yet however specific the intention of French authors to defend a particular state form, the same linguistic usage was widespread among English authors also. Even Whig defenders of the Glorious Revolution and the Hanoverian accession had no secular sense of revolution to substitute for revolution as structureless turbulence. What the Whigs did use was a legitimating device familiar to their opponents also when the turn of Fortune's wheel had proved advantageous for them: Providence. In the Anglophone world of the seventeenth and eighteenth centuries, the place taken in France after 1789 by debates on the nature of revolution was filled by debates on the nature and action of Divine Providence.

Providence did not always smile, and her frowns inhibited the English from reconceptualizing their idea of revolution. This was especially the case after 1776. The resistance of the Thirteen Colonies in 1776 had eventual consequences far beyond the goals affirmed by the majority of American colonial activists in the 1760s, namely the restoration of a mythic golden age in transatlantic constitutional relations: the relationship, it was argued, that was held to have prevailed before the Peace of Paris in 1763. This extensive outcome was both unforeseen and unintended by those colonists who brought on the rebellion, since it could not be conceptualized in advance within Anglophone discourse. Nevertheless, a revolution having everything in common with seventeenth-century understandings of that term was sufficient to devastate the social order which had prevailed in North America until that point. The American war, and American independence, were world-shattering events, but not because they were revolutions in the twentieth-century sense. The events of 1776 were indeed sometimes hailed as 'the birthday of a new world'. Yet acceptance of this perspective was patchy, and its loudest proponents, including Paine, Price and Priestley, were men with powerful religious motivations. In some cases, these men had begun to express such ideas of apocalyptic transformation a decade earlier, for reasons unrelated to colonial disputes but closely related to their theological opinions.

Although the events of the 1640s and 1689 remained (to varying degrees) in the popular memory, those episodes were not in any strong sense prototypes for the events of 1776 or 1789. Certainly there were strong connections between specific episodes, like the attempted revolutions of 1715 and 1745, or the achieved revolutions of 1776 and 1789;[27] but in no strong sense was there a 'revolutionary tradition' within English and colonial American discourse which would have linked episodes of governmental collapse or popular resistance into a sequence. Only much later was the hypothesis framed and propagated that a small number of episodes in European and American history were united by structural similarities, so that each would rank as an instance of a process which finally came to be seen almost as a natural process. Historical analysis can now rescue these episodes from this sort of typological distortion and restore their specific causation. This reinterpretation does more than restore the essential unpredictability of catastrophe: it reveals the groundlessness of utopian revolutionary analysis, and it reinstates the uniqueness and importance of those episodes, especially the American and French revolutions, in which the Western world did something new, of fundamental ongoing significance, departing from its ancient path of minor vicissitude to affirm a new dawn for mankind, a new ideal of purposeful destruction on a scale hitherto inconceivable.

The absence in colonial America of convincing, well-informed explanations for events in the public realm contributed to the characteristic Manichean idiom of American discourse. The assumption that cosmic forces of evil were attempting to subvert ancient liberties by means of vast conspiracies,[28] frustrated only by the interposition of Providence, militated against attributing to political processes a self-sufficient secular logic of their own. In the years of constitutional conflict between 1763 and 1776, American activists almost never incited their fellow colonists to make 'a revolution'. American colonists almost never said, in 1776 or after, that they were re-enacting the model of the Glorious Revolution or reverting to its principles. When John Locke was invoked, as he (though only as one among many other theorists) sometimes was by the early 1770s, it was in providing grounds for a future dissolution of government, not in providing a consensual interpretation of the structure of revolutionary change. Even after independence, the example of American resistance proved strangely weak in England: although it was a powerful incentive to the French intelligentsia in the years to 1789, their English counterparts, and English plebeians, were singularly unmoved.[29]

English Whigs, Edmund Burke among them, found ways of retrospectively sanitizing 1688, arguing that it was 'a revolution, not made, but prevented': they thereby defined as non-existent the divisions and conflicts, ideological, religious, political and military, that persisted for sixty years after the Glorious Revolution. Ascribing the American Revolution to the implementation (indeed, to the manifest destiny) of Enlightenment liberalism[30] was equally a way of sanitizing it. The bland version of that event that was taught to the folk memory of the new republic systematically obscured the bitterness and savagery of the conflict of 1776–83, the revenge and counter-revenge of local militias, the shattering effect on colonial society of the breakdown of legitimate authority and the ensuing war. All this was retrospectively removed from the story by the public myth that the revolution, or the settlement of America itself, had created 'this new man, the American'.[31]

Only in retrospect does it seem remarkable that few in England perceived the American Revolution as a fundamentally new departure that would have major and diversifying implications for the mother country and for Europe. The first reaction of many of them was bewilderment at a catastrophe that seemed infinitely larger than its ostensible causes could explain.[32] Even Burke scarcely sensed any essential novelty in the American Revolution, despite his sensitivities on the same theme in 1789. Equally, given the basis of colonists' arguments up to 1775 in a demand for the restoration of a happy constitutional order which they claimed had prevailed before 1763, it is remarkable how few Americans, after the conclusion of the war in 1783, hailed their new condition as a restoration: revolution as restoration was not a powerful trope. It was more evident in the new republic that rebellion, war and social upheaval had produced a quite different society.[33] Yet even Americans who hailed this *novus ordo seclorum* were inhibited from describing it as a product of conscious will, or of revolution as a process, by the very rhetoric which had justified the Declaration of Independence in the first place.

Although many Americans hailed their newly independent republic in terms of Providential destiny or the inner logic of the ideology of equality and natural rights, many did not. The historians of early America, in contrast to its clergy, consciously attempted to free themselves from Providential history and gave systematic attention instead to the role of contingency: again and again during the War of Independence, the momentous outcome of battles had hinged on minor causes, often pictured as accidental causes. The role of contingency could not be denied to a generation that had lived through the fortunes and ill-fortunes of war, yet nor could the revolutionary generation be argued out of its desire to treat independence both as an inevitable consequence of the rightness of American principles, and as exemplary, or catalytic, for the rest of mankind.[34]

The leading figures in the revolutions of 1688 and 1776 were equally constrained from developing a modern idea of revolution by the way in which they explained resistance. A violation of established authority could be justified only on the grounds that it was the misconduct of that authority itself that had terminated established allegiance. An act of resistance was involved, but it was unique: a revolution was justified, but only as a singular act. The Glorious Revolution and so in turn the American Revolution were presented as exceptional situations, defensive in nature, implying no authorization of the proactive use of violence, justified only on the grounds that they would never be repeated. Although liberties were to be defended, therefore, even Whigs saw revolutions as to be avoided. Where they had occurred, Whigs had to explain them away rather than reify them.

In *Reflections on the Revolution in France*, Burke therefore sought to distinguish the French events of 1789 – a terrifying project to remake society on a wholly new basis – from the English events of 1688 – a defensive attempt to restore the *status quo ante*. He did indeed mention the English Civil War as a precursor, in its religious fanaticism, of the anti-religious fanaticism he diagnosed in the chaos, the minor violence and the lofty ideals of the summer of 1789. More remarkable, however, was Burke's failure to explore his analogy with the 1640s. It was enough for him to prove that 1789 was not modelled on the blueprint of 1688. In his attempt to rescue the England of the 1790s from chaos, murder and expropriation, Burke shied away from the fact that English history had already itself contained just such an episode of shapeless, dynamic, uncontrollable horror.[35]

The revolutionary tradition from 1776 or 1789 onward was not distinguished by its 'modernity' in contrast to the 'pre-modernity' of an *ancien régime. Ancien* in this sense merely means 'previous', not 'ancient'. The essence of the hegemonic social order established in England in 1660 was exactly its attempt to transcend the old problems which had haunted Europe since the Reformation: 'revolution' is not therefore usefully analysed as essentially a liberation from archaic, feudal survivals. More often in world history, phenomena described as revolutions have been popular reactions against processes of modernization initiated and imposed by elites, as in 1776. In the eighteenth century, English travellers to the American colonies reported both the similarity of material circumstances and the archaism of American society: with the outbreak of rebellion in 1776, many observers, German as well as English, saw in colonial conflicts a throwback to Europe's wars of religion of the seventeenth century. Revolutions were not inherently modern episodes.

The events of 1776–83 in North America and 1789–93 in France were proposed as exemplifications of a closely related ideology, egalitarian rather than hierarchical, presentist rather than prescriptive, republican rather than dynastic, rights-centred rather than revelation-centred. This ideology was indeed shared, and indeed had the influence claimed for it; but it does not follow from the presence of such a doctrine in the colonies that Americans reified the events of 1776–83 into a 'revolution' in the sense coined by the French in the early 1790s. The fact that Americans did not, and initially pictured their acquisition of independence as a specific and unique event, analogous to the Glorious Revolution, acted to limit the impact of the American example until the French Revolution multiplied its international significance. Many other states, closer to the centres of the civilized world, had demonstrated the power of the new egalitarian ideology,[36] and the American example was neither a necessary nor a sufficient condition of its spread. Not until *Rights of Man. Part the Second* (London, 1792) did Paine propound the theory of the domino effect of revolutions that was so profoundly to influence men's ideas about the contagiousness of chaos.

Only during the French Revolution did Frenchmen living through repeated uncertainty begin to inspire or to console themselves with the idea that chaos was really a *process* with a *history*, a process which might be analysed into certain stages, a process which might be speeded up or slowed down by human agency. Only in 1791 and the succeeding years did their failure to complete the great experiment by encapsulating it in a constitution open to them the prospect that revolution as such, once begun, was open-ended, impossible to terminate, always threatened by enemies, continually to be revitalized and remade.[37] Yet this was an experience that was missing in England, and, despite the profound effect of the French Revolution as an example or a menace, English discourse did not quickly join French discourse in mapping out new meanings for the idea of revolution itself.

V. THE EROSION OF THE SOCIAL-STRUCTURAL MODEL FROM WITHIN

The analysis of English understandings of 'revolution' helps to explain why the English polity during the 'long' eighteenth century was so profoundly unrevolutionary (in our sense of the term): it had no model to follow. Yet the social-structural argument that, on the contrary, England did have a revolutionary character from the previous century has recently been progressively modified even in its own terms.

The claim that the English civil wars of the 1640s constituted one of the great archetypal revolutions such as 1789, and a bourgeois one at that, was advanced by Guizot, Marx and Engels in the early nineteenth century. Lawrence Stone helpfully distinguished their case into three arguments: first, that 'the opposing forces represented two different attitudes towards labour and property'; second, that 'the Parliamentarians consciously willed the resulting destruction of feudalism'; third, that 'the outcome was a distinctively bourgeois society characterised by the ideal of possessive individualism'. In 1985 Stone, reviewing evidence for the political alignments of innovating landowners, wrote (in contrast to his position in 1965): 'One is forced to conclude that this evidence not only does not support, but tends directly to contradict the theory that bourgeois attitudes towards land management led to support of Parliament.'[38]

It has been argued, mostly more recently, that religion rather than production was the best predictor of allegiance in the civil wars of the 1640s,[39] and wars of religion tend to be explained by their participants in other than social-structural terms. Early-modern Europe was familiar with the desire of various minority groups for collective public events which would be redemptive in nature and would cleanse mankind from ancient and accumulated evils. Such aspirations were almost always expressed as demands for religious reform.

On the basis of new data on the alignments of landowners, without reference to religious affiliation, Lawrence Stone in 1985 abandoned the first two of the arguments which he set out to test, but fell back on the third: that 'the English Revolution [of the 1640s] resulted in a significant psychological and political shift towards free enterprise and possessive individualism'; in short, that

> the English Revolution was not caused by a clear conflict between feudal and bourgeois ideologies and classes; that the alignment of forces among the rural élites did not correlate with attitudes towards ruthless enclosure; that the Parliamentarian gentry had no conscious intention of destroying feudalism; but that the end result, first of the royal defeat and second of the consolidation of that defeat in the Glorious Revolution forty years later, was decisive. Together they made possible the seizure of political power by landed, mercantile and banking élites, which in turn opened the way to England's advance into the age of the Bank of England, the stock-market, aggressive economic liberalism, economic and affective individualism, and... agricultural entrepreneurship.[40]

It is this end-point to the conflicts of the seventeenth century that has been fundamentally revised since 1985, so that Stone's third argument is now left without a point of arrival in the eighteenth century. We now appreciate how mercantile wealth and technological innovation were not antithetical to a monarchical, aristocratic society, being fervently promoted by Charles II and James II in person; how hegemonic Anglicanism patronized natural science; how the Glorious Revolution was not a rejection of the counter-revolution of 1660 (and therefore a reaffirmation of the promise of the 1640s) but rather a confirmation of the state form of 1660 on a more securely Anglican basis. 'Possessive individualism' is another concept that has not survived in the 'long' eighteenth century, that most unrevolutionary third of modern English history whose boundaries have been set in 1660 and 1832.

Unrevolutionary, yet turbulent, the long eighteenth century contained within it a whole series of violent or potentially violent challenges to the hegemonic dynastic and ecclesiastical social order in England, Scotland, Ireland and the American colonies, especially that most formative episode of subsequent history in the West, the American Revolution.[41] The period was, furthermore, terminated in England in and around 1832 by the breakdown of a social order far more marked than any that divided the England of the 1630s from the England of the 1660s.

The attempted overthrows of the established order in this period were legion: the insurrectionary underground of the 1660s; the Rye House plot; Monmouth's and Argyll's rebellions; 1688 itself, and its analogues in the American colonies; a whole series of colonial rebellions; a sequence of Jacobite conspiracies, and the rebellions of 1715 and 1744–5; the American Revolution; England's alleged near revolution of 1780; the Irish Rebellion of 1798; the mass disorders in Britain after the Napoleonic Wars; the 'Great' Reform Act of 1832.[42] Yet a characteristic of all these episodes, in the light of recent scholarship, is that none of them fit within the threefold typology proposed by Guizot, Marx and Engels, as described by Lawrence Stone.

If this typology correctly identifies what an upheaval would require to constitute a rite of passage, a necessary stage in the transformation of societies from pre-modernity to modernity, three conclusions are suggested by recent scholarship: first, that there is no such dividing line between the modern and the pre-modern, however much we might wish to be more subtle and nuanced in proposing that alleged transition; second, that revolutions are not the points of articulation in a securely grounded stadial theory of social evolution; third, that to account for those major changes that did occur, and the vicissitudes to which societies were often subject, we must look elsewhere.[43]

VI.   RITES OF PASSAGE, THE CONTINGENT AND THE COUNTERFACTUAL

Social-structural analysis previously disposed historians to believe that 'powerful socioeconomic sources of discontent may have been necessary to transform a revolt or a rebellion into a revolution'.[44] Just as we now see that such 'socioeconomic' features were not significant in the 1640s, 1688 or 1776 (or even in 1789), so we can now dissolve the related distinction between 'great' national revolutions, those mythic rites of passage, and mere *coups d'état*. The distinction was one of degree, not of kind; of success, not of typology; and a success explained by complex conjuncture, not by the simple triggering of preconditions.

Yet social-scientific typological analysis was intended to negate the role of the counterfactual, of contingency, and of Divine Providence.[45] This was the force of Lawrence Stone's claim that 'everyone is agreed in making a sharp distinction between long-run, underlying causes – the preconditions, which create a potentially explosive situation and can be analyzed on a comparative basis – and immediate, incidental factors – the precipitants, which trigger the outbreak and which may be nonrecurrent, personal, and fortuitous'.[46] Incidental factors, by being fortuitous, were by implication unimportant: some trigger could be expected to set in motion a precondition, if correctly diagnosed. No more effective way could be imagined of privileging the interpretation by denigrating the evidence that might call it in question.

Social-structural analysis had the effect of greatly strengthening the confidence of social scientists in treating revolution as a response to the prior existence of a 'revolutionary situation', a set of underlying causes or preconditions, identified by the social scientist himself, which could be known in advance to cause revolutions.[47] In the rare cases where a revolutionary situation was diagnosed but no revolution followed, a major paradox was created and an academic conundrum was framed for historians to undo: '*la révolution manquée*', the revolution which should have happened but did not.

Typological analysis was a way of seeking to diminish the number of variables in the historical equation, an attempt to reduce to order the teeming chaos of fundamental change. In sharp contrast, the forms of historical analysis which admit the counterfactual and ultimately the contingent are ones that accept the vast diversity, variety and unpredictability of the causes which actually operate in the world of events, of *l'histoire événementielle*. Readmitting this insight pointed to the relevance of other bodies of evidence that have recently assumed ever greater prominence in the attention of historians.

In 1969, John Elliott expressed his scepticism of the thesis of a 'general crisis of the seventeenth century', dominated as that discussion was by typologies. Historians had given priority to the theme of class conflict, but this was, Elliott argued, a retrospective projection: 'Consciously or unconsciously, nineteenth- and twentieth-century historians have looked at revolts in Early Modern Europe in the light of the late eighteenth-century revolutions, and of their assessment of them.' By contrast, work in

German on linguistic usage had shown how slow and uncertain was the transfer of the term 'revolution' from the heavens to politics, and Elliott pointed to the difficulty of bringing religiously inspired movements of the sixteenth century into 'the category of ideological innovation' that 'revolution' required. Instead, Elliott quoted Estienne Pasquier's late sixteenth-century analysis of the causes of 'mutation' in a state: 'huge debts, a royal minority, and a disturbance in religion', and added others: threats to national identity; challenges to 'a corporate or national constitutionalism'; the defence of a heritage; the state's countermeasures against religious dissidence; foreign intervention.[48]

If Elliott had argued from the distorting effect of late eighteenth-century revolutions, in 1974 H. G. Koenigsberger argued for the misleading influence of a model even further removed from early-modern events. Social scientists, he observed, had based their theories of revolution almost wholly on nineteenth- and twentieth-century evidence. The political and social structures of early-modern Europe, added Koenigsberger, would yield different results. In particular, he questioned whether early-modern evidence allows a distinction between long-term structural preconditions of revolution, which can be compared and made the subject of a theory, and short-term accidental triggers, which cannot. The social-scientific concept of a society in equilibrium that was then destabilized by the emergence of 'dysfunctions' would not apply to an early-modern Europe in which the basic structures of power, status and wealth were almost beyond challenge, but in which instability was endemic.[49]

Koenigsberger pointed away from social-structural considerations and towards other explanations of fundamental upheaval, located by him in the realm of contingency. Dynastic continuity (kings being succeeded by adult male heirs) was one major precondition of political stability and of monarchical absolutism, a precondition which contingent demographic disaster often frustrated. Another precondition was the absence of centralizing, monarchical attempts to strengthen a monarchy's hold, especially over its outlying provinces. Attachment to ancient liberties, especially as expressed through representative assemblies, and problems of royal finance were at least as important as social-structural preconditions, revolution 'from below'.[50]

If these points are valid, and they have won increasing acceptance, we are more at liberty to ask how such disturbances and discontinuities of government were devised by those whose conceptualizations produced them.[51] Perception and categorization are central to the nature of the act itself, and this argument has rested on the claim with which we began, that men cannot perform an action which they cannot conceptualize.[52] England and France came to differ fundamentally in this central respect, with lasting long-term consequences. It is demonstrably the case that 'revolution' came to be reified in French political culture in the 1790s (as, later, it was reified in other European cultures). English historians of 1789, by contrast, long declined to follow their French colleagues in visualizing the French Revolution as the embodiment and acting out of abstract principles. English historians, like the English political classes in general, saw instead the actions of individuals rather than of generalized forces, and wrote of avoidable rebellion rather than inevitable process. The contrast was even greater with the typological analysis adopted as a self-evident truth within American political science.[53]

In English historiography, individual agency and the dominance of contingency were the characteristic features (obscured in the twentieth century but finally reasserted), sometimes accompanied by a desire to pass moralizing judgements on the individuals held responsible for catastrophes.[54] Where nineteenth-century French historiography increasingly dealt in collective entities, often in abstractions, and culminated in the *Annales* school's systematic demotion of human agency, nineteenth-century English historians increasingly found allies in Germanic archival scholars, and increasingly stressed the specific case and the uniqueness of nations, institutions and political conjunctures.[55] The political analogue is clear: where France was condemned periodically to re-enact what it had conceptualized as its revolution,[56] English politics continued to follow a path in which revolution was avoided, and piecemeal reform effected, through the free play of political contingency.

In the twentieth century this older disposition changed: some English historians now retrospectively projected assumptions and categories generated in France in the 1790s on to the England of the 1640s. For presentist political reasons, they created the myth that a revolution is a thing in itself, and that 'one such event, or set of events, and one only, should be expected to occur in the life of a nation'. Laslett identified the position he called into question:

Now that the revolutionist ideology predominates in so large a part of the globe, and every nation, to be a nation, has to have had its revolution, it is a necessity, an urgent necessity, to decide whether the first revolution of them all did take place in our own country in the seventeenth century. It could be argued that to have had the first social revolution to which the name of a nation could be joined is as significant as to have had the first industrial revolution.[57]

It is no coincidence that both revolutions have now been reconceptualized: the 'Industrial Revolution', a phrase adopted into English discourse only in the late nineteenth century (and then from French usage), and intended to denote a swift, violent process with an inner logic, has been reclaimed by professional economic history as a diverse collection of phenomena, some related, others not; some swift, most slow; a pattern of piecemeal, incremental change against a background of substantial continuities rather than a liberating transformation in which entrepreneurs and inventors took the parts of the Dantons and the Robespierres.

It is no coincidence, furthermore, that the collapse of the metaphor of 'revolution' for explaining social change has removed that label from the events of the 1640s also. England's history is still central to the world history of these concepts, but it is central as a warning against the misuse of historical argument to persuade people of the inevitability, and therefore the legitimacy, of murder and expropriation. Interested parties have often attempted to gather support for such causes by redescribing the injustices which go with political chaos in terms of the inevitability of revolutions as agents of progress. Yet 'inevitability' failed to validate itself by yielding predictability: although some change was forecast in the years before 1642, 1688 and 1776, expert observers were no more successful in predicting what was soon to occur than were political scientists in 1933 or 1989.[58] However effective as political rhetoric or political science, such appeals to inevitable processes have never been made credible as historical analysis.

The thesis that each nation experiences a 'great' revolution established a canon of the episodes that were allowed to fall into that category, but that gallery of 'great' revolutions has now been dispersed. As a result, we can see the frequently more momentous nature of other causal patterns which had been excluded from it, often overlapping the boundaries of the nation state: the Renaissance, the Reformation, the Counter-Reformation, or the dramatic effects of war, including the shifts in the balance of power effected by the world wars of 1756–63, 1776–83 and 1793–1815. Revolutions in the modern sense have not been the only locomotives of history, nor always the most powerful.

In retrospect, we can identify a phase of European and North American history in which 'revolution' was reified into a national rite of passage, but we can declare that phase to be over. In retrospect, too, we can see that as a strategy this was not only an intellectual mistake; it was also profoundly normative. The revolutionary project was one of self-willed emancipation: the end product of this process of self-fashioning was to be a new man and a new world. Such a project was both vainglorious and hubristic. No new men were born, and no new worlds were constructed. The present always exists in its old interrelationship with the past, and we have no reason for thinking that the end result of revolutionary efforts since 1789 has been other than to increase the vicissitudes to which mankind is subject.

2

STATE FORMATION AND NATIONAL IDENTITY

The case of England

I.   DEFINING THE TERMS

If identity is an invented tradition, more recent than we think, shallowly rooted, easily malleable, then the greatest prize in the contest of historical reinterpretation becomes that of the state itself. We began with the insight that 'class' was an idea rather than an objective structure, a reinterpretation that has had important consequences. We progressed to the contention that the individual was formed by a process of 'self-fashioning', and this has had even more extensive implications. But by far the largest consequences are those contained in the recent critique of national identity. One Marxist tradition had long but unavailingly denounced nationalism as 'false consciousness'; postmodernism, or low-level borrowings from postmodernism, now also targets national identity as the 'big idea' which can most effectively be deconstructed for present advantage, and does so with much greater effect.[1] Part of the critique is undoubtedly correct: to take the archetypal case of England, it is clearly the case that national identity has always been changing. But does it follow that national identity is recent, fragile, shallowly rooted or in flux?

National identity, nationalism, patriotism, state formation, and their present-day policy implications now constitute one of the most vital areas of scholarship on British history. In no other period is the debate currently as focused as it is in the long eighteenth century, that crucially contested territory in which older assumptions about a fundamental transition between pre-modernity and modernity have now been called into doubt. This chapter offers an overview of recent work. It argues that much writing on these years has framed misleading models both of state formation and of national identity. It adds that this period is nevertheless a key in revealing that the processes at work in sustaining collective identities in the British Isles did not originate with 'nationalism' in its historically correct meaning, and need not follow its trajectory.

The diversity and proliferation of recent scholarship in this field suggests that we might sharpen discussion at the outset by setting out the most tenable understandings of the key terms that the historiography has reached. By 'state formation' is meant the process in which the geographical territory of a polity is created. This took different forms in different cases: some states (ancient Rome) expanding by the conquest and absorption of similarly developed neighbours; others (Australia) by settlement in thinly populated areas; others (the young American republic) by the expropriation of nomadic peoples. The polities of medieval and early modern Europe generally grew by dynastic accretion, often by the attachment (in different constitutional formulae) of smaller kingdoms, principalities or fiefdoms to a core kingdom: this was the experience of England and her neighbours,[2] finally constituting a polity completed in its recent form in 1801, before the age of ethnic nationalism.[3] These different scenarios in the practicalities of state formation have significance for concepts of 'national identity' also. This term denotes the images of the polity in the minds of its members, and forms part of the individual's sense of personal identity. It is one of the ties binding subjects or citizens to their political organization, and becomes a constituent of ideas of 'society' as distinguished from the state. The way in which visions of shared identity were formulated and adopted is the subject examined here. 'Nationalism' is a third key concept, formerly either a loose synonym for 'national identity' or, more accurately, signifying the particular form of it generated in the nineteenth century by the modern state – that is, by the populism, homogeneity and vernacular unity of industrial society.[4]

If nationalism was thought to be present only in industrial society, the identification of an earlier origin seemed a gain in knowledge. The first stage in this recovery of national identity was to attend to pre-nineteenth century states of collective awareness, to give them the distinguishing term 'patriotism', and to deny that this constituted a primitive form of nationalism.[5] Yet this model of just two possible forms of identity, patriotism and nationalism, was only a stage on the road towards a more historical picture. The methodologies evolved in the history of political thought in recent decades have shown that the categories of political science are not eternally applicable. It can now be appreciated that 'patriotism' and 'nationalism' are the proper names of two ideologies, two historically located theories of the nature of national identity, two ways of explaining this identity and so mobilizing it for practical use.

'Nationalism' and 'patriotism' are both now located as terms coined in particular times and places to describe, to redescribe, and to shape some of the changing forms that collective consciousness has taken over many centuries. 'Nationalism' was a novel nineteenth-century ideology that claimed as its rationale and as the intellectual matrix for collective identities the alleged constants of race, language and culture; it ascribed to these things a unity and a purposive, evolutionary force. As a doctrine devised in continental Europe, it carried the programmatic assertion that 'peoples' who shared language and culture (and ultimately race) would and should form polities that were homogeneous in these respects. Proponents of nationalism held their ideal to be the naturally arising means by which the individual might relate to his polity.

Yet this was a set of assumptions not found in earlier ages. The long currency of the term 'nation', itself carrying changing meanings, failed for many centuries to generate 'nationalism' in this sense.[6] Recent scholarship establishes that peoples were well able to become aware of themselves as English or French, but the most effective intellectual matrix which contained their collective consciousness from the medieval period to the age of revolutions was a dynastic one the chief components of which were law and religion.[7] In the form of national consciousness which Dickens's Mr Podsnap was meant to satirize, the two dominant components were libertarian constitutionalism and providentialism: it was their coincidence that gave them their peculiar force.[8] Powerful collective self-images did not have to wait for nineteenth-century ideas of ethnic unity.

'Patriotism'[9] was a far weaker ideology, but similarly specific: it was devised in England in the 1720s to give shape to a claim by the Whig opposition to superior public virtue. In twentieth-century discourse the term was appropriated to denote a more decorous, libertarian, non-aggressive form of nationalism;[10] in the early eighteenth century, patriotism involved a militant Protestantism, a rejection of public corruption, and an aggressive international stance based on naval power.[11]

In so far as nationalism was assumed to be natural, spontaneously generated 'from below' out of popular culture, its history was severed from the much older history of state formation. As long as ethnic-linguistic nationalism was assumed as the secular norm, and assumed to be a dynamic phenomenon that overrode the claims of states not premised on it, other possible matrices of collective identity were neglected. The assumption of the revolutionaries of 1848 was long widespread, that 'peoples' (Germans, Italians, Irish) naturally and legitimately seek incorporation into a state coterminous with their ethnic 'nation', and resist state forms imposed upon them from above that are not coterminous: 'the state', in this vision, became at best an imposition. Although this theory became self-validating in so far as it was widely believed, historians now point to the many other state forms before the nineteenth century which were supported on different rationales, which shaped different ideas of collective identity in their populations, and in which religion, not race, was often central. Recent historical attention to national identity has appropriately been accompanied by the reintegration of religious history into accounts of other areas of history that had formerly been secularized. The specific implications of this reintegration are explored here.

II.   THE REDISCOVERY OF THE STATE

This understanding of these key terms was not easily attained, and recent scholarship illustrates different stages on the road to its achievement. To speak of a 'road', indeed, implies too great an order and purposefulness in a variety of studies. 'The state' had long been unproblematic as a subject in Britain because of its maritime boundaries and the inability of Wales or Scotland to threaten encroachment on England: England's cartographical tradition was of Admiralty charts, not (like Germany's) of historical maps focused on disputed border regions. Patriotism was a taboo subject within much of British historiography after 1945; champions of the primacy of politics meanwhile assumed a secure national identity as the obvious corollary of that key functional unit, Thomas Cromwell's bureaucratic machine. If states had functional origins, it seemed, identities could be left to look after themselves.[12]

As recently as the 1970s almost all varieties of historical opinion equally took the existence of a secure and stable state for granted in their research strategies, and the problematic coherence of the dynastic state in the period of its apogee, 1660–1832, was obscured by assumptions of a timeless 'nationalism'. High-political historians took the overall framework of the state as fixed in order to refute progressivist political science by minutely documenting the play of contingency within the parliamentary arena. Students of popular politics similarly took the state's political infrastructure for granted, preferring to give substance to the categories of exploitation and oppression by showing how oligarchs captured and used the mechanisms of state power rather than by studying how those mechanisms had been put together in earlier ages. Social and economic historians took the state for granted in setting the boundaries of the market: even the most politically engaged were concerned to record those emergent features of social life and action which would challenge the capitalist state and produce its abstract withering away; they spent little time in exploring the powerful causes which had generated geographically-specific structures of state power long before capitalism, or in explaining the survival of the state in terms of the antiquity or strength of those structures. Because state formation was assumed, as late as the 1970s national identities were neglected also, relegated to the same limbo as pre-war concepts like 'national character'.[13]

The return to the themes of state formation and national identity antedated the collapse of communist regimes and the reassertion of the nation state in Eastern Europe after 1989. In England, this revival was related most parochially to the frustration of plans for devolved government in Wales and Scotland, anticipated in the Kilbrandon Report of 1973 and sidestepped by clever political footwork at Westminster after Scots and Welsh referenda held in March 1979.[14] Secondly, it related to academic incredulity and indignation at the displays of mass emotion evoked in Britain by the Falklands War of 1982. The symbolic frustration of anti-statist devolution and the triumphalist reassertion of a unified nationalism were frequently received by the English intelligentsia as affronts, calling for an academic response in order that these setbacks to a modernist project might be explained away. Attention to state formation and identity thus sometimes carried the implied agenda of an attempt to dismantle both. Analytically, however, one can identify five main sources of scholarly innovation on this point, within which political purposes sometimes had a role.

The first source was political science and sociology, beginning in the 1970s.[15] Sociology had not ignored nationalism, of course; but where it had formerly traced its origins no earlier than Kant,[16] one distinguished student now antedated national consciousness and traced its origins over several millennia to ethnicity,[17] a subject still out of bounds to many historians. The mid 1980s saw a cluster of books, often from North America, produced by the further realization that sociology had ignored the idea of state.[18]

The second source was provided less by writings on European history than by the political movement for European union. It was this that provoked J. G. A. Pocock's initial challenge, when a 'special relationship' with New Zealand was disrupted in the early 1970s by Britain's entry into 'Europe'.[19] The escalating project of integration stimulated both Euro-sceptic and Europhile surveys,[20] as well as an officially funded collective enterprise. Between 1989 and 1992, a group of scholars addressed a set of largely structural and functional themes sponsored by the European Science Foundation project on 'The Origins of the Modern State in Europe, 13–18th Centuries', a project with a clear contemporary agenda.[21]

Thirdly, internal stresses within the British Isles had been paralleled by renewed academic attention (especially in Scotland, Ireland and Wales) to what was defined as the 'British question': the assembly of the United Kingdom out of long-existing component parts, or its attempted disassembly, and the cultural and political relations of those components. By contrast, not many historians in England accepted Pocock's challenge to see British history as the history of geographical components for some years after that challenge was made. This theme found its main academic home at the Folger Library in Washington: there an influential series of seminars was held between 1984 and 1987, organized by John Pocock, Lois Schwoerer, Gordon Schochet and others. Although these seminars sailed under the flag of the history of political thought, their content came to be increasingly dominated by religion, national identity and state formation. The proceedings, first published informally, are now beginning to appear in formal guise.[22] This initiative in the field of political theory, with

Quentin Skinner's study of the early-modern emergence of the concept of the state,[23] provides the most sophisticated account now available of the theoretical dimension of the question.

The most influential analogue in political history was the 'four nations' analysis of the British Isles, stressing the internal dynamics resulting from the United Kingdom's formation as a dynastic state.[24] A pioneering book in this genre had been written by an American,[25] drawing on American sensitivities to questions of colonialism. It was Britain's debates of the 1970s on devolution which placed this issue on the agenda for modern political commentators, most famously from a left-wing Scottish viewpoint;[26] from the late 1980s this model connected with the reinterpretation of the 'English' Civil War as a war between the three kingdoms, pioneered by Conrad Russell,[27] a vision which became widely influential within English academe.[28]

There was a fourth source. 'Nationalism', a European term, had long been inescapable as a leading theme of continental European historiographies. Yet historians of continental Europe had often denied that England experienced nationalism in the sense familiar to them, and historical works addressing the continental European dimension had little immediate impact within the historiography of Britain's long eighteenth century.[29] In this area it was the political Left that reopened the debate in Britain.[30] A debate had existed within such circles, notably from Perry Anderson and Benedict Anderson,[31] without extending beyond that political milieu; the extension of this debate was due in large part to the growing interest in 'identity' created by postmodern methodologies. Beginning with the individual, the postmodern subject matter grew steadily more generalized: the identities of race, class and gender were eventually extrapolated to end with national identities as a whole. Here, above all, were targets for authors who saw national identities as ones unthinkingly sustained by their political opponents and open to deconstruction.[32] 'Class' was, in reality, a token presence in this new trinity: to a large degree, historians of this persuasion turned to nationalism in response to the breakdown of a traditional class-based historical analysis.[33]

Fifth, ecclesiastical history led us back to a mode of consciousness that had been a key matrix of national identity.[34] Unexpectedly, this discipline revealed that the concept of an English national church, and that of a people with a destiny mapped out by Providence, both preceded the Reformation;[35] the implications of this work are explored below (section V). The theme of the role of religion in shaping national consciousness had never disappeared from writings on the Reformation,[36] but such surveys had long had little impact on other historians' ideas of English identity in a later period. Such insights were now felt even in French Revolutionary studies, hitherto most dominated by assertions of secularization: the link between religion and national identity in continental Europe's resistance to Napoleonic aggression began to be stressed from the mid 1980s. In Spain, but not only in Spain, a holy war against atheistic Jacobinism was combined with a movement of national emancipation and a religious revival. But a revival presupposes something to be revived, and many of the details of military mobilization against invading French armies reveal the reassertion of existing local devotions, priestly leadership, the veneration of saints or relics, the invocation of an historic national role in fighting heresy and defending the motherland.[37]

It remained to be seen how these intellectual influences would affect the way in which national identity was explained in that paradigmatic case, England. There were to be two false starts, one exploring the theme of the 'military-fiscal state', the other exploiting the idea of 'the invention of tradition', but both contributed to an evolving understanding of the subject. Nevertheless, the significance of the years 1660–1832 was to be clear only when the period was seen within a much wider time-frame.

III.   THE FAILURE OF FUNCTIONALISM

The idea that the formation and survival of states can be adequately explained in functional terms was now reasserted on the basis of research on taxation, linked with earlier work on war. The thesis of the importance of war in state formation had already been lucidly stated by Samuel Finer and Anthony Smith, and had substantial validity.[38] The English and British state after 1688, in the Whig model of Macaulay and Trevelyan, was pictured as libertarian because loosely governed and lightly taxed. How, then, had such a state enjoyed such spectacular success in war, overseas expansion and economic growth in the following century and a half? Work by Peter Dickson, Peter Mathias and Patrick O'Brien[39] showed that Britain had, on the contrary, been one of the most heavily taxed states in *ancien-régime* Europe. 'Money is the sinews of war'[40] was a maxim better known to historians of colonial America and of the American Revolution, for the major traumatic episode of the eighteenth century in which the British polity was disassembled arose, ostensibly, from a dispute over the authority and ability of the metropolitan government to finance its military defence. This insight was made the basis of an analysis of Britain as a strong state by John Brewer in a work which focused on administrative structures and military logistics, and said little about national identities.[41]

In 1990 Lawrence Stone chaired a seminar at Princeton on state formation, the proceedings of which were published in 1994. None of the contributions dealt directly with religion. Not many of them addressed national identity as a necessary precondition to or analogue of state formation. War, not national identity, religion, culture or law was the key component of Stone's own explanations, and for Stone 'war is above all a matter of logistics', not of morale, belief, mission, ideology or politics. Stone indeed dismissed these: the state, he argued, 'has been described, cynically but accurately, by Eric Hobsbawm as "a people who share a common misconception as to their origins, and a common antipathy towards their neighbours".' It followed, he claimed, that 'victory in war was a question of money, not men'.[42] Stone found explanations of victory by adapting the Whig political scenario that had always gone with his social-structural scenario: 1688 created a strong state, but one the bureaucratic machinery of which was 'uniquely decentralized' into the hands of the local gentry. This decentralization rather than a strong salaried bureaucracy, argued Stone, explained the paradox that Britain could be so highly taxed yet remain 'relatively liberal', the wielders of power having some regard for the rule of law, at least for property law. Stone contended that, after 1688, it was 'the parliamentary system, which had been a handicap to the Stuarts' that 'now became the critical element in creating Britain's fiscal capacity'. Brewer urged that it was the tax-collecting bureaucracy which was critical.[43] They were not that far apart.

These shared assumptions had the effect of restricting the themes on the agenda of national identity to the characteristics of what John Brewer had termed 'the military-fiscal state': taxation levels, debt, the tax-collecting bureaucracy.[44] First came the state, assumed Stone, then came nationalism: 'British nationalism certainly developed in the period 1790–1810, but the credit must go mainly to the fears engendered by, first, the radical ideas of the French revolutionaries and then, the ambitions of Napoleon for world hegemony'.[45] Nationalism was evidently a late consequence, not an early cause, of national success. Indeed much writing elsewhere about eighteenth-century riots, impressment, smuggling, coining and the unpopularity of public criminal punishments left the consistent impression that the state was strongly unpopular, a regime to be understood in functional terms rather than in terms of consensual acceptance, ideological hegemony or shared national identity.[46] Although Brewer contended that the British state was more like its continental counterparts than had previously been thought, and although Stone replied that 'In many important ways, the British state remained different',[47] they both argued their case on a functional level, largely omitting national consciousness, and wholly omitting political ideology, law and religion.

The Stone–Brewer vision was of the imperial and military formation of 'the state', an abstract concept and one which did not clearly distinguish England from Britain or Britain from the United Kingdom. At that early stage of the subject this part of the picture was made to do duty for the whole. The thesis was also proleptic, too secure about the outcome; yet this confidence rested on a circular argument. Britain could raise the taxation to win its wars because it was sufficiently libertarian. How do we know it was sufficiently libertarian? Because it raised enough taxation to win the wars. It might be objected that in the long eighteenth century there was no such security, either about national wealth or military victory. Each war, each rebellion, hung in the balance. The most crucial episode of state formation of all, the American Revolution, never featured in Stone's or Brewer's scenario, yet that episode is central in revealing the nature of the ideological processes involved.[48] Scholarship outside the long eighteenth century had already revealed that the longer term scenario of state formation in the British Isles, as on most of the European continent, was essentially dynastic (and therefore ideologically, not merely functionally, expressed) and that it was essentially concerned with England's relations with Scotland, Ireland and Wales. This at once illuminated both that process and its constraints. It replaced on the historical agenda the theoretical underpinnings of the state in ideology and law; and it highlighted the salient role of religion. All these called for integration into a functional model.

IV. ELEMENTARY POSTMODERNISM: THE LONG EIGHTEENTH CENTURY

Functional models of state formation found an alternative from 1987 in research which arrived at a familiar end-point from unfamiliar materials. A pioneering work in the study of national consciousness argued on the evidence of cultural history for a reformulation of early Hanoverian English identities in reaction against French cultural hegemony, a 'philosophical transformation' of 'mere patriotism' into nationalism 'essentially between the mid-1740s and the mid-1780s'.[49] This essay in the analysis of discourse was nevertheless overshadowed by another influential work that depicted nationalism as false consciousness by drawing on ideas of the 'invention of tradition'. Linda Colley's *Britons*[50] had two main explanatory theses, in the areas of war and religion, and one main argument about chronology. The first thesis (echoing Lawrence Stone's seminar of 1990) was that 'War played a vital part in the invention of a British nation after 1707'. The second thesis concerned religion: 'It was their common investment in Protestantism that first allowed the English, the Welsh and the Scots to become fused together, and to remain so, despite their many cultural divergences.'[51] The book's chronological scenario was that Britishness was invented after 1707, fundamentally recast after 1815, and open to easy reinvention in the present. These three elements will be examined in turn.

First, war. The main research for *Britons* was on the militia during the French Revolutionary and Napoleonic Wars: what were the reactions of the rank and file to military service? Who was unwilling to serve, and why? What effect did the geographical mobility of regular and militia units have on people's sense of their identity? The author extrapolated this research, pointing to the series of wars with France – begun in 1689, ending only in 1815, and each larger than the former – and argued for their novel importance in defining English identity antithetically against a foreign enemy. Yet this argument was inconclusive, for if wars are formative influences on collective self-awareness, it seems likely that an English national identity was forged much earlier, and may have established itself before the shared 'British' identity allegedly created by military cooperation after 1707. We shall see that this was indeed so (section V below).

It is not clear what, if anything, the addition of the term 'the Other' added to this argument, yet this was the term continually invoked. This antithesis meant that the complex *impact* of war was explained in only one way, in terms of 'Britons' defining themselves against 'an obviously hostile Other'. More influences of war on society might be expected,[52] and the tensions and lasting disunities created by wars must be weighed against the unities they (perhaps temporarily) demanded. Colley's argument that 'men and women decide who they are by reference to who and what they are not'[53] shifted attention to situations, especially military-fiscal situations, and away from thought and belief. Yet unless people already had a fairly good idea of their own substantive characteristics, it is unclear why they would perceive the Other as the Other at all.[54]

Britons also treated wars in this period as having one main sort of *outcome*: uniting Britons, and especially the English, Scots and Welsh elite, against the outsider. There were, nevertheless, countervailing forces, for wars in the long eighteenth century often opened up internal tensions as much as they resolved them. Whig wars against France under William III and Anne stoked Tory–Jacobite resentment, and France frequently played on the possibility of an invasion to restore the Pretender. One consequence of such a restoration after 1689 would have been a redefinition (or disaggregation) of the constitutional relations of England with Scotland, Ireland and Wales: this possibility was present as late as the abortive French invasion attempt of 1759.[55] Although the Seven Years' War was a triumph for Britain within Europe, American historians have revealed how it sowed the seeds of disunion in the Thirteen Colonies.[56] The War of American Independence was a British civil war, profoundly dividing opinion on both sides of the Atlantic[57] and almost leading to the loss of Ireland. Equally, a French invasion attempt in 1797 and an Irish rebellion in 1798 mark points at which Britain's war with revolutionary France almost ended in defeat and dismemberment.[58] Without these major episodes, any account of state formation would exclude the essential counterfactuals.

The second explanatory thesis of the book concerned religion as a matrix of identity. *Britons* rightly attached importance to this theme, which had already been reintroduced elsewhere in scholarship on the long eighteenth century. Yet *Britons* enlisted Protestantism chiefly as a way of strengthening its simple antithesis in which 'Protestant Britain' confronted 'Catholic France'.[59] There is most truth in this explanation between the Glorious Revolution and the end of the Seven Years' War, but it is not an exclusive truth: before 1688 the obvious enemy was another 'Protestant' power, the United Provinces, as it was during the American War of 1776–83. Imperial expansion also contributed to break up any simple denominational perceptions of 'the Other'.[60] As we now realize, the correlation in England during these years was strong between the 'friends of America' and theologically heterodox Dissent, but weak between pro-Americans and Protestant Dissent as a whole. Britain had Roman Catholic allies at many points in the eighteenth century, including Portugal; France itself from 1716 to 1731; and Austria during the War of the League of Augsburg, the War of the Spanish Succession, and the wars against France after 1793. Alliances with Orthodox Russia caused equally little difficulty.

By contrast, the accession of a Calvinist monarch as William III in 1689 and a Lutheran one as George I in 1714 created major difficulties, despite their unchallenged Protestantism.[61] After 1763 it mattered less and less that France was Catholic, and after 1789 anti-French sentiment flourished after the Roman Catholic Church in France was shattered. Throughout the early and mid eighteenth century, 'a virulent anti-Catholicism was compatible with the entire spectrum of political positions in England'.[62] A simple dualism of Protestant versus Catholic will not do as an explanation of a putative consensual national identity.[63] A more informed approach to religious phenomena would show that, especially from the forging of a new Whig ideology in the 1670s, the enemy was less Roman Catholicism as such than 'Popery', a heady cocktail of power, luxury, uniformity, universal monarchy and pride which could be diagnosed in a number of enemies: some Englishmen saw it in the United Provinces in the 1660s,[64] some colonial Americans saw it in George III's rule in the 1760s.

Because the object of the concept of 'Protestantism' in *Britons* was chiefly to establish an antithesis between 'Britons' and 'the Other', the book offered little on the nature of that religion although this was one of its key themes. Despite brief acknowledgement of Protestant Dissent[65] it treated 'Protestantism' without further discussion as essentially one thing, where the reality was much more complex. This relative disregard of the content and continuities of religion also contributed to one of the book's less persuasive assumptions. The author wrote repeatedly of 'the invention of

Britishness', of Great Britain as 'an invented nation', 'this essentially invented nation', 'an invention forged above all by war'.[66] Such an approach assumed to be valid the message of an influential text:[67] an implication that nationalism is false consciousness, the irrational result of what *Britons* termed 'a vast superstructure of prejudice'.[68] Such a formulation does not reveal what true consciousness might be; but since everything is at some moment done, thought or felt for the first time, it can never be more than a truism. The trope of false consciousness is particularly unhelpful when it implies a high degree of credulousness on the part of the people and of deceit on the part of undefined elites, as when scenarios of national development embodied in ecclesiastical history are dismissed as 'pious lies... what [people] were told in church'.[69] With the idea of false consciousness went assumptions about real motivation: 'an active commitment to nation was often intimately bound up with an element of self-interest... From patriotism, men and women were able to anticipate profits of some kind.'[70] Why this should be more true at this time than at any other, and why it should therefore be determinative of national identity, are unclear.

An inattention to denominational and sectional differences went with a neglect of the differences between British and English. The book's subject was British national identity, Britishness defined as the unitary identity to which some appealed in order to ratify the Union of England and Wales with Scotland in 1707 and to replace Englishness and Scottishness. But the novelty of 'Britishness' is not evidence that national identity as such was new, that it was false consciousness, or that it was weakly grounded. It can be shown, as we shall see, that Englishness, though continually evolving, was very ancient. A stress on the novelty and impact of the Union of 1707 was insufficient to demonstrate that the inhabitants of the British Isles did come to see themselves as a single people or were often urged to do so.[71] Before the nineteenth century, they probably shared an identity less unanimously than did the citizens of the USA after 1776 or of France after 1789. A few unified national ideas and symbols were devised and adopted, but they never erased sectional consciousness; lasting differences often threatened the dissolution of the state which had been so laboriously built up. It had already been established that Wales and Scotland possessed separate identities from England's into the nineteenth century, albeit fragmented ones: the end-point of *Britons*, a unified identity, was in doubt even before the book was published in 1992.[72]

A model of national consciousness is required that gives proper attention to the considerable degree to which 'British' identity was consistent with ancient sectional identities rather than replacing them with the Whig vision of 1707. Such a model would account for the way in which travellers from the British Isles in continental Europe, even into the nineteenth century, normally used 'British' of political or commercial matters to describe the component parts of the United Kingdom acting together, almost never to imply a shared 'British' national identity, except occasionally to indicate something praiseworthy about the 'British character' in war.[73]

If 'nationalism' was born in 1707, how did it relate to the *ancien régime*? *Britons* suggested that it did so chiefly as a solvent; that the 'plebeian patriotism' enlisted to defend Britain against the French Revolution had such democratic overtones that it undermined as much as defended the old order, with results evident after 1815: patriotism, or nationalism, was presented as 'radical'.[74] Yet much of the evidence advanced to support this argument can be paralleled in earlier periods. Doubts about the reliability of the militia forces were entertained equally in the 1640s and in 1688. The elite after 1660 feared putting arms into the hands of potential Levellers, and the extent of Jacobite disaffection after 1688 made impossible the organization of a national militia until the Act of 1757.[75] The fact that significant numbers of men would not fight in a particular war, or fight at the behest of a particular ministry or monarch, did not mean that they were lacking in awareness of or identification with their national identity. On the contrary, it might mean that they were so highly conscious of that identity as to possess cogent reasons for thinking that the government of the day was betraying it. As research had earlier shown, during the Napoleonic Wars it was chiefly Dissent, especially 'rational Dissent', that most resisted official efforts to promote military service, and not surprisingly: 'at this time religion usually set the terms of the debate about loyalty'.[76] It was Anglicanism, especially when influenced by evangelicalism, that was most resolutely statist, and it has long been known that a similar link can be observed at the same period in Germany.[77]

The third element in *Britons* was its chronological scenario. A special significance was claimed for the period 1707–1837. The author argued that 'it was during this period that a sense of British national identity was forged'; it saw 'the invention of Britishness'.[78] If valid explanations of major developments are being offered, those explanations will indeed place the phenomena chronologically with greater precision than before. Yet this argument was unsupported in two major ways. It rested on a lack of comparison even with other eighteenth-century examples: instances of deliberate attempts to frame a national identity in the USA after 1783 and in France after 1789[79] show that any analogous efforts in Britain to devise national symbols, to integrate provincial and regional consciousnesses in a new Britishness, were relatively few and fragmented. One can find a small number of unlikely bedfellows, from Daniel Defoe[80] to Lord Bute, who consciously tried to promote such a united identity, but their aspirations were of secondary importance in comparison with repeated attempts to devise and project images of religious denominations and of the dynasty, attempts which were already very ancient. Second, the argument for the special importance of the period 1707–1837 was unsupported by any comparison with what had occurred in previous centuries, yet it was just such a comparison that it now became possible to make.

Britons indeed had an underlying purpose which looked forward rather than back: 'Britain is bound now to be under immense pressure', it announced, threatened by loss of empire, by the decline of Protestantism, by European federalism.[81] The inspiration of much writing at that time was indeed Tom Nairn's 1970s text *The Break-up of Britain*, a work disclosing a secular, left-wing Scot's lack of historical understanding of the substance of Englishness, and Benedict Anderson's work, chiming with that of Hobsbawm and Ranger on the invention of tradition, and claiming the malleable, impermanent, and indeed terminal nature of national identity.[82] Linda Colley volunteered the importance of her Welsh background,[83] and a similar concern to promote devolution or dissolution may have been at work here, too. A nation 'invented', as she described it, could easily be de-invented, once the external stimuli were removed. This was the book's confessed present purpose: 'if Britishness survives (and it may not)', *Britons* expressed the *hope* that it would take a different form.[84] Its main omission was all the more puzzling: without investigation, the book treated 'patriotism' and 'nationalism' as synonyms and ignored their analytical relationship to 'Britishness'.[85]

V.   LONG CONTINUITIES: THE RETURN OF THE
ANGLO-SAXONS

Both of these false starts embodied some valid general principles: state formation, war and taxation were indeed interrelated, and national identities did indeed evolve over time. Yet both were much older than nineteenth-century nationalism or the Union of 1707. The related processes of state building, and the interaction of religion and law in the conceptualization of a national identity, can be traced back beyond the personal Union of crowns with Scotland when James I became king of both realms in 1603 and beyond the Union with Wales in 1536.[86] There are grounds for antedating the strong state earlier still, and a major displacement in our perspective on these questions has been compelled by the work of medievalists. Anglo-Saxon governments have been shown to have operated the most effective financial system in Europe between the Romans and *c.* 1300, and a state form able to avoid civil conflict by bringing the earls under central jurisdiction. Much evidence points to a wide extent of 'emotional and ideological commitment' to this state.[87] Anglo-Saxon law and religion now emerge as the origins of English perceptions of group identity at later periods too.[88] As Elton argued, the united kingdom of England can be dated to the political union of 927, a dynastic arrangement which henceforth embodied what Wormald had identified as 'a remarkably precocious sense of common "Englishness"' defined, for the literate, by the ecclesiastical historian Bede.[89]

Merely structural considerations, even including military ones, were themselves insufficient explanations of this achievement. This could be shown by a functional comparison of the English kingdom of Edward the Confessor and the German polity of the Emperor Henry IV, the two most powerful monarchies of late eleventh-century Europe. Both polities were challenged by localist revolts of nobles; but whereas the revolt of 1073 'sounded the knell of effective kingship in much of medieval Germany',[90] the northern rising of 1065 did not destroy the integrity of the English monarchy, any more than did a whole series of northern risings in subsequent centuries. England remained a relatively unified, centralized polity; others in Europe did not. Why were so many polities of Western Europe, existing in recognizably modern shape in about AD 1000, broken up and reconstituted only much later? Why did England, remarkably, retain much the same shape to the present day? England's 'governmental apparatus' was 'bafflingly elementary', argued Wormald[91] (we might add that it continued to be so throughout the eighteenth century, in comparison with many continental states, however much we have recently learned about the customs and excise or the militia). The answer must lie elsewhere, and one sociologist was independently moving in the same direction in his work on the question of ethnic survival, asking 'how and why some *ethnie* were able to perpetuate their cultures, albeit with changes, over centuries, even millenia, while others, some of them politically much stronger, dissolved and fell into near-oblivion'. He suggested that 'among the complex of relevant factors, religious conditions of salvation and their texts, liturgies and clergies, were vital elements in the retention of ethnic forms among many communities'.[92]

The structural explanations that might explain England's exceptionalism were insufficient, argued Wormald, since 'each was more or less available to hegemonies elsewhere in Europe that did not survive'.[93] A Roman inheritance of political unity was not effective in Britain, but certainly found in *Italia, Hispania* and *Gallia. Britannia*, after the Roman withdrawal, collapsed politically; even the Saxon invaders achieved no greater unity than the Heptarchy, with no inherent trend to unification. The inclusive English kingdom of Aethelstan (927) had many functional similarities with its Carolingian prototype, including oath-bound allegiance to the sovereign as a political guarantee and as the defining element in a legal jurisdiction which safeguarded property; none of this eliminated powerful localist pressures. Even the Conquest in 1066 does not sufficiently explain English unity thereafter. How was the new French-speaking ruling elite 'persuaded to accept a style of government which was in effect that of the kingdom acquired north of the Channel, and definitely not that of the kingdom left behind south of it?... Why indeed did they so soon come to think of themselves as English? The Norman Conquest cannot have been the *making*, even if it was the saving, of England. England, as its name implies, was made already'.[94] Another scholar has also traced 'an increasing sophistication in the development of a self-conscious perception of "English" cultural uniqueness and individuality towards the end of the ninth century'.[95]

What, then, created the difference? One clue was that England had another characteristic from, at the latest, the twelfth century: a sense of mission to bring civilization to its neighbours.[96] If England consolidated itself and expanded at this early period with only elementary bureaucratic mechanisms, its distinguishing feature was a formative ideology, and from a yet earlier date. 'England' and 'English' were terms denoting a 'well-established ethnicity' even before the early tenth century. What was its source? The most successful polities of early medieval Europe were those that responded to the identification of a common enemy: this was articulated partly by writing a people's history, partly by depicting it as a people chosen by God, a warrior people with a mission, specially chosen by the God of battles. The inclusive identity of Angles, English, was established by Pope Gregory's mission: 'a single English kingdom was anticipated by a single English church'.[97] Ecclesiastical authority was then 'reinforced by a supreme masterpiece of the world's historical literature', Bede's *An Ecclesiastical History of the English People*. Bede was a biblical scholar, and his underlying theme in his *History* was 'God's dealings with his original Chosen People'.[98] Bede interpreted the traumatic history of his island since the Roman withdrawal in terms of divine pleasure or displeasure, reward or punishment. Englishness became providential.

In Bede's vision, the '*gens Anglorum*' became 'a people of the Covenant', with a powerful image of their past and their destiny. The dynasty of Alfred exploited it; Bede's *History* was widely circulated in Latin and in English translation; Alfred's lawbook in turn 'took the Old Testament model further than Charlemagne'. 'Old Testament logic was that the cause of political disaster was sin and crime. To obey God's law was a *sine qua non* of lasting worldly success.' Anglo-Saxon experience, whether of the Northumbrians, Mercians, Kentishmen or West Saxons, was that 'Bede's implied warning had almost come to pass when another pagan people crossed the North Sea and threatened to remove their own hard-won promised land as the punishment of their backslidings'. By the early eleventh century, the English kingdom could look back on a time of trials overcome. After the Conquest, this vision of English unity and purpose was absorbed by the spokesmen of the new regime, as in William of Malmesbury's *Gesta Regum Anglorum* and Orderic Vitalis's *Historia Ecclesiastica Gentis Normannorum*.[99] Bede meanwhile achieved wider and wider circulation. By the 1130s, another edifice was built on this foundation, Geoffrey of Monmouth's *Historia Regum Britanniae*.[100] Nor was a national identity an attribute of medieval England alone: Scotland, Ireland and Wales all displayed a variously defined sense of their integrity, widely shared among their populations, which made their relations with England a key dynamic of state formation in the British Isles.[101] English expansion, however fitful, was informed by this sense of Englishness from at least the mid twelfth century;[102] England was a special case in a Europe-wide process of the expansion of core kingdoms over Slavonic, Celtic or Iberian peripheries.[103] These were processes which, in England's case, offset and finally extinguished the fluid, transnational allegiances of the medieval period.

The theme of the impact of war on collective consciousness is important to medievalists, and beside the divisive effects of conflict, powerful until 1485, must be set unifying influences. Service in the nationally organized Anglo-Saxon militia must have had such an effect, and the way in which the concept of 'the community of the realm' was reinforced by military service can be traced from the reign of Edward I (1272–1307); this obligation was enforced by persuasion or propaganda in which the interests of the people and the kingdom were openly equated, a 'common obligation to defend the realm'[104] which appealed over the heads of the barons, bound as they were by more clearly defined and more limited feudal obligations. One scholar has pointed to the twelfth century as the era in which the Irish (and also the Scots and Welsh) were redefined by English chroniclers as alien, barbarous and hostile: 'One of the consequences of this was the emergence of a sense of Englishness based upon what were perceived as significant differences between English and Celtic societies',[105] a sense which long pre-dated Protestantism. Another scholar had stressed the Englishness of this phase of expansion, and argued that what happened in the British Isles in the twelfth and thirteenth centuries was 'the second tidal wave of Anglo-Saxon or English colonization',[106] despite lasting conflicts over control of the Anglo-Norman empire.

War demonstrably contributed to national feeling during the Hundred Years' War with the French: this acted to focus an English identity, though one clearly different from that which came later.[107] For the sixteenth century, Elton similarly stressed the importance of English self-definition against 'another body of people, habitually hostile [the Scots], opposing whom meant identifying more consciously with your own kind on a national scale'.[108] The emotionally charged wars with Spain of that century were expressed in terms of a religious antithesis[109] and gave rise to a 'Black Legend' sharply contrasting Spanish and English character types.[110] Yet war was not necessarily a causeless cause: national identity preceded external war in the seventeenth century and was not chiefly dependent on it.[111] Nor was war against an external 'Other' necessarily paramount: in the 1640s, 'Civil war was a forcing house of national identity'.[112] The three Dutch wars of the seventeenth century had their own distinct impact, and related to the dynamics of denomination and identity in yet another way. Nor did this side-effect of war end in 1815. Ecclesiastical historians of nineteenth- and twentieth-century Britain have shown that the interplay of war and religion continued in new settings;[113] the two world wars of the twentieth century and the major social changes that followed warn against a claim that any earlier war forged a lasting sense of identity. The First World War was the prelude to the breakup of a shared, empire-wide sense of Britishness;[114] the Second to a redefinition of British ethnic identity also.

The progressive rejection of a nineteenth-century model of nationalism has revealed ways in which national feeling can arise even despite linguistic diversity, a diversity which existed before 1066 and survived to the fourteenth century. Law provides one such example. It has long been known that 'The earliest and most ardent statements of the theory of *de jure* as well as *de facto* independence of kingdoms came from canonists and theologians largely of England, Spain and France, from the late twelfth to the mid-thirteenth century and later'.[115] The Englishness of the English common law can be dated to at least 1210, when King John took with him to Ireland a charter to ensure that 'English laws and customs' would be observed there.[116] Similarly, literary scholars, addressing thought and belief rather than structural questions, have long been aware of a national consciousness in medieval England. Older work tended to treat it as a fifteenth-century innovation,[117] an insight progressively extended back to the mid thirteenth. In that century authors using Latin and French also 'expressed their sense of England as a nation'. That the concept of the nation coincided with the whole people was an idea disseminated, deepened and consolidated by writers in English in the fifty years before the outbreak of the Hundred Years' War in 1337, defining a nation in terms of its territory, its people and its language. No longer can it be maintained that 'national consciousness was held in check by a dominant supra-national organization, the Church', since 'multiple and overlapping identities co-exist without cancelling one another out' and since 'it was in the interests of the clergy to promote a sense of national identity as a way of claiming common interest with their lay audience'.[118]

A Providential framework for these national identities long preceded the Reformation: the parallel between England and Israel, in order to illuminate God's design for the first as well as the second, was introduced as a truism in the chancellor's opening speech to the Parliament of 1376–7.[119] Where Norman kings of England were initially cautious about claiming sovereignty over Wales, Ireland and Scotland, their archbishops such as Lanfranc and Anselm did claim that the jurisdiction of Canterbury extended over all the British Isles.[120] It was not a consequence of Protestantism, then, that 'an ideologically engendered allegiance is... the key to the antiquity and resilience of the English state'.[121]

The ancient identity of the *Ecclesia Anglicana* meant that the Reformation did not at once create a unitary national identity. As a religious message of universal validity, Protestantism initially implied a reaction against the national subdivision of the universal Church; only subsequently were some sections of 'Protestantism' identified with national churches and so with national identities.[122] One strand of the Reformation stressed a pan-European solidarity between believers in the Reformed traditions, a shared sense of a supranational destiny.[123] Since the English had 'a long-standing reputation for xenophobia' even by 1500, it did not help that Protestant theology was originally associated with German reformers; not until the reign of Mary I (1553–8) were reformers 'given the opportunity to sail for the first time under Protestant colours'.[124] Anti-Popery, too, could be an international phenomenon, and not until Elizabeth's reign did an assumption become prevalent that England had a special, or even the leading, role in that drama.[125] The Church in England only adopted the label 'Protestant' for itself in the first decade of the seventeenth century, and then in order to distinguish itself from both Rome and Geneva: Anglican Protestantism did not become pan-European. In Scotland and Northern Ireland the Reformation went much further: confessional differences have been basic to the emerging 'three kingdoms' explanation of the dynamics of state formation in the British Isles,[126] and when Wales acquired a distinct confessional identity from Protestant Dissent in the late eighteenth and early nineteenth centuries, that principality took its place as a fourth component in the model.

Reformation and Counter-Reformation meant that the sixteenth century saw a replay of many of the challenges and crises of the tenth: extensive evidence for national consciousness survives from the sixteenth century to the mid seventeenth, importantly dependent on a sense of Providential destiny.[127] Wormald depicted Richard Hooker giving expression to a doctrine of national unity and purpose that would not have been unfamiliar to Archbishop Wulfstan.[128] The transmission of this sense of Englishness in the interim is now a subject for future research, but, as Patrick Wormald has argued,

> the *onus probandi* lies on those who would deny that such a sense remained embedded in the bulk of the English population throughout this long period. Unless a sense of English identity had penetrated towards the roots of society, it is very difficult to understand how it survived at all... The political education of European peoples recommenced in the aftermath of Rome's fall with the simple but explosive idea that God might single out a distinct culture for His special favour in return for its enforced conformity with His Will as its authorities perceived it. That idea bore its first fruit in the concept of the English. The indestructibility of their political *persona* is the proof of its power.[129]

This formation survived the Reformation and was enhanced by it in a multiplicity of ways. English translations of the Bible consistently rendered as 'nation' a variety of words in Hebrew and Greek that were not synonymous with that term. In this usage, the vernacular also went far beyond the Latin Vulgate Bible, and is not to be explained by it.[130] The vernacular did not have to carry a national message, but it did so as men assumed the translated Scriptures to be a ratification of an idea of Providential national identity. The individual was tied to the polity by allegiance, and Christianity was the ideology that interpreted that tie. It was an ideologically engendered allegiance which characterized English society in the long eighteenth century, and which fell into schism in 1776 at a date demonstrably before the emergence of 'nationalism' as we now know it.

Protestantism was never just one thing. A theoretically articulate history of the Church of England, including its ecclesiology, ecclesiastical polity, and political theory, would suggest cautions. However deep-rooted our assumptions, it may be questioned whether 'Protestant' and 'Catholic' were simple, antithetical, ontological identities. They are more intelligible as political labels, generated in a tactical context, and used with all the tactical subtleties that normally surround such terms. 'Protestantism' was not a fixed, unambiguous concept which could be used to explain that ambiguous one, national identity. Into the eighteenth century many argued, from a Low Church and Dissenting stance, that the Church of England was not Protestant – that it was still compromised by Popish survivals. Others, on the High Church wing, also argued that the Church of England was not Protestant – that it possessed continuity with the medieval church. Historians may not simply announce that 'England was a Protestant country', that it embodied 'Protestantism', or claim that they can easily read off, from any such religious identity, data about national identity or patriotism. Religion nevertheless mattered. If 'nationalism' is an anachronistic term for the form taken by national identities before the nineteenth century,[131] and if shared history, law and dynastic allegiance constituted an alternative, it is possible to see how large a part religion played in that matrix of ideas.

The diversity of 'Protestantism' had major practical significance. Denominations not in communion with the see of Rome differed widely. They differed in ecclesiastical polity: some were Episcopalian, others Presbyterian, others Congregational. They differed in theology: some were Trinitarian, some Arian, some Socinian. In soteriology, some were predestinarian, some double predestinarian, some Arminian. Some adhered to solafidianism, others not. Some had an apocalyptic eschatology; some, in addition, were millenarian; others not. They differed in pastoral strategies: some were revivalist; others were quietist. They were as different as Methodists, Baptists, Quakers, and continental European migrants, Lutheran and Calvinist. Nor were these things merely grit in the machinery: they were the machinery itself, centrally connecting with political thought and political conduct.[132]

These are not just optional finer points, 'subtle divisions'.[133] The major episodes of state aggregation and disaggregation throughout the seventeenth and eighteenth centuries were profoundly related to differences, even conflicts, *within* Protestantism. It would be hard to explain the Bishops' Wars of 1639–40, the proximate cause of the 'English' civil wars, as anything else. A shared 'Protestantism' was not enough in the eighteenth century to bring many of the Protestant Irish into the Anglo-Scots Union of 1707, even if Britain engaged in war with a Catholic power.[134] Within England, the confessional basis of electoral behaviour into the nineteenth century has been an emerging theme of research,[135] but this was chiefly a matter of the antagonism between the Church of England and Protestant Dissent which led to partial disestablishment and the fracturing of the confessional unity of the polity.[136] In 1982, Professor Robbins rightly gave prominence to the argument that 'The Christian religion in the British Isles, in its divided condition, has... been deeply involved in the cultural and political divisions of modern Britain and Ireland' in the nineteenth century.[137] In 1988, he demonstrated at length this central point for England's relations with Scotland and Wales;[138] it applies to domestic English identities also.

A perspective beginning in 1707 would also obscure the role of the Church in state formation, since the reversion to a Presbyterian organization for the Scottish Church had been imposed by William III in 1689 in response to the dynastic disloyalty of Scottish episcopalians to the new regime: 1707 was exceptional in entrenching religious difference as a route to political uniformity. The role of religious uniformity as a route to political unification had been clear in the history of the British Isles for centuries; it was reasserted in the Union with Wales of 1536 and in the Union with Scotland of 1603, came under increasing strain in British–colonial relations, decisively failed in 1776, but was reasserted in Ireland in 1798. No study could be complete which omitted these wider features in order to make plausible a secularized picture of a 'short eighteenth century'.

The greatest reverse for the British state, the loss of the American colonies, cannot be understood apart from the denominational dynamics that gave social shape to political theories.[139] 'Protestantism' was indeed shared in Britain and America, but this did not prevent the revolution. This argument about America will come as no surprise to historians of the British Isles who are used to dealing with the Civil War, the Glorious Revolution, the Irish rebellion of 1798, and Catholic Emancipation. In the face of the threat of the return of a Catholic Stuart dynasty, many Protestants in Britain did make common cause (though many did not: even here, Protestantism was a weak cement). But Jacobitism was *la révolution manquée*, the revolution that did not happen. The revolution that did happen, the American Revolution, a civil war among 'Protestants' that changed Anglophone history irreversibly and fundamentally, features too little in the historiography of the British Isles.

Protestantism alone was not enough. In that fertile seedbed of Dissenting Protestant denominations, the Thirteen Colonies, the sects played no clear role in generating a shared American identity before 1776. Only in England did the Henrician union of church and state provide a matrix within which a sense of normative ethical identity might ideally coincide with a political unit. It was the Church, not the sects, which possessed both an institutional, legal expression and a clear sense of national identity. Despite its internal differences, Anglicanism, not Protestantism, should be our key term.

VI.   SORCERER'S APPRENTICES: THE MISUSE OF HISTORY

Neither war, nor law, nor religion alone created an English identity, but their interaction in a Providential setting. Tracing their contributions shows how national consciousness can be discerned long before the 'nationalism' classically exemplified in 1848 or sometimes antedated to 1707. It reveals that processes of state formation were much older than the long eighteenth century; that their nature was essentially dynastic; that the influence of religion was profound long before the Reformation. Protestantism is not the key.[140] 'British' was an identity similarly owed to the Union of crowns in 1603 and the creation of a shared legal matrix of 'nationality' by *Calvin's Case* (1608), and long preceded any Whig cultural project associated with the Union of legislatures of 1707.[141]

A new identity did not necessarily erase older ones. The English did not cease to speak of 'Englishness' in 1603 or 1707: as their horizons widened, they sometimes used 'England' and 'English' to stand for all the communities of the archipelago. Even Edmund Burke (1729–97), a loyal Irishman, could write of himself as 'an Englishman'[142] to indicate his second identity as a member of the larger polity where one might now expect him to use 'British': nineteenth-century nationalism had not yet created its antagonisms. Into the nineteenth century, travellers within the British Isles nevertheless remained acutely aware of differences between Wales, Scotland, Ireland and England, and often found that travel only made them more appreciative of, and attached to, their identities as English, Irish, Scottish or Welsh. Regional differences within these countries were similarly emphasized; a shared British identity was appealed to only in specific contexts and for specific purposes, as a category inclusive of sectional identities, not as an identity that replaced its components. A 'British constitution', or 'British soldiers' engaged in 'British expeditions', did not necessarily imply an overriding British identity.[143]

'British' as a term in general usage has therefore had at least two senses. One was a spontaneous or encouraged Unionist identity allegedly felt equally by the Scots, Irish, Welsh and English. This may indeed have been problematic. But another usage was more prevalent: as employed by the four groups, usually when abroad, 'British' was an official, political euphemism for one's sectional identity, whether English, Welsh, Irish or Scottish: it was to a considerable degree synonymous with, and not a substitute for, sectional national identities. If so, it matters less that 'British' in the sense of the Whig defenders of 1707 had shallow foundations: 'Britishness' in its prevalent sense rested in large part on the ancient and massive foundations of Englishness, and the equally ancient if differently formulated identities of England's neighbours.[144]

On the basis of evidence reviewed above, we can be more cautious of deconstructionist programmes. Britain was not invented; it developed. It was not devised by a small number of cultural entrepreneurs, acting as advertising executives to package and market a new product; it grew, the often unintended result of actions by men and women in many walks of life and often, too, the result of conflicts and cross-purposes. Consequently, it misses the point to argue that 'Britain' was invented recently: its origins in England (not to mention Wales and Scotland) were very remote indeed. Those origins are often beyond the reach of present-day categories: one scholar has postponed the arrival of the abstract 'state' in England until it was given analytical expression in the late nineteenth century by the philosopher T. H. Green.[145]

The long track records of England, Scotland, Ireland and Wales have given rise to a variety of forms of national identity, continually evolving yet displaying long continuities; conceptualized by elites, yet validated by peoples; widely contested, yet widely held.[146] English history has always been a counterpoint of cosmopolitanism and introversion, both themes being present together. In general, the pattern within the British Isles has been the resilience of a diverse and plural system of identities, rather than the rigidity but final shattering of a unitary one.[147] This produced a polity with strengths and weaknesses: although it could not mobilize an ethnically homogeneous 'people', it had the strength of accommodating regional differences in a system which imposed on England, Scotland, Ireland and Wales no novel, abstract formula.[148] It had the greater strength of seldom demanding of its members a deeper acknowledgement of kinship with their neighbours than they were willing, informally, to give.[149]

The experience of imperial expansion and major war in the nineteenth and twentieth centuries never persuaded the English, at least, that they were a 'race':[150] lacking this idea and its attendant problems, the United Kingdom's plural national identities showed themselves to be, in functional terms, highly effective in two world wars. With the exception of southern Ireland (scarcely a modern or a postmodern problem) the United Kingdom survived the twentieth century with its unities impaired far less than other composite states such as Russia and Austria-Hungary. When the challenge of European integration became insistent from the 1980s, the UK's identities – in part a working survival from the old regime – did not fade away, nor was there any historical logic that demanded they do so. On the contrary, people with presentist agendas to pursue had to find means of de-historicizing those identities, suppressing the historical dimension in which public policy issues had long been discussed. But these are questions with the most explosive practical consequences. Whether some recent historians of the subject will prove in this context to be merely sorcerer's apprentices is a matter for urgent public as well as professional concern.

3

WHY WAS THERE NO NATIONALISM
IN ENGLAND?

I. THE PROBLEM

Nationalism has dominated Europe in the last two centuries: so much is
obvious. It has also dominated European historiographies; that is, its
existence has seemed to be self-evident, calling only for praise or blame. In
a modernist perspective, nationalism came to be seen as a natural formation, an unavoidable if generally undesirable response to urbanization,
industrialization and the emergence of 'mass society' in the late eighteenth
or early nineteenth centuries. In this perspective, nationalism emerged out
of earlier and anachronistic forms of collective consciousness but was little
indebted to them: it was a new state of being in a new world. The 'old
world' sustained, at most, 'patriotism'; from that phenomenon it was a
major transition to 'nationalism'.[1] Modernist historians sought to place
England squarely within a nexus of which nationalism, imperialism and
racialism were related facets. Problematically, to some historians of
continental Europe in the nineteenth and twentieth centuries it seemed
obvious that England had never experienced this new phenomenon of
'nationalism', yet their insights were hardly incorporated into the
historiography of England.

The emergence of nationalism, then, rested on a contrast with older
forms, yet this alleged transition was never adequately explained. How
did European states move from 'patriotism' to 'nationalism'?[2] How, the

question implies, did they develop from 'patriotism', a form of collective self-consciousness that was inward-looking, unwarlike, modest, moderate, premised on law and the defence of historic liberties, an ideology which was internationalist as least as much as it was aggrandizing, to 'nationalism', a virulent form of collective consciousness that was in many ways the opposite of all these: outward-oriented, warlike, hubristic, extreme, premised on race and language, and which blasted the internationalizing prospects of Enlightenment Europe in favour of the mutual destruction experienced between 1914 and 1945?[3] How, that is, do we move from patriotisms defined in opposition to 'despotism' to nationalisms that have been a key support of despotism? How do we explain this alleged unfolding logic of historical stages, a logic that (if real) was so strongly against the interests of so many who were affected by it?

In the aftermath of 1914 and 1945 it was natural to pose the problem in these terms. Yet this is nevertheless a *question mal posée*; it will be argued here that, in the case of England, patriotism did not develop into nationalism because both were doctrines not natural phenomena, and therefore linked by no teleology. Acorns may develop into oaks (or sometimes fail to do so), and we can frame explanations of how and why this happens. But we should have nothing to say about why apples fail to develop into oranges. If there is no such teleology in the English case, an alternative scenario becomes possible: that certain ways of conceptualizing group identity (let us not presume an answer by calling it *national* identity) were so well developed in England, and occupied the intellectual terrain so thoroughly, that there was insufficient conceptual space for nineteenth-century ideas of nationalism to flourish.[4] Just as there was no English nationalism in the exact sense of that term, the Britishness that followed the Anglo-Scots Union of 1707 was not a British nationalism either. England, Britain and the United Kingdom comprised a society that was highly self-aware, but one which normally took as symbols of identity a shared libertarian culture, and institutions that promoted the advance of civilization, law and history.

This being so, nationalism becomes a key problem for historians of England, resembling the classic conundrum 'why was there no socialism in America?'[5] It is a question all the more striking because of the much larger degree to which nineteenth-century nationalist assumptions or ideologies were adopted in England's neighbours: Wales, Scotland and Ireland. Yet the modern English experience has been significantly different, as the general absence of ideas of race from recent studies of English identity have unintentionally revealed.[6]

This problematizing of 'nationalism' gains plausibility as the modernist assumptions of the 'Age of Ideology' have collapsed. No longer can historians treat ideologies or '-isms' as reified and hypostatized actors on the world stage, striding like dinosaurs across the nineteenth and twentieth centuries. As their reification has weakened, so these ideologies have ceased to be explanatory tools, linked by teleologies or opposed in necessary antitheses, and have become historical phenomena which themselves demand historical explanation. We can no longer say: 'nationalism emerged in nineteenth-century Europe'; we must now say: 'in nineteenth-century Europe, certain individuals devised and propagated a novel doctrine concerning the nature of group identity, called nationalism. It was new in the following ways... ; it was propagated for the following reasons... ; it was partly adopted, but partly resisted; its trajectory was as follows...' Instead of persuading ourselves that we can find earlier and earlier examples of nineteenth-century phenomena, we now take the eighteenth-century phenomena seriously. Inevitably, the nineteenth century will need to be reinterpreted in the light of the eighteenth.

II. THE ABSENCE OF NATIONALISM

Nationalism and patriotism must be located as neologisms, as doctrines coined in a particular time and place.[7] In the absence of a proper history of concepts, called by German historians *Begriffsgeschichte*, even the second edition of the *Oxford English Dictionary* is only a preliminary guide. The *OED* does at least make clear that the term 'nation' was current in English discourse long before the coinage of the term 'nationalism'. Its first example of 'nation' is dated 1300, and 'national', 1597. Many instances follow. 'National' is defined as 'Peculiar to the people of a particular country, characteristic or distinctive of a nation' (1625) and 'Patriotic: strongly upholding one's own nation' (1711). To this family of terms belongs 'nationality', defined as 'National quality or character', with an early but unusual usage in 1691, when it is defined differently as 'In literature, art, etc. the quality of being distinctively national', a meaning not again exemplified by the *OED* until 1827.

The term 'nationalism', by contrast, came late and is given only a superficial entry in the *OED*. Its first definition, as a theological term, 'The doctrine that certain nations (as contrasted with individuals) are the object of divine election', is illustrated with an example from 1836, but this seems to be a usage that did not survive. The second meaning of 'nationalism', defined inadequately as 'Devotion to one's nation; national aspiration; a policy of national independence', is not illustrated until examples from 1844, 1853 and 1880. Even then, the definition is given a special sub-heading, 'The political programme of the Irish Nationalist Party', examples dating from 1885 and 1899, and echoing a definition of 'nationalist' as 'One who advocates the claims of Ireland to be an independent nation', an example of which is given from 1869. Evidently Oxford's lexicographers never caught up with Wales or Scotland. The *OED* gives examples of 'nationalist' from 1715 and 1716 to illustrate its unhelpfully combined meanings 'One characterised by national tendencies or sympathies; an adherent or supporter of nationalism; an advocate of national rights, etc.', but these two earlier examples are unusual, and are not followed by another until 1873. Nor are the *OED*'s definitions of 'nationalist' precise enough, since its own evidence shows that the examples from 1715 and 1716 do not illustrate a meaning given as 'an adherent or supporter of nationalism'.

Readers of the second (1989) edition of the *OED* will assume it to be a recent work. Yet comparing the entries for 'nation', 'national', 'nationalist' and 'nationality' with the first edition shows that the second edition retains the definitions of the first and, in the main, merely adds further examples without generating deeper insights into the core phenomena.[8] The *OED*, in other words, is itself an historical document. It seems likely that the *OED*'s lexicographers in the late nineteenth century were dealing with a new phenomenon which they only partly understood, and for which they offered functionalist or positivist definitions that did not capture the novelty of what was happening in Europe.

Seeing more than the *OED*'s original compilers, we can better distinguish between 'nation' and 'nationalism'. It is true that the term 'nation' was given enhanced significance in the Authorized Version of the

Bible (1611),[9] but even then within an older framework of ideas: 'nation' was primarily understood in terms of 'kingdom', and the failure of English republicanism in the 1650s preserved that monarchical identity. 'Nationalism' as a political noun awaited import from continental Europe in the mid nineteenth century. Even then it was not immediately adopted in England: nationalism was something that other peoples had. It may be relevant that until the mid nineteenth century 'ethnic' meant 'Pertaining to nations not Christian or Jewish', or 'pagan'; only later did it come to mean 'Pertaining to race'.[10]

Patriotism, moreover, was not a synonym for nationalism but the proper name of a quite distinct doctrine. 'Patriotism' can be dated equally to a particular political project, this time a specifically English one: the attempt from the 1720s to define the platform of an opposition to the Whig ascendancy that took root after 1714, and to do so in terms that did not depend on the main element in the political opposition, the Tory/Jacobite element, but that offered scope for making common cause with extremist Whigs to bring down Sir Robert Walpole.[11] Patriotism was proposed as a jealous defender of constitutional liberties; a vigorous asserter of English self-interest abroad, by mercantile and military means; an enemy to public corruption; and a firm champion of Protestantism. When English politicians in this idiom sought to disparage the Scots, as they commonly did from the Union onwards, they did so, like John Wilkes in *The North Briton*, for the Scots' perfidy, avarice and slavish political preferences; even Wilkes's scathing attacks were devoid of claims that the Scots were racially different from or inferior to the English.[12]

It was this specific political formation, and not loyalty to one's country in general, that Samuel Johnson termed 'the last refuge of a scoundrel':[13] he referred topically to the abandonment of the Opposition by its leading Whig Patriot members when they were lured away by offers of place and financial reward in the administration formed in 1744. Since 'patriotism' was defined in terms of political programmes and personal integrity rather than of social constituencies, it was regularly open to betrayal and disillusion. After 1744 the most notable episode of disillusion was that improbable alliance of opposites, the Fox–North coalition of 1783, a disreputable deal which turned much principled political opinion (including the Nonconformists) against the Whigs and paved the way for the ascendancy of William Pitt.[14]

'Patriot' and 'patriotism' nevertheless continued in English discourse for the rest of the eighteenth century and into the twentieth: the terms had imprecise associations with the principled promotion of a public good, but were seldom the subject of any debate on the relative meanings of 'patriotism' and 'nationalism'. In the early eighteenth century, 'patriot' retained its specific older associations with a stance of opposition to the ministries of the day; later, as ministries found themselves at war with the American and French revolutions, patriotism tended to lose its bellicosity and to become pacifist; to lose its pursuit of parochial self-interest and become professedly cosmopolitan.[15] In a general sense, 'patriot' was widely available as late as the twentieth century to describe admirers of a paternal but libertarian and constitutional order whose integrity imposed duties, station and, ultimately, a call to self-sacrifice.[16] Neither 'patriotism' nor 'nationalism', therefore, definitively identify English ideas of collective identity; both were in origin specific attempts to appropriate such ideas for political purposes, which became imprecise over time.

III.   THE ARRIVAL OF NATIONALISM: 'RACE'

The *Nineteenth-Century Short Title Catalogue* allows us to be more precise than the *OED*, suggesting that nationalism entered English discourse only in the mid nineteenth century. Remarkably, the *NSTC* records only one title containing the term 'nationalism' published in Britain before 1871, and that with a theological meaning.[17] The clearest analogy with continental European developments was not English, but appeared in works like Hugh Scott's *The Creed of the Scots Nationalists* (London, 1850). Even from the 1880s, most English sources discussed nationalism as an overseas phenomenon.[18] The same applies if we turn from 'nationalism' to the slightly different, but essentially related, locutions 'nationalist'[19] and 'nationality'.[20] When such terms were eventually accepted into English discourse, it is not clear how far they modified still-prevalent English meanings: Gladstone, announcing in 1887 'I affirm that Welsh nationality is as great a reality as English nationality',[21] was complimenting the Welsh not with any racial awareness that was beginning to match that of the English, but with an historical identity of the familiar English sort. If the Welsh, Irish and Scots were allowed to be 'nationalities', it might follow merely that the English had been (without knowing it) a 'nationality' all along. Moreover, the United Kingdom itself, in the words of James Bryce, constituted a 'greater nationality' (a use of the word that European nationalists would have regarded as a contradiction in terms).[22]

The framework of English understandings of group identity had been different, essentially concerned with allegiance, shared history, liberty, law, superior civilization and the polity's place within a scenario of the historical development of Christendom. If 'nationalism' became the dominant way of defining the premises of the nation state, it is centrally relevant that England, Great Britain and the United Kingdom were not nation states but dynastic states, formed earlier and within a different matrix of ideas.[23] Moreover, this polity turned into an ethnically plural world empire without passing through the stage of the nation state.

One reason for the late and limited response of England to the European nationalism which secured classic expression in 1848 was the restricted sense still given to the word 'race' in English discourse. The history of the idea has been obscured since 'race', like 'class', was a word current from an early date; what is important is how, when and to what extent its meanings changed. Into the second half of the eighteenth century 'race' meant, chiefly, 'a group identified by descent' or 'a family', and was illustrated in the familiar way by reference to long-standing debates drawn from Scripture history over the origin of mankind and its divisions.[24] The *OED*'s examples under 'Race' (I, 2b and 6b) do not clearly show a shift of meaning from 'descent' to 'genetically determined tribe' until 1856 and 1863, and then only with reference to the slavery question in the United States. The two meanings were, of course, related, yet they were sufficiently different for their practical consequences in the public realm to diverge very greatly.

This older meaning of the term 'race' as 'descent' could be applied to Germans, Welsh, Scots or the family of Stuart, but with no heavy emphasis or reification.[25] The meaning 'descent' allowed any anthropological connotations to be eclipsed by a much more frequent usage, 'the human race', identified as the descent from Adam. Yet this locution was of considerable importance, for 'the human race' implicitly denied the importance of essential biological differences among peoples that European racial theories held to be fundamental. Despite early European awareness of what we now call anthropological difference,[26] English churchmen adhered to the theory now known as monogenesis, the development of mankind from a single, common ancestor; its opposite, polygenesis, asserted that men originated in separate races and that the differences between those races were therefore ineradicable and basic. As the Rev. J. Dingle argued at the meeting of the London Anthropological Society in 1864, the doctrine of polygenesis had been used for more than a century to 'justify the most outrageous oppression, and to palliate the most disgusting cruelty' towards what he thought of as backward peoples.[27] The wide acceptance of monogenesis in England also had much to do with England's early attention to anti-slavery questions.[28]

In contrast with this persisting English usage, it seems that by far the most frequent, novel and insistent emphasis on the category of biologically determined and essentialist race in the English-speaking world was provided by American discussions of slavery, mainly from the 1840s onward; it was this that gave early American anthropology an engagement with a question of public policy,[29] and in a way that did not bear on English problems. American ideas of essential racial difference and racial competition were well developed before Charles Darwin's *The Origin of Species* was published in 1859. In England itself, old usages survived alongside new, and still very academic, ethnological ones;[30] bibliographic evidence suggests that what changed was, initially, the way in which the term 'race' began to be applied to the Irish question from the 1860s,[31] yet this was of modest importance compared with the problems of the United States. There, in the 1840s and 1850s, 'the rise of a new sense of American nationalism' had 'clear racial overtones'.[32]

If the transformation of the idea of 'race' in public discourse occurred first in the United States,[33] it is understandable that the image of Victorian England as being quickly dominated by racialist thought and attitudes has been urged with most insistence by recent American academics.[34] For 'race' as for 'nationalism', such authors seldom distinguished between English, Scottish and Irish discourse, or even between a homogenized 'British' discourse and continental European ones;[35] yet the differences are a key to the diverging political history of those countries as the twentieth century progressed.

It is hardly surprising that practical political issues had a great influence in shaping public discourse. This being so, the consequences of academic anthropology for late nineteenth-century English culture as a whole may have been exaggerated.[36] English ethnologists in the early nineteenth century, including the most influential, the evangelical Anglican and anti-slavery activist James Cowles Pritchard (1786–1848), 'still maintained the religiously orthodox position that there was one human species descended from Adam through Noah'; Pritchard overtly 'refused to believe in the inherent inferiority of any race'.[37]

Changes came slowly; indeed the foundation of the Anthropological Society in 1863 has been ascribed to Dr James Hunt's wish to break free from the monogenist ideas dominant in the Ethnological Society of London. The English tradition of monogenesis remained strong.[38] Discussions of 'race' and 'racial' characteristics were not uncommon in mid- and late nineteenth-century England, but it has not been established that a biologically essentialist meaning of 'race' ever became dominant in English public discourse.[39]

The older genealogical, Scriptural and cultural meanings of the term evidently retained their currency. Examined more closely, even social-Darwinist discussions of racial difference in England can be seen to depend on the older idea that race was a superficial characteristic; what mattered about race was only its role as a marker of the very different degrees of development among peoples along that path of progressive civilization which would lead to a post-nationalist outcome.[40] Beside the works of English ethnologists should also be placed books like William Dalton Babington's *Fallacies of Race Theories as Applied to National Character* (London, 1895) and John M. Robertson's *The Saxon and the Celt* (London, 1897), overtly sceptical of heredity and arguing for the priority of environmental influences.[41]

IV. RELIGION AND ETHNICITY

Yet if new ways of picturing 'race' were being injected into public debate from the American Civil War and the mid-century recurrence of the Irish problem, why did England not adopt these new ideas more widely? Recent scholarship on England's history makes this a much easier question to answer than it would have been a few decades ago. In England, unlike the new American republic and Ireland, older ideas of group identity were in full repair. An established church provided a public doctrine for a clear majority of the population, and did so with all the resources of an established intelligentsia. Its teaching of monogenesis tended to fuel missionary endeavour rather than encourage a view of other races as irredeemably inferior. English ideas of the polity had long owed much to English religion. As we have seen,[42] ideas of the nation had been first formed in England in the age of Bede in an ecclesiological mould. A series of events in the sixteenth, seventeenth and eighteenth centuries reinforced the idea of England as a polity the integrity of which was identified by Providential deliverances rather than by ethnic homogeneity or linguistic purity. The most recent of these events is also the largest, the Second World War: many of its episodes remain in the English popular memory within this Providential explanatory scheme, notably Dunkirk and the Battle of Britain; the most famous visual image of those years, St Paul's Cathedral rising miraculously untouched amid the flames and smoke of the Blitz, was so memorable because it illustrated a theme that was already deeply rooted.

English understandings of identity before the nineteenth century had much to do with religiously inspired ideas of the divine institution of peoples and Providential provision for their fortunes, little to do with social-anthropological ideas of innate characteristics. When Daniel Defoe published his poem *The True-Born Englishman* in 1701, asserting the long-standing genealogical diversity of the English, his purpose as a Nonconformist was to resist a unifying hegemony of the Church of England; he provoked few counter-assertions that the English represented a pure and unmixed stock, even though the poem was continually reprinted throughout the century.[43] Indeed, it was the English who normally satirized the Welsh, Irish and Scots for boasting of (or for being uncertain about) their fathers;[44] the English seldom insisted on the purity of their descent, even when they praised the achievements of their illustrious ancestors. The more common English locution was not 'true born' but 'free born', and works depending on this idea in their titles were commonplace.[45]

Into the nineteenth century, ideas of Englishness continued to be bound up with ideas about the integrity of the English Church. This appeared to be called in question by the Oxford Movement, at least as depicted by its opponents, but this perspective has been recast by recent scholarship: we now see the Oxford Movement as very much more English, stemming from pre-Tractarian High Churchmanship,[46] and indeed denounced for its alleged un-Englishness by critics such as Charles Kingsley[47] in ways that effectively inhibited most of the movement's Romanizing potentialities. The Oxford Movement began as a protest against the English state's betrayal of the English Church, but the emotionally fraught reaction against Tractarianism paradoxically had the result of strengthening the association of Church and State within the older mind set.

The churches of England and Rome did not reunite in this period, and the strength of English anti-Catholicism was a powerful bulwark of an older form of national identity.[48] To be anti-Catholic was, however, to be Anglican or Nonconformist, not (as in France) to be primarily secular and in need of a secular substitute for religion such as nationalism. Keen Protestants like Charles Kingsley preserved an idiom of anti-Catholic collective consciousness that looked back to the sixteenth century, as in texts like *Westward Ho!* (1855), or even further back in time, as in his last novel *Hereward the Wake* (1866),[49] and did not openly appeal to nineteenth-century European innovations.

In the nineteenth century it might be suggested that the more remarkable thing was the limited extent and influence of European racial speculations within England.[50] Even before the European events of the 1930s, historians like Ernest Barker were writing sceptically about ideas of race as a basis for national identity.[51] Racialist-essentialist thought can indeed be found within England, but its scale in the nineteenth and twentieth centuries was small compared with European parallels. The most clear-cut case of an English racialist, Houston Stewart Chamberlain (1855–1927) is revealing: finding no sufficient support in England, he made his career in Germany and took German citizenship.[52]

V.   LANGUAGE AND LITERATURE

Language is an historical theme that demands more detailed comparative approaches than can be provided here, but it is relevant for its social function that the English language developed far more than French or German from the fourteenth to the sixteenth centuries. Its development into an international language, a language that eagerly absorbed new terms from other languages rather than resisting contamination by them, was facilitated by the undecided outcome of a controversy among eighteenth-century English grammarians over whether English should imitate classical models or be brought closer to its Anglo-Saxon roots: failing agreement, linguistic purity did not become an English ideal, and group self-definition built around an ideal of linguistic purity did not become widespread.[53] Where Samuel Johnson's *Dictionary of the English Language* (1755) omitted 'low' words and was openly normative, the *New English Dictionary on Historical Principles* (1888–1928; later titled *The Oxford English Dictionary*) was far more undiscriminating, and its chief editor sought merely to record words actually in use.[54]

With new European ideas of race went new ideas about its relation to European languages. Yet the sweeping victory of English within the British Isles by the eighteenth century[55] meant that the 'Celtic' languages were spoken by too few to be easily and quickly used as emblems of Scottish and Irish nationalism, and also, more importantly, that the English language did not function for the English as a way of differentiating them from their nearest neighbours. Linguistic differences within the British Isles became mainly ones of dialect, and Scottish and Irish accents might easily be thought to differ less from the norms of Standard English than extremely impenetrable English accents like Geordie or Scouse. English became taken for granted in England and hardly became a badge of nationalist identity.[56]

In a wider setting, English was already far too widely spoken in the world by the key year of 1848 to be adopted as an index to ethnicity. Where French, German, Italian, Polish or Russian could plausibly be identified with a homeland and a people, English was already spoken by and accessible to very many who were not English by historic settlement or culture, and this obvious diversity of English-speakers steadily escalated.

VI.   ENGLISH AND EUROPEAN DIFFERENCES

Different polities developed in different ways with respect to identity. The political unity of the kingdom of England was already very ancient, as was a sense of collective identity not premised on the nineteenth-century nation state or on nineteenth-century understandings of 'race'.[57] In Europe, the track records of those forms of anticlericalism and religious scepticism later called, for short, 'The Enlightenment', were different from

England's. So were the political dynamics of conquest and revolution unleashed after 1789. Increasingly, French identity came to be expressed by a series of secular goals summed up in that reification 'The Revolution'. Subscription to abstract metaphysical conceptions of rights became available as a means of defining parameters of group identity, and in a post-Christian setting this paved the way for the rephrasing of those conceptions into equally abstract ones of race and culture, notably in the work of Joseph Arthur, Comte de Gobineau (1816–82). As with Houston Stewart Chamberlain in Germany, the intellectual coherence of ideas of race in France was aided by an émigré of Welsh extraction, William Edwards (1776?–1842), born the child of a slave-owner in Jamaica and a long-term resident of Belgium and France.[58] Edwards's contribution was intended to demonstrate the essential affinity of Celts and Gauls, not effaced by subsequent conquest: his scheme did nothing for the English.

German nationalism before the 1840s owed more to philosophical and philological enquiries than to the sort of ethnology already established in France. From the 1780s, Johann Gottfried Herder expounded the spirit of a nation as residing in the people rather than the government. Jacob Grimm and Wilhelm von Humboldt used philological scholarship to identify a national spirit in the German language. Although polygenism was influential in Germany, and German philosophers' prior emphasis on an internal basis for German identity prevented the early dominance of biological determinism,[59] the resistance of the German 'people' to Napoleonic invasion fused an identification of 'nation' and 'state' in an intellectual context already framed by cultural essentialists.

In areas of continental Europe which defined themselves antithetically against the Revolution, Spain, Germany, Italy and Russia all took on far more emphatic moral and religious *personae* in the struggle to resist first Jacobinism, then Napoleon. Yet perhaps the processes at work were not as different as they first appear. Religion rather than monarchy or aristocracy was the chief casualty of the Revolution, even in those continental European states that fought most resolutely against France. If the churches championed the peoples, the churches also ratified the secular terms in which those peoples were increasingly described. Race and language were even more prominent in the developing identities of those countries where the Roman Catholic or Orthodox churches survived the revolutionary onslaught.

In England, although the 1832 Reform Act can in some ways be interpreted within a process of secularization, its consequences in this direction were limited: true, Holland House's programme for the revitalization of Whiggery at that time had much to do with the unbelief of a small coterie of intellectuals,[60] but the 1832 Act itself was passed after a wave of public mobilization which had far more to do with demands for the rights of Englishmen. Although Lord Grey's Liberalism and Sir Robert Peel's Conservatism became secular creeds, the rank and file followers were by no means secularized: English politics to 1914 continued to a great degree to express a polarity between Church and Dissent.[61] In that conflict, each side sought to establish its superior Englishness by the use of moral and ecclesiological arguments, not racial ones. The theological preoccupations of William Ewart Gladstone (1809–98) alone would not have been sufficient to sustain this idiom into the 1890s, but the wide diffusion of politicized Nonconformity as the electoral base of the Liberal Party made it plausible until the First World War.

In popular culture, recent scholarship has emphasized the survival and robust independence of popular forms. No longer can we endorse the modernist model which claimed that the common man was culturally disinherited by the experience of urbanization and industrialization, deprived of the resources of an older (by implication, libertarian and egalitarian) popular culture and left without resources in a harsh urban environment to invent a new one. By implication, such a new invention might well be 'false consciousness', a coerced or mystified assimilation into 'nationalism', expressed in the jingoism of the music hall.[62] Students now explore continuities as well as discontinuities, and the survival of older national stereotypes and older xenophobia now calls into question the degree to which English popular consciousness in the nineteenth century was influenced by any distinctively new contemporary European nationalism.

Victorians who responded most openly to biological theories of racial difference often prove, on examination, to be either not English, or increasingly eccentric, or both. Robert Knox's *The Races of Men: A Fragment* (1850) with its quotable assertion that 'race is everything in human history' was a response to the European revolutions of 1848, but Knox was a Scot, an anatomist whose behaviour had become increasingly odd after the public odium he suffered when his suppliers of cadavers for dissection in Edinburgh were revealed as having procured their bodies by murder.[63] The author of the provocatively titled article 'Occasional Discourse on the Nigger Question' in *Fraser's Magazine* (1849) was the equally Scottish Thomas Carlyle.

Given the different track records of England and continental Europe with respect to collective consciousness, it becomes easier to explain how England lacked counterparts to many European figures, or how very different the closest English analogues were. In the field of popular political mobilization Ireland indeed had Daniel O'Connell (1775–1847), an organizer whose Catholic Association achieved its aims in 1829; but this only highlighted the absence of populist mobilization or charismatic leadership in the parallel 'emancipation' of English Protestant Dissenters in 1828 and the securing of parliamentary reform in 1832.

The Risorgimento could have no exact parallel in an England already united. Giuseppe Mazzini (1805–72) had his potential analogue in Sir Francis Burdett (1770–1844), but Burdett's mental framework was a backward-looking celebration of English liberties rather than a demand for the self-realization of a people. The same constitutional orientation characterized English Chartism from 1838 to its decisive failure in 1848. Mazzini, in exile in England from 1837, came to believe that the English were unable to grasp the idea of nationality in the new European sense.[64]

In the field of politicized men of letters, it would be difficult to point to any English figures who filled the roles carved out by men like Johann Gottlieb von Herder (1744–1803), Johann Gottlieb Fichte (1762–1814) or Gabriele D'Annunzio (1863–1938). English knowledge of German literature was far too restricted to allow for widespread practical imitation.[65] The more obvious parallels were with Scotsmen like James MacPherson, the inventor of 'Ossian'; Welshmen like Iolo Morganwyg; and such Irish authors as Sophie Bryant, Alice Stopford Green, Lady Gregory, Edmund Hogan, Douglas Hyde, Fiona Macleod, Standish O'Grady, George Sigerson, J. M. Synge and W. B. Yeats. English historical scholarship in the nineteenth century presents what seem the closest parallels to continental nationalist historiographies, but here too qualifications must be made.[66] English romantic history addressed to a mass audience in the early nineteenth century was identifiably English, not British, holding up images of an English social life that was not indebted to elite ideas about institutions or to academic ideas about race:

folk customs, rituals, celebrations and manners designed to identify a robustly plebeian, hospitable and egalitarian Englishness.[67]

Rudyard Kipling (1865–1936) might seem to be the archetypal example of an English writer whose career depended on exploiting an English nationalism with heavy racial overtones; it is therefore important to focus particularly critically on his work. It might be suggested that the central themes in his consciousness were the coherence or continuity supplied not by race but by custom – indeed the strange and ineluctable force of a tradition which imposed duties, even a duty of self-sacrifice, in the name of the group. This meant, for Kipling, the importance of the worthiness of the individual over rank and status. In that sense his theme was not that particular races were superior to others but instead that discipline, courage, duty and sacrifice could win success for any race. It was only on such conditions that 'Yours is the earth and everything that's in it' ('If—', *Rewards and Fairies*, 1910). 'Lesser breeds' were identified as those 'without the Law' ('Recessional', 1897), not without the race. His poem including the lines 'take up the white man's burden' was a call to thankless trusteeship, a burden taken up out of altruism not racial superiority, and a poem addressed to the racially diverse United States. In 'Norman and Saxon' (1911), the identifying characteristic of the Saxon is placed in 'justice and right' and the Saxon's words of defiance to the Norman are 'This isn't fair dealing'.[68]

VII.   ENGLAND AND ANGLO-SAXONISM

The history of English Anglo-Saxonism, like other uses of concepts of 'race', has been obscured by the stadial assumptions quietly present in much of the history of ideas: first one meaning was prevalent; then the intellectual landscape was transformed, and another took its place. In the light of such attitudes, it seemed to a recent American historian that 'A belief in Anglo-Saxon freedom, once used to defend popular liberties, had by the middle of the nineteenth century been transformed into a rationale for the domination of peoples throughout the world... an increasing number were swept away in an emotional tide of racial theory'.[69] Such an assumption made redundant any attempt to trace the survivals of old usages; on the contrary, it led to searches for the earlier and earlier origins of new ones. Yet powerful survivals rather than tenuous origins are precisely what are at issue here.

Attention to Anglo-Saxon history revived in the 1860s and 1870s, but it was English Liberals who were chiefly involved in this process, and their aims were democratic not organicist. They drew on the most recent scholarship in the area, which was indebted to J. M. Kemble's assertion that England's political stability was owed to 'our customs [of] right and justice'.[70] What then emerged was a phenomenon that has been labelled 'democratic Teutonism'; in this work the term 'race' functioned as a rhetorically heightened marker of progress. The historian E. A. Freeman, who made the most emphatic use of the category 'race', also argued that 'Man is in truth ever the same' and that whatever the ancient differences among the inhabitants of England there was 'now no practical distinction' between their descendants.[71] Liberty, prosperity and Protestantism became a creed, and one that gave its followers a world mission, at least until 1914. As such, it called for unity, a downplaying of domestic differences in the name of higher ideals. Where Celticism could more easily be made to seem the cultural badge of a small oppressed minority and so linked to nationalism, Anglo-Saxonism at once led beyond England's borders to continental Europe, North America and the empire: a specifically English nationalism was difficult to build on it.

It is clearly the case that many Englishmen at the end of the nineteenth and into the twentieth century used the term 'race', but the question is what exactly they meant by it. As its president pointed out to the Anthropological Society in 1863, 'hardly two persons use such an important word as "race" in the same sense'.[72] One historian of the subject has written of 'the typical nineteenth-century confusion of race with culture',[73] and it may be that this conflation, to us a confusion, is evidence of the persistence of an older and non-essentialist understanding of 'race'.

Examples of the use of 'race' should be examined in the light of this distinction. In 1913 the imperialist Lord Milner wrote that 'It is the British race that built the Empire, and it is the undivided British race which can alone uphold it'.[74] Yet Milner's phrasing deliberately ignored the differences among the peoples of the British Isles, just as talk of 'the human race' implicitly denied the importance of those variations among mankind that the term 'race' in another sense emphasized. It was in the same inclusive vein that the Welsh Wesleyan Methodist Hugh Price

Hughes, in July 1898, declared that 'God has committed to the Anglo-Celtic people the defence of human freedom, the vindication of the race's conscience, the protection of the weak and the propagation of Scriptural Christianity', a claim in which a sense of shared Protestant mission eclipsed any possible ethnic difference between English and Welsh.[75]

The 'Anglo-Saxon' theme that characterized British attempts at diplomatic alignment with the United States in face of the rise of Wilhelmine Germany is often cited as an expression of social-anthropological racialism, but this too is open to doubt. Take Arthur Balfour in 1895: 'We have a domestic patriotism as Scotchmen or as Englishmen or as Irishmen, or what you will. We have an Imperial patriotism as citizens of the British Empire. But surely, in addition to that, we have also an Anglo-Saxon patriotism...'[76] The British, Anglo-Saxons, or even Anglo-Celts, could be pictured as a constitutionally generated composite rather than as a biologically generated species.

The theme of alleged Anglo-American kinship was prominently a constitutional and libertarian one. Had it not been, it would have been useless as a way of persuading US opinion to favour Britain as an ally over yet more Anglo-Saxon Germany. It was in this sense too that the idiom was directed pacifically towards the new German empire, and that the Bishop of London, preaching a sermon at Sandringham in 1899 to a congregation that included the visiting Kaiser, declared that 'the Teutonic race has the same fundamental ideas'.[77]

Whatever the resonances of Anglo-Saxonism, they were all comprehensively negated in 1914: racial terminology in any sense was discredited in twentieth-century England above all by the experience of war against a people who had so recently been identified as kin, and perhaps by the tardiness of the involvement of another nation, the USA, which had been much more emphatically so identified. When US involvement eventually came, it was also expressed in the very different idiom of Woodrow Wilson as a championing of 'liberal democracy' or of nationalist self-determination in ways consciously aimed against dynastic, multinational regimes like the UK. 'Nationalism' could still seem to the English to be an alien state of mind and a practically threatening one.

Even English Conservatism seldom explored romantic, organic, corporate nationalism: local imperial diversities meant that only the empire as a whole could be easily identified as a unity, whatever play could be made with the 'unity' of its white settlers.[78] There remained, perhaps, a potential for a nationalism of another sort, one that was never realized. In the lines of Gilbert Keith Chesterton (1874–1936), 'For we are the people of England, that never have spoken yet',[79] was some sense that the 'nationalist' possibilities of the English had not been properly expressed. They never were: no party was eager that those possibilities should be developed in a genuinely populist direction. Even the British Fascist movement was not only very small in its appeal compared to European movements; it also received a markedly sceptical reaction among the working class. In England, populist opinion was not obviously 'nationalist'.

VIII. ENGLAND, SCOTLAND, IRELAND, WALES

If the United Kingdom was a composite state, it was appropriate that 'Every Briton in 1800 possessed a composite identity';[80] yet this was to change, for many Britons, in different ways, in the two centuries that followed. Four ancient and still significantly different societies were to follow significantly different paths in respect of their developing identities, and, in some ways, England was the odd one out: England continued to resist racialism where her three neighbours were in different degrees more open to it. Ireland was to terrorize and expel its Anglo-Irish elite, break in two on confessional or ethnic lines in a way familiar in 1848, and achieve partial independence in the violent idiom of European racial nationalism: the Irish Republic remained neutral during the Second World War. Scotland was to adopt new emblems of heavy industry and (eventually) public provision that marked her off more sharply from England as the heroic phase of industrialization receded, and by the late twentieth century came increasingly to interpret this distinction in nationalist terms. Wales was to a greater degree than Scotland or Ireland to revive (or invent) and celebrate emblems of a Romantic folk culture, but with the fewest separatist political consequences. These three different cases nevertheless shared a common political discourse: nationalism. So far has this preoccupied recent historians that widespread Welsh, Irish and Scottish unionism in the nineteenth and twentieth centuries is in danger of becoming a neglected subject. The form of nationalism that has attracted the adjective 'Celtic' is widely glamorized.

Paradoxically, despite England's far greater power, confidence and cohesion, historians are now much more familiar with the rise of Irish, Scottish and to a lesser extent Welsh nationalisms in the nineteenth and twentieth centuries than with any English equivalent.[81] Despite origins that were ethnically more fragmented and politically less unified than England's in the period before c. 1066, the Scots, Irish and Welsh at different times in the nineteenth and twentieth centuries often came to conceive of themselves as 'races' in a more biologically determined sense than the English and to invent components of nineteenth-century 'nationalism' that had been largely absent in their cultural inheritance.[82]

This was, as we have seen, much less true in England. If the English saw Britain largely as an extension of and a synonym for England, then the growing degree to which the Scots, Irish and Welsh held prominent positions in public life before 1914 may have checked the development of any exclusively English nationalism.[83] From an English perspective, 'England' was the wider polity to which these minorities assimilated; in comparison with that daily political reality, the existence of a unitary concept of 'Old England' was relatively weak in its practical consequences. It was the English who used 'England' and 'Britain' as synonym in ways that annoyed the Welsh, Irish and Scots, but a few of the latter can even be found doing the same thing. Yet if this casual attitude to identity characterizes the English experience, it highlights England's differences from her Anglophone neighbours.

All of them, to some degree, eventually came to appeal to language as an index of ethnicity, but not to the extent or with the effects witnessed on the continent. Welsh collective consciousness in the nineteenth century had most to do with Nonconformist Protestantism; in the twentieth, an image of Welsh culture and, especially, language became the more frequently cited foundation. As late as the census of 1891, 54 per cent of the population was recorded as Welsh-speaking: aspirations and fears were expressed in the slogan *Heb Iaith, heb Genedl* (no language, no nation).[84] But this proved a steadily weakening foundation, for Welsh speakers declined to 19 per cent by 1981.[85]

Wales showed the most widespread adherence to its ancient language, but was the weakest of the three in its nationalism.[86] In Ireland and Scotland Gaelic had to be deliberately and with difficulty revived from a lower base by politically inspired movements working through popular education. In eighteenth-century Scotland, James MacPherson's Ossianic poems, written in English, drew primarily on the surviving emotional force of Homeric imagery and were not very effective as the cultural mobilizers for his own day that he probably intended them to be. There, too, literature in Gaelic did not obviously suit nineteenth-century European preoccupations: religious divisions tended to override what linguistic unities there were, and in so far as plebeian Gaelic survived, it embodied a disaffection that was dynastic rather than *volkisch*.[87] Ireland was the most successful example of a linguistically identified ethnicity, although even here the nationalist movement was divided on whether to tie itself exclusively to Gaelic.[88]

It is important not to overstate the strength of the 'nationalisms' of Scotland, Ireland and Wales, or the role of ethnicity within them. Scottish, Irish and Welsh nationalisms were dramatic and disruptive only by comparison with an un-nationalist English norm. In comparison with continental Europe, their successes were limited. Nevertheless, by the standards of a composite monarchy, the impact of Welsh, Irish and Scots nationalisms on the UK in the nineteenth and twentieth centuries was considerable. Yet, and remarkably in the light of the powerful surviving religious premises of group identity in Ireland, the ideology of Sinn Fein became distinguished by its 'racialist tone'; when this ideology was applied, 'Irish history was interpreted in racialist (or ethnic) terms'.[89] More remarkable again, and more remarkably unstudied, was the extremely muted nature of the reactions of the English to these developments.[90]

The story of English responses to these profound changes in consciousness among its neighbouring societies is normally told in terms of high-political answers by English politicians to a series of 'questions', the 'Irish Question' even acquiring a slightly satirical reification and a capital letter. Expressed in this way, the failure of a succession of English politicians to find the answer to the 'Question' seemed to the English to call into doubt the good faith of the Irish or Scots who posed it, rather than the English understandings of what was at issue. Yet the latter may have been as important as the former.

The English elite's appreciation of Irish and Scots nationalism was problematically shallow: as an Anglo-Irish Assistant Commissioner of Police in Ireland argued, Ireland could not be a nation because 'the population of Ireland is not homogeneous... in other words... there is no Irish nation. And racial differences, instead of disappearing as they tend to do in other lands, are maintained and accentuated by religious strife'.[91] As Sir John Lubbock MP wrote to *The Times* on 18 March 1887, 'the defence of Home Rule, on the ground that there are four "real nationalities" in our islands is entirely without foundation': not only did the areas of their predominance not coincide with England, Wales, Ireland and Scotland, but Lubbock cited the anthropologist John Beddoe to argue that the racial components of these four societies were present in all, and predominant in or 'peculiar to' none.[92] This was also Arthur Balfour's position in arguing against Home Rule. There was, he wrote, 'no sharp division of race at all' between England and Ireland. 'We must conceive the pre-historic inhabitants both of Britain and of Ireland as subject to repeated waves of invasion from the wandering peoples of the Continent.'[93] Such politicians argued from sound scientific premises to the erroneous conclusion that Irish nationalism was merely a popular misunderstanding which could be easily cleared up.

Popular English reactions to Irish and Scottish nationalism were also remarkably muted. Even in the face of Irish terrorism in England, English reactions tended to be pragmatic and limited. It is as if Irish, Scottish or Welsh nationalisms hardly registered in English minds.[94] Similarly, popular English reactions to Mussolini and Hitler began in incomprehension and progressed through satire to xenophobia, all very old forms, without passing through a rival English nationalism. Why this was is a question that remains unresearched, but it may be suggested that England's quite different form of collective self-awareness predisposed many or most English observers to reinterpret nationalism or racialism as evidence of other peoples' less advanced level of civilization, rather than as evidence of an ineluctably different mindset which would have violent consequences.

In contrast with English dispositions, not only did the 'Celtic revival' in Ireland come to echo European racial nationalism; substantial Irish migration to Scotland from the 1840s often provoked racialist reactions in the Scottish native population.[95] From the 1990s onwards, the experiment of devolved government in Scotland and Wales, and the boost that this gave to Scottish and Welsh nationalist parties, was accompanied by some concern in England that the English might be encouraged to follow suit and develop a parallel English nationalism. Such a novel phenomenon would give rise to widespread alarm; already observable Irish, Scottish and Welsh nationalism hardly registers.

The term 'nationalism', of course, lost its specific references in English discourse and widened to become synonymous with 'the assertion of a group identity'. In that sense England was nationalist in the nineteenth and twentieth centuries, but in that functionalist sense it had been so at all times as far back as the seventh or eighth. Historians now attend to the need to sharpen the use of terms so that precise questions can be asked and answered. In the original sense of the word, it can be said that England was influenced by that new coinage, nineteenth-century nationalism, but not dominated by it.[96] The different ways of conceptualizing and responding to group identities explain much about the differences between England and Europe into the twentieth century; even about the differences between England, Scotland, Ireland and Wales.

4

HOW IDEOLOGIES ARE BORN

The case of radicalism

I.   ORIGINS: FROM 'RADICAL REFORMERS' TO 'RADICALS'

A problem with facile postmodernism is that, paradoxically, it makes change harder to explain. If all identity is of its nature superficial and in flux, historical development becomes a trivial matter: reduced, in the pages of postmodernists, to an account of how (unwelcome) identities were manufactured by their political or social enemies for inadequate reasons. Yet change is the central and most obvious problem for the historian. To establish the importance of the discipline of history it is not enough to assert that the past was complex and intractable, nor even that long continuities can be set against short-term flux. It is necessary to show that a better account of the emergence of 'modernity' and 'postmodernity' can be offered by the historian than can be offered either by modernists or postmodernists.

A key component of the emergence of modernity has been the formation of its central concepts. Radicalism has been prominent among these, and has generally been acknowledged until now as a concept that explains other historical phenomena without itself being in need of explanation. To overset that assumption is extremely difficult.

The history of radicalism, liberalism, socialism and conservatism has been obscured by two processes, themselves integral to the historical evolution of nineteenth-century ideologies. First, each began with a fairly clear and novel set of meanings which became diluted as more and more attempts were made to appropriate the original position and steer it in new directions: so a term which was at its outset specific became steadily more imprecise and plural in its content. Second, the favoured term was projected backwards in time, and a spurious genealogy invented in order to invest a newly coined doctrine with an air of timeless validity.[1] The most notorious capitulation to this need to find retrospective validation was perhaps Alexander Gray's book *The Socialist Tradition: Moses to Lenin*, but when first published in 1946 this exercise did not seem illegitimate. Gray was himself no hagiographer,[2] and was not consciously attempting to celebrate what he recorded: his book is evidence of the wide acceptance of assumptions about the timelessness of categories. Only recently have such assumptions begun to be discredited.

The terms 'radical' and 'radicalism' were leading beneficiaries from this process of retrospective projection. German historians had applied the adjective 'radical' to the Reformation at least from the 1950s,[3] and that description of it was given wide currency in English from George Williams's monograph of 1962.[4] Despite debates over sixteenth-century phenomena, the category itself was strangely immune from historical challenge, so that by 1991 one might read that 'Radicalism in the sixteenth-century Reformation first appeared in the stormy years of the movement in Germany and Switzerland'.[5] In the light of all that has happened in the methodology of intellectual history in recent decades, we can now see why such a sentence is the historical equivalent of the philosophical statement 'All square circles are French'. A sentence may be correct in grammar and syntax and yet convey no meaning. The use of anachronistic categories merely creates a world of shadows and fictions in which no clear questions can be asked and no clear answers can be given. To ask whether the origins of English 'radicalism' can be traced to the 1640s or 1760s is to ask a question which is only not wrong because it is meaningless.

In locating 'radicalism' in the 1820s, we now adopt the conclusions of many specialized enquiries. It is no longer possible to see the 1760s as the key decade in initiating a novel phase in reform, or to see John Wilkes as a catalyst of a new ideology; no longer do we seek an English radicalism before Wilkes. We no longer see something called 'American radicalism' being born in these years through the communication to the colonies of a Commonwealth tradition, nor do we see the American revolution acting as the 'ideological midwife' of English reform.[6] We do not even see the intellectual groundwork of 'radicalism' being laid in Dissenting Academies. We appreciate that

Thomas Paine did not call for universal suffrage,[7] and we do not credit him with creating 'Paineite radicalism'. We no longer see late eighteenth-century English society as having been swept by a transformative 'Industrial Revolution' which explains either the 'making of the English working class' or 'the rise of the middle class'.[8] Neither industrialization, nor class formation, nor popular protest will do. None of these things now suffice as an explanation of that specific ideology newly termed 'radicalism'.

Disorder and disaffection, alienation and marginalization did not await the formulation of the ideology of radicalism in the 1810s and 1820s. Englishmen throughout the sixteenth, seventeenth and eighteenth centuries sometimes expressed the most profound antagonism towards their rulers, local or national, in Church or in State, in agriculture or in manufacturing, and for a wide variety of reasons. Yet, even after this diverse experience, 'radicalism' was something new. Its conceptualization was a distinct and special episode that must be correctly located in the early decades of the nineteenth century, part of that wider and momentous process in which a whole vocabulary of political terms was coined, terms which quickly became basic to a new conceptualization of politics and society.[9]

In that conceptualization, the new ideology of radicalism did not spring at once into being, fully formed. Many of the component parts of radicalism can be found at earlier dates, but what counted in the conceptualization of this as of other ideologies was the novel and unpredictable assembly of those components. It was a process in which old usages survived and were added to, and transformed by, new usages. 'Radical' had long been a familiar term in etymology, referring to the 'roots' of words, and this usage continued.[10] 'Radical' was familiar also in medicine. John Mudge offered a remedy that 'will immediately and radically cure a complaint very troublesome and fatiguing'.[11] This usage, too, continued.[12] 'Radical' in political discourse might therefore merely mean 'fundamental', without any implication of social levelling or reconstruction.[13] Samuel Johnson's usage was not new or controversial when he wrote that the American colonies 'were kept flourishing and spreading by the radical vigour of the Mother-country';[14] nor was Lord Stormont's in 1792 in extolling 'the radical beauties of the Constitution'. Paine quoted Stormont's speech to deny its substance, but he used the adjective in the same way to denounce 'the radical and practical defects of the system'.[15] William Wilberforce similarly claimed that man was 'tainted with sin, not slightly and superficially, but radically and to the very core'.[16] Even the noun did not have to signify membership of a group: in 1845 one Tory critic of Sir Robert Peel granted him the title, and predicted (rightly, as it happened) that Peel would subvert 'Conservatism'.[17]

This imprecision began to change with the formulation of the new doctrine of universal manhood suffrage by heterodox theologians, and its adoption as a practical political goal by their co-religionists in the late 1770s and early 1780s. Increasingly, the term 'radical reform' came to be applied exclusively to parliamentary reform.[18] It was in this sense that the Rev. Christopher Wyvill (whose theological opinions were scarcely orthodox) called for 'a radical reformation' in 1781, and the openly Unitarian John Jebb demanded 'a substantial and radical reform in the representation' in 1784.[19] In this sense 'Radical Reform' became increasingly reified, and acquired capital letters. In 1801, Christopher Wyvill called for 'nothing less than the attainment of such a redress of grievances, such a correction of abuses as may secure the future enjoyment of Liberty... it ought to be a Radical Reform, on the Principles of the Constitution'. But John Cartwright's adherence to universal manhood suffrage would prevent the success of a national reform movement, urged Wyvill, since it would alienate 'the Rich'. 'This, I sincerely think, will be the consequence of consulting Theory alone.' Wyvill recommended Fox's solution, 'viz. to extend the Right of Suffrage to Householders not receiving alms':[20] this, presumably, still counted to Wyvill as a radical reform.

Neither the American nor the French Revolution was inspired at its outset by the idea of universal suffrage: the old diversity of meanings of 'radical' could continue. When the idea of universal manhood suffrage rose again to prominence in the years after 1815, Sir Walter Scott could observe in 1819 that 'Radical is a word in very bad odour here, being used to denote a set of blackguards a hundred times more mischievous and absurd than our old friends in 1794 and 1795'.[21] 'Radical' was now a shorthand for 'Radical Reformer', and the clearest and most extreme definition of that term was 'a believer in universal manhood suffrage'.

Not all usage was equally exact, however. The old senses of 'radical' in medicine or etymology meant that many men could still try to appropriate the term. In 1835 even a heterodox churchman could do so: Jonas Dennis used the term when congratulating himself on his 'voluntary sacrifice of professional emolument' and his 'consciousness of personal integrity, and persuasion of divine approbation' in his task of detecting 'radical errors, ecclesiastical and sectarian', that is, faults in the doctrine of the Church of

England. Dennis wrote as an opponent of Catholic Emancipation and the repeal of the Test and Corporation Acts to protest that the Church of England was 'a solitary instance of a religious community deprived, through crooked state policy, of the exercise of its unalienable right to efficient synodical assemblies', as a result of which, 'heresy, scepticism and infidelity, are encouraged and diffused to a terrific extent'.[22] Another author in 1820, who believed that the 'mill-stone' of the national debt was 'the sole cause of the public distress', proposed a national lottery and encouragement for 'domestic fisheries' to reduce it:[23] this was his 'radical' solution, one which clearly had nothing to do with 'radicalism' in its extensive later meanings and expressed no sense of alienation from the social order.

In popular discourse, then, the key terms were often inexact and open for appropriation. One journal, launched in 1833, announced that 'our principles are most decidedly liberal, radical and Christian... It shall be our endeavour to make the *Truth* as agreeable as possible to all classes and parties'.[24] Out of the diversity and imprecision of daily usage, a new doctrine, 'radicalism', nevertheless emerged, and came to be seen as a reified actor on the national stage in what was eventually characterized as the 'age of ideologies'.[25] Radicalism was not a timelessly applicable category, nor did it have such close functional equivalents in earlier centuries that the term can be used without regard for its specific subject: it was a concept freshly minted in the early nineteenth century. If that process of conceptual innovation can be dated and analysed, 'radicalism' can be recovered as a valid term of historical analysis.[26] Such a recovery will show us not only what the phenomenon was, but also why it is merely a solecism to invoke the term in any period before the phenomenon existed.[27]

II.   ENEMIES: THE ANTI-JACOBIN CONTRIBUTION

Both the friends and the enemies of fundamental reform took part in shaping the emerging concept in the years after 1815. The enemies tended to look to the recent past, and to argue for a fundamental affinity between the radical reform of their own day and the revolutionary Jacobinism of the 1790s; they tended to counter the disturbances of the post-war period in the same way that they had resisted revolution in the 1790s, by arguing that radical reform was synonymous with religious infidelity, and that it could only be effectively countered at local level by a return to Christian piety.

This strategy was present as early as the 1790s. For the satirical poet George Huddesford (1749–1809), 'radical reform' was evidently a synonym for 'Jacobin reform'. He denounced both in classically learned doggerel verse:

> As, when "Revenge Timotheus cried,"
> And maudlin Greeks electrified,
> His strains inspir'd ferocious joy,
> And zeal to level and destroy:
> Such furious joy the Factious feel,
> Such transports of destructive zeal
> Inflame the disaffected swarm,
> At sound of RADICAL REFORM.

Such men, claimed Huddesford, looked to the day

> When Jacobin Reform uncheck'd
> Shall take its radical Effect![28]

This anti-Jacobin idiom can be traced in recognizable form from the 1790s at least to the 1820s, and survived in the novels of John Galt (discussed below) to 1832. Within this idiom, a satire of 1820, combining visual images with political verses, emphasized the identity of the radical and the Jacobin: the slogans of 'Universal Suffrage' and 'Liberty or Death' on the banners of the mob were held to lead directly to mob violence, summary execution, the destruction of Magna Carta and the Bill of Rights, and an assault on the three-columned temple of King, Lords and Commons.[29]

One friend of the constitution tried to use the new term in its defence. 'The term Radicals is commonly applied to all who wish to destroy or infringe on the constitution', he argued; this term therefore applied to the ministers themselves, whose attempts to deal with political corruption in a rotten borough, Grampound, interfered with customary rights.[30] Successive constitutional milestones had guaranteed that constitutional rights would not be taken from the people without their consent, but 'it remained for the present days of Radicalism to advance a contrary doctrine: a complete revolution in our constitution is now about to take place, not by consent of the people, but by the efforts of a Radical Ministry'. They could claim no mandate from the people for such a change, since the electorate numbered only 400,000 in a nation of 18,000,000, and since 300 of the 489 English MPs were nominated by 'proprietors or patrons of Boroughs'. The constitution needed 'that reform... which alone can save the country from Radicalism', namely the end of the 'borough system'.[31]

Another observer relied on the theory that 'nations, like animals and vegetables', passed through the stages of origination, maturity, reproduction and annihilation in calling for 'extraordinary, judicious, and decisive measures' to rejuvenate a Britain that had quite possibly 'passed her meridian'. He was no friend to what was generally called '*a radical Reform*', however, which he saw as synonymous with 'anarchy, or a general pillage'. His argument was that 'too little attention has hitherto been paid to the encouragement of virtue', and his amateur schemes, devoted to that end, culminated in a defence of the constitution against 'the Catholic claims'. Not that he was against parliamentary reform: only, the franchise in the hands of so many of 'the lower orders', as it currently was, encouraged dissolute lives. The solution was the representation of 'interests, rather than individuals'.[32]

Satirical narratives in the anti-Jacobin tradition could dwell on the ignorance of ordinary people about the precise beliefs and proposals of the radical reformers, as in a cottage conversation between Jenny and Hannah:

[Jenny]: 'there's to be great doings in London, to-day. Hunt and all the patriotics are to meet in Spa Fields, and get things to rights abit; so my husband and a few friends are spending the day at the Anchor, to drink success to the good cause.'
[Hannah]: 'What cause, Jenny? What are they to meet for? And what are they going to set to rights?'
[Jenny]: 'Why, I can't tell you all the particulars, Hannah; but they are going to order it so, that every body shall have plenty of work and plenty of bread.'[33]

The unspecific promise of radical reform had its practical advantages. In 1819, 'Britannicus' was aware that

> there have risen up men, from amongst the lowest of the people, who rend the air with clamours in favour of a remedy which they represent to be abundantly competent for the removal of all our evils. This much boasted specific is *Radical Reform* – a thorough change in our whole political system – a complete renovation of our civil and ecclesiastical establishments.

His practical instance of this was France during the Revolution.[34] Real reformation, insisted Britannicus, could only come from a return to religion: this constituted the only effective 'Radical Reform'. His opponents, by contrast, had a secular analysis:

> The Reformers assert that our distresses are the result of immoderate taxation – taxation occasioned by extravagant expenditure – extravagant expenditure upheld by political corruption. Their summary method of cure, therefore, is to strike, as they conceive, at the root of corruption, by establishing *Annual Parliaments and Universal Suffrage*.

The result of this could only be 'universal anarchy' and general impoverishment. Scripture taught that 'war, and famine, and pestilence... are dispensations of Providence by which rebellious nations are chastised': the only remedy was 'true religion'.[35]

Those who wished to urge biblical morality (prudence, thrift, delayed marriage) on needy labourers as a means of raising the 'subsistence wage' could see themselves as recommending a 'radical reform' in the old sense: a reform of human nature.[36] It is easy to read such moral tracts as simplistic and condescending if their sophisticated economic under-pinning (Malthus, Chalmers) is overlooked. Whatever their economic analysis, such men were generally led to a particular view of the recent political origins of the problem. According to John Harford, a leading Evangelical, in 1819, Richard Carlile's republication of *The Age of Reason* during his trial and newspaper reports of the proceedings, 'have given, of late, an unusual currency to the name and to the opinions of Paine. The Radical Reformers are also grown bold enough to acknowledge him as their Apostle and their Idol'. Outlining Paine's career up to the publication of *Rights of Man*, Harford concluded: 'It is impossible to overlook the striking resemblance which exists between the Revolutionists of 1793, and the Radicals of 1819. – They all belong to the same family, and are wedded to the same principles.'[37]

Now as then, there was a plan for elections to a Convention that would bypass Parliament. 'The whole system of 1793, and that of 1819, are equally founded on Thomas Paine's doctrines of the Rights of Man':

> not only in their general system of proceeding, but in almost every minute particular, the Radicals of 1819 are copyists of the Revolutionaries of 1793. The same inflammatory language belongs to both. With both, kings are tyrants, religion a fable, its zealous friends hypocrites and knaves, the rich, plunderers of the poor, all employers oppressors, rebellion another name for patriotism, and the assassination of those whom they deem the enemies of their cause, the acme of public virtue... As to the scheme of universal Suffrage and annual Parliaments, a notion borrowed from Paine, which is the watchword of this party, it is so triumphantly absurd as hardly to justify a serious refutation.[38]

Paine was the clue to the true nature of the Radicals, argued Harford: 'For some time we heard only of "universal suffrage" and "annual parliaments", and were left to guess the ultimate objects of the party; but the whole truth is now displayed in a broad day light, and the evidences of a deliberate conspiracy to overturn the government are no longer wanting.'[39]

Perhaps significantly, Harford did not use the term 'radicalism': his interpretation of 'Radical Reform' was backward-looking, and he did his best to identify it with Jacobin revolution. For Harford not radicalism but 'Modern Infidelity, with Faction and Revolution in his train, is the grand enemy whom we have to oppose'.[40] He did not appreciate those newly emergent features that were to provoke the conceptualization of a new ideology. His preoccupations were those of the activist Evangelicals with whom he associated.[41] He was preoccupied not with *Rights of Man* but with *The Age of Reason*. The 'one great and impassible barrier' to the success of Paine's schemes, insisted Harford, was 'the influence of Christianity'. It was a 'pillar of national principle and happiness', since the Bible 'teaches its disciples on the same principle that they serve God to

honor the King'. What the nation needed was a religious revival, 'a RADICAL
REFORM, such as the world has never yet seen'.[42]

Harford was undiscriminating in his denunciations. Many of the points
to which he objected were no part of Paine's teaching. The undoubted
attachment of Paine to natural rights had not logically entailed universal
suffrage[43] or a hostility to employers as such. Harford's tract was mostly
concerned with retailing scandalous biographical information about
Paine and stories of the horrors of the French Revolution; he said little
about the exact points of connection between Paine and the radical
reformers, which was his central claim. Harford's object was to disparage
the radicals of 1819 by asserting an obvious identity between them and the
irreligion and threats of revolution of the 1790s. The differences were
important, however. Although Carlile did indeed republish Paine's Deist
tract *The Age of Reason,* and although it obtained a wide currency, it is
suggested here that radicalism was novel and important in adding an
economic analysis of debt, taxes and distribution to the natural rights and
Deistic agendas of the 1790s, an economic analysis which then came to
dominate and obscure the others in a context not of Deism but of atheism.

The emergence of that economic agenda will be examined below. The
anti-Jacobins were rightly sensitive, however, to one central aspect of
radicalism's economic component. The Christian message was embodied
in the Church, but this institution had an earthly dimension and
presented a material target. 'We have long had our *radical reformers,*' wrote
one pamphleteer, 'foretelling instant and inevitable ruin to the State... This
is not reformation – it is revolution.' He specified its targets:
'Retrenchment is the plea; confiscation is the object – confiscation of all
appropriated revenue – subversion of all established institutions. And
church revenue, and the church establishment, are the first, marked,
objects of aggression.' He suggested a series of agrarian reforms to mitigate
the burden of tithes.[44] So an economic analysis came to focus not on
capitalism, but on the Church.

What came to preoccupy radical reformers, it seems, was not just taxes
in general, but tithes in particular;[45] not merely property in the abstract
but Church property and landed estates, the nexus of squire and parson.
This was not dictated by existing alignments, since anti-Jacobins did not
ordinarily define themselves as being pro agriculture and anti industry:
before Ricardo, they were more able (despite Godwin's attack on 'landed

inequality') to see land and manufactures as complementary rather than antithetical. In one pamphlet, 'a manufacturer' was presented as advising his radical reformer son that his son's favourite writings 'contain nothing new. The same fallacies have been often used and detected'. But 'You think, no doubt, that the wise and sagacious authors of them have just now discovered, that the Bible is false, and the Government is wicked; and that the one ought to be burnt, and the other overturned without delay'. The author bracketed 'Infidels, and pretended Reformers' together and refused to see anything new in the world after 1815. The Christian message, he argued, contradicted the claim of the perfectibility of government and the equality of property which were basic to 'Radical Reform'.[46] This perspective was not wrong, but it was too limited. It omitted the way in which pre-existing elements were being brought together in a crucial process. New ideas, and new terms to describe them, arrived together.

III.   THE LIFE-EXPERIENCE OF THE RADICAL: 'NATHAN BUTT' AND SAMUEL BAMFORD

Not all who were sceptical towards radical reform entertained as static a view of its nature as did the anti-Jacobins. One shrewd observer in particular implied a theory of its development over time which deserves to be tested against the evidence. John Galt[47] was better known for his minor classic, *Annals of the Parish* (1821), a penetrating exposure of Scottish foibles through the genre of the fictional autobiography, but this remarkably prolific author had an insight into politics also. In the early 1830s, he returned to the genre in which he had recorded his biggest success. *The Member* (1832) concerned the adventures of a Scots nabob, MP for the aptly named borough of Frailtown. *The Radical* (1832) was a similar satire on the life of the fictitious 'Nathan Butt', depicted as dedicating his autobiography to Lord Brougham, a man who had released 'property from that obsolete stability into which it has long been the object of society to constrain its natural freedom'.

Butt recounted with pride his struggles, from his infant years, against 'misrule, the lot of all, under the old system': he began with a story of how, as a baby, he had bitten his grandmother, who had tried to intervene to stop him from strangling a kitten: it was emblematic of 'the divine right of resistance'. Punishment for stealing apples while a schoolboy confirmed 'my abhorrence of coercive expedients in the management of mankind'.[48] Butt rationalized his conduct: 'It was not the sordid feelings of the covetous thief that drew me into that enterprise; but an innate perception of natural right'. Chastisement by his father, after being expelled from school for leading a rebellion, 'gave me both black and blue reasons to resent the ruthlessness of that false position in which children and parents stand, with respect to each other'. In the family as elsewhere, maintained Nathan Butt, 'the impulses of nature are justly acknowledged as superior to all artificial maxims and regulations'. Such a young man was a natural admirer of the French Revolution: 'It was delightful to contemplate the triumphs of liberty among them, and how they hallowed their cause with blood.'[49]

The ascendancy of Napoleon, who betrayed this revolutionary promise, made the fictional Butt and his fellow radicals 'shrink back into ourselves, and seek to obscure our particular opinions by a practical adherence to the existing customs of the world – errors and prejudices which we never forgot they were'. His marriage was tolerable, though marred by a family quarrel over the baptism of his child when he made public his belief that there was nothing in religion 'beyond the ingenuity of those who in different ages had invented its several rites, as a mode of levying taxes for the maintenance of their order'. Napoleon's restoration reawakened his public hopes; but 'the battle of Waterloo blighted my expectations; and with a sick and humbled heart, I acknowledged that the cause of philanthropy was, in consequence, suspended'.[50]

Nevertheless, after 1815, Galt made Butt declare, 'the rumours which then began to rise of discontents in the manufacturing districts, assured me that the great cause still lived, and that the candle, though low in the socket, was not extinct'. When the violence of these mass meetings failed, the radicals turned to argument. 'Nothing could be more galling to the latent indignation of the country, than that so many should enjoy the fruit of the taxes – should revel in elegance, or wallow in opulence, on the hard-won earnings of the industrious poor; and we took up this obvious truth as our theme.' Fortunately, Butt could exploit what he sensed was an important social change going on around him: 'an ebb or subsidence of anxiety for the interests of posterity, – an ancestral error in the feeling of patriotism or public spirit, which occupied a high station in the minds of our predecessors'. This now came to include the question of property. Butt was not completely unhappy at the prospect of post-war distress: 'Radicalism thrives by it and the general world is turned more towards the question of permitting property to continue in such large masses.'[51]

Butt now began to advocate 'the breaking into pieces of the great masses of property' as a way of alleviating beggary. Rents, not taxes, were the root cause of distress, and the solution called in question 'the existence of that class or order called "landlords"'. It was at this point in the novel that Galt placed Butt's refusing to hear the deathbed request of his uncle and business partner from the Presbyterian clergyman who had attended the deceased: 'Were all men to treat the members of the privileged orders [of priesthood] as I have done, the nuisance of being troubled with them would soon be abated.'[52]

Butt's political goals were still outlined by Galt in highly generalized terms, 'nothing less than the emancipation of the human race from the trammels and bondage of the social law; although, certainly, I did abet rational undertakings to procure parliamentary reform, as among the means by which my own great and high purpose might be attained'. Parliamentary reform was evidently a means to an end, and not the only means at that.[53]

> The truth is, that the [parliamentary] Reformers and the Radicals are two very different parties. It is not impossible – and I say so, having studied their predilections – that the former may hereafter amalgamate themselves with the Whigs and Tories, which the latter never can. Radicalism is an organic passion, and cannot be changed in its tendencies; it goes to the root of the evil that is in the world, and discerns that, without an abolition of the laws and institutes which it has been so long the erroneous object of society to uphold, the resuscitation of first principles can never be effected; and nothing less than that resuscitation will be satisfactory.

Reformers sought 'a moderate measure of amendment in things that have fallen into abuse'; Radicals sought 'a new system – a revolution'. Butt now realized the quite different nature of the two groups. The same conclusion was impressed on him when he was elected to Parliament in time to support the 1832 Reform Bill: he as a radical urging it forward merely as the prelude to future reforms which would finance poor relief out of 'the parks, palaces and grandeur of the aristocracy', a reformer arguing against him that 'we should be thankful and content' with whatever could be obtained.[54]

Galt was a brilliant satirist: his novel is evidence for the perception of the radicals by a friend of the old order like himself from the perspective of 1832, more than for the historical trajectory of the reform movement. Nevertheless, his satire suggests some important hypotheses. Radicalism, Galt's account implied, was not a clearly conceptualized ideology from the 1790s or earlier. It had its antecedents, instead, in less sharply defined Jacobin aspirations of limitless progress and human perfectibility. Nevertheless, this disposition began to acquire clearer shape in the world from 1815, as Galt began to sense the radical reformers' impatience with both 'Whigs' and 'Tories',[55] and as the theme of the levelling of property, and the breakup of great landed estates, became more prominent in the radicals' agenda.[56] The theological element was nevertheless present throughout: as Butt's friend Mr Cobble, the Reformer, tells him: 'you behold evil in all things'.[57] What Galt did not record, or seek to satirize, was Butt's encounter with any new and clearly defined ideology: 'radicalism' did not present itself to Butt as a school of thought, with a philosopher as its patron and mascot; but it acquired its parliamentary impact as 'knife and fork questions' rose to practical prominence. Life also could imitate art. When John Stuart Mill founded a group to propagate his philosophy, he called it the Utilitarian Society, borrowing the term from John Galt's *Annals of the Parish*, 'in which the Scotch clergyman, of whom the book is a supposed autobiography, is represented as warning his parishioners not to leave the Gospel and become utilitarians'.[58]

From fiction, we return to authentic testimony, which suggests that Galt was not wrong in discerning an element of individual emancipation in 'radical reform'. One tradesman recommended such emancipation to his fellows through an autobiography whose leading theme was 'the spirit of independence against wrongs... the spirit of independence against sufferings of a poor deserted child, a defenceless orphan'.[59] The same life-experience informed the memoirs of Samuel Bamford,[60] a work designed to record 'some of the most remarkable and interesting events that took place in the manufacturing districts of Lancashire, and other parts of England, during the years 1816 to 1821'.[61]

An underlying theme of his book was how much the radical agenda had changed in his lifetime. Looking back, Bamford recorded the resolutions of the twenty-one Hampden Clubs of the area around Manchester, held in the neighbouring small town of Middleton on 1 January 1817:

> resolutions were passed declaratory of the right of every male to vote, who paid taxes; that males of eighteen should be eligible to vote; that parliaments should be elected annually; that no placeman or pensioner should sit in parliament; that every twenty thousand of inhabitants should send a member to the house of commons; and that talent, and virtue, were the only qualifications necessary. Such were the moderate views and wishes of the reformers in those days, as compared with the present: the [secret] ballot was not insisted on as a part of reform. Concentrating our whole energy for the obtainment of annual parliaments and universal suffrage, we neither interfered with the house of lords; nor the bench of bishops; nor the working of factories; nor the corn laws; nor the payment of members; nor tithes; nor church rates; nor a score of other matters, which in these days have been pressed forward with the effect of distracting the attention, and weakening the exertions of reformers...

who would all, he argued, stand much more chance of success in a House of Commons elected on universal suffrage.[62] Yet since Bamford's memoirs, published in 1841–2, covered only the years 1816 to 1821, they offered no systematic account of the broadening of the reformers' agenda that was to occur in the 1820s. It is open to argument that that extension into the field of the redistribution of property came when the agenda of universal suffrage, familiar since the 1780s, was linked in an explosive way with that most sensitive issue of Church reform. No single individual did more to make this connection than Bentham.

IV.   FROM 'RADICAL REFORM' TO 'RADICALISM':
JEREMY BENTHAM AND THE REV. JAMES MILL

It was Bentham who, above all, provided a term, 'radicalism', at a moment in which men were open to a new definition. The French visitor Louis Simond had been surprised in 1810 to find the great number of people in the opposition; that is, those who disapprove, not only the present measures of ministers, which have not been of late either very wise or very successful, but the form and constitution of the government itself. It is stigmatized as vicious, corrupt, and in its decay, without hope or remedy but in a general reform, and in fact a revolution.

He divided people into three categories in this respect: 'whigs, tories, and absolute reformers'. Their categorization would be easy, 'for there are a few principal topics, which, like cabalistic words, it is enough to touch upon, to know at once the whole train of opinions of those with whom you speak'.[63] Simond's 'absolute reformers' were, within a decade, to see themselves as 'radicals', expressing a position which was recognizable when identified as 'radicalism'. In that process, Bentham's 'deep-rooted hatred, not only of revealed, but also of natural religion'[64] was fundamental.

Yet because Bentham founded so powerful a school, the nature of his achievement was identified, over succeeding decades, largely in the secular and utilitarian terms which the school itself dictated. It is this later secular assumption that must be dispensed with if a properly historical account of the origin and conceptualization of radicalism is to be established. The first category to be rejected is, of course, 'philosophic radical' itself. Elie Halévy began the first chapter of his classic study with the birth of Jeremy Bentham in 1748; only in an aside did Halévy disclose that the term 'Philosophical Radicals' did not begin to be used of a group until seventeen years after Bentham's conversion to universal suffrage, and authorship of *Radicalism not Dangerous*, in 1820.[65] As William Thomas has now shown, the term 'philosophic radical' was coined by John Stuart Mill in 1837 in reaction against what he then perceived as the narrowness of the ideas of Bentham and James Mill.[66] Far from explaining the phenomenon, the term itself becomes a subject for historical explanation. Consequently, the idea that one might write 'a continuous or comprehensive history of a body of ideas called philosophic radicalism, utilitarianism or Benthamism' must be rejected: the scholarly conclusion is, rather, 'the variety both of theoretical outlook and of political response within the group'.[67]

Bentham's own early intellectual formation therefore assumes much greater importance, for the later term 'radical' does not explain it. This formation was obscured in the nineteenth and twentieth centuries, not least by the pious Unitarian John Bowring's omission of Bentham's virulent writings against religion from the 1838–43 collected edition of Bentham's *Works*.[68] Nevertheless, Bentham's crusade against the Church, its liturgy and its teachings in the years 1809–23 can be traced back to his own loss of faith in an Oxford where subscription to the Thirty-nine Articles was a central public affirmation of identity and soon became the centre of controversy.[69]

Bentham dated his revulsion from the Church, and the loss of faith in its teachings, to the expulsion of six Methodist undergraduates in 1761.[70] Later, in London in *c.* 1773, Bentham drafted (but left unpublished) contributions to the controversy of 1768–74 over the subscription required of Oxford and Cambridge undergraduates. In 1774 appeared a translation of Voltaire's *Le Taureau Blanc*, with an anonymous lengthy Preface by Bentham himself which expressed not merely scepticism at formal biblical exegesis but a blasphemous hostility towards the claims of Christianity as such to historical veracity.[71] Already, then, in this work and in the manuscripts on subscription, conventional religion had been cast as the enemy of mankind in a way which fully anticipated Bentham's published writings of 1817–23.

The subscription controversy arose at the time that Bentham was drafting his attack on the man who had emerged as the leading Anglican defender of the nexus of Church and State, Sir William Blackstone. In his anonymously published tract of 1776 attacking Blackstone's *Commentaries*, Bentham singled out as the very first passage to which he objected Blackstone's paragraphs on the Dissenters, a passage inspired, according to Bentham, by 'the first transport of a holy zeal'; the youthful critic cited in his support the tracts by the Dissenters Priestley and Furneaux, which seized on Blackstone's harsh account of the laws against Nonconformity.[72] In 1790, when writing to congratulate the Unitarian Duke of Grafton for his anonymous pamphlet attacking the establishment, Bentham condemned 'the tyranny exercised by the church over the consciences of men' and 'its pernicious influence on the public morals'.[73]

These expressions of belief were, however, private. Bentham was remarkably reticent in public, and in published work, about his religious opinions. As late as 1831 he acknowledged that he had concealed his irreligious opinions from a Calvinist reformer, pretending to be committed merely to 'universal toleration'.[74] In one case, the *Traités de législation civile et pénale* (Paris, 1802), Bentham's editor Etienne Dumont excised his patron's 'plea for atheism' and softened many other irreligious passages.[75] There seems little doubt that Bentham knew that the massive commitment of English society to Christianity, whether within or outside the Church, would result in hostility towards him if his views became known. It might even mean prosecution.

The fragmented nature of Bentham's published work during his lifetime has generally been ascribed to his self-absorbed pattern of working, for he often abandoned a good project before its completion for a better. Much of the delay in publishing his writings on Christianity is, however, explained by the legal penalties then enforced against views as extreme as Bentham's, and by the government's anxious response.[76] In 1809, the failure of the Walcheren expedition and a wave of satire against the army and its commander, the Duke of York, was met with a series of prosecutions for seditious libel. Bentham's attention was drawn to the system of picking more reliable men to serve on the 'special juries' used in these cases; he denounced the system in *The Elements of the Art of Packing*, a work revised for him by James Mill.[77] While the book was being printed, the publisher became alarmed, and halted work. Bentham consulted the reformer and MP Sir Samuel Romilly, who advised that the Attorney General, Sir Vicary Gibbs, would certainly prosecute. So the printing was finished in 1810, but the book was not openly sold until 1821 (although it had some private circulation). Similarly Bentham's *Plan of Parliamentary Reform*, drafted in 1809, was not published until 1817; *Swear not at All*, an attack on the use and nature of oaths, was printed in 1813 but not published until 1817.[78]

The most legally sensitive of issues was still religion, and it was here that Bentham's writings centred after he became interested in the subject of judicial procedure in 1802. In 1809, he began drafting a work entitled 'Church', part of his critique of English institutions: this grew in size and proliferated, resulting in works published between 1817 and 1823[79] which have been characterized as a campaign to extirpate religious beliefs and practice as a necessary precondition of the establishment of a utilitarian society. For powerful philosophical reasons, Bentham was an atheist, and, for him, law and religion were inextricably linked.[80] A society in which Christian belief was widespread would presumably resemble the society in which Bentham actually found himself: to arrive at his ideal form of society through the action of innumerable individuals in the pursuit of utility, it was necessary that the members of that society understand pleasure in atheistic terms.

Atheism could be made explicit in Bentham's writings, but where it was, these works had normally to be published under pseudonyms. Atheism was, however, implicit in all of his works, especially those which dealt with a legal system which still claimed that Christianity was a part of it.[81] After John Stuart Mill finally edited and published Bentham's *The Rationale of Judicial Evidence* in five volumes in 1827, John Henry Newman commented: 'Mr. Bentham made a treatise on Judicial Proofs a covert attack upon the miracles of Revelation.'[82] For Bentham, therefore, a commitment to reform in law and administration had coexisted throughout his life with hostility to orthodox Christianity and to the Church. It was this integral role of Bentham's theological views that the positivist and anticlerical Halévy had obscured.[83] In the late 1810s, however, Bentham took three steps of major importance. He began to publish his irreligious works; he became converted to universal suffrage; and he coined the term 'radicalism' to describe his position, the ideology which identified the precise agenda or targets for utilitarian reform. Universal suffrage as a political goal was not new: it had originated in the 1760s and 1770s, but among a small group of heterodox Dissenting intelligentsia.[84] Bentham relocated its premises within atheism, and this was to give it a far larger social constituency in the urban-industrial society that now began to develop.

These doctrinal changes were reflected in the evolving language of politics. Halévy thought the expression 'radical reform' had 'first been in fashion for a time round about 1797 and 1798, when Fox and Horne Tooke, derided by the *Anti-Jacobin*, had come to an agreement in order to demand a "radical reform"... Then the expression seems completely to have disappeared and does not occur again before about 1810... The adjective *radical* and the substantive *reformer* are used henceforward with increasing frequency... But it appears that it was not until 1819 that the adjective Radical was used, by an abbreviation, as a substantive'. Halévy related this to the publication in 1817 of Bentham's *Plan of Parliamentary Reform, in the Form of a Catechism*, an event which led to his cooperation with Sir Francis Burdett, and Bentham's adoption of the goal of universal suffrage.[85]

It was soon after he met James Mill that Bentham had drafted what was later published as *Plan of Parliamentary Reform*; perhaps he was influenced by his Scottish disciple.[86] Bentham was undoubtedly frustrated at official resistance to reform and alienated from the government in 1809–10, but he was not thereby converted to 'radicalism':[87] there was no such pre-existent position to which to convert except universal suffrage. Yet Bentham was not yet an exponent of that doctrine: it seems that his conversion to the opposition in 1809–10 arose from his adoption of the belief that 'abuses in the law and abuses in parliament were symbiotic'.[88]

Bentham's draft *Plan of Parliamentary Reform*, which Cobbett refused to print in his *Register* in 1810, did not then include universal suffrage among its goals:[89] the secret ballot, not a universal franchise, was as yet Bentham's key device. Although he favoured a 'uniformly large' electorate in each constituency, that electorate was to be controlled by a property qualification, and this was only one of many political reforms primarily designed to check a malevolent monarchy.[90] From a wide franchise, envisaged by Bentham in *c.* 1790, it was a quantum leap to 'virtual universality of suffrage' in 1817. Bentham's development in politics and religion owed much to cooperation and discussion with Mill, his needy but forceful disciple whom he had known since 1808. The evidence does not establish that either converted the other;[91] nevertheless, they had important commitments in common, and probably encouraged each other in similar directions in the next decade.[92]

The young James Mill (1773–1836), son of a shoemaker, had gained his start in life through the patronage of Sir James Stuart, who intended to help his protégé become a Presbyterian minister. Mill indeed read theology at the end of his course at Edinburgh University (1794–7) and was licensed to preach in 1798, but failed to obtain a parish; in about 1807–11 he lost both his vocation and his faith, and soon became as ardent an atheist and anticlerical.[93] His thought, however, never lost its 'strongly moralistic element': 'He may have come to reject belief in God, but some form of evangelical zeal remained essential to him.'[94] His censorious disapproval of the clerical and patrician elites of the England in which he struggled to make a living as a journalist, often disguised for tactical reasons, only became more embittered with time.[95] Although Mill's *Essay on Government* (1820) was reticent about precisely what he sought in the realm of parliamentary reform, his views on that topic in 1817–18 have been rightly described as 'very radical, not to say apocalyptic'; they included universal suffrage.[96] This, and Mill's covert atheism, has led one scholar of Mill's unpublished papers to stress 'the well concealed contents of his private thoughts'.[97]

Bentham's public interventions in 1817–23 were part of a wider pattern. In the late 1810s, the disaffected intelligentsia often returned to the question of the existing state of parliamentary representation as the major barrier standing between them and the implementation of their schemes. It was in these years that the idea of 'radical reform' became sharpened and acquired an identity as 'radicalism', an ideology combining a central commitment against revealed religion and the Church of England with critiques of the Church's main props: the unreformed Parliament, the monarch, and the landlord.[98] This re-ignition of the reform agenda coincided with a renewed wave of prosecutions for blasphemous or seditious libel, beginning in 1817,[99] and a renewed government campaign against subversive political association that culminated in the 'Six Acts' of 1819.

In 1817, Jeremy Bentham cast his tract advocating parliamentary reform 'in the Form of a Catechism'. Its apocalyptic quality was precisely the reason for his rejection of 'moderate reform' in favour of 'radical... reform': 'reform or convulsion,' he insisted: 'such is the alternative'.[100] England was compared with the predicament of France under the restored monarchy: there, 'the wardrobe of the Holy Virgin will be supplied with a new gown, and every prison in the country with a new set of torture-boots and thumb-screws'. Bentham defined himself against a social system of nobility, of corruption and sinecures, of endless and unnecessary war, the whole personified in the person of a monarch, whose nature was 'to draw to himself in the greatest quantity possible'. This constituted a system:

And here we have one *partial*, one *separate*, one *sinister* interest, the *monarchical* – the interest of the ruling *one* – with which the *universal*, the *democratical* interest has to antagonize, and to which that all-comprehensive interest has all along been, – and, unless the only possible remedy – even parliamentary reform, and that a radical one, should be applied, – is destined to be for ever made a sacrifice: – a sacrifice? – yes: and, by the blessing of God, upon the legitimate and pious labours of his Vicegerent [the king], and the express image of his person here upon earth, a still unresisting sacrifice. Omni-presence, immortality, impeccability – equal as he is to God, as touching all these 'attributes' (ask Blackstone else, i. 270, 250, 246, 249), – who is there that, without adding impiety to disloyalty, can repine at seeing any thing or every thing he might otherwise call his own, included in the sacrifice?[101]

In this predicament, the 'ultimate end' was not merely improvement, but 'political salvation', namely 'democratical ascendancy' via 'virtually universal suffrage'. Bentham's definition of this omitted only idiots, infants and those incapable of 'exercising it to the advantage either of others or of themselves'; it included women.[102] In another pamphlet, Bentham attempted to explain his proposal:

> *Universal Suffrage, Annual Parliaments,* and *Election by Ballot.* – At Public Meetings, these are the words commonly (it is believed) employed, for expressing the essential features of Radical Reform.
>
> Another expression, however, there is, which in some respects seems to afford a promise of being more apposite. This is – *Secret, universal, equal, and annual suffrage*; or say, *Secrecy, universality, equality, and annuality of suffrage. Suffrage* is the common subject, to which all these qualities are referable: it presents a bond of union, by which all these elements may, in our conception, be knit together into one whole.

Bentham rebutted an accusation: 'Under Radicalism, all property, it is said, would be destroyed.' Clearly this was not the case in Pennsylvania. There, 'for these forty years, radicalism has been supreme: radicalism without Monarchy or Aristocracy: radicalism without control, and not any the slightest shock has property there ever received'.[103]

Bentham's *Plan of Parliamentary Reform* (1817) was swiftly followed by a related and much larger work, extending to 759 pages, a pertinacious assault on the legal framework and the doctrine of the established Church.[104] Bentham prefaced it with an explanation: the former work had given 'a sort of sketch... of one of the two *natures*, of which our constitution, such as it is, is composed, viz. the *temporal* one. In the present work may be seen a portrait of the other nature, viz. the *spiritual* one'. The sketch in 1817 had been 'a miniature'; the attack on the Church was 'more particularly delineated' in his new volume.[105] Bentham candidly recounted his own intellectual formation as a churchman; the clergymen among his ancestors;

the daily devotions 'in every part accordant to the rites of the established Church'; his father's membership of a club in which he was the only one not to be a clergyman of the Established Church; his own disillusion with Oxford at the expulsion of Methodist undergraduates. Bentham likened the proceedings against them to the Inquisition. At that moment, 'that affection which at its entrance [to Oxford] had glowed with so sincere a fervor, – my reverence for the Church of England – her doctrine, her discipline, her Universities, her ordinances, – was expelled from my youthful breast'. In 1818, Bentham devoted himself to proving that the Church's Catechism was 'a bad substitute' for the Bible, and a system of education based on that Catechism, that of the National Society, was an '*Exclusionary System*', dedicated to promoting '*Prostration of understanding and will*', in other words, 'slavery'.[106] Persuaded by his review, Bentham announced the 'utter rottenness' of the Anglican 'system of Church Government' and its 'complete ripeness for dissolution'.[107] It was an inflammatory work, and internal evidence suggests that James Mill may have had a hand in its composition.[108]

Why did Bentham now openly commit himself to universal suffrage, and publish *Church-of-Englandism* over his own name? The agitation for reform in the nation was growing; mass unrest might seem to point to an impending crisis, in which Bentham might at last intervene to effect. The Home Secretary, Lord Sidmouth, moved to press magistrates to bring prosecutions for blasphemous and seditious libel. It was in this gathering crisis that Bentham's *Plan of Parliamentary Reform* (1817) and *Swear not at All* (1817)[109] appeared. We know that *Church-of-Englandism* had been held back. Bentham had shown the draft of *Church-of-Englandism* to Romilly, seeking reassurance. Romilly was appalled: many passages seemed blasphemous and would leave Bentham to open to prosecution; he advised restraint. In three highly publicized trials (17–19 December 1817), the bookseller and Freethinker William Hone was acquitted on three counts of blasphemous libel.[110] At last, it seemed, the tide of public opinion on religious freedom had turned. Bentham could come into the open, and in 1818 *Church-of-Englandism* was released for sale. Yet if Bentham thought the danger over, he acted too soon. Prosecutions of Richard Carlile for blasphemous libel began in January 1819, and he was convicted in October.[111] Bentham and his circle had a crusade against orthodox religion still to fight.

Not only James Mill, but others of Bentham's inner circle shared this interest, though with a quickly reasserted caution. George Grote[112] heavily edited, or reworked, a set of Bentham's manuscripts to produce a volume entitled *Analysis of the Influence of Natural Religion on the Temporal Happiness of Mankind*, published in 1822 and ascribed to 'Philip Beauchamp'.[113] Its publisher was listed as Richard Carlile, who, already in prison for a similar offence, may have been seen as immune from further prosecution. The book professed not to deal with the truth or falsehood of natural religion, but claimed to show that it was 'the foe and not the benefactor of mankind', so calling into question whether 'any alleged revelation' was sufficient to 'neutralise the bitterness' of natural religion's 'fruits'. Natural religion alone 'invariably leads its votaries to ascribe to their Deity a character of caprice and tyranny'; it 'must produce the effect of encouraging actions useless and pernicious to mankind, but agreeable to the invisible Dispenser'. Since epistemological scepticism was normally directed against revelation, and often assumed an inherent benevolence in natural religion, this was a shrewd strategy. The tract culminated in a denunciation of the clergy, who, it demonstrated, 'cannot fail to be animated by an interest incurably opposed to all human happiness'; moreover, 'between the particular interest of a governing aristocracy and a sacerdotal class, there seems a very peculiar affinity and coincidence – each wielding the precise engine which the other wants'.[114] It has been rightly observed that Bentham's critique, despite its disavowals, here extended beyond natural to include revealed religion also. Bentham's unpublished manuscripts went much further, to the complete extirpation of all religion. In this he came close to abandoning the central axiom of utilitarianism that each man is the best judge of his own interests.[115] But it was essential that he do so if utility was not to mean what it meant in the works of Archdeacon William Paley: that man naturally pursued an idea of the good implanted in him by God. In Paley's Christian universe, as Sir William Blackstone had explained, the institutions of government and society could claim an authority quite independently of the personal preferences of individuals: in a general sense, the nature of things was the result of God's design. Secular utility implied a different scale of values.

Meanwhile, Francis Place, a supporter of universal suffrage, annual parliaments, the secret ballot and republicanism, was organizing another set of manuscripts on which Bentham had been working since *c.* 1815 into a work published in 1823 as *Not Paul, but Jesus*, claiming as author the fictitious 'Gamaliel Smith'.[116] Here, in print, Bentham now turned to revealed religion. The book argued that 'all the mischiefs, which have been imputed to the religion of Jesus' were the result of Paul's teaching doctrines that opposed those of his master, and doing so from 'inducements of a purely temporal nature'. Chapter XVI summarized Bentham's conclusions: '*Paul's Doctrines Anti-apostolic. – Was he not Anti-Christ?*' He answered clearly: 'here is an Antichrist, and he an undeniable one'.[117] Despite Place's editorial role, only the first third of the work was printed (it still ran to 403 pages). Bentham's request that the rest be published after his death was ignored, and Bowring suppressed it.[118]

In 1819–20, Bentham wrote (but left unpublished) a defence of his pamphlet *Bentham's Radical Reform Bill*. It was, as he made prominently clear, an attempt to rescue radicalism from the destructive criticism of Tories and Whigs alike, and from the charge that 'radical reform' would mean 'a general destruction of property'. This was logically impossible, Bentham showed (to his own satisfaction). Fear of radical reform rested only on the assumption of the 'consummate excellence' of the government, the 'consummate depravity' of subjects – 'the supremely ruling *one* [the king], sharing with the Almighty in his attributes, as Blackstone, who enumerates them expressly, assures us he does; those in authority under him a little lower than the angels; the subject-many devoid of reason, and in shape alone differing from beasts...'[119]

Bentham carefully rehearsed the examples of America since the Revolution, and the Volunteer Movement in Ireland during the American revolutionary war, to prove his claim: 'Radicalism not Dangerous... democratic ascendancy has nothing dangerous in it'. Remove the Church, the king, the aristocracy – the evil forces in society – and all the rest, including its institutions, the pre-eminence of the social elite, and private property itself, could remain unchanged. Bentham in his formal pronouncements sought in this way to limit both his analysis of the problem, and his solutions. In recent years,

> In our Islands, the distress has had two causes: the deficiency of [economic] demand as in the United States for produce, and that excess of taxation which has been produced by vicious constitution and misrule. The misrulers place it of course, the whole of it, to the

commercial account; no part to the financial and constitutional: but the people, who not only feel but see what the taxes are, as well as in what state the constitution is, are not to be thus blinded.

The solution therefore was that offered by 'the features or elements of radicalism', namely '*secrecy, universality, equality, annuality of suffrages*'.[120]

Yet if radicalism had not already contained so potentially powerful a redistributionist threat, Bentham (and others) would not have had to labour so hard to deny it. The redistribution of property had been a theme never wholly absent in Christian thought, especially since the Reformation, and derived from the interpretation of Genesis. Patristic commentators like Ambrose and Augustine had expounded God's grant of the world to mankind in common. Some more recent commentators claimed that this implied an equal grant to men in the present. John Locke encountered this position as a possible corollary of his argument for the natural equality of man by creation, and had to devise elaborate theories of property to account for and excuse the wide inequalities of wealth in his own society.[121] It was nevertheless possible to cite Locke's doctrine of property in an egalitarian sense, and this usage recurred in works like William Ogilvie's anonymous *An Essay on the Right of Property in Land* (1781) and George Dyer's *The Complaints of the Poor People of England* (1793).

Locke was not a necessary source, however, since all reformers could appeal much more obviously to Scripture. Paine's ideas of the equality of 'natural' rights and the legitimate redistribution of landed estates via punitive taxation were equally based on creation: 'every child born into the world must be considered as deriving its existence from God. The world is as new to him as it was to the first man that existed, and his natural right in it is of the same kind'. Paine proved his point by quoting Genesis.[122] A sermon by Richard Watson, Bishop of Llandaff, entitled *The Wisdom and Goodness of God, in having made both Rich and Poor* provoked Paine to publish *Agrarian Justice*, which proceeded from the argument that 'It is wrong to say that God made *Rich* and *Poor*; he made only *Male* and *Female*; and he gave them the earth for their inheritance'.[123]

The dependence of Locke's argument on premises about God's intentions was well understood, however. Thomas Spence, the most consistent advocate of the redistribution of land,[124] in 1793 linked Locke's

Two Treatises with Leviticus.[125] Spence's father was a member of a fundamentalist sect, the Glassites; he himself was inspired by the firebrand Presbyterian minister James Murray.[126] In 1797, he praised Paine's *Agrarian Justice* for its use of Locke and its invocation of the biblical teaching that 'God hath given the earth... to mankind in common', but went far beyond Paine's limited proposals.[127] At his trial in 1803, Spence invoked Locke and the Bible once more to support 'this my Millennial Form of Government'.[128] It may indeed be that Spence's 'millennium was secular',[129] but it may also be doubted how secular such an idea can become. Before 'radicalism' and 'socialism', there were few secular sources of powerful imagery. Charles Hall, author of *The Effects of Civilization on the People in European States* (London, 1805) and sometimes wrongly classed as an early socialist, similarly 'seemed to have found more inspiration from the Old Testament than any other source' for his plans to give labourers access to land.[130]

It is, of course, conventional to trace mid seventeenth-century projects for material redistribution (as with the 'Digger' Gerard Winstanley) to theological roots, to posit an hiatus for more than a century thereafter, and to treat redistributionist ideas in the early nineteenth century as self-sufficiently secular in nature.[131] Although this is not the place for a full investigation of the subject, this explanatory scheme now seems ripe for re-examination. If radicalism was formulated following a religious critique of landed inequality, it is understandable that this critique should have been carried over to become one element of the new but secular ideology. It was not, however, a preoccupation of that quintessentially urban intellectual Bentham himself: the priest, not the landowner, was his target.

Nevertheless, as socialists were soon to argue, general economic redistribution beyond the issue of land was not central to radicalism. If it was not, however, the question becomes harder to answer: how did the 'radicalism' of the 1820s differ from the phenomenon of the 1790s so widely (though inaccurately) called 'Jacobinism'? An answer, at least in outline, now begins to emerge. Jacobinism was normally premised on natural rights, although not because it was drawn from any deep knowledge of natural rights theory; its enthusiasm about the rights of man was inseparably linked to Deism, that worship of a Supreme Being that shaded so easily into the 'religion of humanity'. Radicalism (although it sometimes used the rhetoric of abstract rights and the rhetoric of historic constitutional liberties) was normally intellectually premised upon utilitarianism, which, in Bentham's fa..ious phrase, regarded natural rights theory as 'nonsense upon stilts'. It too was firmly atheist, since atheism was (as Bentham well knew) a necessary precondition of the sorts of reform he expected from utilitarianism. Radicalism was, moreover, both utilitarian and atheist in a context created by Ricardian economics, that essential theoretical constituent of the critique of the old order of squire and parson.[132] Radicalism was, therefore, far more powerfully redistributionist than Jacobinism ever became. And yet the targets of radicalism were still highly selective, as another new ideology – socialism – was now to demonstrate.

V.   RADICALISM VERSUS WHIGGISM AND SOCIALISM

It was not only the anti-Jacobin idiom that stood outside radical reform and acted to promote its self-definition; other self-consciously reformist traditions also came to be contrasted with radical reform as it developed into radicalism. Whigs, too, had their agenda, and despite long years in the wilderness it was their hour, not that of the radicals, which came in 1830.[133] As radical reformers increasingly inclined to distrust the Whigs for the covert limitations the Whigs placed on their intentions, radical reformers found themselves threatened from 'the Left' as the new ideology of socialism itself found a way of explaining why even radicalism was too limited. For 'socialism', too, was conceptualized in these years, considerably earlier than is often supposed. Socialism did not stand on the shoulders of radicalism; it was defined in contrast with it. Most notably, where radicalism was generally irreligious, socialism was frequently driven by Christian ideals of community.[134]

In these circumstances radicals began to extend their genealogy backwards in time, where even Paine's intellectual horizon in the 1790s had extended only as far back as the sanitized Whig triumph of 1688.[135] In 1819, the first issue of the periodical *The Radical Reformer* set out its creed:

> Impressed with a deep sense of the awful situation of the country, and convinced that an ignorance of, and *contempt* for the NATURAL RIGHTS OF MAN, are the sole causes of the corruptions of government and

public grievances, some admirers of the genuine principles of the Constitution have come forward to lay the foundation of the present work.

This did not entail novelty, however, for the authors sought to locate themselves within a tradition, 'what Algernon Sydney called "THE GOOD OLD CAUSE"'.[136] Natural rights, and an appeal to an historical constitutionalism, were still present among radical reformers; ahistorical utilitarianism did not at once sweep the board. Nineteenth-century radicals went on to construct a genealogy for radicalism that ignored religion and instead stressed patriotism to establish a link with the Levellers, but that is another story.

Even the most strident of the radical reformers could still profess a scrupulous respect for most forms of private property. Richard Carlile, in Dorchester jail from November 1819 to November 1825, conducted an extensive and influential publicity campaign that scarcely touched on issues of redistribution.[137] Only on the land question did Carlile adopt a redistributionist scheme with an explicit acknowledgement of Thomas Spence: in *The Republican* for December 1822 he explained how the products of industry were private and could not be taxed, but land was public property, held only conditionally by the landlord, and subject to taxation considered as 'a rental, or a payment from those who hold to those who do not hold'.[138] Henry Hunt, another champion of universal suffrage, annual parliaments and the secret ballot, took a similar position. His newsletter *To the Radical Reformers* was written from 'Ilchester Jail', or as he finally called it, 'Ilchester Bastile', from 1820 to 1822.[139] Hunt used it to review the issues of the moment and incite indignation over the Queen Caroline affair, the anniversary of 'the Manchester massacre', and the treatment of prisoners. In the midst of his endless and strident invective, Hunt indeed professed that 'The Radicals have always said, and honestly said, that they want nothing new, they only want the constitution; and a reformed House of Commons, chosen by the *whole people*, would at once restore that constitution'; 'rational liberty' could only be brought about 'by holding all private property sacred and inviolable'. As Hunt replied to an address from 'the Committee of Female Reformers of Manchester', 'Be but the friends of *Universal Suffrage* united, then our tyrants will fall and you will be free'.[140]

Assurances like these did not always persuade a wider audience. The author of the homiletical tale *Will Waver* evidently saw the first and main threat of radical reform in 1821 to be the expropriation of the squirearchy and the division of landed estates. Almost equally prominent was the theme of the fictional village radical Jem Gudgeon's irreligion: 'I would have a man use his reason, and not be priest-ridden; I would have him follow his nature, and not a parcel of lies, invented by the priests to keep folks in order.'[141] Christian apologists, although sensitive on this point, were also aware that radical reform had acquired an economic theory from Ricardo which systematized a widely held critique (seen, for example, in Cobbett) in which high taxes to fund an enormous national debt were identified as a prime cause of poverty, and in which rent was identified as an unjustified extortion by what Ricardo in 1817 defined as 'the unproductive class', the landlords.[142] Even John Harford, though preoccupied by what he saw as the lasting legacy of Thomas Paine, identified the preoccupations of 1819. 'The DEBT, the DEBT, is now the hue and cry of the whole party', he wrote of the radicals.[143]

A new journal, *The Radical*, posed the question 'What is a Radical?' in its first issue (1831) and answered it:

a Radical is one who, impatient of enormous taxation imposed by a set of tax-imposers, over whose rapacity he has no control, is determined to procure a remedy for such a foul disease. He is acquainted with the cause: he is aware that it is the present system of government by which the irresponsible, almost self-elected, aristocratical *Few* contrive to exclude the *Many* from the deputation of Representatives to the Assembly where the taxes are imposed; he is desirous of *eradicating* such a monstrous, unjust, detestable system: he is conscious that a Whig or *partial* remedy will prove insufficient for a cure; he honestly proclaims every quack, pretended remedy to be inefficacious; he is not such a fool as to imagine that a *partial* or *moderate* dose of political medicine will relieve the People. If a man has a fever, he must be cured *radically*, not *partially* or *moderately*. On the same principle the honest political physician will prescribe a course of medicine which will go to the *radix*, or root of the national disease. He will physic, purge, bleed, – he will ERADICATE, – he will be a RADICAL.

This is a *radical*, efficacious, certain, safe cure. Recipe: —

EVERY MAN (*not incapacitated by crime or extreme ignorance*) A VOTE IN ELECTING A REPRESENTATIVE *in the Assembly where the Laws are made.*[144]

In 1820–22, Henry Hunt stressed the consistent hostility of the Whigs towards the Radicals. The Whigs had not been libertarian in their legislation 'in 1807, when they were last in power; and what has been their conduct ever since? have not many of them, upon all occasions, joined the minister to make laws to put down the radicals?'[145] Certainly, the Whigs shied away from universal suffrage, and many of them were hesitant about any measure of parliamentary reform in the first three decades of the nineteenth century.[146]

By the time the Whigs achieved power in 1830 and found themselves unexpectedly united behind a parliamentary reform bill, the position of the radicals had moved further still. For them, universal suffrage was now even more clearly only a means to an end. After its ringing opening declaration in favour of the franchise for all, *The Radical* specified its grievances: the tax on newspapers; unemployment; tithes; the death penalty; the question of distribution:

> An abundant harvest will not suffice to alleviate efficaciously the cruel sufferings of the poor man; for it is not the *insufficiency* of *produce* which reduces him to misery and famine – it is its *unjust distribution*. The poor man often dies of hunger, not on account of there being no bread to eat, but because he, who prepares it, has none to eat!
>
> The working-man has it not in his power to buy sufficient bread for his family, because all the instruments of labour are subject, under the name of *rent*, &c., to enormous subtractions made for the profit of the *do-nothings*; so that, these deductions being effected, there remains for the unfortunate labourer out of the produce of his labour, but a scanty and insufficient portion.[147]

Despite its attempt in its first issue to be most things to most men, the new journal *The Truth* displayed what was by 1833 one hallmark of the radical position: it included as its leading principle the claim that, since 'nature... gives to all an equal right to the soil', the great landed estates should be broken up.[148]

This was the undisguised message for an audience presumed to be sympathetic. For the parliamentary classes, the nature of radicalism could still be described in minimal terms. In 1830, the *Westminster Review* placed the question of the franchise first in its discussion of radical reform. The anonymous author reassured his readers: 'Let no man be startled at the term radical; does any man but the guilty, desire a reform that is not radical? "Radical" means that which shall do something effectually; and "not radical" means not doing it at all. Does any man go to a doctor, and ask for a cure that is not radical?' It followed that:

> the time cannot be far off, when the middle classes, and those of the highest who are not entered of the plot, will come forward to join their influence to the cause of the starving poor... The time will come when rich and poor will combine to make every man eat out of his own dish; and the actual agent in this cruel operation, will be a radical reform in what is called the commons house of parliament.[149]

Thanks not least to the crises surrounding the Reform Act, by the 1830s 'the Radical party' had been reified as an actor in parliamentary elections.[150] Yet no sooner was this identity established than, in the same decade, another new ideology, socialism,[151] began to define itself in contrast with radicalism.[152] In 1835, Robert Owen's socialist weekly *The New Moral World* recorded a meeting of the London 'Great Radical Association' and briefed its readers on the contrasting principles of the radicals. 'These are, – "universal suffrage, equal representation, annual parliaments, vote by ballot, and no property qualification". Radicals were 'informed that the *root* of the evil by which they are oppressed and enslaved, is not in the constitution of the monarchy, not in the constitution of the House of Lords; no, these are only *branches* of the root; but the root itself, is in the constitution of the House of Commons'. This was all very well, argued the Owenite, but how would it help the common man?

> We will suppose that the new Parliament was assembled, elected according to these new arrangements, and that they immediately proceeded to make the monarchy elective, or to determine to have a President, who should be satisfied with a salary of 5000 *l.* per annum; that they would abolish the House of Lords, or make that an elective

body; that they would separate the church from the state, abolish tithes, and make the voluntary principle, for the support of the clergy, the law of the land; that they would annihilate the pension list, and abolish all useless places and sinecures; disband the standing army; and, in short, reduce the expenditure of the government of this country to a level with that of the United States; supposing all this accomplished within the space of the next two years, – and few of our Radical friends calculate upon a more rapid accomplishment of their wishes, – we then again enquire to what extent the condition of the labouring population will thereby be improved?

A reduction of public expenditure would throw many labourers out of work;

and this would go on, until the wages of labour would be reduced to the same relative scale as at present; that is, *to the mere subsisting price;* which, as the political economists tell us, is the natural reward of labour: and, notwithstanding all this change, therefore, in two years after, the industrious classes would find that they were just in the same state as before.[153]

By 1838, another observer could contrast socialists and radicals even more sharply:

Embracing in its objects the political equality and self government aimed at by the Radicals, the scheme of the Socialists superadds a new principle of morals, and a new system of marriage, the destruction of priestcraft, and community of property. The means too proposed by the latter for the accomplishment of their views, vary essentially from those which have been adopted, or contemplated to be used, by the Radicals.

The radicals were not homogeneous, he acknowledged; 'a large section are favourable to, at least, the economic views of the Socialists, and seek political power merely as an effective instrument for removing the competitive principle from society'.[154] But the views of the 'anti-Socialist section' of the radicals could be listed:

The purely political Radicals say that through the following gradations, beginning with universal suffrage as a first step, might be reached the maximum of human liberty and happiness.

First. A really responsible, justice-loving, and cheap government.

Second. A relieving of the people from the ascendancy and dominion of any religious sect, and the government from all care about religion.

Third. A good education for every citizen; the removal of all fiscal restraints from, and the utmost possible extension of, knowledge.

Fourth. An equal chance of participation in all state honours and emoluments.

Fifth. An equitable, simple, and comprehensive code of laws, impartially, cheaply, and readily administered.

Sixth. The abolition of private property in the soil.

Seventh. The suppression of all other monopolies, and the utmost possible freedom, both local and national, given to the competitive principle.

Eighth. An unexceptionable circulating medium.[155]

Samuel Bower's eight components of radicalism were highly generalized, or unobjectionable, or utopian; some were already familiar, even dating back several centuries. What was new was the way in which this list of aims had been fused together, given a unity and a coherence by the existence of a view of man. For the secular, free-standing, omni-competent individual, the Church and the institutions of society that claimed a divine sanction were the barriers to the maximization of utility. How far would this programme go? Would this critique condemn the squire as well as the parson? Some radicals extrapolated their analysis of the unreformed political system and the origins of the national debt to include reform of landownership, but others did not. Bower added a footnote to his sixth point concerning land:

This has not been found a place in the programme generally given to the public. Some, however, of the most honest and fearless of the Radicals have shown the institution of private property in the soil to be what it really is, namely, an evil of the first magnitude, and one the abolition of which must be an early fruit of the political enfranchisement of the people.[156]

There was much in this of which the socialist Bower approved; but 'the system of individual competition', he argued, would still preserve 'the classification of society into master and servant, and richer and poorer'. This would in practice 'destroy the assumed political equality'.[157]

By the late 1830s, then, distinctions between the creeds of radicals and socialists had been drawn with some clarity. Radicals could perceive Chartist disorders as proof that the diagnosis offered by radicalism was a correct one. One radical insisted that 'Our grievances, in short, are, – Enormous Debt, and habitual Extravagance disabling us from paying it'. Since 'The interest of the Debt is defrayed by heavy taxes laid on the poor', argued Francis Newman, a professor at the new University of London, this was the grievance on which 'all the rest turns'. 'As long as it exists, it is morally certain that poor men will become disaffected to the existing constitution as fast as they gain political information.'[158] Socialists, by contrast, 'located the cause of working-class misery within economic activity and no longer thought of political corruption (the debt and taxes) as the cause of poverty and inequality. Their attention was less on the owner of land than on the owner of capital, less on the farm, the landless, and the unemployed than on the factory and the working poor.'[159]

Although radicalism expanded far beyond its starting point, it had never expanded as far as to include this socialist agenda. Socialism and radicalism were henceforth alternatives, competing for the allegiance of a mass audience. They were not, however, unchanging ideologies. With the passage of time, they developed, notably by the steady elimination (at least in the eyes of the intelligentsia) of the theological element in their origins, and with the substantial assimilation of many elements of radicalism (anti-imperialism, financial reform, religious pluralism) by the Liberal party.[160] By the late nineteenth century, this process of amnesia was largely complete. Viewed from Balliol College in the 1880s, it seemed that

> The old Radical creed may be summed up in three words – justice, liberty, and self-help. To obtain justice and liberty they believed all classes should be admitted to the suffrage; to promote self-reliance they believed that every restriction on trade should be abolished, that labour and commerce should be as free as the winds. Two things are observable in this creed, the intense dislike of the old Radicals to State interference, and their complete faith in the people.[161]

But this was only part of the story. 'Radicalism' had begun life as an ideology intended to negate the 'old society': in order to do so, it had to propound a new view of man that replied to man as he was. Universal suffrage was not a self-evident idea for the secular utilitarians. In the eighteenth century it took its rise within Arianism and (especially) Socinianism, theologies which carried to the most articulate theoretical extreme Dissent's idea of the individual as free standing, with immediate personal access to God. As such, the appeal of universal suffrage was, at first, narrowly framed and strangely limited. It was only when an alliance was forged between universal suffrage and utilitarianism that 'democracy', understood as individual agency, could become a potent force. The conceptualization of 'radicalism' was a key to the forging of that alliance, but the secular world to which radicalism appealed was not self-generated. The secular ideologies of the nineteenth century emerged only out of a profound engagement with religion. Their conceptualization did not prove the emancipation of modern man from his past. On the contrary, they showed how profoundly shaped by his past he was even in the act of seeking to escape from it.

5

CHALLENGING THE AMERICAN PUBLIC MYTH

I.   THE INEVITABILITY OF AMERICAN HISTORY

If postmodernism is to be shown to be inadequate, better general accounts of fundamental historical change must be provided. Yet a major obstacle to such provision is the American Revolution, for its interpretation has become set in the concrete of a national myth of origins and propagated by the highest ideals of its subscribers.[1] History, indeed, labours under a major handicap in all societies suffused with a sense of their own rightness or inevitability. Whether driven by secular ideologies, shared religious beliefs or consensual optimism, such societies devise intellectual strategies to blot out their earlier sense of the paths that were not taken, their number, their feasibility and their attractiveness to those who, knowingly or unknowingly, with foresight or without it, made the fatal choices. Although England has at times been archetypal in all these ways, no culture has been more systematic and more consistently successful in this retrospective reordering than the United States. American exceptionalism is still a powerful collective myth, and one whose origins can be traced to an event reified with a leading capital as the Founding. The United States is therefore peculiarly vulnerable to post-modernism, since its public culture embodies few scenarios of fundamental change apart from revolutionary, emancipatory ones. The reinterpretation of the American Revolution is therefore central to the development of history, both in method and substance, as well as in many other areas.

It is not surprising that so few American historians have ventured seriously to question the 'manifest destiny' of the United States by pursuing counterfactual inquiries. Those few writers who have imagined American history without independence have tended to treat the idea as a joke.[2] The early American historians of the new republic at least tried to escape from the sense of inevitability created by the prominence of Divine Providence in their Puritan heritage, and did their best to give proper attention to the importance of contingency; but the attempt did not last. The pressure to celebrate the manifest destiny of an independent United States made impossible any serious respect for the two greatest counterfactuals of modern history: the absence both of an American Revolution and of a French. For without the American Revolution, and the financial burden placed on the French government by its participation in the American war, it is unlikely that the old order in France would have collapsed as it did in 1788–9, and with such widely acknowledged finality. What is at stake in the recreation of the counterfactuals of 1776 is therefore not any trivial flattery of injured British sensibilities but rather the possible avoidance of that alleged sequence of 'great' national revolutions[3] of which 1789 was seen as the second instalment, and which devastated the culture of the *ancien régime* across Europe. Historians' adopted role of celebrating this sequence of collapsing dominoes gave those authors no reason to question the inevitability of the American episode that had triggered the sequence in the first place.

The lack of intellectual challenges to American self-sufficiency from outside the American republic is one of the French Revolution's unnoticed legacies. Yet, in the case of Britain's relations with her former North American colonies, this lack of constructively critical engagement is more remarkable. Partly the cause was definitional: independence in 1783 seemed to remove the American question from its former place as a problem integral to British history and to establish it as a separate subject, with questions and answers relevant only to itself. More important, the absence of British analyses of American counterfactuals reflected the substantial absence of such analyses within British history. Until quite recently, British historians evidently felt little need to consider what might have been when the actual outcomes appeared, from their perspective, to be so agreeable. The teleology built into the 'Whig interpretation of history' was entirely congruent with its American counterparts. Whig historians might briefly allow themselves to dwell on the might-have-been, but only in order to highlight its abhorrent and unacceptable nature. With the counterfactual as with the ghost story, Victorians might frighten themselves with the intolerable, safe now in the knowledge of its impossibility.

Some writers have more recently ventured to reopen the questions which English historiography had traditionally defined as closed. Geoffrey Parker used a counterfactual framework to set out evidence for the strength of the Spanish land forces in 1588 and the weakness of their English counterparts, and to speculate on the wider consequences of even limited military success had Spanish troops landed in England.[4] A still more provocative reversal of the orthodoxies was provided by Conrad Russell in a parody of an explanation of James II's victory over William of Orange's invasion force in 1688, an explanation which dismissed short-term contingencies and ascribed the triumph of Catholicism and absolute monarchy in England to deep-seated and long-term causes.[5] John Pocock too, examining the ideological consequences of the Revolution of 1688, pointed out that the governing classes would never have consented to James II's deposition had he not fled the country.[6] Such enquiries therefore have their justifications, for if, as Russell has suggested, there was nothing inevitable about the Glorious Revolution of 1688, then we can hardly avoid posing counter-factual questions about the American Revolution too. The term 'revolution' confers no special status, either modernist or postmodernist, on the avoidable events to which it is applied.

II.   STUART ALTERNATIVES

To understand the case of America, we need to place it in a wider context: a counterfactual scenario extending back to the later Stuarts, and including their successors in exile. This is necessary if the constitutional framework of Britain's transatlantic empire is to be established, since one option for North America in the eighteenth century was as a British possession in an empire still ruled by that strangely fated dynasty. Such an outcome might have embraced either of two quite different constitutional settlements, both of which might have strengthened the empire's long-term coherence. The first would have applied had James II's plans for the reorganization of colonial government succeeded, and had he retained his throne in 1688. The second might have obtained had one of his successors regained the throne which James lost, and had the relations between Britain and her colonies thereafter mirrored the constitutional relations between the component kingdoms of the British Isles.

It might be argued that James II's plans for the American colonies illustrated an inflexible commitment to bureaucratic centralization and against representative assemblies. His plans were a more considered response to American realities, however, for his involvement in colonial affairs was extensive, and came early. As Duke of York, James was granted the proprietorship of the colonies of New Jersey and New York in 1664 after their conquest in the Second Dutch War. While proprietor of New York, his experience of colonial conflicts made him consistently resist local demands for an assembly: he conceded such a body with reluctance in 1683, and promptly abolished it on his accession to the throne in 1685 when New York was reorganized as a crown colony.[7] Massachusetts, equally, lost its assembly when its charter was revoked and reissued in 1684. James then went further still, combining the colonies of Connecticut, Massachusetts, New Hampshire and Rhode Island into a new body, the Dominion of New England, under the control of a Governor General; later it was enlarged to include New Jersey and New York, raising fears that James intended it to be the model for amalgamating into two or three Dominions all the American colonies.[8] The suppression of colonial assemblies, and the magnification of the powers of the Governor General, was probably intended primarily to turn the colonies into defensible military units, and only secondarily to impose religious toleration on recalcitrant Congregationalists. But the combined effect of these two implications was to raise in full form the spectre of 'Popery and arbitrary power' already familiar in England, and to unleash sudden resistance when news arrived in the colonies of James's deposition in December 1688: America, too, had its Glorious Revolution.[9]

Without the events of 1688 in England, however, it is not clear that American colonists at their then stage of development could have resisted the centralization of their governments into three 'Dominions' and the elimination or diminution of colonial assemblies. Without the structure provided by those assemblies in the eighteenth century, it is unlikely that colonial constitutional debate would have taken the form it did. An America effectively subordinated to an English executive at an early stage, and paralleled by a constitutional settlement at home in which the Westminster, Edinburgh and Dublin parliaments – but especially Westminster – played much lesser roles, would have been an America with a much smaller potential for resistance in the 1760s and 1770s.[10]

This first alternative assumes, as Whigs at the time firmly believed, that Stuart rule would mean the end of parliaments. This is at least open to qualification: if it was chiefly conflicts over religion that made it so hard for Charles I, Charles II and James II to work with their parliaments, one might frame an alternative scenario in which a compromise on religious questions would have left the Stuarts no more averse to democratic assemblies in practice than other dynasties. Stuart history after 1688 gives some support to this, for James II's exile in 1688 did not settle the dynastic question. Conspiracies for a restoration 'were hatched, exploded or investigated in 1689–90, 1692, 1695–6, 1704, 1706–8, 1709–10, 1713–14, 1714–15, 1716–17, 1720–22, 1725–7, 1730–32, 1743–4, 1750–52 and 1758–9. Foreign invasions inspired by the Jacobites were foiled by the elements and the Royal Navy (in almost equal parts) in 1692, 1696, 1708, 1719, 1744, 1746 and 1759.'[11] Yet these attempts were increasingly accompanied by proclamations from James II, his son and grandson professing elaborate respect for the constitutional forms they had previously seemed to threaten. After 1689 it was supporters of William of Orange, Whigs and Hanoverians in turn who tended to treat representative assemblies with minimal patience, and the Stuarts in exile who came to call for free parliaments, uncorrupted by ministerial malpractice.[12] Along with the exiled Stuarts' goal of the liberation of the Westminster, Edinburgh and Dublin Parliaments went a legitimist constitutional theory which, by emphasizing the monarchy, meant that the unity of the kingdoms of England, Scotland and Ireland was expressed solely in terms of allegiance to a common sovereign. The restored monarchy in 1660 had deliberately undone the Cromwellian unions with Scotland and Ireland; the Stuarts, bidding for Scottish support, were committed to undoing the Union of 1707 also. Scottish Jacobites looked for a restoration of a Stuart dynasty and the Edinburgh Parliament together, and Irish Jacobites anticipated by many decades the arguments most loudly made by Irish Whig politicians in the 1780s about the legislative equality of England and Ireland.[13] If James II had not been destroyed by his religious zeal, such a constitutional *modus vivendi* might have been feasible for him also.

Such a structure would have been as helpful in North America as in the British Isles. Until the 1770s, colonial Americans too sometimes expressed a desire for greater legislative autonomy within the reassuring framework of the empire. They reverted to an argument which, to Hanoverians, appeared shockingly Tory, associated with excessive deference to the Crown: the assembly of each colony was claimed to be equal in authority to the Westminster Parliament, and the component parts of the empire were, Americans claimed, united only by their allegiance to a common sovereign. Nor was this argument confined to a handful of American colonists. It could be found in England too, in the writings of reformers like the Dissenting minister and philosopher Richard Price.[14] Just as Jacobitism in its later stages began to take on something of the air of a protest movement, adding to its dynastic doctrinal core a series of social grievances which anticipated the platform of John Wilkes, so too its constitutional doctrines began to find echoes at many unexpected points in the political spectrum. A Stuart Britain might have appealed to constituencies on both sides of the Atlantic.

After independence, the victors made it seem that American colonists had always been ruggedly anti-monarchical. Parts of the writings of the Founding Fathers could indeed be interpreted in this way. In 1775, for example, John Adams, one of the earliest of his generation to campaign for full independence and later the second President of the USA, argued that the idea of a 'British empire' in America was unwarranted in constitutional law, 'introduced in allusion to the Roman empire, and intended to insinuate that the prerogative of the imperial crown of England' was absolute, not including Lords and Commons.[15] But most colonists were attracted by the convenient and seemingly patriotic argument that each colony was linked to the empire solely through its link with the crown. This remained an appealing model for many Americans even after independence. In 1800, reflecting on the then balance of power between the federal government and the states, James Madison, Virginia revolutionary, co-author of *The Federalist* and in 1809 fourth President of the USA, argued that

The fundamental principle of the Revolution was, that the Colonies were co-ordinate members with each other and with Great Britain, of an empire united by a common executive sovereign, but not united by any common legislative sovereign. The legislative power was maintained to be as complete in each American Parliament, as in the British Parliament. And the royal prerogative was in force in each Colony by virtue of its acknowledging the King for its executive magistrate, as it was in Great Britain by virtue of a like acknowledgement there.[16]

This was an old idiom of debate, revolving around charters, statutes and common-law privileges. Of course, colonial arguments came finally to be expressed in a quite different natural law idiom that proved explosive. The origins of this change of idioms came late, in the mid 1760s. In 1764, for example, the Boston lawyer James Otis, one of the first patriot controversialists, appealed to Locke's anti-Stuart natural law argument to contend that the government was dissolved whenever the legislative arm violated its trust and so broke 'this fundamental, sacred and unalterable law of self preservation', for which men had 'entered into society'.[17] The revolutionary doctrine that, by 'the law of nature', men leaving the mother country [by implication, Britain] to found a new society elsewhere [by implication, in North America] 'recover their natural freedom and independence' was heard in 1766 from the senior Virginia politician and pamphleteer Richard Bland. According to Bland, 'the jurisdiction and sovereignty of the state they have quitted, ceases'; such men 'become a sovereign state, independent of the state from which they separated'.[18] After the Revolution, such arguments were retrospectively organized into a high road to independence. Yet this transition to a natural law idiom was not inevitable and did not become widespread until the 1770s. Had the empire already, since 1688, been structured in terms of the separateness of the colonies and their personal tie to the king, natural law claims of this kind might not have been generated. Anglo-American disputes might have gone on being addressed in the concrete, negotiable language of specific liberties and privileges.[19] Compromise rather than revolution might have been the consequence.

English law provided another area in which the debate could have taken a different direction. Formally, all lands in America had been granted to settlers by the Crown in 'free and common Soccage' as if they were located in the manor of East Greenwich in Kent.[20] Such lands were, in law, merely part of the royal demesne. Benjamin Franklin ridiculed this ancient doctrine of English land law in 1766, but others were to put it to use in the republican cause.[21] It was a doctrine to which both sides might appeal. John Adams cited it in the interest of independence to establish that English law, to the reign of James I, made no provision for 'colonization', no 'provision ...for governing colonies beyond the Atlantic, or beyond the four seas, by authority of parliament, no nor for the king to grant charters to subjects to settle in foreign countries'.[22] The argument was still sufficiently powerful for colonists to use it in order to place a particular interpretation on the transatlantic constitution. Others could use the same doctrine differently, however: the argument that men reassumed their rights by the law of nature in quitting the kingdom was always vulnerable since the king had a common-law right to prevent such emigration (given effect by the writ *ne exeat regno*). If colonies were royal grants, some colonists could argue (contrary to Bland's claim that the colonies were already free and independent states) that they were still part of the realm of England and therefore entitled to all the rights of Englishmen, including 'no taxation without representation'. Complete independence was not the only or inevitable outcome of the remarkable flowering of constitutional and political theory seen in America between 1763 and 1776.

Despite natural law arguments and the self-evident truths of the Declaration of Independence which natural law arguments generated, this older constitutional idiom remained basic up to the outbreak of the war. In 1775, the Lord Chief Justice, Lord Mansfield, in a debate in the House of Lords, argued that colonial grievances focused on the principle of British supremacy, not the detail of controversial legislation.

> If I do not mistake, in one place, the Congress sum up the whole of their grievances in the passage of the Declaratory Act [1765], which asserts the supremacy of Great Britain, or the power of making laws for America in all cases whatsoever. That is the true bone of contention. They positively deny the right, not the mode of exercising it. They would allow the king of Great Britain a nominal sovereignty over them, but nothing else. They would throw off the dependency on the crown of Great Britain, but not on the person of the king, whom they would render a cypher. In fine, they would stand in relation to Great Britain as Hanover now stands; or, more properly speaking, as Scotland stood towards England, previous to the treaty of Union.[23]

Or, as it would have been politically tactless for him to have said, before the Revolution of 1688.

Constitutional doctrines and practical purposes were thus mutually dependent. In an eighteenth-century Britain ruled by Stuart monarchs, such doctrines might have been more easily used as a way of redefining imperial relationships to cope with increasing colonial population, prosperity and political maturity. Imperial devolution was to be the path eventually explored by the metropolis after the Durham Report of 1839; it is possible that a continued or a restored Stuart regime would have found itself committed to a constitutional formula within the British Isles which unintentionally promoted the process of imperial devolution at an earlier date, and so accommodated American ambitions rather than resisting them. No such Stuart restoration recast the political landscape, of course, and a forward-looking Britain found itself increasingly committed to the Blackstonian doctrine of the absolute authority of the Crown in Parliament which a backward-looking America, still obsessed with the seventeenth-century jurist Sir Edward Coke, finally resisted with armed force.

III.   TWO TYPES OF TRAGEDY? 1688 AND 1776

The revolutions of 1688 and 1776 shared a number of essential features: their initial seeming improbability; the reluctance of most men, however critical of the government, to resort to armed force; a high level of eventual unanimity that something had to be done; a considerable degree of disagreement, in historical retrospect, about the causes of what actually was done; a powerful political need subsequently to claim that the meaning of the revolution was profound and unambiguous. Yet in respect of causation, the two episodes now appear very different. The fall of James II came about in a narrow time-frame, as the result of a set of events which contemporaries saw as bewildering and recent historians explain as having been dominated by contingency. It was a revolution which then seemed and now seems incomprehensibly underdetermined. By contrast, historians of the conflicts of the 1770s and 1780s have always treated the Revolution as overdetermined, the long-delayed result of long-rehearsed social, religious or ideological conflicts. This is equally true of those who pointed to British policy and of those who, more recently, explain the revolution chiefly as the result of causes internal to the colonies themselves.[24]

The readmission of contingency to our accounts of 1776 both reopens the counterfactuals and reveals the character of the American Revolution as a *civil* war, each side embracing a plausible reading of shared doctrine, rather than a consensually supported war of colonial liberation aimed at driving out an alien occupying power. Where the majority of both English and Scots had sat on the fence in 1688, waiting to see which side would prevail, the pattern in the Thirteen Colonies in 1776 was strikingly different. There, men had often been politically mobilized and pre-committed to one side or other by principled conflicts and local coercion dating as far back as the early 1760s. In England in 1688 a change of government was peacefully effected, but followed by agonizings over the theoretical implications of what had been done; in 1776 American colonists had already had their theoretical debate and were now swiftly drawn into bitter civil war with neighbouring communities of the opposite allegiance. Only the permanent exclusion of the Loyalists from 1783 and the subsequent wave of triumphalism created the illusion of a unity of national purpose and the inevitability of a wholly independent United States.

This seeming over-determination therefore conceals two counter-factuals, two distinct and irreconcilable alternatives: a British America, ever more securely integrated into a British modernity of Church and King, commerce and science; or a republican America, stepping back into a mode of plebeian politics, sectarian conflict, and agrarian self-sufficiency[25] which to many English observers recalled the 1640s and 1650s. Political contingencies defined these options, of course, for the British model of a future American society was not forcefully proselytizing. It did not include any sustained attempt to export nobility and gentry to the plantations, where colonial society was already sufficiently receptive to English patrician ideals. It did, however, include an attempt to promote the Church of England in America as the basis for a tolerant regime in a plural society, an ambition which many colonists, and not only Dissenters among them, saw quite differently as a sinister bid for spiritual power.[26]

English hegemony was often interpreted as insidious, since it increas-ingly found its expression through the processes of cultural emulation: consumerism, with its cargo of English aesthetic and commercial norms, was giving American polite society an increasingly English orientation.[27] Later, these forms of English influence were quickly overlaid by the exultation of the new republic at its independence and at the initial success of its experiment in devising a constitution. The vision of a young society rejecting old-world political corruption in favour of republican innocence[28] and spurning the tainted luxury of modern consumerism for rustic simplicity[29] fused in a national myth. When corruption and luxury returned, as return they must, they paid obeisance to that myth and were not allowed to overturn it: colonial cultural exceptionalism, it was assumed, had pointed the way to American political independence. Yet only in retrospect did it seem obvious that the evolution of American values had made independence inevitable.

Before the 1770s the path of rebellion and autonomy seemed anything but likely. The British *ancien régime,* a state form devised in England in the 1660s to make impossible any lurch back into the horrors of religious war and social upheaval that scarred early seventeenth-century Europe, had done its work all too well. Many contemporaries regarded the momentous and atavistic events unfolding in the mid 1770s with awe and disbelief: it was a common reaction to say that the ostensible causes were wholly inadequate to explain the scale of the unfolding tragedy, and so they were.

Although some commentators had predicted the hypothetical independence of America at an unspecifically remote date, almost none had expected a crisis as soon as the mid 1770s. Benjamin Franklin, testifying before the House of Commons on 13 February 1766, during its deliberations on the repeal of the Stamp Act, classically identified what colonial republicans came to argue had been the status quo before 1763: the colonies then, he claimed,

> submitted willingly to the government of the Crown, and paid, in all their courts, obedience to the acts of parliament. Numerous as the people are in the several old provinces, they cost you nothing in forts, citadels, garrisons or armies, to keep them in subjection. They were governed by this country at the expense only of a little pen, ink and paper. They were led by a thread. They had not only a respect, but an affection, for Great Britain, for its laws, its customs and manners, and even a fondness for its fashions, that greatly increased the commerce. Natives of Britain were always treated with particular regard; to be an Old England-man was, of itself, a character of some respect, and gave a kind of rank among us.[30]

Even experienced colonial administrators might share this perspective. In 1764, Thomas Pownall, who had been Governor of Massachusetts from 1757 to 1759, looked to the strengthening of the hold of the metropolis on a mercantilist empire through strengthening the tie between Whitehall and each colony individually, while carefully avoiding any possibility of a union of colonies. According to Pownall, developing commercial relations made a transatlantic breakdown impossible:

> if, by becoming independent is meant a revolt, nothing is further from their nature, their interest, their thoughts. If a defection from the alliance of the mother country be suggested, it ought to be, and can truly be said, that their spirit abhors the sense of such; their attachment to the protestant succession in the house of Hanover will ever stand unshaken; and nothing can eradicate from their hearts their natural, almost mechanical, affection to Great Britain, which they conceive under no other sense, nor call by any other name, than that of *home*.[31]

In the second edition of this work, published in 1765 after the colonial outcry against the Stamp Act, Pownall left this passage unchanged and merely prefaced his tract with a Dedication to George Grenville which explained how the recent tumults had been produced by 'demagogues'.

> The truly great and wise man will not judge of the people from their passions – He will view the whole tenor of their principles and of their conduct. While he sees them uniformly loyal to their King, obedient to his government, active in every point of public spirit, in every object of the public welfare – He will not regard what they are led either to say or do under these fits of alarm and inflammation; he will, finally, have the pleasure to see them return to their genuine good temper, good sense and principles.[32]

These expectations explain men's astonishment at the Revolution. The Virginia Congressman Edmund Randolph wrote later of the famous protest of Patrick Henry in the Virginia House of Burgesses in May 1765 against the Stamp Act:

Without an immediate oppression, without a cause depending so much on hasty feeling as theoretic reasoning; without a distaste for monarchy; with loyalty to the reigning prince; with fraternal attachment to the transatlantic members of the empire; with an admiration of their genius, learning and virtues; with a subserviency in cultivating their manners and their fashions; in a word, with England as a model of all which was great and venerable; the house of burgesses in the year 1765 gave utterance to principles which within two years were to expand into a revolution.[33]

Joseph Galloway, Speaker of the Pennsylvania Assembly between 1766 and 1775, argued from the perspective of 1779 that during the Seven Years' War 'there was no part of his Majesty's dominions contained a greater proportion of faithful subjects than the Thirteen Colonies... The idea of disloyalty, at this time, scarcely existed in America; or, if it did, it was never expressed with impunity'. Galloway had, unknown to him, already received remarkable confirmation from none other than George Washington. On the very eve of the fighting, Washington had replied to an enquiry from a British army officer, alarmed that events were taking such an ominous turn:

I think I can announce it as a fact, that it is not the wish or interest of that government [Massachusetts], or any other upon the continent, separately or collectively, to set up for independency... I am as well satisfied as I can be of my existence that no such thing is desired by any thinking man in all North America; on the contrary, that it is the ardent wish of the warmest advocates for liberty, that peace and tranquility, upon constitutional grounds, may be restored, and the horrors of civil discord prevented.[34]

This only created the paradox: how could such deep-rooted attachment be so suddenly reversed? Galloway asked:

How then can it happen, that a people so lately loyal, should so suddenly become universally disloyal, and firmly attached to republican Government, without any grievances or oppressions but those in anticipation?... No fines, no imprisonments, no oppressions, had been experienced by the Colonists, that could have produced such an effect...

If we search the whole history of human events, we shall not meet with an example of such a sudden change, from the most perfect loyalty to universal disaffection. On the contrary, in every instance where national attachment has been generally effaced, it has been effected by slow degrees, and a long continuance of oppression, not in prospect, but in actual existence.[35]

Galloway's solution to the paradox implicitly relied on contingency: the colonists in general were not disaffected, as some zealots for republicanism had claimed, and might be won back to their allegiance. It was an argument that still challenges the received explanation of the Revolution as the culmination of long-prepared American nationalism.

Nor was Galloway alone. The Boston judge Peter Oliver argued that the Revolution was a '*singular*' phenomenon: 'For, by adverting to the historick Page, we shall find no Revolt of Colonies, whether under the *Roman* or any other State, but what originated from severe Oppressions.' America had been 'nursed, in its Infancy, with the most tender Care & Attention... indulged with every Gratification... repeatedly saved from impending Destruction'; this was 'an unnatural Rebellion', instigated by a small minority of the colonists only, 'a few abandoned Demagogues'.[36] The Earl of Dartmouth's under-secretary for the colonies, Ambrose Serle, observing events in New York, reacted in the same way to news of the constitutions of New Jersey and Virginia: 'An Influenza more wonderful, and at the same time more general than that of the Witchcraft in the Province of Massachuset's Bay in the last Century! The Annals of no Country can produce an Instance of so virulent a Rebellion, of such implacable madness and Fury, originating from such trivial Causes, as those alledged by these unhappy People.'[37] 'Will not posterity be amazed,' wrote the Massachusetts lawyer and politician Daniel Leonard, 'when they are told that the present distraction took its rise from the parliament's taking off a shilling duty on a pound of tea, and imposing three pence, and call it a more unaccountable phrenzy, and more disgraceful to the annals of America, than that of the witchcraft?'[38] Only after their initial incomprehension at the justifications of the patriots did such men come to explain the revolution as a volcano, erupting in response to enormous internal pressures.

The tragic quality of the Revolution of 1688 lies in the trope of

Boccaccio's *De Casibus Virorum Illustrium*: 'the fall of great men'; the malign turn of Fortune's wheel that reduces the most noble and splendid to the most base, and does so from trivial causes. It is, in retrospect, the tragedy of contingency. The same is true, it might be argued, of 1776; yet the need retrospectively to integrate the events of the mid 1770s into the founding myth of a great nation has created a different impression. The tragic quality of 1776 now seems to lie in the inexorable logic of an approaching doom, a chain of events, unfolding to catastrophe, triggered not by a tragic error but by the pursuit of high ideals and good intentions. The historian is entitled to doubt whether such chains of causation were as inevitable at the time as they were later made to seem. And to abolish historical inevitability is to open up counterfactuals.

IV.   'EXTERNAL CAUSES' AND THE INADEQUACY OF TELEOLOGY

Until recently, historians' accounts of the causes of the revolution of 1776 tended to be a familiar – and teleological – litany of the stages of British policy and colonial responses to it, both expressed in a secular constitutional idiom: the Stamp Act, the Townshend duties, the Boston Tea Party, the 'Intolerable Acts'.[39] The decision to declare independence made it necessary to argue that the causes of the Revolution were external to the colonies, so that the 'ostensible causes' of the conflict were the true ones: these innovations in British policy alone were sufficient to explain the colonial reaction to them.[40] Such a pattern of explanation was implicitly counterfactual, but inadequately so: it had to suggest (without conviction) that slight changes in colonial policy at Westminster and Whitehall would have left the empire intact. Although metropolitan policy should indeed be questioned in this way, presenting the problem in these terms alone obscured the options plausibly available for colonial Americans; in particular, it systematically removed their major counterfactual, the obvious and central path of peaceful colonial development within the empire in the direction of greater political and less cultural autonomy.

In deference to national cultural imperatives, it has been an assumption shared with remarkable unanimity by recent American historians of the American Revolution that the causes of that event were external to the colonies.[41] Two scholarly and powerful versions of that thesis are currently prevalent, and it is important to establish that, despite their merits, neither should be accepted as it stands. One is owed to Bernard Bailyn, and was devised in the 1960s. In this model, colonists in the early part of the eighteenth century adopted from England a political rhetoric derived from the 'Commonwealthmen', a rhetoric that identified political virtue in landed independence, representative institutions, religious scepticism, gentry dominance and a militia, and saw political corruption in standing armies, placemen, arbitrary taxation, priestcraft and assertive kingship. In the early 1760s, colonists thought they saw these evils in British policy. Given the nature of British politics and innovations in colonial policy, argued Bailyn, it was rational for them so to think.[42]

The second variant of this 'externalist' interpretation has much older origins, but its most modern version was formulated by Jack P. Greene. It depicts the emergence by the early eighteenth century of a consensual, tacitly accepted legal and constitutional structure for relations between colonies and metropolis. That structure allegedly ensured *de facto* autonomy to each colonial assembly, and produced a quasi-federal system of colonial self-rule. According to this thesis, it was the colonists' consensual understanding of already extensive American autonomy that was challenged by British policy in the 1760s and, with the British persisting in their infringements of an agreed constitution, armed resistance was the final and natural response.[43] Without substantiating the point, both Bailyn and Greene implied that the colonial tie with Britain could have survived unchallenged for a long period, but for metropolitan innovations.[44] Colonial demands, they assumed, could all have been accommodated within the empire had the British government acted differently. This being so, it made sense for historians to frame counter-factuals in British politics rather than in American politics:

The chance that brought one man and then another to the place of power in Whitehall played its part in bringing on the imperial civil war. At almost every turn events might have proceeded differently – if George III had not quarrelled with Grenville in the spring of 1765; if Cumberland had not died that autumn; if Grafton and Conway had not been so insistent in early 1766 that Pitt ought to lead the ministry; if Pitt, now Earl of Chatham, had not allowed the reluctant Townshend to be foisted on him by Grafton as his chancellor of the exchequer; if Chatham had kept his health, or if Townshend's had given way twelve months earlier than it did; if the Rockinghams had not, by combining in a trial of strength to bring down Grafton in 1767, forced him into the arms of the Bedford party; if Grafton as head of the Treasury had had the firmness of purpose to insist on his own fiscal policy (with regard to the tea duty) in 1769. Either armed conflict might have come earlier when the colonists' resources were less developed and when they were less prepared, materially and psychologically, than was the case by 1775; or prudence might have prevailed, causing adjustments within the Empire, which clearly had to take place ultimately, to be pursued with less animosity and without violence.[45]

The two distinguished authors of that passage, one British, one American, in a work published in 1976, strikingly omitted a similar list of counter-factuals on the colonial side. Yet although these counterfactual insights into metropolitan politics have not been refuted, attention has increasingly shifted to the social and denominational conflicts, the ideological debates in law and religion, that explain the colonies' swift conversion from loyalism to disaffection.

Recent scholarship has steadily converted to the view that whatever the vicissitudes of British ministerial politics between 1765 and 1775, and whichever individuals were in office, the options available within British colonial policy were unlikely by themselves to have made a major difference to the outcome. The best-informed colonial administrators of the 1750s adopted diametrically opposite views on whether the colonies should be subdued by force or won by kindness; yet even such contrasting figures as Henry Ellis, a hawk who favoured force, and Thomas Pownall, reputedly a dove, had much in common in asserting metropolitan authority. Pownall in 1764 looked to strengthen the hold of the metropolis over a mercantilist empire by strengthening the tie between Whitehall and each individual colony while carefully avoiding any possibility of a union of colonies. Nevertheless, argued John Shy, Pownall's supposedly pacific policy in fact anticipated 'The Sugar Act, the Currency Act, the Stamp Act, the Townshend Acts, the extension of vice-admiralty jurisdiction, the creation of West Indian free ports and a Secretary of State for the Colonies, even threats to the Rhode Island charter, the alteration of the Massachusetts Council, and adamant opposition to intercolonial congresses.'

It follows that 'if Thomas Pownall and Henry Ellis are taken to represent the limits of what was conceivable in American policy between 1763 and 1775, then the range of historical possibilities was very narrow indeed'. By contrast:

> A great deal of historical writing on the American Revolution contains at least the suggestion that there were available alternatives for British policy, and that what actually happened may be seen as a sad story of accident, ignorance, misunderstanding, and perhaps a little malevolence. George Grenville is narrow minded, Charles Townshend is brilliant but silly, Hillsborough is stupid and tyrannical, Chatham is tragically ill, Dartmouth is unusually weak, and the King himself is very stubborn and not very bright. But if politics had not been in quite such a chaotic phase, perhaps the Old Whigs or an effective Chathamite ministry would have held power, been able to shape and sustain a truly liberal policy toward the Colonies, and avoided the disruption of the Empire. So the story seems to run.

Given the absence (as historians now acknowledge) of a new, liberty-threatening master-plan for the empire in the minds of British politicians in 1763, especially that of George Grenville, it can seem plausible that 'A little more knowledge, a little more tact, a little more political sensitivity, and it all might have turned out differently'. But if even such an instinctively pro-American observer as Thomas Pownall was not at odds with the policies adopted, there is a 'prima facie case that British colonial policy in this period was neither fortuitous nor susceptible of change... The impulse that swept the British Empire toward civil war was powerful, and did not admit of any real choice'.[46]

V.   THE STRATEGIC COUNTERFACTUALS

Before accepting so fatalistic a diagnosis, however, we need to examine those points at which, as some have argued then or later, a different line of policy could have been adopted which would have retained the colonies within the empire (however that empire might have been redefined). One such set of policy options concerns the strategic setting of the Thirteen

Colonies. Given the appeal by many Americans in the 1760s and 1770s to the status quo which, they claimed, prevailed before the Peace of Paris in 1763, the first such change of direction has been located in the Seven Years' War of 1756–63, an episode decisive, in some accounts, in re-establishing metropolitan control, abrogating customary relationships, and asserting novel powers including a right of taxation. Many scholars, but especially Americans, discerned a new attitude towards empire in these years as Britain adapted to the responsibilities and opportunities created by the defeat of France in North America.[47]

Even if the Seven Years' War meant a decisive realignment, British military successes in the second half of that war were by no means assured, as a series of reverses in its first half, including the loss of Minorca, emphasized to contemporaries. Wolfe's victory at Quebec was a classic military contingency, and it could not be foreseen that Canada, once conquered, would be retained. The key French Canadian fortress of Louisbourg, captured by a colonial expedition in the previous war, had been returned at its end in 1748. A debate raged between 1759 and 1761 over whether Canada or more immediately valuable conquests in the French West Indies should be retained at the peace, if both could not be kept;[48] the eventual choice of Canada might easily have gone the other way. Few statesmen at the time entertained the visionary belief in an empire of vast geographical extent in North America or saw its potential for commerce. Even William Pitt, speaking against the Treaty of Paris and in favour of the retention of Guadeloupe, argued that 'The state of the existing trade in the conquests in North America, is extremely low; the speculations of their future are precarious, and the prospect, at the very best, very remote'.[49]

Canada might not have been won; when won, it might not have been kept. True, in the debate over its retention, William Burke famously predicted that the removal of the French threat would also remove a powerful inducement which kept the other British colonies in subjection to the metropolis: Guadeloupe should be retained, Canada returned to France. The prospect of a colonial bid for independence was already entertained as a hypothesis: 'If, Sir, the People of our Colonies find no Check from *Canada*, they will extend themselves, almost, without bounds into the Inland Parts... by eagerly grasping at extensive Territory, we may run the risque, and that perhaps in no very distant Period, of losing what we now possess... A Neighbour that keeps us in some Awe, is not always the worst of Neighbours.'[50] But this was hardly a disinterested argument, for William Burke had obtained the posts of secretary and register of Guadeloupe when that island was conquered in 1759, and was to lose them again when it, rather than Canada, was returned at the peace in 1763. The possible future loss of the mainland colonies of British settlement was evidently a remote possibility to most observers. Despite warnings of the future independence of North America, what weighed more with British statesmen was the need to defend the colonies as a whole against the French threat. Canada was retained in order to make British possession of its more southerly colonies secure. That this retention would provide a necessary condition of the independence of colonies to the south was, as yet, a counterfactual to which few people gave weight.

In 1760, Benjamin Franklin argued passionately in reply to William Burke's pamphlet that Canada should be retained at the peace, and that this posed no threat to Britain's hold over her other North American colonies. Writing anonymously, and adopting the character of an Englishman, Franklin argued: 'A people spread thro' the whole tract of country on this side of the Mississippi, and secured by Canada in our hands, would probably for some centuries find employment in agriculture, and thereby free us at home effectually from our fears of American manufactures.' Indeed, they would be tied by dependence on British manufactures. Franklin predicted that rapid population increase in America

would probably in a century more, make the number of British subjects on that side of the water more numerous than they now are on this; but I am far from entertaining on that account, any fears of their becoming either *useless* or *dangerous* to us; and I look on those fears, to be merely imaginary and without any probable foundation.

Even the fourteen North American colonial governments already in existence found it impossible to combine:

Those we now have, are not only under different governors, but have different forms of government, different laws, different interests, and some of them different religious persuasions and different manners. Their jealousy of each other is so great that however necessary an union of the colonies has long been, for their common defence and security against their enemies, and how sensible soever each colony has been of that necessity, yet they have never been able to effect such an union among themselves, nor even to agree in requesting the mother country to establish it for them.

If the colonies could not unite against the French and Native Americans, 'who were perpetually harassing their settlements, burning their villages, and murdering their people; can it reasonably be supposed there is any danger of their uniting against their own nation, which protects and encourages them, with which they have so many connections and ties of blood, interest and affection, and which 'tis well known they all love much more than they love one another?' Such a union, predicted Franklin, was 'impossible' (though he at once added a rider: 'without the most grievous tyranny and oppression').[51] The retention of Canada, then, was the first major consequence of the chances of war.

A second consequence stemmed from the manner in which it was terminated. What was crucial was the decision of a restructured British ministry to end the conflict in circumstances interpreted by Frederick of Prussia as abandonment of him. As a result of this decision, Britain went into the American war in 1776 without a major ally on the European continent. Britain, undistracted, might have been able to contain or suppress a rebellion in her American colonies, but in the 1780s Britain was drawn into a major war against both the Bourbon powers, France and Spain, and the League of Armed Neutrals. Continental alliances had been essential to sustaining British naval supremacy, argued one historian: 'Neither administrative weakness, nor military and naval ineptitude was responsible for the humiliating disaster' of Yorktown. 'The dominating factor was political isolation.'[52] A continental alliance might have made a difference in the years 1763–76. But the absence in this period of a French expansionary threat on the European continent meant that no other major continental power had an interest in fighting Britain's continental battles for her.[53] From this perspective, Britain's failing hold on her American colonies was largely the consequence of her own overstretched military resources. But this was not widely foreseen, any more than were the consequences of the retention of Canada.

Strategic speculation on the long-term future of transatlantic relations normally focused on another theme. Some commentators speculated that the changing balance of population between Britain and America would eventually bring about a redefinition of imperial relationships. By 1776, this could be used as a decisive argument for the inevitability of independence by a friend of America like Richard Price:

> They are now but little short of half our number. To this number they have grown, from a small body of original settlers, by a very rapid increase. The probability is, that they will go on to increase; and that, in 50 or 60 years, they will be *double* our number... and form a mighty Empire, consisting of a variety of states, all equal or superior to ourselves in all the arts and accomplishments, which give dignity and happiness to human life. In that period, will they be still bound to acknowledge that supremacy over them which we now claim?[54]

Yet, even among those who so argued (and such arguments can be traced back many decades), none foresaw the immense cataclysm of the 1770s. Even Price himself had not done so, writing to Benjamin Franklin on colonial demographic data in 1769. In the version of his letter intended as a paper to the Royal Society, Price added a sentence on the colonists, 'Formerly an increasing number of FRIENDS, but now likely to be converted, by an unjust and fatal policy, into an increasing number of ENEMIES.'[55] Even here, it was British policy that Price sought to blame, not some inexorable logic of demography.

Price's correspondence before the outbreak of the Revolution shows no anticipation of that momentous event, an apparent blindness that he shared with almost all of his contemporaries. The constitutional conflicts of the 1760s had, after all, been settled by negotiation; the explosion of the mid 1770s caught by surprise even colonists who were soon to be in the forefront of the movement for independence. The Dissenter Price's interest in American affairs was first attracted when the colonists were seen to be engaged in a battle like his own against those 'enemies to truth and liberty', bishops: 'If they once get footing there, it is highly probable that in time they will acquire a power (under the protection and with the aid of their friends *here*) that will extend itself beyond Spirituals, and be inconsistent with the equal and common liberty of other religious persuasions.'[56] These atavistic English Dissenting phobias, not the imminent independence of America or its constitutional claims, were Price's starting point.

With the advantage of hindsight, of course, men were able to argue differently: by 1773, Thomas Hutchinson, lieutenant governor of the colony of Massachusetts, locked in controversy with his colony's assembly, looked back on the retention of Canada as the great mistake. Without it, 'none of the spirit of opposition to the Mother Country would have yet appeared & I think the effects of it [the acquisition of Canada] worse than all we had to fear from the French or Indians'.[57] In this sense, the acquisition of Canada is now acknowledged as 'a major cause' of the American Revolution.[58] But it was a necessary, not a sufficient, cause: it established the context in which a rebellion might occur, but it did not determine that it would. The same causes (the removal of a neighbouring threat) obtained equally within Canada, but it was not Canada that sought to break its political ties with the metropolis in the 1770s.

VI.   DOMESTIC COUNTER FACTUALS: COLONIAL UNION, TAXATION AND DEMOCRACY

A second set of policy options concerned developments within the colonies. One reason for thinking an American revolution unlikely was, as Franklin suggested, the marked lack of enthusiasm for plans for colonial union in earlier decades. The scheme discussed at a conference at Albany, New York, in 1754, would have vested very substantial powers, including those of taxation, in a Grand Council nominated by the lower houses of colonial assemblies; but so dominant did such a unified government seem that the provincial assemblies themselves unanimously rejected the scheme.[59] When a more modest plan of intercolonial cooperation in military and Native American affairs was drawn up by Lord Halifax at the Board of Trade in 1754, Charles Townshend dismissed it: 'It is... impossible to imagine that so many different representatives of so many different provinces, divided in interest and alienated by jealousy and inveterate prejudice, should ever be able to resolve upon a plan of mutual security and reciprocal expense.' Nor would the colonial assemblies, thought Townshend, pass the act of supply necessary to fund a union: it would run counter to their 'settled design of drawing to themselves the ancient and established prerogatives wisely preserved in the Crown' by steadily gaining control of each colony's finances.[60]

Yet even this 'quest for power' on the part of colonial assemblies, if real, did not create an assumption that independence was inevitable. Even the man regarded as the greatest catalyst of the Revolution did not claim it to be the outcome of a trend which the colonists had long understood. In *Common Sense*, published in Philadelphia in 1776, Thomas Paine wrote of the colonists' policies of 1775: 'Whatever was advanced by the advocates on either side of the question then, terminated in one and the same point, viz. a union with Great Britain; the only difference between the parties, was the method of effecting it; the one proposing force, the other friendship.'[61] In the words of Jack Greene, the 'latent distrust' that lay behind transatlantic relations could not 'become an active cause of disruption between Britain and the colonies so long as the delicate and uneasy accommodation that had been worked out under Walpole continued to obtain. That it would not obtain was by no means predictable'.[62] Given the commitment of colonists to the constitutional practices they claimed as a shared inheritance, it is understandable that so many at the time regarded transatlantic controversies as open to negotiated settlement. However, Paine's claim was contradicted by much evidence of which, as a recent migrant, he was probably unaware. In the early 1760s, long before he set foot in America, the political rhetoric of many colonists had moved in a relatively short period from eulogies of the liberties they enjoyed, as Englishmen within the empire, to denunciations of the corruption and tyranny into which English society, in their perception, had fallen. 'It is when viewed amidst this widespread and enthusiastic acclamation for the English constitution', as Gordon Wood has observed, 'that the American Revolution takes on its tone of irony and incomprehensibility – a tone not lost to the Revolutionaries themselves.' By a rhetoric which sought to take its stand solely on the English constitution, 'the Americans could easily conceive of themselves as simply preserving what Englishmen had valued from time immemorial... Yet this continual talk of desiring nothing new and wishing only to return to the old system and the essentials of the English constitution was only a superficial gloss'.[63]

On the classic constitutional points at issue, the 'ostensible causes' of the Revolution, colonists themselves proposed a counterfactual. In the 1760s, responses to the Stamp Act often assumed that all would be well if the novel legislation were repealed. John Dickinson's best-selling *Farmer's Letters* implied the same argument against the Townshend duties of 1767.

Governments might adopt wrong measures: 'But every such measure does not dissolve the obligation between the governors and the governed. The mistakes may be corrected; the passion may subside.'[64] In 1769, Benjamin Franklin wrote:

> Of late a Cry begins to arise, Can no body propose a Plan of Conciliation? Must we ruin ourselves by intestine Quarrels? I was ask'd in company lately by a noble Lord if I had no Plan of that kind to propose? My Answer was, 'Tis easy to propose a Plan; mine may be express'd in a few Words; *Repeal* the Laws, *Renounce* the Right, *Recall* the Troops, *Refund* the Money, *Return to the old Method of Requisition.*[65]

Congress itself, in its address *To the people of Great-Britain*, dated 5 September 1774, argued that the constitutional relationship prior to the Seven Years' War was legitimate; it was only at its conclusion that 'a plan for enslaving your fellow subjects in America was concerted [...] Place us in the same situation that we were at the close of the last war, and our former harmony will be restored'.[66]

Yet this was a counterfactual substantially disproved by events, for the metropolitan government showed a repeated willingness to compromise on the points at issue in the 1760s.[67] It can now be shown that British policy towards colonial trade underwent no profound sea change from mercantilism to imperialism in the early 1760s, as an older historiography once argued. The Sugar Act of 1764 attempted to raise a revenue in the colonies, at the same time attempting to encourage trade to flow within traditional mercantilist channels. The same was true in 1767 of Chatham's reduction of the duty on tea re-exported to the American colonies.[68] Likewise, inflation in the colonies, the result of colonial issues of paper money, was checked by Westminster's Currency Act of 1764; after colonial protests, this measure was relaxed in the case of New York by an Act of 1770 and in the case of the other colonies by an Act of 1773: on this basis, it is possible that the issue might have been resolved.[69] George Grenville later admitted in a debate in the Commons that he 'did not foresee' the degree of opposition to the Stamp Act, and, had he foreseen it, would not have proposed it.[70] This was plausible: given that a revenue had to be raised by the imperial government in the colonies, a small stamp duty was an ineffective method of raising it. The anticipated revenue from the tax was only £110,000, of which £50,000 would come from the West Indies.[71] Without broaching issues of internal taxation, the ministry in London might have raised far larger revenues through the existing customs and excise legislation, vigorously enforced by the use of naval power and adjudicated by an augmented version of the existing vice-admiralty courts. After colonial protests, the Westminster Parliament repealed the Act.

If the Stamp Act was passed with no anticipation of colonial resistance, so too was Townshend's Revenue Act in 1767: it raised no questions of internal taxation, and seemed to be based on the colonists' own distinction between legitimate external and illegitimate internal taxation. Not even the colonial agents forecast what was to come, or warned against it.[72] Benjamin Franklin himself, in an article in the *London Chronicle* in April 1767, had accepted the constitutional correctness of imperial taxation on external trade, protesting only against 'internal taxes'.[73] In turn, it is difficult to resist the conclusion that the outcry against the reduction of the duty on tea from one shilling to three pence per pound was manufactured by colonial merchants who stood to lose from the suppression of the lucrative smuggling trade. If the earlier use of the Royal Navy in North American waters to eliminate smuggling might have pre-empted this before it became a political hot potato, it remains true that, in the absence of serious coercion, there was little room for compromise on the American side. Contingency was not dominant in 1776 as it had been in 1688, but it was nevertheless important.

Historians who adhered to the traditional scenario of 'ostensible causes' could not progress beyond too simplistic an alternative to conflict. On 1 May 1769 the Cabinet met to consider the mounting colonial protests against the duties passed by the Commons in June 1767 on the initiative of Charles Townshend, then Chancellor of the Exchequer. Now, the Cabinet voted for the repeal of all but one. By five votes to four, the conciliatory First Lord of the Treasury, the Duke of Grafton, was outvoted in his move to abolish the tea duty. 'This fateful decision', it has been claimed, 'was to prove the point of no return in the sequence of events leading to the American Revolution. Without a tea duty there would have been no Boston Tea Party and no consequent final quarrel between Britain and her colonies.'[74] This confident judgement seems less plausible as colonial causes of rebellion are admitted to the historical record. Counterfactuals can indeed be framed in respect of British policy, yet the more important counterfactuals all concern the patterns of social development and of ideological conflict within the colonies themselves.

These colonial counterfactuals do not chiefly involve the classic constitutional issues, the 'ostensible causes' of inevitable revolution. The problem of representation was the most obvious obstacle to a settlement, yet it may be that even this was not the insuperable barrier that it later appeared to have been. Taxation and representation were, of course, linked issues. Yet if questions of revenue seem to have been more open to a negotiated settlement (taxation being a feature of all governments, including republican ones), questions of representation tend to be regarded as more principled, and more irreconcilable. This was not necessarily the case, however, even with the constitutional fiction generally identified as the weakest link in the metropolitan argument, that of virtual representation. As Thomas Whately argued, 'All *British* subjects are really in the same [situation]; none are actually, all are virtually represented in Parliament; for every Member of Parliament sits in the House, not as Representative of his own Constituents, but as one of that august Assembly by which all the Commons of *Great Britain* are represented'.[75] In other words, apart from those men sitting in Parliament as members of the House of Lords or House of Commons, all Britons related to their MP not as a delegate but as a representative, a representative unpaid by his constituents and not bound to accept instructions offered by them. The problem with this doctrine of virtual representation was not that it was self-evidently untrue, but that it was a truism, and therefore introduced into the debate unrehearsed and with no theoretical explication. But it could have been given the sort of theoretical basis which would have contributed to a better understanding both of imperial relations and of the actual working of politics in Britain itself.

It was a truism that a British MP represented the whole polity, not just his constituency; represented all the inhabitants, of both sexes, including minors; represented the eight or nine tenths of the populace who were not voters; represented those electors who had voted against him, or had abstained, as well as those who had given him their votes. This was, of course, a necessary fiction of government. But it bore more relation to the daily working of government than did the succeeding myth that a man could only be represented if he himself cast a vote, a theory which, in a system of universal suffrage, by definition subjected to a majoritarian

tyranny all non-voters, all voters for defeated candidates, and all voters for
MPs on the losing side in parliamentary divisions. In both cases, states
were effectively run by small minorities; in the first case this reality was
less disguised and more dignified. Except for the political elite, virtual and
actual representation were equally formal concepts. Here too, just as in the
replacement of divine-right monarchy by representative democracy,
historians are now obliged to dispense with a scenario in which a logic of
historical inevitability led men to replace early-modern 'fictions' with self-
evident modern 'truths'.[76]

To be sure, William Pitt in 1766 declared that 'The idea of a virtual
representation of America in this House, is the most contemptible idea
that ever entered into the head of a man; it does not deserve a serious
refutation'.[77] This was a political gambit, however, for Pitt himself only
represented a variety of tiny constituencies including, as his first, the
depopulated borough of Old Sarum, which boasted (on a good day) an
electorate of about seven. From 1757 to 1766 he sat in the Commons as one
of the two Members for Bath: it fielded an electorate of about thirty. Even
in that seat, Pitt never had to face a poll.[78] Despite his rhetoric, it is not
clear just whom William Pitt represented, either in the Commons or when
elevated to the Lords as first Earl of Chatham. American adulation of him
as a democrat overlooked the fact that he fought only one contested
election in his entire parliamentary career. Even that was in the tiny
Cinque Port of Seaford.

However contemptuous some orators might be of the concept of virtual
representation, their desire to create an American nation reintroduced it.
Thomas Paine hailed the cause of independence: ''Tis not the concern of a
day, a year, or an age; posterity are virtually involved in the contest, and will
be more or less affected even to the end of time by the proceedings now.'[79]
Although the colonists rejected 'virtual' representation, their 'actual'
representation in the Westminster Parliament was generally sought neither
by themselves nor by their British supporters: since the relations of colonies
and metropolis were debated in terms of mutual self-interest, this would
only have imported the conflict into the House of Commons, not resolved
it in a new context of Anglo-Saxon solidarity. The only viable alternative
was to work with and through the growing power of the colonial
assemblies. Even Joseph Galloway, later remembered as a resolute loyalist,
was explicit at the First Continental Congress in Philadelphia in September

1774 that Acts of the Westminster Parliament did not bind the colonies;[80] if a man so well-disposed could only envisage a redefinition of imperial relations along federal lines, it is unlikely that there would have been substantial backing in the colonies for a solution which failed to include the principle of equivalence between the Westminster and colonial assemblies.

The rise of these assemblies as against the power of the governors was, indeed, a marked feature of the half century to 1776. Yet although these assemblies showed a clear desire to assert growing colonial wealth and population, they had shown few overt signs of extrapolating these trends into a bid for separation from the mother country. Even in 1774–6, it was not the assemblies that articulated the claim of independence, but groups of zealots bypassing each assembly to set up a self-authorizing representative body. Well-informed and practical individuals like Galloway continued until a late date to act on the belief that a negotiated compromise was still possible. On 28 September 1774 Galloway proposed to the Continental Congress a plan for reconciliation based on the establishment of an American legislative council, under a president-general appointed by the crown, its members chosen by the colonial assemblies.[81] Congress voted on that day by six colonies to five to lay the plan on the table for subsequent consideration, so effectively killing it;[82] had the vote gone the other way, a positive response from London might have cleared the way to negotiated settlement. For there, the ministry remained open to the idea.

In January 1775 the cabinet agreed on North's so-called 'olive branch': backed up by coercive measures to halt the trade of those colonies perceived as being uncooperative, the proposal was for Parliament to forbear to exercise its right of taxing a colony if that colony, through its normal and legal channels, would contribute its proportion to the common defence and pay the expenses of its civil government and administration of justice.[83] It was a proposal which inevitably ignored the Continental Congress: for Parliament to have addressed it would have been to recognize its legitimacy, which was the point at issue. At the same time, it expressed the reasonable hope that by dealing with each colony separately, their common front might have been broken. It was the Second Continental Congress that rejected North's proposal as inadequate: it did not meet the colonies' demand for recognition of a right of granting whatever they thought fit, at their sole discretion, and did not address Parliament's claim of a right to legislate for the colonies in other matters, most recently in the Coercive Acts and most generally in the right to alter colonial charters.[84] Had Galloway's proposal been adopted, a compromise might still have been reached.

In its absence, the most dramatic and decisive solution to the problem was that proposed by the Dean of Gloucester, Josiah Tucker. He saw clearly that, by this stage, the claims of the two parties had been defined in terms which precluded compromise. Britain's interests, however, lay in trade with her colonies, not political control over them. Tucker's solution was 'to separate entirely from the *North-American* Colonies, by declaring them to be a free and independent People'.[85] Such a pre-emptive act would have at once deprived the republican movement of its *raison d'être*. If adopted at any time before the colonial Declaration of Independence had stigmatized George III personally, a British Declaration of Independence would have caught the colonists at the moment of claiming equality with the Westminster Parliament by talking up their personal loyalty to the Crown: independence would have removed most incentives to distance themselves from this royalism. Americans would have been locked into the position of being subjects of George III, though a George understood to be a very constitutional monarch.

Equally, the absence of a war to win independence would have prevented the emergence of the single main cause of colonial unity. Even the tenuously confederal system embodied in the Articles of Confederation was agreed to only in response to dire military necessities. Without war, the jealousies, rivalries and diversities of the North American colonies would probably have produced only a much weaker association, if any. The new states, lacking a natural focus of unity, would have been likely, therefore, to preserve their allegiance to the monarch as a valuable guarantor of the legitimacy of their civil governments and an emblem of their cultural equality with the old world. For a marked feature of political debate in the decades before 1776, even in the last decade before the revolution, was the absence of a key component which, in retrospect, appears natural and obvious: republicanism.

Colonial Americans had seldom, before the publication of Paine's *Common Sense* in 1776, denounced monarchy as such and still less often had they speculated on alternative, republican, models for colonial governance or society.[86] *Common Sense* itself contained no extended discussion of republicanism: it was a negative critique of existing constitutional arrangements, not a blueprint for new ones in the future. Few such blueprints were available to colonists in 1776. Equally, although democracy became a shibboleth of the new republic, it was not a cause of the Revolution. Since these two 'ostensible causes' tell us little about why the Revolution occurred, they cannot be invoked as explanations of why it was inevitable. Without the breakdown of 1776, transatlantic relations would not have run on in unchanging tranquillity: the powerful ideological pressures mounting in the colonies would have seen to that. But it remains true that the traditional 'ostensible causes' did not make inevitable the exact form that the Revolution took.

VII.   THE PROBLEMS OF REPRESSION IN
A LIBERTARIAN POLITY

Early-modern rebellions were as often provoked by lax government, permitting the growth of practices and expectations of local self-rule, as by active tyranny. A more efficient exertion of Britain's legal sovereignty over the colonies from an earlier date might have been another way to retain executive control, and it is necessary to explore the reasons why this was apparently so difficult to achieve. For there is an immense contrast between the metropolitan responses to the threatened rebellion in Ireland in 1797–8 (which largely aborted a carefully prepared rising) or the Indian Mutiny in 1857 (similarly repressed by military force) and the relative restraint employed by Englishmen towards fellow Englishmen in America before 1776.

Even before the fighting, Whitehall officials might systematically have resisted the many small steps by which colonial legislatures built up their power. The metropolis might have stipulated that colonial grants of revenue to colonial budgets be for long periods, or indefinite; that the salaries of the governor and other officials be shielded from local political pressures; that the colonial treasurers be royal appointments; that the governors' powers of local patronage be built up and exercised by the governor, not the ministry in London. Such steps might plausibly have been taken under the energetic and reformist Earl of Halifax, President of the Board of Trade from 1748 to 1761, had he received the necessary backing from his ministerial colleagues. One reason why he did not, of course, was that ministers were wholly preoccupied with the need to secure the full cooperation of the colonies in the war with France.[87] Yet there were other reasons too, in particular the ministers' unwillingness to revert to the administrative ethic associated with the later Stuart monarchy.

The rare exceptions to this administrative quiescence help to illustrate the rule. In Massachusetts, Lieutenant Governor Thomas Hutchinson sought to force the issue in January 1773 by instituting an exchange with the assembly on the questions of constitutional principle involved. This initiative had the opposite effect to that which Hutchinson wished, however, for the assembly, especially the House of Representatives, took the opportunity to turn their *de facto* resistance to certain metropolitan measures into a defiant *de jure* rejection of metropolitan authority. Lord Dartmouth, the Secretary of State for the Colonies, was appalled: 'The governor had upset Dartmouth's hopes that the controversy might subside and even perhaps disappear in time if only the parties would avoid raising the critical issues that separated them. To Dartmouth, Hutchinson had reopened a wound that might have healed if only it had been neglected or ignored.'[88] Although this seems implausible in the light of later events, it is open to argument that it represented one possible avenue of development.

Politics destabilized policy in London, too: throughout the 1760s, indeed up to the end of 1774, British policy towards the colonies was rendered indecisive and vacillating by the instability and internal conflicts of ministries. Had George III been the tyrant that Americans later painted him, this would not have been the case. As it was, with many possible policies being advocated by different groups in the Lords and Commons, the natural response of many politicians was to frame a compromise or leave policy ambiguous, firm in principle, indecisive in practice. True, in a world of greater consistency of conduct and clarity of intentions, American resistance might have come earlier. On the other hand, in such a world it might not have come at all.

In part, the ineffectual nature of British policy reflected early Hanoverian phobias about arbitrary power, represented by the hypo-statized threat of a Stuart restoration. This meant that successive Whig ministries under the first three Georges were often inhibited about using the power of the executive against equally Whig opposition. By contrast,

Roman Catholics, Jacobites, Nonjurors and their fellow-travellers had often been subjected to persecution, sometimes sanguinary, and the Tory and Jacobite press had suffered legal harrassment and judicial suppression. Successive ministries treated Whig and Dissenting opponents gingerly, fearful of the charges of 'Popery and arbitrary power' that they could level against the authorities. In the colonies from the early 1760s, therefore, imperial officials did almost nothing to prevent a quasi-treasonable opposition from organizing itself. Colonial governors largely failed to muzzle seditious newspapers and pamphlets, take printers and authors into custody, prosecute inciters of disaffection or prevent the growth of organizations like the Stamp Act Congress which might be the bases for rebellion. Countermeasures like these had often been used in England under the first two Georges to smash the Jacobite underground, and had been used with success. A self-consciously libertarian regime in England had then ruthlessly defended itself against the threat of populist subversion by whatever means were necessary to achieve its ends. After the defeat of the Stuart menace that had come to a head in the 1740s, however, the Hanoverian regime dropped its guard. It is worth considering what the outcome would have been in colonial America had the vigilance of the imperial authorities been maintained at its former level, and redirected against the activities of Dissenters and Whigs.

This was, of course, not done. The British army in America, which, after some delay, was adopted as a symbol by agitators to play on colonial memories of late Stuart rule, was – even in the occupation of Boston in 1768–70 – almost never used to control civil disobedience: officers were still inhibited by the legal dangers which surrounded such interventions in England.[89] Even when the ministry decided in the summer of 1768 to send British army units to Boston, the troops found on their arrival that the civilian authorities who alone could requisition the assistance of troops (the Massachusetts Council and justices of the peace) were opposed to their very presence. Up to the outbreak of the revolution, there was no such legal requisition. British troops in Boston were subjected to continual harrassment in local courts staffed by hostile colonists:[90] this had not been foreseen, and Parliament had taken no steps to change the statutory context within which military power was exercised in America. Had it done so, and from an early date, a preventive military occupation of colonial capitals might have been feasible. In February 1769 Lord Hillsborough, the then Secretary of State for the Colonies, indeed urged on the Cabinet and the king firmer measures against Massachusetts Bay, including vesting nominations to the colony's Council in the Crown, and envisaged a forfeiture of Massachusetts's charter. George III accepted that such measures might be a last resort, 'but till then ought to be avoided as the altering of Charters is at all times an odious measure'. That, of course, had been James II's fatal policy. Nor was there agreement in the House of Lords on altering the charter, an alteration Governor Bernard of Massachusetts had urged.[91] Although it was rumoured that a Bill for charter reform was imminent in 1770–71, at the outset of North's ministry, no such Bill was introduced into Parliament.[92]

The novel presence of a 'standing army' in America after the peace of 1763 was later elevated into a major grievance; it is not obvious that it need have been. Far from being part of a metropolitan plot to extinguish American liberties, the stationing of regular troops in America was a natural response to the strategic problems created by the conquest of vast new territories during the Seven Years' War, the need to hold down conquered populations and make real the claim to sovereignty. The distribution of British troops reflected this: of fifteen battalions deployed, it was intended to station three in Nova Scotia, four in Canada, and four in Florida. Only four remained for Britain's older possessions, many of which would be assigned to defend the frontier.[93] At the time, it was natural that few colonists protested. 'The decision to maintain a British army in postwar America was not, as such, a matter of controversy. The size and deployment of the force were largely determined by the essential functions it would be called upon to perform.'[94]

Occasional military commentators in earlier decades had suggested that the stationing of British troops would help to ensure the loyalty of Americans, but the evidence does not suggest that the Grenville ministry considered the prospect of resistance to their policy of raising a colonial revenue or the prospect of coercing the colonies. George Grenville's lack of foresight was shared by many colonists, however, including Benjamin Franklin. Even when metropolitan taxation began to be challenged in the colonies, the target of colonists was the principle of taxation as such, not the army.[95] Only later, in a more heightened emotional atmosphere, were the thinly scattered detachments of redcoats built up into a symbol of tyranny. There was nothing inevitable about this invention of a demonology, however, and an alternative scenario is plausible in which no such heightened imagery was employed.

In most areas of Britain's North American possessions, the minimal presence of the army remained non-controversial. The troops sent to America brought with them the assumptions about their role in society which had, by then, become ingrained in the army's mentality in England: they attempted to stay out of politics. The army did not interfere in colonial elections, and did not coerce colonial assemblies. Only with great reluctance did it take on the police role of preserving civil order. The flashpoints, the moments of friction with the civilian population, were few. It is reasonable to ask whether this state of affairs might have continued. Certainly, it made coercion extremely difficult. In the autumn of 1774, the commander-in-chief in North America, General Gage, warned correctly that the situation in New England already amounted to rebellion, that imperial authority could only be reasserted by military force, that his own resources of 3,000 troops were inadequate, and that a force of 20,000 was needed to re-establish control. This advice, unwelcome in London, was not acted upon.[96] But what course might the conflict have taken if large numbers of troops had been committed to New England at an early stage?

Even after the outbreak of fighting, many different outcomes remained possible. The war was long and indecisive partly because of its character as a civil war, driven by powerful social constituencies unwilling to accept defeat, and partly because the conflict revealed the existence of little outstanding military talent on either side. Neither the British nor the republican colonists produced a single dominant general: no Marlborough, no Wellington fought decisive campaigns, and the war dragged on, ebbing first one way, then the other. Thomas Gage offered his home government good advice, but was unable to snuff out the revolution in Massachusetts. The three major-generals sent to reinforce him (John Burgoyne, Henry Clinton, William Howe) did little better. On the other hand, neither the colonial rebels nor the colonial Loyalists produced any military geniuses. The characteristics revealed in battle were generally ones of stubborn determination and dogged endurance rather than swift and triumphant conquest. But from the British point of view the war was worth fighting even if the possibility of a sweeping reconquest of the colonies was remote:

military force had good prospects of compelling a negotiated peace in which the constitutional points at issue would have been compromised, and some form of political tie retained. The forces of both sides recorded victories during the land campaigns in North America; it is easy to imagine military scenarios in which even slightly more successful British commanders could have made an important difference.[97]

As it turned out, British military action was fatally divided between the alternative goals of a negotiated settlement based on the conciliation of fellow countrymen, and the decisive military defeat of an enemy at any cost to their lives and property.[98] It was similarly divided between a strategy of maintaining major bases on the American seaboard, seeking thereby to control American trade, and a strategy of attempting to conquer large tracts of territory inland, often in liaison with Loyalist forces.[99] The failure of the British authorities to exploit this social constituency was an important feature of the conflict. As a result of lack of preparedness in previous decades, during the Revolution 'the potentially enormous military strength of Loyalism remained inert, almost untapped as a means to put down rebellion'.[100] In return, Loyalists were the best-informed and most unsparing critics of British military commanders. Joseph Galloway posed the question:

> How then, since the British Commander had a force so much superior to his enemy, has it happened that the rebellion has not been long ago suppressed? The cause, my Lord, however inveloped in misrepresentation on this side of the Atlantic, is no secret in America... Friends and foes unite in declaring that it has been owing to want of wisdom in the plans, and of vigour and exertion in the execution.[101]

The military history of the Revolutionary War is thick with pivotal incidents which, decided otherwise, might have had major effects on the final result: Howe's failure to destroy Washington's army in Long Island and on the Delaware River in the autumn of 1776, when he seemed able to do so; Burgoyne's failure to lure the American forces into an ambush that would have reversed the outcome of the subsequent battle of Saratoga; the escape of the American army from its British pursuers after the battle of Cowpens; and Washington's decision to strike south in late 1781 rather than adhere to his intended attack on New York, a decision which led to Yorktown.

VIII.   MANIFEST DESTINIES? THE DENIAL OF AMERICAN
COUNTERFACTUALS

The details of military conflict have a wider significance. Had the course of the war been different, it has been suggested, the shape of the America that emerged from the fighting might have been different also. Had British arms been more successful, and been overcome only by a more systematic American response, 'The consequence might have been a very different American public culture, one that stressed the national state more than the individual, obligations more than rights'.[102] Yet military conflict is as uncertain in prospect as the result seems triumphantly assured in retrospect. Contemporary American historians of the Revolution knew this, for they were close to and often confronted by the awkward fact that the outcomes of battles had hinged on minor events. They uneasily reflected on this truth, as did William Gordon: 'On incidents of this kind may depend the rise and fall of mighty kingdoms, and the far distant future transfer of power, glory, and riches, of arts and sciences, from Europe to America'.[103] Gordon's inconclusive discussion of such incidents, suggests a modern analyst, marks a point at which American historians broke with their Puritan, predestinarian past by attempting to give some historical rigour to the force of contingency and to equip their new republic with a serious, professional account of its origins; but they emancipated themselves only in part. They

> destroyed the traditional concept of providence by blurring the line between providence and chance. They used the terms interchangeably and they used both descriptively to suggest only that the improbable, unexpected, inexplicable event had indeed occurred. In addition, they used both the language of providence and the language of chance not as modes of historical explanation but precisely to reserve judgement about causes when they were unknown. By destroying the distinction between providence and chance, the historians made clear that providence was no longer for them an adequate mode of historical explanation.

Providence survived only for 'ideological and aesthetic purposes'.[104] Not God but American manifest destiny became the final cause within this national myth of origins.

It might be suggested that the American Revolution thus represented an important stage in the secularization of historical explanations. Henceforth, trivial events (inexplicable contingencies) and grand counterfactuals (Providential destinies) were no longer united within a Providential order, and so were potentially at odds with each other. Yet this too may have been an unintended outcome, if Lester Cohen's account of early patriot historians of the Revolution is correct: 'by conflating providence and chance, by destroying the traditional use of providence as a mode of explanation, and by using chance independently of providence', those historians meant to achieve the same ends as Hume and Gibbon: 'to reinfuse history with a sense of contingency, and to present causation as a complex problem'.[105] They only succeeded, however, in giving America's history a new, though secular, purposiveness.

These historians 'wanted it both ways. On the one hand, they aimed to write impartial history, dedicated to truth and the service of humanity and pure in language and style; while on the other, they meant to develop a distinctively *American* history, intended to justify the Revolution and to inculcate the principles of republicanism in future generations of Americans'. Moreover they 'saw no contradiction between their efforts to be objective and their insisting upon the principles and values of the Revolution',[106] a problem which, it might be suggested, has persisted in some quarters. The counterfactual was not to be entertained in the new American republic, any more than it had been in the Puritan phase of colonial history. Puritan theology, the revolutionaries' heritage, had regarded the future as unknown only to man: the future had, however, already been predetermined from the Creation by God, and man lacked the power to change it by acts of free will. By contrast, the new 'zealous rhetoric' of the revolutionaries manifested 'the sense of urgency, anxiety and challenge presented by an indeterminate future and by the feeling that people are responsible for the future's shape'.[107] They were to be free to shape it, but in only one way.

These historians of the Revolution, then, attempted to devise a more sophisticated, more professionally historical version of their nation's founding. They did so not least by qualifying Puritan predestinarianism with a new sense of the force of chance. But they were unable to proceed more than a part of the way towards this professionalism, because the logic of contingency had to be made subservient to a single, predetermined end, the rightness and inevitability of an independent United States. The alternative counterfactual, which pointed to another and equally feasible scenario for the development of a British North America, was implicitly excluded from the outset. So the real dynamic of history, the interplay between counterfactuals and contingencies, was never grasped. Instead, the Revolutionary historians used a residual notion of Providence as a way of hinting at their purposive understanding of American destiny, and were led to use contingency only as a device to secularize Providence rather than as a means of eliminating teleology. In this way were the broad outlines of the current historiographical problem established at an early date.

IX.   THE MARGINALIZED, THE EXPROPRIATED AND THE OPPRESSED

It was not only the white colonists whose futures were at stake. If a British America might have taken a more libertarian, less populist direction, it is worth considering the implications of such a polity for the two groups that were to be so massively disadvantaged in the new republic: Native Americans and African–American slaves.

Before the Seven Years' War, each colony had determined its own policy towards the Native Americans. These policies had enjoyed little success in alleviating the continual friction, sometimes flaring into savage conflict, which resulted as the settlers dispossessed the natives. Assimilation largely failed: Native Americans showed a marked unwillingness to accept enslavement or to surrender a nomadic for a settled way of life, and pastoral for arable farming. Settlers, especially when they were Calvinist predestinarians, showed little of the practical desire to convert the natives to Christianity that the Anglican discoverers of the new world in the early seventeenth century had promised. Britain had, however, a major rival on the North American continent. French relations with Native Americans, then referred to as Indians, were far better: the Catholic drive to convert the natives implied far more respect than could be inferred from New England Puritanism; the French reliance on the fur trade similarly argued for a certain reciprocity, where English-speaking settlers aimed at settlement and expropriation.

It was the need to compete with France for the favour of Indian tribes in wartime, especially during the Seven Years' War, that induced the government in London to involve itself in Indian policy. So pressing was this need, as Anglo-French conflicts on the American frontier escalated into a major international conflict, that London was willing not only to regulate trade between the colonists and Native Americans but to address the major problem: land. Three times during the war the metropolitan government signed treaties with Indians (Easton, 1758; Lancaster, 1760; Detroit, 1761) which committed the unwilling white colonists to respect the line of the Appalachian mountains as the limit of settlement: these treaties remained in force after the war was over, and Indian policy was quickly expressed in the royal proclamation of 7 October 1763. From Georgia to Quebec, the same principle now applied: land west of the Appalachians was reserved for Indians, and permission of the imperial government was required before purchase or settlement. Licences were made necessary for traders. *De facto* authority in this area rested with the British commander-in-chief in North America, working through two Indian superintendents. Clearly, the metropolitan authorities were establishing a structure intended to implement a comprehensive Indian policy. It was not proposed to halt westward expansion permanently but to regulate it, in the wake of controlled imperial purchases of Indian territory.

A major Indian rebellion in 1763, Pontiac's uprising, and the haphazard colonial response to it, made metropolitan control of Indian policy more essential, as the imperial government saw it, and a standing army more necessary to police the frontier. It was the cost of these forces that gave additional urgency to metropolitan attempts to raise revenue from the colonists. Whatever the difficulties this caused, the final objective – to free both colonists and Indians from the threat of periodic massacre – was intelligible enough. A British army would have been needed in North America anyway, to secure the older British colonies against the strategic threat posed by newly acquired Canada and Florida, and this in itself would have required a colonial revenue: for the imperial government to have ignored the Native American problem would not have solved the constitutional problems raised by imperial taxation.[108] But a British America might have been one in which the westward migration of peoples was regulated and humanized, freed in part from the stains of massacre and theft which were later to characterize it.

Black slaves might equally have enjoyed a fundamentally different lot in a continuing British America. White colonists interpreted as treachery the decision of the Governor of Virginia, Lord Dunmore, in November 1775, to offer emancipation to slaves who rallied to the British cause,[109] but apart from pressing military needs this episode may also have reflected the faster and further evolution in Britain of opinion on the question of chattel slavery. Similarly, where many groups in the colonies remained rabidly anti-Catholic in a way that recalled seventeenth-century traumas, British opinion was already moving towards a lifting of Catholic disabilities. In 1772 Lord Mansfield's judgement in *Somersett's Case* established at once that the common law dissolved the bonds of slavery for blacks on English soil: with a British America loudly claiming the rights of Englishmen, it would only have been a matter of time before the same principle was communicated to the colonies. How long would it have taken? Within the empire, a supreme political authority in the metropolis, deploying the power of the Royal Navy, was able to end the slave trade following legislation of 1806–11 and proceed to the emancipation of slaves in British possessions overseas after legislation of 1833; in America, political realities compelled the deletion of Jefferson's condemnation of slavery in his initial draft of the Declaration of Independence. Black colonists who fought for the Crown during the Revolutionary War (as many did) fought with some reason.[110] Historians have debated whether the American war of the 1860s was essentially about slavery, or essentially about the rights of the subordinate legislatures to resist by secession Sir William Blackstone's doctrine of the indivisibility and absoluteness of sovereignty. In either case, the events of the 1860s can be analysed as the second American Civil War, a reversion to the problems left unresolved in the first. Had the events of the 1770s developed differently, therefore, it is possible that avenues of negotiation and compromise might have developed which might have skirted the second great catastrophe to afflict the North American continent.

X.   THE LONG SHADOW OF THE TRANSATLANTIC COUNTERFACTUAL

Not only the British and their former colonists but continental European observers also entertained counterfactual reflections on the Revolution's result. The French political economist, Turgot, in a memorandum written in April 1776, expected an independent America to emerge from the conflict; but, should the outcome of the war be the opposite, the scale of British military resources committed to the colonies would inevitably lead to a British conquest of the whole continent from Newfoundland to Panama, expelling the French from Louisiana and the Spanish from Mexico.[111] A transatlantic world of peace and trade would have promoted the economic development and population growth of Britain's American colonies: without the war of 1776–83, which devastated the colonial economy and delayed its development by decades, the wealth and power of a libertarian North Atlantic polity might have promoted meliorist reform in France rather than *philosophe*-inspired revolution. The point is so obvious that it rarely needs to be stressed: had the American Revolution not taken the form it did in 1776–83, it is highly unlikely that the French state would have staggered vainly beneath a fatal fiscal burden and collapsed in ruin in 1788–9.

Such a counterfactual is so large, and so far removed from the actual outcome that it loses touch with the present-day needs of those who have adapted to the actual outcomes. Analysts of the counterfactual must beware of that easy escape offered by the argument that, but for some initial mistake, some tragic error, all would have been well, and mankind released from avoidable conflicts into a golden age of peaceful progress. From the perspective of 1914 or 1939, British observers might easily look back with regret on the great opportunity missed, the opportunity to create a peaceful and prosperous North Atlantic Anglophone polity, united in its commitment to libertarian and commercial values. The Whig–Liberal tradition of English historiography could make such a course seem plausible by ascribing the American Revolution to easily avoidable errors of British policy, and especially to the personal failings of George III. This explanation has become increasingly unlikely, however. Even if conflict had been avoided in the 1770s, as it well might, this would not have guaranteed future tranquillity in perpetuity.

Slavery might, after all, have shattered the peace of this resplendent empire in the 1830s or 1840s, as it tore apart the new American republic shortly afterwards. For if the Stamp Act in the 1760s produced a near-unanimous outcry from American colonies incensed by even so modest an infringement (as they saw it) of their property rights, how much more violent would have been American resistance to a British attempt to emancipate America's slaves? Such a metropolitan intervention in the affairs of the colonies, had it come in 1834, as it did for Britain's other colonies, might have united American colonists with far greater vehemence around an economic institution of vastly greater significance than tea. As it was, the conflict over slavery in the 1860s was one from which Britain was able to stand aside; the result was a victory for the northern states, and emancipation. Had the conflict been fought within a transatlantic polity, American victory might have had the effect of entrenching that peculiar practice even more deeply in the life of the nation. Whig history has (in the English case) been identified as 'winners' history'; postmodern history has been identified as the histories of the losers. What contingency and the counterfactual remind us is that a distinction between winners and losers is not one that modernism or postmodernism could securely identify.

6

THE END OF THE SPECIAL
RELATIONSHIP

I. THE PROBLEM

The declining influence of the social sciences, the increasing historical analysis of central concepts, and the postmodern challenges to the familiar 'grand narratives' can all be understood as abstract debates about method, but that is seldom how they appear in the daily work of academic history. Here they are expressed implicitly, in the course of writing and debating the substance of our accounts of the past. These debates are not undertaken by disembodied intelligences but by historians with identities, loyalties, programmes and ideas of their national identity (however much they might prefer to escape them). It is this that creates another level on which history operates, what we might call the diplomatic relations between historical traditions. For real historians in real states often cohere in national historical professions, and the relations between these national historiographies is the general theme of this chapter and the next. Chapter 6 seeks causes of the partial drawing away of British historiography from that of the USA; chapter 7 explores some causes and consequences of British historiography's partial realignment with Europe and, as a particular case, Germany.

National historiographies are, to begin with, still significantly different from each other: they can develop in different ways, and have very different characteristics, even in the same time frame. Modernism and postmodernism have both obscured these differences without abolishing them. Indeed the assumption that the historical enterprise is an international common currency arises not from the truth of either modernist or postmodern analysis but from the wide influence of one historically grounded national tradition in particular, the historiography of the United States. That nation's unprecedentedly powerful and self-referential historical profession is largely committed to this project by its engagement with the demands of the USA's 'civil religion' and its claims about American exceptionalism.[1] For US historiography, the main index of self-absorption or international engagement is nevertheless still the degree and nature of its relationship to British historiography. This chapter argues that the alleged death of British history in the USA is not a consequence of any failure of British historiography to keep up with modernist or postmodern advances; it is, rather, a result partly of growing intellectual introversion in the host culture, partly of the outdated versions of British history often exported to the American market.

We must first appreciate that a problem exists, for it exists despite the boasted internationalism of modern academe. One result of this internationalism, paradoxically, is to mask the way in which an intellectual engagement between countries becomes progressively harder to achieve. English speakers in general are becoming more isolated from other cultures as communications improve and foreign language skills decline.[2] The English language does not itself guarantee an international perspective in the face of pressures that are all in the direction of making cultures self-referential. Even where language is shared, a people's own nation state is its yardstick, their chief and perhaps sole frame of reference. My Oxford colleague was moved to protest: 'National identity is not the universal touchstone for judging historical significance... it is time for a different approach to American history, one that will view the United States in the context of an Atlantic world.'[3] English history, too, has been called on to see itself in wider contexts (the British Isles,[4] continental Europe,[5] the Atlantic) but the outcomes did not always meet the challenge. The 'three kingdoms' framework for British history, for example, has increasingly been appropriated by those inclined to defend the parochial integrity of Scotland, Ireland and Wales, despite the intentions of its framers to explain a composite kingdom as an achievement in cultural integration.[6] Proposed similarities between British and continental

European history were often resisted. The reconstitution of an intellectually viable Anglo-American dimension has, so far, escaped us.

As postmodernism demanded, the 'grand narratives' which formerly linked the public consciousness across national boundaries have been weakened. The histories of Greece and Rome are no longer exemplary for us. Medieval Christendom, the Reformation and Counter-Reformation have become subjects of scholarship rather than common points of reference. Books on such unifying modernist themes as the Renaissance, the Enlightenment or nationalism now conclude that their chosen phenomena were significantly different in each country,[7] so that we begin to doubt the validity of these unifying categories at all. Few people still maintain modernist international allegiances to class, party or revolution. Preserving the intellectual contacts between cultures becomes steadily more difficult; but this has a particular significance for British history in its international standing. Nowhere is the history of Britain under such threat, and nowhere does its alleged decline have such wide implications, as in the USA.

The numerical decline of students of British history in the USA (and vice versa) is only part of the problem. Domestic cultural dynamics in each country dictate that mentalities continue to diverge. The sorts of history being practised in the two countries are becoming increasingly disparate, as are each country's political science and literary scholarship: more and more, the books which speak most eloquently to American audiences and attract widespread praise in the USA receive only passing notice in Britain, and books which seem at the cutting edge of scholarship in Britain largely fail to engage with a characteristically American academic agenda.[8] Students in either place would seldom now face the challenge that to understand one culture demands knowledge of the other also. Were they to do so, they would encounter another problem. Whatever the subtleties and nuances of British and American historiographies in their native habitats, each presents a public face to the other that is fundamentally simplified, even caricatured. Historical integration is not necessarily achieved by studying best-selling texts.

Simultaneously, the historical perspective as such is in decline.[9] Francis Fukuyama offered a world-historical rationale for what many wished, on other grounds, to believe:[10] people (but especially Americans) increasingly see themselves as already emancipated from historical problems and constraints into a timeless realm of private personal fulfilment.[11] This trend underlies the reorientation of many areas of US life away from an engagement with historic knowledge, texts, formulae, creeds or liturgies and towards the personal, subjective spiritual quest. The section on popular psychology, not history, is at the heart of the modern bookshop; and this was true first, and is especially true, in America. For related reasons, a characteristic of North American and European cultures is the steady forward march of the event horizon, the earliest episode that a society commonly attends to. A century ago, the collective public memory of white Americans extended back to the Mayflower; fifty years ago, to the War of Independence. For US students today the limit of the inconceivably remote in their society seems to be the Civil War; for the less educated, it is, perhaps, Pearl Harbor. Even in Britain, the long sweep of compulsory English history embodied in the old Oxford and London History syllabuses, widely replicated elsewhere and classically satirized in *1066 And All That*, has fragmented under the weight of scholarly specialization: medieval history has almost everywhere lost its compulsory status, and more and more students choose courses in more and more modern time-frames.[12] This increasing myopia means that public memories in Britain and the USA contain fewer and fewer shared elements.

Cultural dissociation nevertheless enhances the importance of British history for the present-day American (and vice versa): for each, the other's history is the most accessible mirror, often the only accessible mirror, which can show us what we are by contrast with what we might have been and what we are not. Britain and America should be studied as each other's indispensable counterfactuals, yet it is this role which is now at risk. Even in academe, the area of US life most open to overseas influence, the language barrier has not prevented the dominant imports being for decades continental European, not British; yet from the *Annales* school, through Martin Heidegger, Hans-Georg Gadamer, Claude Lévi-Strauss and Roland Barthes to Jacques Derrida and Michel Foucault, their general impact has been to promote not internationalism but a parochializing subjectivism, and to help to dismantle those overarching structures of historical explanation that once formed a modernist transatlantic bridge.

The way in which the historical agendas of Britain and America mesh together or, increasingly, fail to do so; the way in which the intellectual preoccupations of the two countries' historians engage with each other, or fail to engage, are therefore increasingly problematic. Recent decades have witnessed important changes in this symbiosis, and in the responses of British and American history to the cultural dynamics of their societies. Increasingly, assumptions about shared structures have been undermined: as British history withdraws into a new geographical arena, the USA's conception of its world mission is seen abroad as more and more exceptionalist and consequently intrusive.

These currents in cultural development will have their political consequences. Scenarios of the two countries' futures which would be the result of policies built on novel historical theories are regularly discussed. The postmodern strengthening of the USA's national myth as a result of postmodern introversion may direct that society towards an ever greater self-absorption. Equally, Britain might commit itself to regional devolution or to a federal Europe on the basis of a similar postmodern historical theory which explained how national differences were 'imagined', national identities 'constructed', national traditions 'invented', and how these were open to remoulding by the modern historical entrepreneur. These options provide good reasons for seeking an historical understanding of the cultural pressures urging societies in different directions. The task of the historian is to discover what history is doing to endorse or question these trends, and to ask whether it has a good intellectual warrant for its public role.

II.   THE PUBLIC FUNCTION OF THE HISTORIAN

Cultural dissociation is not new. History has always been a significantly different activity in Britain and the USA because of its markedly different public functions and methodological commitments. Old differences of public function persist and are accentuated. British academics have a much more immediate access to a unified public arena and public debate than is the case in the USA. Historical education in British universities has always focused on the education of a public service elite,[13] and, after an interesting digression in the 1960s and 1970s, now serves a newly commercialized economy. A public role of this sort calls for pragmatic judgement rather than moral seriousness.[14] By contrast, history in the USA is a leading aspect of that society's social conscience, an embodiment of its moral purposes. In US universities, history plays the salient role in students' acculturation to their country's civil religion; British history is more often an agency of British students' self-emancipation rather than their acculturation. The first generation of American historians, like William Gordon, David Ramsay and Mercy Otis Warren, demonstrated the tension between the desire to establish the intellectual autonomy of their subject and the demand that the history of American independence be written as a ratification of the new republic and its values.[15] The imperatives of public culture still mean that the inner dynamics of American historical writing differ from its British equivalent, where providentialism has played little part since David Hume.[16] In the USA the pressures to write history as the ratification of the present (whether a modernist or a postmodern present) are still profound.

In America the title to enunciate these purposive public moralizings was constructed with the profession itself. History in British universities developed some similar functions,[17] but it had many other functions too, including predominantly what Elton championed as 'history for its own sake'; in the USA Elton's generation reinforced history's identity as a socially purposeful activity in unprecedentedly important universities, each a secular cathedral, a monument to public ideals in a way that their British counterparts were no longer.[18]

Different social purposes generate different controversies. Britain has no arguments about which books to include in the canon of Western Civilization courses; there are no such courses. No reformers seek to redefine that canon in the name of multicultural, non-hierarchical ideals. No conservatives uphold a conception of their society by championing the inclusion of certain items on a reading list. British history is emblematic of no single ideology, as the history of the USA is supposed to embody liberal democracy; the British, or English, even doubt the meaning of Britishness, or Englishness, and explore the implications of challenges to reconstruct those things either from the champions of 'history from below', or from Scotland, Ireland and Wales,[19] or from Euro-federalists.[20] These debates have no US parallels, for the strength of the national myth means that the shape of the polity and its constitution are beyond reform. The British divide now aligns some forms of social history against unifying narrative history told as the history of a state, institution, church or ideology defending itself against successive challenges. Where race, class and gender flourish in the USA within the postmodern myth, in Britain those largely modernist genres labour history[21] and social history have even been diagnosed to be in terminal crisis, and their postmodern successors are hostile to the national myth rather than supportive of it. Modernity itself has been presented as 'a normative project': 'If social history comes to be seen as the outcome of the project of modernity then this may be the signal of its end.'[22] The contrast to the USA is substantial, where debates between modernism and postmodernism have left the public function of the historian essentially intact.

In the USA a leading role was played in this public function by an institution, the American Historical Association. Where the British Academy, the Royal Historical Society and the Institute of Historical Research soon lost most of their early social role, it is still the content of this purposefulness which is debated in the USA rather than the moralizing enterprise itself. In 1991 the AHA's President celebrated the involvement of historians in national politics,[23] but recorded with apprehension a growing number of predictions that 'scholarship can offer no guarantees for the solution of social problems'. The assumption that it could do so is peculiarly American, but this vindication did not address the real problem: the content of some historical writing had been losing credibility by becoming increasingly self-referential.[24] This historical failure also has consequences for America's engagement with a wider world.

In recent years, these problems have been revealingly expressed in two areas: rhetorically charged conflicts over the structure of the US school curriculum, and over what texts to include in the 'sacred canon' of English or Western Civilization courses in US universities. Many of the most revealing discussions have come from a questioning of the composition of the canon, and the challenge that it include excluded writers or groups. Equally, the defence of the canon has disclosed its essential premises. In 1990, a group of historians signed a memorandum of protest to the *New York Times*:

In July, 1989, a task force on minorities, appointed by the New York commissioner of education, submitted a report... calling for revision of the history curriculum... The report, a polemical document, viewed division into racial groups as the basic analytical framework for an understanding of American history. It showed no understanding of the integrity of history as an intellectual discipline based on commonly accepted standards of evidence. It saw history rather as a form of social and psychological therapy whose function is to raise the self-esteem of children from minority groups... We have a further concern: The commissioner of education's task force contemptuously dismisses the Western tradition. Recognition of its influence on American culture, the task force declares, has a 'terribly damaging effect on the psyche' of children from non-European cultures. No evidence is adduced to support this proposition and much evidence argues against it. The Western tradition is the source of ideas of individual freedom and political democracy to which most of the world now aspires. The West has committed its share of crimes against humanity, but the Western democratic philosophy also contains in its essence the means of exposing crimes and producing reforms. Little can be more damaging to the psyches of young Blacks, Hispanics, Asians and Indians than for the State of New York to tell them that the Western democratic tradition is not for them. And little can have more damaging effect on the republic than the use of the school system to promote the division of our people into antagonistic racial groups. We are after all a nation – as Walt Whitman said, 'a teeming Nation of nations' – and history enables us to understand the bonds of cohesion that make for nationhood and a sense of the common good: *unum e pluribus*...[25]

This is less a debate about what the broad outlines of the history of the USA are than a debate about the uses to which a largely consensual modernist account of the Founding of a unified nation ought to be put within the postmodern cultural politics of an ethnically mixed society. In a debate structured as a conflict between multiculturalism and 'the Western tradition', British history scarcely enters: race, class and gender have built few transatlantic bridges. British historians too debated national identity, but not in such terms. In Britain, the debate has been not about the claims of groups to a lead part in the national epic, national unity being beyond question, but about whether to undo the effects of early-modern state-building, and whether to find historically plausible the claims of some Welsh, Irish and Scots to what some of them allege to be an historic nationalist mandate to pursue federalism or independence.

The public functions of history in Britain and the USA have indeed diverged.

III.   AMERICAN METHODOLOGIES

British and American history are also profoundly different in their dominant methodologies, and methodology provides a possibly autonomous variable amidst the pressures exerted by history's public function. As Peter Novick recorded, the American historical enterprise from an early date was consciously built around positivism,[26] a modernist methodology only recently assailed by a variety of (mostly imported) forms of subjectivist relativism. The creation of the American historical profession in c. 1880–1920, and its sense of purpose and self-worth, were bound up with the attempt to make history the arena of demonstrable, scientific and therefore usable truths.[27] This faith created a strong social and intellectual system; but it had its fault lines. Positivism never became sufficiently self-aware. It never identified its premises, which (without explicit justification) seemed more and more like massive columns supporting the neoclassical portico of the official American self-image.

This status made positivism a target from the 1960s: each challenge could be phrased as a demand for a place in the canon, for legitimate space for a newly professionalized specialism. Where in Britain historians who prioritized their public function sought to generalize, to command a national historical debate, in the USA the specializers were also seeking platforms within academe from which their sectional vision could be realized. In Britain, contested concepts like class functioned as 'junction concepts', linking the ideational to the material in order to show the dominance of the latter;[28] as the scales later tipped towards the ideational and away from the material, class proved to be a key point of entry for idealist methodologies into British social history. In the USA, no such Trojan horse existed.

With American positivism went an attitude to texts and to their historical meaning which in biblical scholarship might be called fundamentalist, and which we might term objectivist or essentialist: the working historical assumption that values, being timeless, are based on the essential and objectively unchanging meanings of explanatory categories.

The most fervent statements of the objectivist position have come from the Straussians, but they were unusual only in offering a sophisticated and agitated defence of a position which is widely held. Leo Strauss was clearly an essentialist in this sense. His diagnosis of the crisis of what he saw in the West as a loss of belief in its purpose and superiority was one that he traced to 'late modern doctrines that denied the possibility of rational knowledge of the universal validity of any purpose or principle'. By a related argument, Strauss 'deplored the influence of those thoughtlessly egalitarian historians who debunk, rather than make more intelligible, the greatness of statesmen'.[29] Great statesmen (by implication, the Founding Fathers among them) were those who championed these timeless values. Yet values can only be timeless in an ahistorical society, a society with which a profoundly historicized Britain cannot easily engage.

Allan Bloom's strange notoriety came by defending as a social formation, failing in the face of postmodernism, what Leo Strauss had advocated as a modernist philosophical programme.[30] Bloom's agitated protest was focused on what he diagnosed as a newly pervasive moral and cultural relativism. Students, he claimed, were 'unified only in their relativism and in their allegiance to equality'. Bloom was held to believe that 'Western' civilization is built on 'trans-historic, trans-cultural absolutes', communicated to the USA at the Founding, and structured around 'axiomatic principles exempt from historical criticism'.[31] He allegedly displayed an ahistorical commitment to moral absolutes: for Bloom, 'The facts of history... have really nothing to do with the moral quality of an action'.[32] Peter Novick's *That Noble Dream* accepted a similarly pessimistic account of what had occurred in the American historical profession, recording its earlier modernist unified goals and comparing them with their present fragmentation.[33] Novick approved of this diversification and widening of opportunities with the breakup of a shared notion of objectivity;[34] his book drew attention by its insistence that the old modernist objectivity had indeed irreversibly broken up.

But had it? In the USA, it may be that the old social function (originating with positivism) finally predominated over the disintegration of unified moralizing that postmodernism ought to entail. Post-modernism in America thereby became heir to the most general purposes of an earlier project that it claimed had collapsed (as was also the case in France). Most of the conflicts over teaching values (over hierarchy, gender and multiculturalism) were resolved in favour of the extension of the sacred canon to include new authors and new cultures, not by the abolition of the concept of a canon itself. Even Novick argued that 'relativists share no doctrine' and are identified only negatively, by not endorsing the liberal–conservative social programme of the objectivists.[35] It has been urged against Novick that most scholars on the Left are covertly objectivists too, and that the goals of feminism and multiculturalism are pursued by historians only some of whom would subscribe to relativist methodologies.[36] Conflicts between modernists and postmodernists have revealed a surprising loyalty to objectivist understandings of the agenda for social action.[37]

At many such moments the modernist social function of history in the USA outweighed the deconstructionist challenge, especially through the weight of those majorities everywhere who subscribed to the vision of the Founding embodied in the work of best-selling historians like Daniel Boorstin (born 1914) and Henry Steele Commager (born 1902).[38] These assumptions could be given a Straussian spin. In 1988, Gordon Wood noted how the bicentennial celebrations had been marked by

> talk of the 'human soul', of the 'moral foundations' of American politics, of the 'founding principle', of 'virtue' and the threats to 'virtue', of 'character', and of religion and its relation to the polity... Perhaps the most remarkable fact about the scholarship of the bicentennial celebrations is the extent to which that scholarship has been colored by the students and followers of Leo Strauss...[39]

From a British perspective, it is evident that after the conflicts of the 1960s and 1970s had died away, the stars of American positivism and the stripes of American objectivism are seen still flying on the citadel of purposeful civic enterprise.

Given recent subjectivist fashions in US methodologies, it was not obvious that this should have been so. From a British perspective, Straussianism's relative isolation of its chosen texts both from authorial intentions and from a wider context of related texts as a frame of comparison seems to have much in common with deconstructionism; but where deconstructionists claimed to deduce a nihilist relativism from their approach,[40] Straussians sought to defend the timelessness of certain categories and the values built on them.[41] Straussians were a sect preaching a prophetic message to a society seen as irreversibly secularized, but in need of moral guidance: redemption involved a new way of reading the sacred scrolls of America's civil religion.

Both Straussianism and postmodernism were ahistorical or anti-historical; but Straussianism left undamaged (indeed was intended to reinforce) the enormous residual power of the USA's founding myth. In the 1960s and 1970s, that national myth seemed to be under threat from a variety of sorts of new history, especially the histories of race and gender. From our later vantage point, it seems that areas of US academe which committed themselves to subjectivist introversion deprived themselves of the ability to revise the USA's civil religion and could, at most, hope to be incorporated within it. By the 1990s, the ability of America's public ideology to absorb and accommodate these new testaments was manifest. The life experiences of women, Native Americans and Black Americans had been grafted into the public image of the Founding; multiculturalism and feminism were celebrated as if they were among the goals of Washington and Jefferson. The new American litany of race, class and gender was eventually sung in the old cathedrals of public purposefulness.

IV.   BRITISH INNOVATIONS

Most historical writing is within familiar frameworks of ideas, yet this is not always the case. Much has changed in British historiography, and this must inevitably have its effect on how we view Anglo-American relations.[42] In Britain the characteristic social functions of post-war historians (including endorsing a welfare-statist consensus, if indeed there was one, or hastening a Marxist revolution) were to be subverted by shifts in methodology. Whatever the changing party labels for these dispositions, the broad distinction in Britain has been between those committed to a reductionist methodology and those attracted by an idealist one, that system of ideas by which Bishop Berkeley emancipated the English from Lockeian empiricism and R. G. Collingwood emancipated English historians from Victorian teleologies of material progress.[43] The difference was summed up in John Stuart Mill's account of the contrasts between Bentham and Coleridge. Both, said Mill, were 'great questioners of things established'. But where Bentham asked 'Is it true?' Coleridge asked 'What is the meaning of it?' Mill continued:

The one [Bentham] took his stand outside the received opinion, and surveyed it as an entire stranger to it: the other [Coleridge] looked at it from within, and endeavoured to see it with the eyes of a believer in it; to discover by what apparent facts it was at first suggested, and by what appearances it has ever since been rendered continually credible – has seemed to a succession of persons, to be a faithful interpretation of their experiences.'[44]

These dispositions had later equivalents, of which the clash between modernists and postmodernists was merely the most recent.

In Britain, the positivists had their social role through being reductionists; they were identified by their assumptions of 'underlying' causes, and found them in economic and demographic phenomena. Thus armed, the positivists were generally eager social commentators, even if their confidence in assuming a public role was, in retrospect, surprisingly un-self-reflective until modernism was assailed by postmodernism in debates within British social history.[45] Elsewhere in British history since the mid 1960s, however, two parallel but related developments of method fundamentally revised the substance of the story: one in the history of political thought, one in narrative political history.

US academe did not need to make the history of political thought more than a minority interest, even then often heavily influenced by Leo Strauss and essentialist in its method, drawing on a culture long predisposed to appeal to natural rights as self-evident; but in Britain the history of political thought became central, has been adorned by scholars whose approach has normally been contextualist (i.e. anti-essentialist), and has opened up points of contact with historians of many other areas. Its destructive impact on the old Whig canon having been outlined by Laslett, its methodological foundations having been laid especially by Pocock and Skinner, this school has recast perspectives on a swathe of English thinkers in the early-modern period.[46] Its flourishing went with a related anti-essentialist development in the writing of political history: this was devised by authors who initially addressed, in a tactical setting, the significance of contingency in its action upon the eternal truths formerly assumed by political science. In the USA, the nature of politics and its attendant historical narrative remained self-evident within a world of timeless categories.

In the history of early Stuart and Victorian Britain, however, central categories (including 'class' and 'the social') were first challenged by authors who gave renewed attention to political narrative and to political manoeuvre.[47] In the 1960s and 1970s they laboured at the task of escaping from the hegemony of positivist history by seeking to show how politics (at that time neglected by social history) was not determined by 'underlying' phenomena; how it was, on the contrary, an autonomous mode of human experience and action (echoing Oakeshott), not even necessarily to be understood as a purposeful, problem-solving activity; and how it was to a large degree a matter of contingency rather than of long-term necessary causes.[48] Narrative history rather than typological analysis became the point of access to this mode of experience: by contrast, the lessons drawn by historians from the social sciences had until then been reductionist ones, and this school of political historians spurned such sources. Their idealist critique initially had two targets. One was political science, then the most obvious champion of the practice that Oakeshott had condemned as 'abridgement', a discipline issuing in the 1950s and 1960s in the constitution-mongering associated with Sir Ivor Jennings.[49] The second target was the sort of political history which had embodied in a naive narrative similar assumptions, derived especially from Victorian 'constitutional history'.[50] By the early to mid 1980s, this idealist critique had been markedly successful.[51] The political studies written in the 1960s and 1970s did not at once lead to new synoptic accounts of British history, but they did profoundly compromise the familiar, Whiggish forms of political narrative. By that success, this genre abolished itself in the early 1980s. It had been located chiefly in the nineteenth and twentieth centuries, but it could point to equally far-reaching achievements in the seventeenth, where one narrative of the outbreak of the civil war was undertaken with similarly overt methodological intent.[52] In whatever century, it had been drawn to the weak points of the Whig scenario, like successive parliamentary reform bills, and had made explicit its dissent from existing practice.

By its success, this genre opened up new avenues of enquiry.[53] Its initial object was to show what political action was not like and not about. Only when an interlocking nexus of misconceptions had been removed was it possible to discern those areas of human experience, often familiar enough to historians before 1914, that had passed into the shadows since that date. So in the 1980s many historians of high politics or economic policy, often secular in their priorities at the outset, found themselves writing, via political thought, on that largest and most central area of thought before the age of ideology, religion.[54] The same reintegration of religion was observable in the histories being written of the seventeenth,[55] eighteenth and nineteenth centuries: it was a result of a fundamental methodological shift, widely and independently influential on scholars with different, but weak, conceptions of history's social function.

This was, in itself, a notable reversal. British history from the 1930s into the 1970s had joined in a general borrowing from adjacent social sciences: as Lawrence Stone recorded in 1976, 'In this perpetually moving frontier the most influential discipline changes from decade to decade'. First economics, then in turn sociology, demography and anthropology (with psychology an uncertainly acknowledged intruder), enlivened an historiography allegedly otherwise confined to the bread-and-water diet of high politics and diplomacy. In a preface of 1981 to a collection of essays reprinting this analysis, Stone recorded that the 'heroic phase' was over: in the next fifteen years 'it is probable that intellectual stagnation will set in' marked by 'quiet consolidation of received wisdom'.[56]

From today's perspective we can see that the outcome in the years that followed was quite different. This period was one of fundamental reconstruction, not quiet consolidation. In this perspective much of what happened can be analysed as the consequences of the widespread addition of theology and the partial addition of law and political economy to Stone's list of influences from adjacent disciplines. As a result, the general map of the British past is now unimaginably different from its appearance even when Stone surveyed it. As the old teleological certainties faded, rooted as they were in early twentieth-century political purposes, British historians returned in large numbers to the fields of political theory and religion: ideology now became the autonomous variable. This was not the case in the USA, where the separation of Church and State still justified the exclusion of the history of religion from historians' main agendas.[57] There, even those political historians who acknowledged the collapse of the old teleologies returned to a more robust positivism.[58] In Britain, the anti-positivist victory ended differently, by rehabilitating a methodological position that would have been dismissed as heretical in 1981. In episode after episode of modern British history, from the military and the diplomatic to the recovery of republicanism in the history of political thought, scholars have reasserted the counterfactual: we look differently at what did happen, in the new knowledge that other avenues of development were as plausible, sometimes more so.

In political history, two things have combined: the contextual approach to the history of political thought, and a 'high-political' focus on short-term events, stressing the contingent and the counterfactual. Together, they have led on to a 'new' political history[59] characterized by a 'linguistic turn', a sensitivity to the terms in which conduct is described. This new school deals with parties as discourse rather than structure; it attends to identities in a way which allows 'class' to be explored in its relations with 'nation' more than with production. Although identified as 'postmodern', especially by its modernist critics,[60] works employing this idiom can be as archivally based as their immediate forerunners, and the label is as unhelpful as that empty category, 'revisionist': terminology borrowed from literary criticism does not always identify what is really going on in historical scholarship.

V.   BRITISH HISTORY FOR AMERICANS

Given these differences of methodology and public function, what image of British history was most easily projected to an American audience by its British practitioners? Two scenarios may be noticed among several not dissimilar candidates.[61] They achieved some currency by relating most simply to American preoccupations. One scenario was devised from the perspective of urban history, and derived its positivism from unimpeachably materialist-reductionist credentials. It was a thesis of national archaism and decline, a decline promoted when an exciting historical profession was subverted in Britain by hostile politicians. British society, in this vision, was hopelessly antiquated because it contained a monarchy and an aristocracy. Aristocratic values were a continual check on British modernization.[62] This thesis pointed to what it saw as promising trends: from 1945 to 1979, it claimed, the dominant ethic was socialist, futuristic, statist, egalitarian and international in outlook. It was an ethic sustained by a dynamic historical profession happy to see the triumph of these themes in 'revolutions': the Industrial, the Agricultural, the Scientific, and, above all, the 'English Revolution' of the 1640s.[63] Then, in 1979, a 'thunderbolt' struck British academe with the election of a government not easily assimilated to this scenario. Soon the mood of the profession was one of 'gloom, despondency and alarm'. Historians were 'spurned by the politicians and shunned by the public'. The exciting, innovatory, socially relevant message of the 1960s was no longer congenial to the governments of the 1980s, and they subverted it. In a wider setting the decline of British history was presented as a reflex of the decline of British power. With the fading of world power status, the immediate relevance of Britain's track record faded too. It followed that 'we must fashion a new version of the national past which can regain its place in our general national culture, and become once again an object of international interest'.[64] Yet that new version was never explicitly identified, and could only be reconstructed, by inference, as the antithesis of the demonology.

Such an account of British history superficially engaged American audiences whose priorities of race, class and gender left Britain as merely providing a contrasting model of racialism, hierarchy and patriarchy. However, it neglected the recently retrieved historical record of a Britain in which a hitherto powerful peerage lost its hegemony after 1832 and most of its residual power after 1914. Rather, it drew its intellectual credibility from the work of an American, Martin J. Wiener.[65] It was also a rhetorical rather than an historical response to Conservative governments since 1979, for they consciously embraced a reforming individualism which either ignored the ceremonial trappings of British society or was unfriendly towards them. Party fortunes were in reality irrelevant, since the scenario of aristocratic decline accorded ill with the fact that since the Second World War the long-term growth rate of GDP per head had been higher in Britain than in the USA whichever party was in power, Labour and Conservative, Republican and Democrat.[66]

Historical interpretations exist in groups, and sometimes support each other for reasons of social function despite apparent methodological dissonances. The positivist thesis of the collapse of a putative British patrician social structure as an analogue of national decline went with a related thesis, echoing, in a simplified way, postmodern subjectivist methodologies[67] about the imminent collapse of British national identity. The alternative to the old teleology of the nation state was presented as a new teleology of European integration.[68] One such theory (explored in chapter 2 above) sought to define 'Britishness' as synonymous with Whig efforts to present, package and celebrate England's Union with Scotland of 1707.[69] The argument runs that the surrounding challenges, which made this union work, no longer exist. Its necessary preconditions were the external threat of 'the Other', in the eighteenth century provided by Catholic France, and the internal phenomenon of a shared Protestantism.

Here too, historical writing in Britain (again reviewed in chapter 2) uncovered the limitations of a thesis framed in an American context. By showing how both a sense of Englishness and the role played by law and religion in framing that sense are much older than the Union with Scotland, British historiography revealed the extent to which they survived long after the historical setting of that treaty had been modified. When *Britons* repeatedly asserted 'the invention of Britishness', it was to assert that Britain's was a national identity little older than that of the USA. In deference to US positivism it presented national identity as an offshoot of 'a vast superstructure of prejudice', evidently a disguise for 'an element of self-interest' (not all subjectivist methodologies were as idealist as they purported to be). The local significance of this interpretation in the USA meshed with a wider US imperative: this historical scenario was less an attempt to understand the past than to emancipate readers from it. More widely, terms like 'construct', 'invent' and 'imagine' in the titles of historical works[70] show a new but characteristically American emphasis on the role of the liberated subjective imagination and a de-emphasis on engaging with intractable evidence, an engagement which is difficult precisely because that evidence recedes from us in historical perspective.[71] 'Construction', 'invention' and 'imagining' are terms repeated like a litany in the titles of papers at historical conferences on both sides of the Atlantic, but most of all in the USA.

Declinist scenarios of British history may have a short-term congruence with the leading preoccupations of US historiography, but lack the qualities necessary to dictate the terms of debate in that arena. What, then, are the major themes in British history that need to be included in a better assessment of its links with US history? One author complained that the impact of the 'new, professional version of British history' published in the

1980s had been wholly destructive: 'the great generalizations which gave the subject its shape, substance and success in its welfare-state heyday have been overturned by the inexorable workings of professional research, but no new interpretations of comparable significance or interest have yet been put in their place'.[72] This was inaccurate even when published in 1987 and is doubly so today. The years following Lawrence Stone's prediction of 1981 actually saw a fundamental reconstruction of many of the basic components of British history.

A variety of scholars have proposed theses which now join up to form a new outline. We have seen (chapter 2 above) that the origins of the English polity and of Englishness are very much more ancient than we thought, in the Anglo-Saxon 'strong state'; the origins of England's sense of manifest destiny can be traced to the ecclesiastical history of the English in the face of Scandinavian invasion, as propounded by Bede and systematically adopted by later chroniclers. State formation, nationalism and liberal pluralism do not necessarily go together: the USA can hardly be depicted as normative either for the nineteenth century or the twentieth. The image of medieval England as a 'feudal society' conforming to the Marxist model, inherited by the social anthropologists, has been replaced with a picture of law-governed market relations, and affective individualism, from an early date.[73]

In this sense 'English individualism', as much as Puritanism, travelled with the *Mayflower* and (as is argued in chapter 1) revolutions like those of 1642 or 1776 can no longer be explained as 'passages' from 'feudalism' (or its equivalents) to 'modernity'. Puritanism itself has been relocated within an Elizabethan Calvinist mainstream, and schism rather than liberty becomes the key term for English as for American history. English 'absolutism' was a position much closer to its constitutionalist critics under James I and Charles I than had been thought: the American constitutionalist tradition from C. H. McIlwain to J. H. Hexter has been invalidated. If the English Civil War was no decisive watershed between 'ancient' and 'modern', and had no long-term social-structural causes sufficient to explain it, the same tropes, applied to 1776, now look equally implausible. Instead, the civil war of the 1640s had many features of a war of religion,[74] and involved the relations within a dynastic composite state between England, Scotland and Ireland.[75] Some of the building blocks of early American sectarianism and constitutionalism are clearer to us. The restoration of the monarchy in 1660 re-established a polity comparable to many continental European states, especially in its overriding aim of preventing the recurrence of wars of religion; if this state form was effectively redefined rather than rejected in 1688–9, it was this state form which failed in the Thirteen Colonies in 1776 but survived in England.

The population history of England has been securely reconstructed, and shows the demographic constraints that structured the 'old society' until the early nineteenth century: the loss of 'the world we have lost' is no longer part of the antecedent causes of 1642, 1688 or 1776. This was, then, a wholly different picture of early-modern Britain to that found in the pages of Christopher Hill or Lawrence Stone, and accepted from them by Eric Hobsbawm. It also provides a related model for colonial American society before the Revolution, recently paralleled by Gordon Wood.[76] With respect to ideology, the Glorious Revolution clearly did not institute a Lockeian or a civic humanist idiom as the dominant idiom of political thought. American historians had been debating whether the ideology of the Founding was essentially to be understood as Lockeian liberalism or as republicanism. In the new setting of British scholarship, we can see that this is a *question mal posée*, and that the answer is 'neither'.

If late eighteenth-century England still possessed central features of a confessional state, it can be shown to follow that 'nationalism' is a misnomer for the self-identities formed within a monarchical, Anglican intellectual matrix, and that 'radicalism' took its rise later, primarily from a series of theologically driven antipathies to this order.[77] The building blocks of the modern world are no longer self-evident truths on either side of the Atlantic, although Thomas Paine becomes easier to explain. It follows that 'nationalism' and 'radicalism' are equally solecisms when applied to colonial America. We must look elsewhere both for American self-images and for the source of that explosive transformation that unfolded after 1776. Because the social dynamics of early-modern English-speaking societies remained to a significant degree denominational, the American Revolution too was in part a war of religion, an aspect of that resistance by Protestant Dissent to an Anglican hegemony which, for ecclesiological reasons, exploited divisions within the Church of England itself. Anglo-American relations are inescapably on this new agenda: geographically as well as thematically, a wide reference is demanded.[78]

It follows that 'liberal democracy' was a phenomenon wrongly diagnosed in the American tradition of Louis Hartz.[79] British scholarship calls for a reconsideration of the origins of the democratic ideals apparently shared on both sides of the Atlantic. No longer, for example, can British political reform be interpreted as the following of a US model. The American Revolution, centrally, did not stem from any significant debate on the franchise or the representative machinery. The series of reform bills that widened the parliamentary franchise in 1832, 1867, 1884 and 1918 have been reassessed (in the light of earlier work in the 1960s and 1970s) and freed from the teleological implication of inevitably broadening democracy with which one Victorian account credited them. Victorian politics in general have been emancipated from their purposive, Whiggish assumptions and replaced in the realm of contingency, a realm in which action and ideology cannot be taken for granted or read off from 'underlying' material structures. The interrelationship of the languages of class, radicalism and nationalism is now central, and alternative genealogies are being explored for the liberalism and socialism of the 1880s which fill the alleged 'caesura' which divided that era from Chartism. 'Society' and the sphere of the social have begun to be examined critically as explanatory devices of historians rather than accepted as natural formations which validated an autonomous 'social history' excluding the state.

No longer can 'class' be used to demonstrate Britain's tardiness in emulating the social forms that modernism designated as archetypal (i.e. as prevalent in the USA). Class and class formation in Britain are now studied as part of a history of discourse, disengaged from sole dependence on the too familiar reductionist setting of urbanization and industrialization. Where the old materialist historiography made the USA a paradox in which industrialization inexplicably did not produce class, the new historiography opens up a whole new agenda, yet to be fully explored, of Anglo-American similarities. The necessary triumphs of liberalism and of socialism (those un-American terms) now reside in the cabinet of historical curiosities; collective ownership and welfare-statism now figure as historical formations with identifiable trajectories rather than inevitable matrices of modernity. The classic question, 'why was there no socialism in America?', might be nearer to a solution in the light of the recent track record of socialism in Britain.

Given this vitality in British historical writing, it seems likely that one reason for the weakening relevance of Britain's history in the USA is that a discerning but different American audience has too often been provided with superficially appealing but deeply inadequate versions of what Britain's historic track record has actually been. It may be flattering to Americans to be told that Britain is a recently invented nation, little older than the United States, but such an historical thesis would not only be a misleading partial truth; it would also hinder Americans in understanding the essential nature of US society itself. Less and less can the British flatter Americans with the argument that the two cultures were always essentially the same, and that the Thirteen Colonies in 1776 merely began to tread sooner a path which Britain belatedly followed in the nineteenth century. New historical agendas demand a sympathetic enquiry into differences, not a triumphalist celebration of apparent similarities.

VI.   TWO TYPES OF EXCEPTIONALISM

The exceptionalism and self-referential orientation seen in parts of American historiography are not to be interpreted as naive parochialism: there are, on the contrary, sophisticated and powerful reasons for the development of these characteristics. They are also related to their British counterparts. British exceptionalism and American exceptionalism were, indeed, linked themes, but the first has been fundamentally reconfigured where the second has grown in strength. On the nature of the latter, American scholars remain divided in part because one argument has not featured in the recent American debate: American exceptionalism was somewhat less immune from external historical analysis than had been thought, since both it and modern British exceptionalism came from a common source. The Whig historiography of Britain, too, had been exceptionalist. Sometimes it wished to argue that Britain was important because it was exceptional in the sense of being irreducibly different (by inference, different from continental Europe and hence similar to America). Sometimes it wished to argue that Britain was important because it was exceptional in the sense of being normal or prototypical, blazing trails which others followed (or in which the USA had, in some ways, overtaken its parent). The more these two assumptions were qualified in recent years, the more the once-obvious linkages between

British history and American history became problematic. American history, too, showed the same unresolved tension between the unique and the exemplary; but whereas post-1945 Britain's myth of origins was being challenged in and after the 1970s, the myth of origins of the USA was strengthening from the same period.

British historiography in recent decades has begun to make progress on the ancient problem of British exceptionalism by widening its frame of reference: it has reappraised the English experience by relocating it in its British and United Kingdom contexts. The British Isles provided a valuable yardstick against which to measure continental European evidence exactly because Britain was related yet not identical.[80] In some (but too few) cases, recent British history has been comparative: often, at first, implicitly; finally explicitly, as a new version of English history allowed scholars of the seventeenth century to re-emphasize England's relations with Scotland, Ireland and Wales; or allowed others to explore Britain's similarities with continental Europe;[81] or as other work, in turn, came to set the British experience in a transatlantic context.[82] This is indeed the most recent (and thinly exemplified) phase of the newer British history, as a decade and a half of research reveals new outlines of English history and so relates that new model to the different yet not wholly dissimilar track records of England's neighbours.

Thanks to these changes, British history has been more fundamentally reconstructed since c. 1980 than at any time in the last hundred and fifty years. This is an unusual experience for any national historiography. In the same period, the American image of America has undergone no such profound change: on the contrary, the USA's national myth has shown itself remarkably able to absorb those historiographical and political challenges which in the 1960s and 1970s seemed to threaten its existence. In the same time frame, the main changes in American academe were not producer-led changes in the substance of the story but consumer-led changes in that story's use amidst the pressures of US cultural politics.

In its public functions, too, American history has evolved away from British history in the last two decades. No symbolic contradiction of reigning orthodoxies occurred in the USA equivalent to the 'disillusion of the clerks' so agonizingly apparent in Britain after 1979 and 1989; in the USA the cultural dynamics have been different. The collapse of communism and the emergence of the USA as the only superpower have reinforced the self-evidence of America's self-evident truths to a degree not seen since the 1950s. An essentially revised history of Britain therefore confronts an essentially reasserted history of America.

From this British perspective, the underlying theme of that ongoing dialogue that is American public life has emerged as a debate about the American Revolution itself. Here two different schools of thought confront each other. One school looks back to the Revolution with reverence as the decisive event in the nation's history, the moment of birth and self-definition. A generation of patriots was forced unwillingly into doing what they did; but they rose to the challenge with both heroism and genius. They produced the intellectual and moral foundations of the USA. They did their job so well that it need never be done again.[83] Rebellion was justified in 1776, but only as a unique event. The USA is henceforth a politically libertarian but socially conservative society.

The other school reveres the Revolution, too. It sees in the experience of the Founding a fundamental emancipation from old world norms, an emancipation which progressively opened up new vistas of liberation for new social groups and peoples undreamed of in 1776. The developing agenda of liberation is to be seen as part of the Revolution itself. Even in 1783 the Revolution had only just begun. For this school, the USA is committed to a public doctrine of continual revolution. American society is still politically repressive, but socially radical: emancipation is not far off.[84] These unresolved rivalries are familiar to British historians, for they are not only at the heart of our explanations of 1776; they are, in essence, the eighteenth-century Whig debate over the Revolution of 1688.

British history illuminates this contemporary American tension as essentially a conflict over America's Founding, and therefore over the USA's relation to Britain. This relevance emerged unexpectedly in the debate generated by the National Standards Project, a Federally funded enterprise to draw up guidelines for the History syllabus in America's schools.[85] Since one of its directors was Gary B. Nash, a professor at UCLA, it revealingly echoed the debate raging within US academe. The points at issue were clearly recognized by an American conservative commentator like Walter A. McDougall as a clash between the ideologies of *e pluribus unum* on the one hand, and multiculturalism and gender on the other. McDougall sided unambiguously with the first, and was a stern critic of multiculturalism and its agenda. Yet he denounced the political correctness of the *Standards'* treatment of the American Revolution in a revealing way: 'What strikes me as idiosyncratic is how *Tory* it is. Students are repeatedly asked whether the English Parliament's position on taxation was not in fact reasonable, whether the colonies' resistance was really justified, how a Loyalist would have viewed the Intolerable Acts, whether a break with England was inevitable. A conspiracy theorist might see here a bias against liberty.' McDougall quoted the *Standards'* challenge, 'students need to confront the central issue of how revolutionary the Revolution actually was': his position evidently required him to minimize it.[86] The position of British historians requires us neither to minimize it nor to maximize it but to explain it in its British setting.

So US public culture embodies a fundamental division over whether the Revolution is unique and completed, or multifaceted and ongoing. This antithesis polarizes much of American cultural politics. The ongoing revolution is associated with the ideologies of pluralism, multiculturalism and gender, and is claimed by its enemies to depend on various methodologies that may be summed up as relativist or postmodernist. The unique revolution is associated with the ideology of *e pluribus unum* and cultural homogenization, and held to depend upon the modernist methodologies of positivism and what might be called objectivism or essentialism. This antithesis tends to polarize choice: either objective truth is attainable and US values are timeless, built on the essential meaning of the classic documents of the Founding; or everything is relative and therefore political, so implicating US values as the product of the oppression of patriarchy, hierarchy and racism. In the 1950s, the 'unique revolution' school was dominant; since the late 1960s, the 'ongoing revolution' school has everywhere gained ground. Meanwhile, British (but especially English) history has been revealed as, in the old sense, scarcely revolutionary at all.[87] If it becomes instead only a story of material decline, political fragmentation and the dissolution of identity, its longer-term relevance to the modern preoccupations of the USA is hard to see.

VII.   THE LIMITS OF ANGLO-AMERICAN REINTEGRATION

This increasing dissonance between two national historiographies makes increasingly difficult the question, why should Americans care about

British history? A viable answer will depend not on sentiment but on the intellectual connections historians are able to draw between those two subjects. Attention to their interactions suggests several conclusions: that the old connections have broken down; that we are urgently in need of new connections; that some versions of British history can provide them, and others cannot. First, a version which cannot. Lawrence Stone, reviewing Conrad Russell's *The Causes of the English Civil War*, posed the same question for his chosen period: why should we care about what happened in England 350 years ago?[88] He answered:

> For Americans it matters a great deal, since if the events were indeed no more than an accidental civil war caused by factional disputes among disaffected noblemen, then the ideology behind the American Revolution and the language of the Declaration of Independence become virtually incomprehensible. If the founding fathers did not have more than a century of individualist and democratic political ideas from England upon which to draw, where else did they get the ideological principles which enabled them first to achieve independence from George III and then to form a union based on the theory of popular sovereignty, the rule of law, the division of powers, and the separation of church and state?[89]

This British Whig–Liberal scenario used to engage easily and without self-consciousness with the American essentialist or objectivist school of Strauss or Bloom, Commager or Boorstin; but it is just this account of British (more exactly, English) constitutional progress that has been fundamentally rewritten. Renewed attention to British history in a US setting therefore implies no return to any traditional library of texts. The revised version cuts across American debates rather than offering easy endorsements to any party. If we accept the new accounts of the 'English' civil war of the 1640s, we need to find new ways of answering Stone's question about the ideology of the American Revolution and the language of the Declaration of Independence, for his answer clearly no longer stands. Moreover, the significance of the American Revolution, if it is reinterpreted as a problem within British history, extends forward and backward in time. It remains to be seen how far new answers to the old problems of historical and historiographical links will be accepted in the USA.

Reinterpretation has revealed a British historiography which not only differs from American historiography as the British nation differs from the American nation, but does so increasingly. Britain has no 'founding' from which its subsequent path, or historical categories, could be deduced. Its past is one of problematically historical continuity, not of problematically ahistorical modernity. It shows the repeated impact of contingency to offset the unfolding of its sense of manifest destiny. It reveals the repeated exploration of counterfactuals, the repeated shifts of historiographical perspective imposed by changes in religion or public ideology. The history of the USA does not. Although some English documents, like Magna Carta, have for periods played roles not unlike the American Constitution, and although some events, like the Glorious Revolution, have for a time replicated the mythic function of the American Revolution, the significance of the British experience over time is Oakeshottian, not Jeffersonian. This is indeed the norm for ancient states. The USA may, one day, follow this path. We can, however, be sure that it will not do so yet. Meanwhile, there is a problem of mutual interpretation; a British historiography that has evolved so far in method and in internal alignments[90] currently offers few olive branches.

New historical agendas have, nevertheless, brought new points of possible reintegration. Research on British and American history, each taken in isolation, will rightly continue; but there are many themes in the domestic histories of both societies that would become fully intelligible only if projected on to a larger, transatlantic screen. We have been wrong to assume that British history and American history could never fundamentally neglect each other so long as they shared that defining event of recent history, the American Revolution. The national myths that have grown up to surround that sharp and painful event, as the oyster turns the grain of sand into a pearl, have influenced historical writing so far that the two countries now engage not via their histories but via their historiographies. In so far as these are free-floating, an opposite trend is also possible: British historiography might be urged to follow US historiography into parochializing subjectivism, and retreat from, or ignore, the gains made in recent years. This, too, would prevent the emergence of more broadly based understandings. It is nevertheless important not to overstate this thesis of historiographical dissociation. No identifiable crisis is approaching. Anglo-American scholarship will continue to explore many detailed interconnections, to which a discussion such as this cannot do justice. Yet it would be wilfully nescient to allow smaller exceptions to obscure a larger truth: the extent of real Anglo-American historical understanding has diminished and is diminishing. There are currently few reasons for expecting that it will be easily increased.

7

THE UNEASY REALIGNMENT WITH EUROPE

I. NATIONAL HISTORIES AND NATIONAL HISTORIOGRAPHIES

Men make their own 'history'. Yet they make their history not in abstract debates but by practical action, and the most general level on which they engage in these practical actions is within the history of their polity. National identities are, for good or ill, powerful, but the perceived shape of a nation's history is often formed by implicit comparisons with the histories of neighbouring states. With little reflection, these general perceptions change over decades, influenced by world events and, at one remove, by professional scholarship. Like the slow movement of land masses, nations realign themselves in their understandings of each other. In just that way, Britain has come to align itself somewhat less with the United States and somewhat more with continental Europe. The diplomatic features of this slow but momentous shift are, of course, well known. The historiographical features are almost unknown, and these deserve our attention. These are features that neither modernism nor postmodernism adequately explain.

How profoundly national our intellectual traditions still are is often overlooked, since we seldom make the relations between them a subject of study in its own right. In substantive rather than metahistorical matters, we often give increasing priority to domestic concerns.[1] Even in an age self-consciously international and deliberately suspicious of the demands of the nation state, nations tend to be preoccupied with their internal political, social or cultural agendas; when a 'problem' or a 'crisis' makes the question of these relations inescapable, they often fall back on familiar and seldom-scrutinized assumptions about the wider setting and about 'normal' patterns of development which in fact depend on implied international comparisons.

Most nation states therefore support an historical profession, and an historiography, which is still chiefly focused on that nation's internal experience. The real contacts between these national historiographies are few; the number of major historians who have devoted themselves to the task of establishing links between different historiographies is negligible by comparison with the body of professional historians as a whole. The international links have often been provided by other disciplines, especially sociology and political science, that are not as self-scrutinizing and not subject to the criteria of historical argument.[2] These disciplines therefore tend to be more openly normative than history. Although it is now a familiar point that all societies have their own myths of exceptionalism, the recovery of their histories has not dissolved those myths in any but a few cases. Moreover, those myths still provide unexamined premises for adjacent disciplines.

Thus national historiographies have a life of their own and relate to the historiographies of neighbouring states via a form of intellectual or cultural diplomacy. Indeed national intellectual traditions as a whole interact in this way. Just as each nation state generates its history, so it sustains its own meta-image of itself, built chiefly around the history of the nation itself, embodying to differing degrees a set of national priorities and purposes, and composed of a heady cocktail the major ingredients of which are historiography, political science and sociology.

This chapter addresses one episode in which answers to momentous international questions were supplied in large part by the extension of an American national tradition of history, itself intellectually dominated by American social and political science. It deals with the way in which an idea of 'the West' was constructed to exclude Germany; it explores the way in which an American intellectual tradition imposed that perspective on Europe in the late twentieth century; and it argues that recent developments in historiography, especially in Britain, have broken up the implied comparisons on which that American public doctrine rested. This, it contends, is the key to the perceived North Atlantic drift that is relocating Britain's intellectual longitude.

Understanding this process involves some appreciation of the history of modern Germany. The events of the early twentieth century clearly acted to demonize large areas of German political and intellectual culture in the eyes of Anglophone commentators, just as the events of the sixteenth century imposed on Spain what in English is known as a 'Black Legend'.[3] Those events in both centuries are matters of historical record, and are in no way denied or diminished here. Nevertheless, it is clear that these two processes of demonization had effects on the historical enterprise that have extended more widely even than the Anglophone historiographies of the countries immediately concerned. Historical understandings were neither properly modernized nor properly postmodernized, but merely distorted.

One means of tracing that distortion is to uncover the way in which a normative conception of 'the West' was formulated and imposed on the historiography of Germany.[4] Different understandings of what is meant by 'the West' are not new: they can be traced to the ancient Greeks, and have been subject to steady change as different polemical purposes were expressed by them. One scholar distinguished twelve versions of the concept.[5] For English, French and Germans in c. 1900, the terms 'the West' and 'Western civilization' could easily seem synonymous with 'European': the United States did not need to be mentioned to explain westernness as an inclusive, transatlantic term.[6] Twentieth-century European perceptions of geopolitical questions long lacked the concept of a 'West' as a formation integrally including the United States.

The idea of a 'West' including the USA is absent even in so notable a piece of post First World War geopolitical reflection as Halford Mackinder's *Democratic Ideas and Reality*; its author treated the 'Teutonic' element as an historic component of 'West Europe'.[7] The Frenchman Henri Massis, in 1928, largely ignored the United States and treated 'the West' as synonymous with Catholic Christendom; it was to be defended against a threat from 'the East', from Asiatic culture.[8] Oswald Spengler's book, translated into English as *The Decline of the West*, contained no such thesis. Its German title, *Der Untergang des Abendlandes* (1918–22) expressed a different perspective on geopolitics. Although Spengler wrote of 'the West-European–American' culture, America featured rarely in his text. For Spengler as for most of his generation, 'Western' art and 'Western' thought referred to Western Europe: America was important only as a geographical area to which that culture had been exported.[9]

Winston Churchill, beginning a history of England and America in the 1930s and publishing it in the 1950s with a ringing call to continued co-operation, used no such notion. The English statesman who most strongly emphasized transatlantic affinities referred to 'the British Empire and the United States', and to 'the Western States of Europe' rather than to a 'West' that included America.[10] That idea came from the USA itself, perhaps as late as the Cold War. Even Russian communism sought, in part, to integrate with that older 'West', to reunite with Western Europe (but not the USA) under Soviet leadership.[11] Nor was the USA early in generating another meaning. Even in 1941, a US defence analyst, warning his country of the need soon to engage in the war then raging, took 'the Western world' or 'the Western Hemisphere' to mean North, Central and South America and the adjoining oceans.[12]

Despite an exceptionalist and normative American cultural project, American culture paid the old world an unconscious tribute: 'Western Civilization' in the titles of courses in US universities[13] initially referred to the civilization of western Europe without reference to America. The USA's relationship to this civilization has long been ambiguous and equivocal, as has most recently been shown by bitter conflicts within American academe caused by challenges to restructure the concept into 'World Civilization' at the behest of the ideology of pluralism. The substantial success of these challenges is evidence less of the growing numerical presence of third world minorities within the USA than of the deliberate but long-standing ambiguity of Americans of European descent towards old world norms.

The United States was, had to be, different. Yet American academic disciplines, like American society, have often been equivocal between interpretations of US exceptionalism: unique and therefore paradigmatic, or unique and therefore isolated.

Sometimes American political science appears imperial in its influence across national boundaries and in defining whole realms of enquiry outside the United States. In other instances, American political science appears closed and withdrawn, preoccupied with peculiarly American concerns while ignoring or radically altering discourses appropriated from elsewhere.[14]

American academe, then, posited 'the West' as the arena for cultural conquest, and that is a thesis examined, and partly qualified, here.

The collapse of Nazism in Germany in 1945 left 'a gaping vacuum that could only be filled by the historical thoughts of the victorious powers', what one historian has termed 'the Allied Scheme of History', an orthodoxy which prevailed until challenged by a rival mythology designed to serve the goal of Western European unification.[15] The strategic prominence of 'the Allied Scheme of History' explains the prominence in the research agendas of US history and political science of themes to be condemned, especially German Nazism, and a calculated neglect within the same agendas of themes which supply the unexamined assumptions of that 'Scheme'.

German nationalism was temporarily destroyed in 1945, and, to a large degree, German national identity was destroyed with it. This has given profound encouragement within Germany to the project of 'modernity': modernization, it was assumed, would dissolve national identities in the name of universal values. Per contra, states still displaying national identities must still be in an earlier historical stage. Defeat in war is not a sufficient explanation of this deconstruction of identity, however, for military defeat is at least as often associated with reassertions or reconceptualizations of identity. One of the peculiarities of the German case in 1945, and a decisive one, was the imposition upon German society of an historical and social-scientific perspective on itself that was substantially derived from the modernist national academic enterprise of the United States.

Defeat in 1945 therefore reversed a project that Germany too had promoted, in a German form. As Friedrich Meinecke argued in 1907, the national ideal and the cosmopolitan ideal were not simply antithetical, each excluding the other: rather, both existed in symbiosis.[16] If a nation were different and special, it would have a message and a mission for other nations. Johann Gottfried Herder's theory of the transmission of arts, sciences and culture from one people to another entailed a universalizing world mission for the nation which had reached its zenith – now, Germany in succession to Enlightenment France. Paul Pfizer found a different rationale for the universal role. 'For Fichte and Hegel, the Germans had been the universal people; for Pfizer they were the "cosmopolitan nation". German nationalism was defined as an amalgam of all the traditions – of the classical and the gothic. It represented a grand-scale synthesis, and was permeated by the belief that it drew together the threads of the world's past.' Herder's or Hegel's sense of Germany as the 'bearer of historical development' was carried directly into Engels's model of Germany as the standard-bearer of revolution. In the wider arena, this tendency was made consistent with the drive to protect German industry by tariffs from England's 'universalist or cosmopolitan economics', free trade.[17]

In 1945, this whole model was thrown into reverse by the imposition of 'the Allied Scheme of History'. For geopolitical reasons, this model proved highly resistant to revision. In 1982, Professor Gordon Craig of Stanford University was clear that there was something called 'the West', external to Germany, with which the German Federal Republic had been allied for thirty-five years, but with which it had enjoyed an ambivalent relationship for three hundred years before that. The distinction between the West and Germany began with Germany's 'arrested development' as a result of 'the religious wars of the 16th and 17th centuries'. This historical background led to a 'resistance to modernity' in the nineteenth and twentieth centuries. The Enlightenment was a 'relative failure' in Germany: 'the clinging of local communities to custom and tradition' and 'the influence of religion, always deeply rooted in the German mind' more than offset 'those ideas of social contract and popular sovereignty that were salient features of the Enlightenment in the West'.[18] This polemical doctrine was, to a large degree, internalized in Germany also. In 1984 Wolfgang Mommsen argued that Anglo-German divisions should be traced 'primarily in particular political circumstances and, secondly, in the different pace of economic and political modernization to which the two countries were subjected':[19] 'modernization' still seemed a self-evident route to the present.

If Germany had missed that path, it had, presumably, followed its own aberrant route, a *Sonderweg*. The *Sonderweg* theory, recently most notable in the work of Hans-Ulrich Wehler, was 'based on a fusion of Marxism and Weberian modernization theory'; this fusion established norms by comparison with which German social hierarchies and values 'remained premodern'. Although Wehler conceded something to the critique of David Blackbourn and Geoff Eley in 1980, examined below, the evolution of Wehler's vision in the successive volumes of his *Deutsche Gesellschaftsgeschichte* has evidently resulted chiefly from detailed research into the domestic history of Bismarck's Germany rather than from transnational comparisons.[20]

Academic history was slow to provide an antidote to such assumptions, even though historical writing is becoming steadily more self-conscious and self-reflective. Writers on the history of historiography tend now to congratulate themselves on having escaped the naively self-referential and judgemental histories of their ancestors. But even these volumes on the history of history tend to be preoccupied with the inner workings of national historiographies and to say little or nothing about the ways in which these national historiographies have interacted.[21] Anglo-American historical dissociation, largely the result of present-day US exceptionalism, has been discussed above.[22] This chapter extends the implications of that analysis to consider the relations of those two countries with Germany.

Our starting point is the substantial present-day intellectual isolation of nations. The rise of national historiographies was a normal counterpart of the rise of the nation state, and these historiographies in turn tended to become more self-sufficient and self-referential over time, though with important differences of substance and evolution. The English case shows how intellectual horizons narrowed rather than widened over several centuries. The Reformation encouraged a broad historiography which extended back in time to the early Christian martyrs, and extended sideways geographically to include the adherents of reformed religion everywhere; yet this was a unity that soon dissolved. Foxe's *Book of Martyrs,* which embodied such an international perspective, was reinterpreted to be a founding text of England's national Church,[23] that union of Church and State which was led forward by self-sacrifice to a Providential destiny. The frenzied vision of the religious sectaries of the British civil wars of the 1640s was shaped more by ideas of national destiny than by pan-European expectations. English revolutionaries even defended their liberties by creating an historical interpretation of the uniqueness of the Westminster Parliament and the English common law. This they used to defend Protestantism from what they saw as the threat of international Roman Catholicism and monarchical absolutism or international Calvinism and republicanism.

At the restoration of the English monarchy in 1660, this exceptionalist historiography of common law and Parliament was made part of the Anglican mainstream. Anglicanism, not sectarianism, became the beneficiary of Providential destiny, and Church and State united around a theory of the immemorial antiquity and the rugged independence of the English common law. Against these exceptionalist assumptions, Enlightenment thinkers protested, largely in vain, that mankind was everywhere alike, and that a modern, professionalized historiography left no room for the action of Divine Providence to design a manifest destiny.[24] International links were not wholly erased: some opposition thinkers in England continued to trace English liberties back to shared Germanic institutions, finding the origin of an English parliamentary tradition in the forests of Germany. But this theory derived from an eighteenth-century reading of Tacitus[25] rather than from knowledge of what was at that time being written in any German state. Indeed, the wide unpopularity of the first two Hanoverian kings in Britain from 1714 to 1760 tended to cast the government of the electorate of Hanover, in many British eyes, as a princely despotism, rather than as a cousin in the enterprise of law-bound, Protestant, limited monarchy.[26] Links with Prussia did not entirely offset this.[27]

The American Revolution then isolated Britain from searching contrasts and comparisons with its greatest counterfactual in North America, just as it isolated the United States from serious reflection on its greatest counterfactual, Great Britain. The French Revolution in turn largely defined Britain as antithetical to the international Jacobin 'religion of humanity': British national survival came to depend on the further development of an idea of exceptionalism. Thanks to revolution both America and France were cut off historiographically from Britain, and although some Americans like Jefferson at once applauded the new French republic, the reaction of his countrymen was mixed: US exceptionalism was still stronger than US universalism, and the restoration of the monarchy in France weakened the hold of US universalism still further. No British Tocqueville explained America to the British until Lord Bryce at the end of the nineteenth century.[28] By the time Bryce's *The American Commonwealth* was published in 1888, the British exceptionalist self-image had taken as deep root as had the exceptionalism of the United States, but in different forms: the British self-image rested on an idea of inimitable privilege, the United States' on universalizing but uniquely American moral norms.

Nevertheless, from the 1890s, a pragmatic myth of a supranational 'special relationship' between Britain and the USA was manufactured (perhaps instigated by the British Foreign Office in response to the rise of Germany)[29] which explained to an exceptionalist Britain and an exceptionalist USA how they were both, in reality, pursuing the same ends. Some public figures, in the idiom of Cecil Rhodes, emphasized the ethnic solidarity of what they termed the 'Anglo-Saxon peoples'.[30] Exceptionalism was defused: the paradox of how two allegedly similar allies could both be exceptional was avoided. Yet this comfortable myth created a mutual admiration society and made deep examination of the relations between the two countries unnecessary. Anglo-American relations, in the sphere of historiography, are even now only beginning to emerge from this phase.

It might have been possible to create a more serious, more scholarly intellectual bridge between Britain and Germany in the nineteenth century.[31] Apart from men at either political extreme, many Germans found much in the British experience to be worthy of imitation (even German Gothicism derived chiefly from English Romanticism).[32] Where British and American historians largely ignored each other, British and German historians until Treitschke found much in common.[33] In the nineteenth century, British historiography tended to align itself with German rather than French examples.[34] Oxford undergraduate historians writing their final examination papers do so in a hall dominated by a portrait of Kaiser Wilhelm II, resplendent in the scarlet robes of an Oxford Doctor of Civil Laws. But the events of 1914 and 1939 checked this development. German history, too, had to be defined as antithetical. For reasons largely geopolitical, British historiography in the twentieth century retained its exceptionalism, an exceptionalism qualified mainly by its partial absorption from the 1960s of the priorities of the programmatic historiography, social and political science of the USA.[35]

Developments in continental Europe had a mixed but limited impact on this English exceptionalism. France's weakness in 1914–18 and collapse in 1940 seriously undermined the claims of French cultural ideals to universal validity. The Third Republic provided few persuasive models for

Anglo-French historiographical links.[36] When French historiography revived its universalist claims, especially from Marc Bloch, the *Annales* school and other recent French universalist schools of historical writing were influential chiefly in that other universalist culture, the United States. In Europe, history and historiography from 1917 to 1989 were dominated by a different geopolitical threat, given theoretical expression by the universalizing claims of Marxism: here too, art (or, at least, history) followed life. In so far as each national historiography tried to escape from the grasp of this international doctrine, it did so alone, by emphasizing that universal Marxist models did not fit its specific national pattern. So the escape from Marxism, in history and in historiography, did not promote historical integration. German historians were still left to explore their sense of a *Sonderweg*.

The European Union looks as if it should be premised upon an already reintegrated pan-European historiography, but this would be hard to demonstrate. Only after the EU had come into being, indeed after it had existed for many years, did its bureaucracy begin to fund historical writing dedicated to revealing unsuspected similarities between the inconveniently diverse track records of European states. So far, this has made little difference to the ways in which the domestic national histories of member states of the EU are constructed. The EU was not built on any previously existing historical theory generated from within Europe: in so far as it was built on an historical theory at all, it was an American one, the result of the post-1945 desire of the USA to promote a United States of Europe as a solution to Europe's political disasters of the twentieth century.[37]

So European historiographies failed in recent decades to build many or strong bridges between themselves. The collapse of Russian Communism left one superpower, the USA, and one superpower in historical writing, again the historical profession of the United States, a profession numerically larger, financially better provided, and more self-referential than any that has ever existed before. It was a profession still widely committed to universalizing goals, formerly described in terms of democracy, now partly redescribed in terms of pluralism and multiculturalism. In Europe, many national historiographies have, to different degrees, been swayed by a massive amalgam of the historiography, political science and sociology of the USA.

Which perspective predominates is a matter of historical diplomacy, especially the mediations which established the relationship between the historiographies of Britain and the USA; yet this relationship is not symmetrical. In Britain during recent decades, scholars of many persuasions have been engaged in research and reconceptualization that have fundamentally altered the general map of the British past; but in the USA, historical initiatives in the 1960s that threatened to have similar effects were absorbed and rendered harmless. The American public myth emerged as essentially unreconstructed, indeed strengthened. Even British historians working in the USA have not systematically challenged this consolidation and reassertion of the American historical self-image. Indeed the models of British history being projected to an American audience in recent years by British expatriates have encouraged an American rejection of the old association of British and American national historiographies, and have done so in ways that cut the USA off from the consequences of recent historiography in Britain.[38]

II. THE NEW HISTORY OF BRITAIN AND ITS GEOPOLITICAL IMPLICATIONS

Wolfgang Mommsen rightly maintained that 'the idea of a German *Sonderweg* is no more, but also no less, a myth than the idealised notion of British progress towards democracy, which served it as a counter-factual model'. He called, instead, for a study of British and German 'developmental paths' which explored both the differences and the similarities: these had 'far more in common with each other than with most other European nations'. British and German divergence, he claimed, really began to accelerate after the defeat of Prussian Liberals by Bismarck in the 1860s, and after German Liberals parted company from their working class in the same decade.[39]

Both countries found historical means of arguing for their special mission in the world: England's proved by the continuity which inscribed broadening libertarian precedent so clearly on the pages of history; Germany's similarly shown by the same quite contrary discontinuities in which some great national achievement was snatched away at the last moment by catastrophe. For Germans, national mission was to be sought in the *Volkseele* and identified by *Geistesgeschichte*; for the English it was to be sought in institutions and identified by constitutional history.[40] For both, it was powerful.

Yet British historiography has developed, and those ancient certainties no longer hold. What, then, are the major themes in British history that need to be included in a better assessment of its links with continental European history? General understanding of the points of contact has not kept pace with the research which in recent years has seen a reconstruction of many of the basic components of English and British history.[41] The picture of Britain that has emerged has often emphasized ideological conflict rather than the progressive consensus that was formerly alleged to have aligned Britain with the USA as distinct from Europe. Against the old picture of steady and continual change, validating a Whiggish teleology, new accounts have balanced long continuities with distantly spaced but catastrophic discontinuities, discontinuities that were formerly sanitized as benign stages of modernizing evolution, but that now appear as dominated by contingency or open to development along alternative counterfactual paths.[42]

From being a precocious but exemplary model of modernity, eventually falling behind the even more advanced modernity of the Thirteen Colonies, British society now seems to have had more the features of a successful *ancien régime*, some persisting even after 1832. But these features had little in common with the caricatures of repression, rigidity, immobility or hostility to intellectual enquiry that the term *ancien régime* once conventionally denoted: that is, British 'modernity' was understood differently from the definitions current in recent American political science. We now see that there are many ways of reconciling authority and innovation; as Shmuel Eisenstadt has shown for the case of Japan, the recent American model is not applicable even in a society which was (like Germany) subject to military conquest and ideological re-education by the USA.[43]

For British history, a variety of scholars have proposed theses in different centuries which now join up to form a new outline. In the pre-Conquest period, scholars have shown the significance of the Anglo-Saxon 'strong state' for the long-term characteristics of English state formation.[44] This is in no sense a shared Anglo-American process, part of democracy's historic mandate. State formation and liberal democracy do not necessarily go together; in European history, they have done so rather seldom. Military survival, bureaucratic centralization and a Providential sense of destiny now emerge as the leading themes. American federalism itself has come under scrutiny as a process of normative state formation not intended by many of those who embarked on the exercise of rebellion.

Nor is state formation, in the English case, any longer an aspect of a process of 'modernization', chronologically located at a debatable date between the 'medieval' and the fully 'modern'. Alan Macfarlane has argued for a quite different model of England's medieval starting-point, a monetarized economy resting on law-bound security of property and the nuclear family. If so, 'individualism' has to be reconceptualized as something consistent with strong corporatist elements of English society clearly present from an early period to the seventeenth and eighteenth centuries, if not later: no longer is 'individualism' the midwife of 'modernity' by being antithetical to the values of an *ancien régime*, and no longer does it seem axiomatic to write of the culture of the USA as individualistic in a sense which England did not share.[45]

In respect of social structures, it follows also that in England there was in no strong sense a 'feudal' social order to be overthrown by a 'bourgeois revolution' in the 1640s. This being so, the whole concept of a watershed between pre-modernity and modernity, a 'transition from feudalism to capitalism', has been undermined. This is more than a rejection of Marxism in its geopolitical dimension: it is a rejection of the myth that an exemplary and programmatic US exceptionalism can be discerned long before 1776, from the earliest period of the establishment of the colonies.[46] Such an argument would realign England, and to a degree the Thirteen Colonies before 1776, more closely to European patterns.

In the history of religion, it no longer seems sufficient to treat England, in any simple sense, as a state whose religious complexion gave her an essential affinity with her North American settlements. The reinterpretation of Puritanism means that Scots and Scots–Irish Presbyterianism, English Dissent and theological heterodoxy after 1660 are now leading themes of colonial intellectual dynamics. Glenn Burgess has shown that English 'absolutism' was a centrist, not an extreme, position:[47] the claim of the American constitutionalist tradition, as described by American historians from McIlwain until Hexter, to be a shared transatlantic tradition invites reappraisal, as do Anglo-European parallels. Cromwell's state was a strong state, the pioneer in efficient tax-raising,[48] and

Cromwell proved to be as impatient of his Parliaments as Charles I had been: republicanism was far from being inherently libertarian, as its history in the 1650s and later in North America sufficiently demonstrated.

It has been argued that the English, Scots and Irish civil wars of the 1640s did not signal the arrival of modernity, any more than did 1776. If so, the American Revolution looks more important in recent historiography than it did before, but important as the definitive establishment of American exceptionalism rather than because it emancipated Americans into a normative modernity. The conflicts in the British Isles in the 1640s had much in common with the pan-European problem of which the Thirty Years' War was Germany's version. Yet the English Restoration of 1660 reversed the events of the 1640s, just as the Peace of Westphalia in 1648 provided a lasting settlement; among the most turbulent episodes of the period, only the revolution of 1776 was never reversed. Although England's demographic regime was significantly different from that of continental Europe, the larger contrasts were between Europe, including Britain and the USA.

In ideological terms, neither the 1640s nor even 1688 created a bourgeois society in England. This dissolution of the bourgeois model of modernity has profound geopolitical implications, and the study of status, hierarchy and the hereditary principle has moved England somewhat towards the intellectual milieux of continental Europe. There were important dissimilarities, but not always ones that identified England as more libertarian. Most notably, Henry VIII's fusion of Church and State created a state form unusually powerful in European terms, and England was no stranger to the continental principle *cuius regio, eius religio*. With respect to political ideology, as to much else, the American republic was not built on British foundations: it was a rejection of them. There was no 'age of democratic revolution', as R. R. Palmer influentially claimed at the high water mark of liberal democracy, either in North America or, by communication, in France.[49] We now see that democracy is not an essential component of a 'western' model.

British historians have finally laid to rest Victorian assumptions of the steady, purposeful unfolding down the ages of a model of Parliamentary democracy and the rule of law. No longer can the American Revolution be traced to a 'democratic deficit' in the England of the 1770s, and no longer is it possible to explain that revolution, or the early American republic, as essentially concerned with democracy. Here again, with respect to doctrines of representative government, there was no single 'Western' model. British scholarship suggests a reconsideration of the origins of the democratic ideals which we had once assumed were shared on both sides of the Atlantic and a reconsideration of their development in the last two centuries.

It was once common for German historians to appeal to an exemplary liberal-parliamentarian image of Victorian England as a critique of Wilhelmine Germany,[50] but that image has been significantly qualified. For the English case, research into the nineteenth century means that liberal democracy has lost its teleology. Liberalism is no longer seen as a simple expression of middle-class or 'bourgeois' self-interest. If there is 'no such thing as society' (that is, if society is an idea and not a natural formation, developed at a particular time as a way of intervening in a debate over the political authority of the state) then the state can no longer be seen as any more of an authoritarian imposition than are any other ways of categorizing the public realm. 'State' and 'society' are both ideas, not things. Each is 'constructed'; neither is just 'out there', with a simple meaning.

The alleged contradiction between a modern, industrial economic 'structure' and an unmodernized political 'superstructure' represented by the persistent hegemony of old elites was a trope of political polemic, latterly most clearly associated with Marxism. Yet it was a model imprecise enough to be stretched to cover many cases. If it was used to create the idea of a German *Sonderweg*, it was used also to reproach Britain's political structure in the nineteenth and twentieth centuries for being out of line with economic 'realities', whether in post-war Marxist historiography or in the party-political polemics of the 1960s. What has changed in historical scholarship is an increasing unwillingness to label some things 'modern', others 'pre-modern'; an increasing scepticism about arranging ideas or social formations in binary antitheses.

The 'Industrial Revolution' in Britain, once seen as the archetype of industrialization everywhere, has been a major target for historical reconsideration.[51] Where an older tradition treated it as a transformative event, occurring in the 1780s,[52] a phenomenon of which all forms of economic and social change were integrally related aspects, recent historiography has disaggregated this fictional unity and replaced a revolutionary model with an evolutionary one. Revolution as catastrophic transformation must now be sought elsewhere, both in its causes and its effects.[53] By contrast, economic change was incremental; its authors and subjects (including even the political economists of *c*. 1800–30) did not interpret what was happening as the replacement of an old world by a new until a late date, and even then only a few of them made that claim.[54]

Economic growth, moreover, followed significantly different pathways in all societies that came to be grouped under the category 'industrial':[55] again, there was no single 'Western' model, outlined by some objective and universally valid inner logic of historical evolution. If the absence of such an inner logic is now clear even in as quantifiable a field as this, the future of ideal-typical models in other fields looks bleak. There were, of course, similarities. Germany was dominated by conflicts between agrarians and industrialists, but Britain had similar debates over the Corn Laws, culminating in their divisive and symbolic repeal in 1846. Differences in political outcomes between Britain and Germany can no longer easily be traced to 'structural' economic differences.

Where an older historiography treated manufacturing industry and agriculture as irreconcilable enemies, in the manner of David Ricardo's economic analysis, recent historiography has shown a much more varied pattern. Many British landowners at all times had interests in commerce and the professions, and many merchants bought land, if not the largest estates. The largest landowners were prominent in urban development and mining. Even manufacturing industry in the nineteenth century did not prove to be as incompatible with the landed interest as the controversy over the repeal of the Corn Laws in 1846 suggests. It was the rise of agriculture in the new world, not the rise of industry in Britain, which produced an agricultural recession from the 1870s. In general, the ideal of the 'middling orders' in Britain was a professional ideal, not a manufacturing ideal, and this professional ideal had long played a major political role.[56] If the German middle orders existed in a close relationship with the old aristocracy, this was a familiar pattern in Britain and perhaps in France also.

Harold James argued that 'Germany's historical peculiarity in the nineteenth century lay in the close association between nation-building and economic evolution',[57] but a comparative study would show a similar association, although of a different shape, in the case of Britain. Where this German model of national identity was destroyed by the First World War, leading to a reassertion of the 'cultural and political versions of nationalism' in the form of Nazism,[58] Britain, by military victory, experienced no such transposition of the rationales for identity. The Weimar Republic (1919–32) reverted to a democratic version of the 'economic idea of the nation', and this in turn was destroyed by economic dislocation. Britain experienced similar, though lesser, dislocation, and this equally produced the destruction of the Liberal Party, the abandonment of the free-trade version of British identity and the temporary suspension of party government. Yet economic similarities did not compel political conformity, and Britain's political response to mass unemployment in the 1930s was quite different to Germany's.

Class and class formation in England is a related area that has seen fundamental historiographical change. Where an older historiography posited three historical actors, the upper, middle and lower classes, which did *this* or failed to do *that*, recent historiography treats 'class' as a descriptive language, not as a reified group.[59] Even social reform has been freed from its implicit Whig teleology and re-examined as a disparate collection of projects with different ideological origins, serving different interest groups, and with widely differing outcomes, some benign, others unhappy. In this respect as in others, the aspirations of a 'bourgeoisie' are no longer synonymous with a normative social modernity.

The new historiography of England and Britain therefore corrects a widespread German misapprehension of English society that can be dated at least to Hegel.[60] It offers a model which does not shy away from the themes of authority, the strong state, the persistence and renewal of elites. In this last respect, British and German experiences diverge chiefly after 1918.[61] During the nineteenth century, Britain was distinguished not by a homogeneous Liberal egalitarianism but by the coexistence of apparent opposites: the meritocratic, free-trading ethic of Bentham, Cobden and Bright, and the patrician, military, public-service ethic of its elites.[62] The same combination was evident in nineteenth-century Germany also, and it was in Germany that the old elites were far more seriously threatened by the late nineteenth century: the socialist revolution was rightly expected in Germany, not Britain.[63]

Something like it indeed materialized in Germany in 1918–19. In Britain, the elites remained in control; the rise of Labour was contained. It may be that the elites' social role was larger in Britain, given British plebeians' persistent resistance to education; yet in the exigencies of war this leadership by British elites was successfully depicted as a national and patriotic act. In Germany, the same elites made a final bid in 1933 to regain control through a deal with Hitler, with results that are familiar. The entire elimination of traditional elites, and the discrediting of hierarchical attitudes, was a consequence of defeat in 1945 and of re-education by an occupying power. This geopolitical experience confirmed a traditional German vision of England, a vision which German historiography has seldom thereafter challenged: for half a century after 1945, German academics were seldom drawn to explore differences between Britain and the USA. In Britain, by contrast, despite powerful pacifist sentiments, victory in two world wars substantially preserved the ideal of the military–public service ethic until the 1960s, and the final revolution against a society of corporatism and prescription has been symbolically dated to the election as Prime Minister of Margaret Thatcher in 1979.

Now that Britain's 'world we have lost' finally *is* lost, it becomes possible to analyse it historically, and to place it on the historical map in relation to its European neighbours. Such a study reveals neither essential similarities nor essential dissimilarities. Claims that Britain is 'at the heart of Europe' or that Britain enjoys, on the contrary, a 'special relationship' with the USA based on essential affinities are in both cases political, not historical.

III.   BRITAIN AND GERMANY: THE CASE FOR PARTIAL
        REINTEGRATION

A German audience may find surprisingly familiar some of the themes in this discussion of the historiographical relations between Britain and the USA, for the debates on British and American exceptionalism are debates on the alleged existence of a shared British and American *Sonderweg*, and must have important consequences for the same debate in Germany too. As English historians have recently understood it, the idea of a *Sonderweg* was a German attempt to identify analytically the features of German history that distinguished it from 'the West' or from 'Western values'. Before 1945 this attempt was often meant to praise those distinguishing features; after the 1960s it generally had a negative connotation; but the analysis was similar. Yet that concept focused almost wholly on one half of the problem, of what the leading characteristics of German history were; little was said about how far opposite characteristics were really shared in the rest of Europe or North America.

Political imperatives still tend to override serious comparison. Most recently, a German attempt to escape from the isolating idea of a *Sonderweg* has taken a form that echoes the integrationist project of the European Union. Some people had argued that what Friedrich Meinecke called the 'German catastrophe' of the Third Reich meant a 'loss of history', a de-historicization of national life in the pursuit of modernist prosperity. But this de-historicization has not worked itself out to completion in Germany. On the contrary, it has led to a reaction: as Hagen Schulze explained, 'One can never begin anew but only pick up the threads of the past and continue. People who believe they have undertaken something completely new in fact do not really know what they are doing'.

Schulze provided a survey reintegrating Germany with the rest of Europe, in which 'The origins of German history lie not in the primeval forests of the north but in Rome... There was no higher status than being a Roman citizen; the apostle Paul was just as proud of it as Hermann (Arminius), tribal chief of the Cherusci, despite their differences with Rome' – in the latter's case extending to his famous defeat of the legions of Quinctilius Varus in AD 9, a 'decisive battle' hitherto often taken to mark the failure of Rome to extend its empire to central Europe and the event that guaranteed the future development of a separate German culture. The key event, for Schulze, was the division of the Roman Empire, producing a lasting dualism: 'Rome and Byzantium, Roman Catholicism and the Eastern Orthodox Church, the liberal West and the Slavophile East, ultimately the culture of democracy and human rights versus the Bolshevist system of the Soviet Union'. Germany was to be identified with the former. By contrast, Schulze dispenses with the idea of ethnic or linguistic continuities uniting a 'German' people since the early Middle Ages.[64]

This reinterpretation is not new, for the idea of German distinctiveness has taken different forms in different periods. In the nineteenth century, most notably in Hegel and Treitschke, it indicated a moral or metaphysical superiority of German civilization and its consequent world mission. After 1945, the valuation placed on this phenomenon was inverted: the *Sonderweg* became the analysis that explained Germany's catastrophe, and assigned responsibility for it. It was an idea which was, however, now increasingly explained in new ways, less and less by a distinct German character or ideology, more and more by borrowings from 'Western' (but in reality mostly American) political science, sociology and history, disciplines that provided structured accounts of an array of functional or structural aberrancies in past German society.

This critique had earlier origins, including domestic German political polemic in the 1890s and the condemnation of Germany framed by Oxford historians during the First World War, but the internalization of this model in Germany must be dated to the decades after 1945. The substantial borrowings of history (but especially American history) from the social sciences in the later twentieth century meant that the contribution of these disciplines was essentially similar, and history did not provide the necessary corrective to the others. In England, the resistance to the social sciences mounted by historians like Sir Geoffrey Elton meant that the picture was somewhat different even in the 1960s and 1970s, and was able to develop in fundamentally different ways in the 1980s and 1990s; but by then a quite different analysis had already taken hold.

Some doubts were indeed expressed. Even in the early 1980s, the point was hesitantly made (in Britain, not Germany) that most German accounts of a *Sonderweg* had assumed the existence of a single Western model, by comparison with which the German experience was aberrant, without examining that Western model closely enough.[65] This argument was not then developed. Since the early 1980s, however, the changes in British historiography discussed in this book must alter the terms in which the German debate has been conducted. It is a development which neither American historiography, still committed to its normative project, nor German historiography, still atoning for national guilt by deferring to that project, has recognized. The significance of new accounts of British history for this debate is to suggest that there is no single Western model, and that the German and the English experiences are closer than was assumed in earlier debates over the German *Sonderweg*. Yet this relevance of the two cases has been overlooked, and initially was perhaps unwelcome.[66]

Unlike British exceptionalism, the idea of German exceptionalism was formed late, in its modern sense in opposition to the French Revolution. German responses to the American Revolution suggest no such alignment. In so far as the war of 1776–83 was international, it was one that aligned Britain and her German allies against Americans and their French allies, and the impact of the American example in Germany after 1783 was far less than its inspirational effect in France.[67] Recent scholarship has emphasized the similarities between 1776 and 1789, where earlier histories written by and for Americans tended to dissociate them. Other states opposed the French Revolution in similar terms, including Britain, Spain and Russia, and with similar results for national self-images. Although each was different, none was unique. After 1789, Britain and many German states were drawn together. Both the American and French Revolutions now encourage us to think of Anglo-German similarities.

In nineteenth-century Germany, German exceptionalism came to be defined as a combination of features that were held to be incompatible elsewhere: it was meant 'to exalt the particular German combination of political, economic, military, and educational institutions: monarchy and industrial success, university and army'.[68] But with the substitution of 'navy' for 'army', such an analysis now seems to have much more in common with the British case than it once did. The strength of the old order in England after 1660 meant that many features survived the sweeping reforms of 1828–35: Victorian England, and still more Victorian Britain, is now seen as a combination of old and new rather than as the achievement of rational modernity alone.

From the 1870s German separatism reasserted itself in the form of a mystical theory of racial community at odds with the cold modernism of liberal economics.[69] These assumptions were manifest in many fields: in history with Heinrich Treitschke, in philosophy with Friedrich Nietzsche, in music with Richard Wagner. Of these, Treitschke departed least from the 'historical–economic consensus' of mid nineteenth-century Germany about the roots of nationalism. Yet here too Britain produced some apparently parallel examples, though never identical copies:[70] in history, J. R. Seeley and J. A. Froude; in philosophy, the idealists T. H. Green and Bernard Bosanquet; in the arts, William Morris, Rudyard Kipling, Edward Elgar, Edwin Lutyens. If German thought had an anti-Semitic component rare in Britain, British identity had an imperialist element that was equally a minor theme in Germany. 'History is not concerned with individuals except as members of a state' was a sentence written by an Englishman, indeed a Regius Professor of History at Cambridge.[71] 'In great extremities the eloquent tongues fall silent. The heart of the nation is in its armies' was a pronouncement of his successor.[72]

Explanations for an alleged German exceptionalism are weak not least because they apply in considerable measure to Britain also, where the outcome was very different. First, the geographical. It is argued that a Germany in a *Mittellage*, caught between East and West, challenged by coalitions of hostile neighbours and with no natural borders, would be more embroiled in military conflict and so less libertarian than a Western 'norm'.[73] Yet a maritime Britain equally lacked natural defences, for the ocean opened the islands to seaborne invasion from every side.[74] The history of the British Isles since the Romans is equally a history of successful invasions (the last now dated to 1688) or invasions repulsed. Despite the naval press gangs, the geographical displacement of the exercise of state power to the high seas meant that England could seem much less authoritarian at home than it did to its maritime rivals, or even than English power did to its Welsh, Irish and Scottish neighbours in the British Isles.

Despite these lasting dangers, the English experience was less and less dominated by politicized armed forces. The apolitical nature of the army was one lasting result of 1642 and 1688. In so far as the disasters of the twentieth century unfolded from the tragic error of 1914, the geopolitical determinism of the *Mittellage* idea depends on an interpretation of the origins of the First World War; yet here, at least for English readers, Fritz Fischer decisively shifted causal responsibility on to human agency and away from any putative inevitable processes.[75] The myth of German 'encirclement' up to 1914 has not survived historical research. 'Encirclement' was not an independent reality, but a perception created in German minds as a result of voluntary German actions: in the early twentieth century, in part as a result of the decision to build a battle-fleet to rival Britain's. 'Their own decisions and actions, taken on their own responsibility, meant that within the first ten years of the new century, the Germans were excluded from the international community and faced a hostile formation around them.'[76] Geopolitical determinism seems more ineffective as an explanation of the American case, for the absence of military rivals on the North American continent has not prevented the emergence of a popular culture in the USA in which interpersonal violence and national military force are notoriously glamorized. Nor does the *Mittellage* thesis explain those many other continental European states, caught between potential enemies on either side, that displayed a quite different pattern of political development to Germany's.

The 'strong state' clearly means different things in different historiographical traditions. Some historians praise it as the necessary agency of sweeping social reform, others value it as a bulwark against such reform; some see the strength of the state in shared law and access to legal redress, others in a police or army able to resist challenges to the authority of the government. The English and German ideas of the strong state include many such divergences, but they include many similarities also. In the German empire created in 1871, historians have suggested that imperial ministers and the military were beyond the control of a Reichstag that was, in itself, highly democratic (it was elected on universal manhood suffrage). In Britain, we now trace the royal appointment of ministers much later than we did, at least to the first decade of the nineteenth century, and the ministry's control of foreign and military affairs, largely unrevised by Parliament, for far longer. The weakness of the House of Commons in the face of party-political and ministerial manipulation is indeed a constant theme of historians of twentieth-century Britain, and that weakness has evidently increased into the twenty-first. In both states, mass political participation in elections did not necessarily mean effective democratic control.

Not all cases of the exercise of state power have catastrophic consequences: historians often implicitly sanction, for example, episodes which fall into the category of 'state formation'. If Bismarck's German state was united around Prussia, the United Kingdom was united by the military power of its dominant component, England. Yet where England exercised an intellectual hegemony which sanitized this process in the name of English values (the rule of law, representative government, Anglicanism, trade), Prussia failed fully to appropriate a German nationalism with deep roots in liberalism. If the German empire had a militarist air, it nevertheless spent little more of its Gross National Product per head on military uses in the years 1870–1913 than did Britain.[77]

The old idea that a 'refeudalization' of German society took place in the late nineteenth century, partly through the purge of liberals from the bureaucracy by the Prussian Minister of the Interior, has not survived recent scrutiny.[78] This development has occurred in parallel with the recovery by historians of political thought of English and British national identity in the eighteenth century as essentially libertarian; one scholar, in the light of this work, has reinterpreted early German 'nationalists' like Wieland, Lessing, Goethe, Möser and Hamann, and found them to be expressing either a principled cosmopolitanism or a virtuous and libertarian attitude to their public duties, albeit one which found its liberty in the positive duties of the *Ständestaat*, and came to attach a special significance to the German language.[79]

If Germany's internal constitution was partly shaped by external military necessities, so was England's: the expedients used to fund the Royal Navy and imperial defence were defining moments in the formation of the English and then the British 'strong state': the suppression of the monasteries, Ship Money, Cromwell's excise duties, the Navigation Acts, the Stamp Act, Pitt's income tax.[80] Thanks to Henry VIII's squandering the revenue from the sale of monastic lands (partly on military attempts to win back extensive territorial possessions in France), the English case was different in the early-modern period chiefly because these fiscal devices did not produce a financially independent monarchy. Nor was Britain without its catastrophes in this area, as 1776 above all showed. If Germany was compromised by expansion in the twentieth century, so was Britain in the eighteenth, with equally disastrous results. The transatlantic empire, uniting Britain with the Thirteen Colonies, was Britain's version of Germany's *grossdeutsch* aspiration; the dismembered empire which survived in 1783 was Britain's counterpart to the *kleindeutsch* reality. Britain survived in 1783, as Prussia survived after defeat at the hands of Napoleon in 1806, but survived making a different use of state power.

In Germany, the *kleindeutsch* model of German unification after Bismarck came to seem obvious and natural: the absorption of the component parts of the Holy Roman Empire in North Germany by Prussian military power and around a Prussian axis, excluding Austria. As at least one distinguished study has now emphasized, this process was in no way overdetermined but was dominated by contingency, most obviously by the extremely narrow margin of the Prussian victory over Austria at the battle of Königgrätz in 1866.[81] In Britain, the 'Three Kingdoms' model of early seventeenth-century conflicts has enforced a similar conclusion on the pattern of state formation around its English core. This, too, now seems dominated by contingency, and a corollary has quickly followed: no longer do we assume the force and homogeneity of a 'British' identity.

A second explanation of the *Sonderweg* has proposed a distinct German mentality which allegedly exalted the irrational, glorified militarism and valued the obedience of the subject. If this model is still entertained by German historians, it is an area where differences with England (though not, perhaps, with a militaristic United States) will be most marked, but they will be less marked than they seemed to be when John Locke was hailed as the framer of the ruling liberal consensus established in England in 1688. Yet this sort of argument from English national character is hardly now maintained by historians. Instead, they acknowledge how, in a different idiom, the duties of the subject and a glorification of naval conquest were features first of English and then aos of British society. The acquisition and administration of the second British empire in the eighteenth century and the third in the nineteenth clearly had effects on British character; it would be hard to argue that British differences from the German case were *essential* differences. The discrediting of racialist theories of history has, of course, undermined one of the original sources of the German sense of separateness; but that discrediting has also, by the same token, undermined the original basis for the idea of an Anglo-American special relationship, the Anglo-Saxon kinship of the 'English-speaking peoples' devised in the 1890s.

A familiar critique of German public thought has focused on its proclivity to reify abstractions and to reduce plural historical experiences to the unified object of *Geistesgeschichte*, a discernment of the unifying spirit of ideas and institutions and the attribution to them of a drive to self-fulfilment. However true this was of an older German historiography intellectually indebted to Hegel, recent English-language scholarship in the history of ideas, and especially the history of political thought, has revealed a similar pattern of reification and the ascription of teleologies acting to inflate the privileged categories of 'Western' (but especially American) values and institutions. The older German methodology has been discredited since 1945; the Anglophone version remains in need of historical explanation.[82]

In so far as German militarism is explained in terms of economic backwardness in relation to Britain (the greater role in German society of the Junkers), this argument is severely qualified by the discovery that landowning was far more concentrated into great estates in Britain than in Germany even in the late nineteenth century: in England, 'Many Junkers would have been considered yeoman farmers'. In respect of the distribution of wealth and income it was again Britain that displayed the greatest inequality, while Germany was 'limping along behind in a crowd together with the liberal republics, France and the United States'.[83]

Most important, German historiography since the 1960s seems to have defended the concept of a *Sonderweg* on a third and different ground. What has been called the 'failure of Western-style liberal democracy to take root in Germany' has been attributed to a structural or stadial failure, a disjunction between economic development on one hand and political forms on the other: 'According to this reading, the central point about Germany's passage to "modernity" was the lack of synchronisation between the economic, social, and political spheres. Germany did not have a bourgeois revolution of the normal kind associated with England, France or the United States.'[84]

This was, in origin, a German argument. The critique of the Wilhelmine state as one dominated by an entrenched feudal elite in alliance with the army, bureaucracy and Church was first mounted by German liberals in the 1880s, continued in the writings of Max Weber, and restated during the First World War by Thorstein Veblen: like England's 'Whig interpretation of history', it was political polemic before it became academic analysis.[85] Its hour came, however, when it was taken to the USA in the 1930s by émigrés like Alexander Gerschenkron and Hans Rosenberg. They then came to typify American perspectives on the question:

> By the 1960s such concepts were reimported into Germany and served as a major intellectual source for contemporary historians such as Jürgen Kocka, Hans-Ulrich Wehler, and Heinrich August Winkler. Ralf Dahrendorf also assimilated them into his influential liberal critique of conservatives and corporatist social-democrats in *Society and Democracy in Germany* [1967]. By the late 1960s the paradigm of flawed modernization had apparently come to dominate German historiography.[86]

The German bourgeoisie was presented in this model as having failed to do what other bourgeoisies allegedly did, namely to emancipate itself and assert self-interested, separate, commercial, liberal-democratic values, in opposition both to the state and to the traditional patrician landed elite. Instead, the German bourgeoisie was held to have compromised, to have entered an association with the Wilhelmine state machine, and capitulated to the values of the Junker landowners, the officer corps, and the Prussian bureaucracy.[87] It has been cogently urged in reply that this picture was misconceived, and that the Wilhelmine state was, in many respects, 'highly modern'.[88] But even in so far as this older model was accurate, it now seems much closer to the British case than it did in the 1960s.

Britain had no bourgeois revolution, for – as historians now admit – there was no 'normal' bourgeois revolution waiting to happen.[89] A central but unexamined assumption of the *Sonderweg* theorists was the authoritarian, anti-rational, illiberal nature of pre-industrial values, surviving into the recent past to frustrate German modernization: here too, recent writing on British history has knocked away this prop by revealing science, technological advance and commerce as consistent with older political and social forms rather than antithetical to them. In eighteenth-century Britain, the middling orders normally subscribed to patrician values and pursued assimilation rather than class confrontation. Britain's schools and universities were most noted for a diversion away from 'scholarship for its own sake' to the creation of an imperial public-service elite, not a meritocracy, still less a class of technocrats and manufacturers.[90] Given the popularity among the middling orders of the values and ideals of the old elite, it is by no means clear what 'bourgeois' values are supposed to have been: perhaps, after all, the 'bourgeoisie' was only an ideal type, nowhere existing in nature.

The Reform Act of 1832 was not a moment of middle-class empowerment. Even subsequent extensions of the franchise in the nineteenth century were limited and ambiguous in their creation of a democratic state.[91] As has been correctly observed,

A comparison with other industrializing countries in the nineteenth century suggests that it is very difficult to maintain that industrialization failed to bring democracy with it only in the German case. France, for instance, underwent authoritarian episodes both after its successful revolution (under Napoleon I) and at the height of the industrialization process (under Napoleon III), while Britain industrialized only under conditions of a very limited franchise and, from the 1790s to the 1820s, with draconian laws against political radicalism that far outdid any of the restrictions imposed on the Social Democrats in Imperial Germany in the late nineteenth century.[92]

In England, the behaviour of the middle orders has often been examined through electoral studies; but here too, 'Why should the behavior in England known as "deference politics", which supposedly helped entrench parliamentary liberalism, be condemned as a prop of the *Obrigkeitsstaat* (authoritarian state) in Germany?'[93]

From an English perspective, insights into the alleged nature of German exceptionalism have been dominated by geopolitical imperatives since 1914 if not before. The early English critique of German National Socialism focused on questions of national character, ideology and individual agency. It sought to construct a long genealogy for German absolutism and realpolitik,[94] or to treat Hitler as an irresistible force.[95] But this was not unique to Nazism: 'it was primarily Oxford historians who developed this interpretation of German history during the First World War'.[96] A more functional interpretation of the 1930s diverted attention from Germany to blame Baldwin and Chamberlain for not resisting Hitler resolutely at an earlier stage, and eventually issued in a functional reappraisal of German foreign policy which treated Germany as one of many players in the international state system, not as a nation marked out from the 'West' by essential differences.[97] This thesis proved controversial for allegedly failing to attend to the enormity of the Holocaust, and in retrospect it is clear that moral condemnation of National Socialism, anti-Semitism and war crimes obscured the separate question of whether German society had been essentially different from its neighbours for a long time before 1914. Only recently, perhaps, is it possible to show how, in some respects not related to anti-Semitism, Nazi policies can be seen as continuations of German policy in former eras, not least in the drive to annex territory and secure a world hegemony that was identified in Wilhelmine foreign policy by Fritz Fischer.[98]

Differences between Britain and Germany were not invented by British historians as First World War propaganda, but were clearly demonstrable in the historical record. The German army was significantly more important, and more autonomous;[99] the bureaucracy stronger;[100] the development of national consciousness later, 1848 being a key moment of its mature emergence.[101] English unity as a state (if not a nation state in the sense of the liberal nationalists of 1848) was as old as the Anglo-Saxons, and centralized currency, law and administration of justice distinguished it clearly even at that early period from the German-speaking territories within the Holy Roman Empire. While the institutions of the Empire at Wetzlar, Regensburg and elsewhere never developed much force as national symbols, the Westminster Parliament did so from an early date;[102] yet it built its Whig myth of steadily broadening representative government on the ruins of those local representative assemblies within the British Isles which it suppressed or absorbed, notably the Edinburgh and Dublin Parliaments.

The differences, then, were real, but the similarities have not been weighed: British success depended on naval victory; the Holy Roman Empire had important traditions of political representation, far stronger than those of France; the Lutheran link of Church and State in the 'magisterial Reformation' was closely related to England's, and distinguished England's reformed but magisterial ecclesiastical polity from Calvinist ones. In 1941, Rohan Butler observed:

> Thinkers of the West who find German thought contemptible might perhaps do well to review the tenets of their own belief and to ponder a little upon those ideals which stand so close to German speculation: the rule of the many by the abler few, recognition of the fact that blood will tell, a community conjoined by ties more lovable than cash and interest, a society in which all work for all, in which efficiency and enterprise find just reward, a social order that is not static but moving with the sweep of life itself, a supernatural order inspired by the splendid scope of the undertaking rather than an international order dependent upon the shifts of politicians, politics that are philosophy made real, the discovery of the new faith that is to carry on where Christianity left off, elevating mankind to nobler achievements and to a higher destiny.[103]

Arno Mayer's picture of an old order being prevalent in Europe until 1914 needs to be rethought in the light of British historiography since the publication of his book in 1981.[104] Perhaps British exceptionalism and

German exceptionalism were both correct, and wrong chiefly in that the exceptionalisms had significant similarities.

IV.   THE NORMATIVE PROJECT OF AMERICAN ACADEME

An old order, then, was more prevalent, and more powerful, than we thought. The differences between European societies, and their real points of similarity despite their differences, have been obscured; and that obscuring of the obvious has much to do with the universalizing claims of modernism. It was during and after the French Revolution that the new American republic evolved in its interpretation of itself and in its perception by others from a unique structure towards a universal model. The American Revolution, in the minds of more and more people, was transposed from being a singular event, justified only because it was unique, into an ongoing process, offering emancipation to all men everywhere. The French Revolution set a similar example, but the lid was repeatedly placed on Pandora's Box by the restored Bourbons, by Louis Philippe, and by Napoleon III. Only the United States was free to develop such a sense of world mission in the long term. Yet even here, America was torn between isolationism (premised on a view of the Revolution as an achievement for the USA alone) and internationalism: Woodrow Wilson's vision of a universally exported new world order was no sooner triumphantly asserted than American voters disowned it.

Its day came not in 1918 but in 1945,[105] and it was given expression by an alliance within American academe of history, political science and sociology; this influence goes far to explain the significance of the concept of 'the West'. In recent American sociology, a 'Western' society is one which has undergone an historical experience denominated 'modernization'. This is, of course, a circular argument in so far as 'modernization' has been inferred from processes observed in the societies already deemed to be of 'the West', but it is not impregnably circular: the identity fails at the point of empirical observation if 'Western' societies have significantly different stadial characteristics. In that case, 'modernization' is shown never to have been an analytical concept and is revealed as being a normative one: from explaining the past, it becomes itself a social formation in need of historical explanation.[106] Such an explanation is offered here.

One route to such an explanation of 'modernization' would be a study of one of its central concepts, the idea that societies evolved stadially and that a key point of articulation was the moment of 'bourgeois revolution'. The idea of a bourgeois revolution not occurring in Germany is normally associated with Karl Marx. Yet in Marx it was specifically tied to 1848, and he did not give it much substance as a general historic form. For Marx, the concept of bourgeois revolution in general denoted at best only a milestone on the road to those substantively important phenomena, proletarian revolution and the dictatorship of the proletariat. The idea of a bourgeois revolution as an essential and momentous rite of passage for modern societies owed more to Max Weber, and was given its immense currency by American political science[107] (and by émigrés from Nazism, often themselves in America)[108] between the 1930s and the 1960s. In that form, bourgeois revolution was the essential matrix less of class domination than of modernity; in that form, and with that backing, the thesis became widely accepted among historians of many persuasions everywhere. From our present perspective, we can see that analysis not as expressing a generally valid 'Western' insight, but as in substantial part a culturally specific United States perspective on European history, a peculiarly American attempt to impose an analysis on the rest of the world.[109] American political science, history and sociology share in many of their provinces a common characteristic: they are (overtly or covertly) normative,[110] both announcing and seeking to promote what it still seems self-evident to term 'the ultimate triumph of Western liberal democracy'.

The most formative expositions of such an ideology have emerged from the United States, most recently by authors like Francis Fukuyama and Allan Bloom. Bloom's account differed from Fukuyama's chiefly in seeing the American ideological heritage as being under dire threat rather than triumphant; their understanding of that heritage was otherwise strikingly similar. This heritage consisted of 'rational discourse' derived from the Founders: 'Their authority was founded not on tradition or revelation but on nature grasped by reason. This was a new beginning, a liberation from prejudice, legitimized by reference to principles of justice assented to by man's most distinctive and most common faculty and persuasive to a candid world... This is the peculiarly American form of patriotism.'[111] Fukuyama posited a twentieth century going out where it came in, with a programmatic confidence in the progressive and beneficial triumph of

'Western' values. Yet the vicissitudes of world history in the intervening decades suggest a different perspective on this insight: the unity is supplied by the consistent purposefulness of the academic analysis. From the origins of the American historical profession in the final decades of the nineteenth century, it has been marked by a desire to embody and promote public values.[112] American political science was similarly characterized, as was American law. The wide complicity of German jurists with the Nazi regime delayed until recent decades an academic comparison in the USA between the modern legal systems of that country and Germany, often to the advantage of the latter.[113]

The uniqueness of this formation is hardly apparent within the United States. From a European perspective, it was easier to discuss 'the idea of a science of politics as an episode and as a tendency in American political thought and intellectual history'. In 1959 Bernard Crick diagnosed American distinctiveness as – to outward appearance – a uniquely strong commitment to the possibility of a science of politics built on 'the method of the natural sciences' and recorded that his interest in the subject arose from a personal rejection of the 'traditional methods of English political studies', especially in T. D. Weldon's nominalist *The Vocabulary of Politics* (London, 1953). In studying American writers, however,

I soon found the nature of my problem changing. As 'scientific' I found them in fact more prone to narrow than to explain the field that I had conventionally thought of as 'political'... there were, throughout their works, some strong assertions of political doctrine, seemingly inexplicable according to their own criteria of truth and method. The habitual confidence of their espousal of 'democracy', indeed the mere fact of their congregation in the United States, began to seem more important to me than their formal claim to be scientific. It was when I tried to discover the quality of this 'Americanness', apparently so different from the autocratic implications of the Enlightenment and the Comtean science of politics in France, that a shift, indeed a turning, began to take place in my own thought – that is to say, in my perception of what problems were important. For the methodology of those books seemed of little help in understanding their own obvious and intense democratic moralism: the presuppositions outweighed the propositions.

It was then like waking up on the other side of the mirror to see the whole school more as an expression of American political thought than of science. Their meaning became clear only when studied in the whole context of the American liberal tradition.[114]

Something similar was true of 'the American sense of history' in the early twentieth century, according to Ernst Breisach: it

acknowledged life's incessant change but found the assurance of continuity in timeless rights and values. It even transformed these, by their nature, seemingly static entities into spurs for change when history was perceived as their ever-fuller realization. Change was no longer chaotic but had acquired a clear direction. It aimed at emancipation from the restraints of the past; change was ultimately progress. America's awareness and affirmation of that progress, together with the institutions of the new Republic, were thought to exempt America from the destructive mechanisms of the Old World: they could even make her the catalyst for history's movement toward a new and better universal order.[115]

If this was the position in 1959, the influence of American political science became far more powerful in Britain during the crucial expansion of the subject in the 1960s, when 'the full brunt of developments in a self-confident American political science was felt at a time when there was uncertainty about what to teach and how to study the subject'.[116] The establishment of the discipline in the German Federal Republic can be similarly dated to the 1950s, its expansion to the 1960s, and was given point by the need 'to build up democracy' in the post-war world.[117] One student has identified a 'normative-ontological approach' which 'heavily contributed to the "Americanization"... of West German political science' through a 'massive import of conceptual approaches and analytical methods'.[118]

Crick noted that 'the style of thought that we sketch has, of course, a wider habitat than political science alone – indeed we will see that it inclines to a sociological rather than a strictly political viewpoint'.[119] Since 1959, the applicability of this insight has more obviously extended to other areas of the social sciences. These themes can be traced in the interconnected disciplines of history and sociology[120] also. A comparison of these shows how American political science is 'lacking in appreciation of historical difference', but as a combination contributes to 'an idealized liberal vision of American society' which only recently came to be challenged by domestic diversity.[121] Even this was an historically created phenomenon, however, for it was only during the period c. 1870–1929 that American social scientists distanced themselves from older German historical models and affirmed the natural sciences as a methodological foundation. The story demonstrates how

> American social science owes its distinctive character to its involvement with the national ideology of American exceptionalism, the idea that America occupies an exceptional place in history, based on her republican government and economic opportunity... The successful establishment of republican institutions and the liberal opportunity guaranteed by a continent of virgin land, Americans believed, had set American history on a millennial course and exempted it from qualitative change in the future.

These early nineteenth-century ideas of exceptionalism were later partly qualified by an acknowledgement of the role in America of the 'forces that were creating liberal modernity in Europe'. But this attempted reorientation of American social science to open it to the historical was incomplete and equivocal: 'many social scientists hastened to subject history to scientific control', and coped with the threats of twentieth-century industrialization and socialism by redefining 'the American exceptionalist ideal in wholly liberal terms', reading back 'those terms to the origin of the Republic'. We must conclude that this enterprise achieved a large measure of success, so that 'American social science has consistently constructed models of the world that embody the values and follow the logic of the national ideology of American exceptionalism'.[122]

The consequence was that the characteristic American understanding of political science, which integrated it with social science more generally,

> assumes a peculiar four-fold relationship between a common notion of *science* as it is found in ordinary American political thought; the idea of a common *citizenship* training; the generalization of the habits of American *democracy*, and, tending to embrace all these, the common belief in an inevitable *progress* or a manifest destiny for American society.[123]

Within this cultural programme, 'modernity' was not a valid historical term: it was normative, not analytical.[124] It follows that we need histories of the normative project of recent writers, and that these will replace histories of 'transitions' to 'modernity' by past societies. This is not a conclusion that follows from the recent history of Britain alone. The historiography of the French Revolution, once more obviously indebted to Marxist models, has similarly emancipated itself from the notion of a bourgeois revolution.[125] This leaves 1776 looking peculiarly isolated, and the time has now come to reinterpret the American Revolution itself in the light of the European norms which the indebtedness of colonial American society to the old world make appropriate.

It has been argued that 'Political science, as a discipline, first arose in the United States to fulfil the practical task of maintaining a belief in the unity of American sentiments'.[126] In that task it initially proved strikingly successful, not least because its goal has been shared by other disciplines within American academe, especially that numerically larger and more diffusely influential discipline, history.[127] Yet, with the passage of time, the immense preponderance which the American political science profession enjoyed in 1945 has been steadily offset by diversification within the USA and by the expansion of the discipline in other countries. By 1991, a survey which demonstrated a concern about 'the imperialism of American political science' could balance it against an appreciation of other national traditions: 'as a weak thesis the claim that political science was an American invention is true but trivial, and as a stronger thesis it was simply incorrect'.[128] Yet what is at issue is not political science alone but an intellectual amalgam in which political science and sociology offered polemical abridgements of the larger component, history.

This increasing qualification of the self-evident truths of the political science of 1945 is not always apparent in historical discussions of large themes and geopolitical relations, where painting with a broad brush still often excuses universalizing assumptions. The American historical profession still often displays a mindset that has encountered no fundamental discontinuity and transformation since an epoch revealingly referred to as the Founding.[129] Consequently, American historiography too often presumes that its categories have a timeless validity and (as with American political science and sociology) those categories are almost never historicized.[130] No movement like *Begriffsgeschichte* has emphasized to Americans how each term embodies an ideology, and shares with that ideology a temporal trajectory. It seems likely, therefore, that the increasing emancipation of European historiographies will have an effect not unlike the development of other traditions of political science outside the USA.

V.   THE LIMITS OF ANGLO-GERMAN REINTEGRATION

There was a variety of ways of explaining the essence of that 'West' into which post-war Germany had been assimilated, but they amounted to the same thing. Jürgen Habermas, who largely began the *Historikerstreit* with a newspaper article of 1986 drawing attention to the significance of the arguments of historians like Ernst Nolte, Andreas Hillgruber, Klaus Hildebrand and Michael Stürmer, condemned their views as necessitating the abandonment of a recent achievement:

> The political culture of the [German] Federal Republic would be worse today if it had not adopted impulses from American political culture during the first postwar decades. The Federal Republic opened itself for the first time to the West without reservations; we adopted the political theory of the Enlightenment, we grasped the pluralism which, first carried by religious sects, moulded the political mentality, and we became acquainted with the radical democratic spirit of the American pragmatism of Peirce, Mead, and Dewey.[131]

In this philosopher's vision, it was the historical idea of a single homogeneous Enlightenment that performed the task of creating a unified 'West'; yet here, too, historians were rejecting the French model of an Enlightenment, adopted as normative by the American scholar Peter Gay, himself a refugee from Nazi Germany, and reasserting the differences between national traditions.[132] In our age, no single historical concept any longer establishes structural norms for the long-term historical development of societies. There is, as Richard Evans has emphasized, little point in revisiting the *Historikerstreit* of 1986–8 over whether the Holocaust was unique, or whether the attempt to analyse it historically was a covert attempt partly to condone it. That debate belongs to an intellectual landscape that has subsequently been fundamentally modified by German reunification.[133] The debate has moved on, yet much may be learned from it.

The wider debate has, indeed, progressed through stages. In the first, it was asserted that there was a single, normative 'Western' path to 'modernity' from which Germany departed. In the second, it was increasingly realized that there were many paths to 'modernity': Germany's might or might not have been one of them. Finally, we see that there was no single normative 'modernity' to which various counterfactual paths might lead: the construction of political or cultural homogeneities or similarities between societies is now shown to be indeed a political and cultural act, not an independent process of nature.

It is a principle of historical enquiry that *tout comprendre, c'est tout condamner*. To argue against the idea of a *Sonderweg* is not to argue that there were no unique features or patterns in German history: clearly, the Holocaust was one such, perpetrated by Germans and not by others. It does not follow, however, that one outcome, even so great an evil, identifies a society's history as essentially different from its neighbours'. Other nation states contain episodes of oppression within their histories that are widely morally condemned[134] without that nation's history being deemed to stand wholly outside more familiar patterns of development. The thesis advanced here offers no exonerations in German controversies: the debate over Fritz Fischer's thesis on the origins of the First World War;[135] the *Historikerstreit* over Ernst Nolte's arguments about the comparative nature of twentieth-century totalitarianisms;[136] or the debate on Daniel Goldhagen's thesis over the extent of responsibility within German society for the Holocaust.[137] Each of these has a unique moral dimension, but in so far as they bear on the situation before 1914, these are, in part, aspects of the same debate: whether the events of the twentieth century totally discredited German society as it stood before 1914 for falling short of what it was once conventional to depict as the liberal, democratic, egalitarian ideals of 'the West', and for creating an historical logic which led to the disasters of the twentieth century.

The argument advanced here has some moral dimensions. It assumes that responsibility for actions attaches to individuals; it does not consider it legitimate to transfer blame to geopolitical locations, structures of power or mentalities. Equally, if we re-establish the counterfactual, we see that many social structures of power have proved viable, and survived subject only to the unexciting accretion of incremental change, had avoidable catastrophes been avoided.

The long-term historical experiences of Britain and Germany displayed more general points of similarity than the models of a German *Sonderweg* or of a homogeneous Western norm allowed, yet these similarities, often structural, did not force Britain to act on the international stage as Germany did in and after 1914. Nor did these points of structural similarity have the effects on domestic British political and social forms that is attributed to them in the German case. Even this degree of similarity elides important internal diversities. The thesis of a greater affinity than has been often acknowledged does not depend on the existence of a homogeneous 'Britain' and a homogeneous 'Germany' whose degree of difference could be simply measured. Both political units enclosed diverse cultures. The diversities and the conflicts within them were, however, points in common between Britain and Germany, and points which distinguished both from a USA which, beginning with old world diversities, systematically homogenized them to produce a society which was, by the early twentieth century, comparatively uniform, especially in its patterns of thought, and in its subscription to certain values in the academic realm.

Unrecognized similarities between the British and the German cases do not establish that there was an ideal type, call it an *ancien régime* or anything else, to which European societies conformed before practical or ideological intervention from without. One fictional cast of historical characters must not be replaced with another. *Anciens régimes* had some structures in common, but their main common feature was diversity, the dominance of prescription, local practice, and 'rights' conceived as specific entitlements. This was especially true of Germany, where unification around Bismarck's Prussia tended to obscure, in retrospect, the marked diversities of the components of the Wilhelmine empire. It was the revolutionary experiences of 1776, 1789, 1917 and 1933 that had the more powerful similarities. But the revolutions of 1642, 1789, 1917 and 1933 have all, in a sense, been reversed: 1776 now stands alone.

We may be left with the conclusion that by the opening of the twentieth century Britain and Germany differed less in their forms or structures of social power than in the tactical uses to which that power was put in 1914, 1933 and 1939. Nor do we have good reason for thinking that the undoubted differences between British and German society were sufficient to determine those divergent uses. Germany between 1914 and 1945 indeed pursued a different path, but this is not necessarily evidence of the inherent uniqueness of German society before that era, still less for the existence of a single yardstick in the historical experience of 'the West' against which any other country can be judged. Our sense of normal patterns of development against which German history before 1914 might be measured has been fundamentally modified. It was above all the First and Second World War alignment of France, Britain and America that created 'the West' and 'Western values' out of a collection of significantly different cases. As that tactical coalition recedes from us in time, as Britain rethinks its history and the USA refuses to do so, it seems increasingly likely that if any *Sonderweg* existed, it was that pursued, not by Germany, but by the United States.

If the historiographies of Britain and the United States are dissociating,[138] the same intellectual currents may in some respects lead to a partial reintegration of the historiographies of Britain and her European neighbours. In that process, Germany will not be immune. Historical analysis is sceptical of claims of the *essential* similarities of widely different societies. In place of these politically generated claims about the affinities of power blocs, historians are able to embark on the more compelling investigation both of similarities and of differences.[139] On this grandest of geopolitical planes, our histories dominate our presents, but not by determining them. Men make their own history; but, as has been well observed, they do not make it just as they please.

CONCLUSION

This work has not urged grandiloquently that modernism or postmodernism be replaced by some other and superior doctrine; it has instead made some more modest but more subversive claims about the practical effectiveness of historical techniques in explaining the assertions and assumptions of postmodernism and modernism alike. Those historical techniques take us beyond pre-formed models to the more complex, more intractable and less escapable historical record; yet here answers are necessarily neither easy nor agreeable, since our deepest needs urge us not to take unwelcome counterfactuals seriously. The 'past' which modernists think ratifies the present, and the 'past' from which postmodernists think they can so easily emancipate themselves, is a 'past' which they first select in order to prove their point.

So we draw a veil over happier possibilities as well as over darker ones; our need to reconcile ourselves with the world in which we live forbids us to raise that veil and take seriously the world we have lost. History challenges that idolatry of the actual when it reveals as improbable and unforeseen many momentous episodes that men found ways of portraying, in retrospect, as inevitable: within Britain's long eighteenth century, my own home ground, the geopolitical transformations of 1660, 1688, and 1776, are of that nature. Equally, attempted actions that had a considerable chance of success are explained away by a hegemonic ideology, diminished in retrospect to the level of wild gambles, like the

French invasion attempt of 1744 or the potentially French-backed Irish rebellion of 1797–8. In both cases, a plan made a domestic rising contingent on foreign military intervention that never materialized; but had the pieces fallen into place, as they did in 1660, 1688 and 1776, the historical landscape could have been transformed.

This aversion from counterfactuals does not abolish their force. Whatever our unthinking preferences for the established certainties and self-evident truths of modernism, or the promised limitless emancipations of postmodernism, counterfactuals implicitly underpin all historical reconstructions of grand events; only strongly purposeful ideologies condemn the open appraisal of alternatives as disreputable, inspired by an impractical nostalgia.

In popular consciousness, nostalgia may be at least an instinctive awareness of options not taken and potentialities never realized. Nostalgia is sometimes securely grounded in the minutiae of past life, although sometimes uncritically reliant on national or sectional myths. But whatever its emotional content, whether well- or ill-judged, the methodological significance of nostalgia suggests that popular under-standings of history tend to be non-teleological.[1] It is with good reason, as Raphael Samuel has reminded us, that the *bienpensant* instinctively reacts against popular attitudes to the past and seeks to denigrate them: however much populist nostalgia reflects an authentic empirical contact with the conditions of existence of past time, its unteleological structure robustly contradicts the thin-lipped commitments of the present age.

Nostalgia is therefore an instinctive contradiction of politicized timelessness, and it is this to which history provides an alternative. In George Orwell's nightmare world, the Party's slogan is: 'Who controls the past controls the future: who controls the present controls the past.' The result is a continuing, changeless present. As Winston, the book's hero, explains it, 'History has stopped. Nothing exists except as an endless present in which the Party is always right'.[2] The historian is always involved in opposing the latest form of this ancient heresy and reasserting the validity of choice.

Yet historians are not strongly supported in this public role: mankind has generally given less credence to counterfactuals than the historian would wish. It is, of course, unprofitable to regret the might-have-been, whatever the logical status of such a stance:

Some natural tears they dropped, but wiped them soon;
The world was all before them, where to choose
Their place of rest, and providence their guide:
They hand in hand with wandering steps and slow,
Through Eden took their solitary way.[3]

Part of the reason for this refusal to contemplate the might-have-been is psychological: a major decision once taken, a major counterfactual once actualized, has to be rationalized in retrospect as inevitable, as rational in the circumstances. Values are then adapted to outcomes to praise the new situation.

A larger reason may be methodological. The philosopher W. B. Gallie offered one such account (perhaps over-complacent) of how disruptive contingencies were absorbed and accommodated in historical explanations, an account which implied that even an 'unparalleled, hope-shattering disaster' in the realm of contingency did not entail the enforced choice of an alternative counterfactual.[4] In spite of contingency, mankind may be free already, in no need either of the consoling inevitabilities of modernism or the encouraging emancipations of postmodernism.

Even if this is true, however, no merely secular doctrine is an unambiguous ally of the historian. The contingent and the counterfactual are only congruent at the outset of any historical enquiry. Soon, they begin to pull in different directions. The counterfactual assumes clearly identifiable alternative paths of development, whose distinctness and coherence can be relied on as the historian projects them into an unrealized future. Contingency, by contrast, not only tells us that unfolding events followed no such path, whether identified by the merits of a case, by the good arguments or inner logic of principles or institutions; it also entails that all counterfactual alternatives would themselves have quickly branched out into an infinite number of possibilities.[5] Mankind cannot greatly lament the path not taken if that counterfactual is quickly lost, itself dividing into a myriad of options determined by the kaleidoscope of contingency. These difficulties ought to be reasons for placing them in the foreground of our enquiries; in daily life, the need for consolation generally overrides the desire for exploration. Historians impressed by the force of contingency and their colleagues who stress counterfactuals could, after all, equally contend that if Eve had not offered Adam the apple, something else might have gone wrong anyway, and that we do indeed live in the best of all possible worlds. The historian needs powerful arguments against this secular counsel of despair.

NOTES

NOTES TO PREFACE

1   Lawrence Stone, 'History and the social sciences in the twentieth century' (1976), reprinted in Stone, *The Past and the Present* (London, 1981), pp. 3–44.
2   Economic history has tended to divide into narrowly quantitative studies and the history of economic thought.

NOTES TO INTRODUCTION

1   How far such a view can be from a thoughtless or romantic preference of 'the past' over 'the present' is shown by Peter Ackroyd, *London: The Biography* (London, 2000).
2   This is a growth area of historical studies, e.g. Jacques Le Goff, *History and Memory*, trans. Steven Rendall and Elizabeth Claman (New York, 1992); Raphael Samuel, *Theatres of Memory* (2 vols., London, 1994–7).
3   Speech at West Point Military Academy, 5 December 1962.
4   This school has begun to provoke effective replies, e.g. John M. Ellis, *Against Deconstruction* (Princeton, 1989); Christopher Norris, *The Truth About Postmodernism* (Oxford, 1993); Terry Eagleton, *The Illusions of Postmodernism* (Oxford, 1996); Keith Windschuttle, *The Killing of History* (New York, 1997).
5   James Ceaser, *Reconstructing America: the symbol of America in modern thought* (New Haven, Conn., 1997), p. 1.
6   Modernism proves to be an historical phase as difficult to date as its successor, but in a variety of areas commentators have placed its inception in the late nineteenth century and its supersession by postmodernism in the late twentieth. The validity of such a stadial theory is doubted here.

7   The materialist dictum of Ludwig Feuerbach, 'Man ist was er isst' (man is what he eats), has been replaced by a parody of René Descartes's argument 'cogito ergo sum': 'I shop, therefore I am'.

8   These simple propositions of postmodernism were concealed behind defensive jargon. Satirists have now devised a computer program that will randomly generate postmodern essays in literary criticism (in reality, all meaningless): www.csse.monash. edu.au/cgi-bin/postmodern. For a candid postmodern claim that 'unproblematic prose' and 'clarity of... presentation' are 'the conceptual tools of conservatism', see Ellis, *Against Deconstruction*, p. 10.

9   See chapter 1 below.

10   For diverse identifications of this cultural formation, see David Selbourne, *The Principle of Duty* (London, 1994); Christopher Lasch, *The Revolt of the Elites and the Betrayal of Democracy* (New York, 1995); Quentin Skinner, *Liberty Before Liberalism* (Cambridge, 1998); Roger Scruton, *An Intelligent Person's Guide to Modern Culture* (London, 1998).

11   For a claim that deconstructionists 'have generally reacted with hostility and even outrage to any serious criticism of deconstruction and thus to any possibility of an exchange with their intellectual opponents', see Ellis, *Against Deconstruction*, p. viii.

12   It was evidently unknown to the proponents of this step that Anglo-Saxon historiography had been experiencing a golden age, with implications discussed in chapter 2 below.

13   The phrase now carries a quite different meaning than it did in Carl L. Becker's article 'Everyman His Own Historian', *American Historical Review*, 37 (1932), pp. 221–36. Becker argued that Everyman already had some participation in the knowledge more accurately established by the professional scholar: 'Suppose Mr. Everyman to have awakened this morning unable to remember anything said or done. He would be a lost soul indeed. This has happened, this sudden loss of all historical knowledge. But normally it does not happen. Normally the memory of Mr. Everyman, when he awakens in the morning, reaches out into the country of the past and of distant places and instantaneously recreates his little world of endeavor, pulls together as it were things said and done in his yesterdays, and coordinates them with his present perceptions and with things to be said and done in his to-morrows. Without this historical knowledge, this memory of things said and done, his to-day would be aimless and his to-morrow without significance'. Although this meant that history was an 'imaginative creation' which Everyman 'adapts to his practical or emotional needs', Becker still emphasized that 'In thus creating his own history, there are, nevertheless, limits which Mr. Everyman may not overstep without incurring penalties'; he was obliged to recall the past with 'much exactness' (p. 228). Becker did not foresee how far his argument would eventually go in writing: 'we [historians] do not impose our version of the human story on Mr. Everyman; in the end it is rather Mr. Everyman who imposes his version on us'. Consequently he could still argue that 'The whole dignity of human endeavor is thus bound up with historic issues' (pp. 223, 228, 235).

14   E.g. Harold Bloom, *The Western Canon* (New York, 1994).

15   *Emilius; or, an Essay on Education. By John James Rousseau, Citizen of Geneva. Translated from the French by Mr Nugent* (2 vols., London, 1763), I, p. 12.

16   Francis Fukuyama, 'The End of History?', *The National Interest*, 16 (summer, 1989), pp. 3–18, at 3–4; idem, *The End of History and the Last Man* (New York, 1992).

17   See below, chapter 7.

18   Fukuyama, 'End of History', pp. 15, 17, 18.

19   Ibid., pp. 8–9. Affinities between Fukuyama's analysis and Marx's are stressed in Windschuttle, *Killing of History*, pp. 159–84.

20   In *The Chicago Tribune*, 25 May 1916. Ford's remark came in an extended interview in which he set out his own philosophy of history: 'What do we care what they did 500 or 1,000 years ago? I don't know whether Napoleon did or did not try to get across there [i.e. invade Britain] and I don't care. It means nothing to me. History is more or less bunk. It's tradition. We don't want tradition. We want to live in the present and the only history that is worth a tinker's dam[n] is the history we make today... The men who are responsible for the present war in Europe know all about history. Yet they brought on the worst war in the world's history.' His conclusion was emphatic: 'There is one thing the United States and the world ought to do this minute, and that is disarm. I'll spend the rest of my life and all I have to see that is brought about.' As so often, Ford's homespun rejection of history was merely the preliminary to a policy commitment based on a simplistic lesson allegedly taught by 'history'.

21   For an attempt to characterize deconstruction not as an ideology but as a 'project', proceeding by a different logic (which is never adequately specified), see Ellis, *Against Deconstruction*, chapter 1. Postmodern politics is sometimes similarly characterized as a 'third way'.

22   Samuel P. Huntington, 'The Clash of Civilizations', *Foreign Affairs*, 72 (1993), pp. 22–49, reprinted in Salim Rashid (ed.), *The Clash of Civilizations: Asian Responses* (New York, 1997). Huntington's article provoked controversy on many grounds. Here, it need only be observed that it seriously understated the potential for religious conflict *within* what the author identified as religiously grounded power blocs.

23   Claude Lévi-Strauss, *The Savage Mind* (London, 1966), pp. 232, 234, 263.

24   For the argument that 'History, as opposed to history with a small "h", is for postmodernists a teleological affair', ineluctably moving towards the discrediting of modernist goals, see Terry Eagleton, *The Illusions of Postmodernism* (Oxford, 1996), pp. 45–68, at 45.

25   See chapter 2 below.

26   For a summary, see Nicholas Henshall, *The Myth of Absolutism: Change and Continuity in Early Modern European Monarchy* (London, 1992).

27   Stuart Sim (ed.), *The Routledge Critical Dictionary of Postmodern Thought* (London, 1998), p. 320.

28   For postmodernists' indebtedness to Nazi supporters and collaborators, see Windschuttle, *Killing of History*, pp. 178–83, drawing on Victor Farías, *Heidegger and Nazism* (1987), trans. Paul Burrell (Philadelphia, 1989); Tom Rockmore, *On Heidegger's Nazism and Philosophy* (Berkeley, 1992); Roger Kimball, 'The Case of Paul de Man' in Kimball, *Tenured Radicals* (1990); Lutz Niethammer, *Posthistoire: Has History Come to an End?* (1989), trans. Patrick Camiller (London, 1992).

29   Eric Hobsbawm, 'Introduction: Inventing Traditions' in Eric Hobsbawm and Terence Ranger (eds.), *The Invention of Tradition* (Cambridge, 1983), pp. 1–14, at 1.

30   Cf. E. P. Thompson, *Customs in Common* (London, 1991).

31 Hobsbawm, in *The Invention of Tradition*, pp. 2–3. This meaning attached to 'tradition' should be compared with that of Lévi-Strauss, for whom invariance was a feature not of tradition but of totemism.

32 It is appropriate to the postmodern project that much recent writing on these themes should take the form of the 'higher anecdotage' rather than critical historical analysis.

33 There may not have been the accidental awakening to affinities that this form of words suggests. In France especially, many postmodernists of the 1980s were ex-Marxists from the 1960s in search of more tenable premises.

34 As is appreciated by Eagleton, *Illusions of Postmodernism*. It is noteworthy that *The Invention of Tradition* also included a chapter by England's last Whig historian.

35 Hobsbawm, in *The Invention of Tradition*, pp. 6–7 and 263–307.

36 The second argument is advanced in chapter 2 below.

37 Eagleton, *Illusions of Postmodernism*, p. 121.

38 The philosophical status of historical knowledge is too large a subject to be explored here, but the approach adopted in this book is indebted to English schools which look to R. G. Collingwood and Michael Oakeshott. It is in no sense a defence of what has been characterized as 'piecemeal empirical research': Quentin Skinner, in Skinner (ed.), *The Return of Grand Theory in the Human Sciences* (Cambridge, 1985), p. 5. No Collingwoodian need suppose that for man to be located within his own linguistic system means that any statement he can make about the world is as valuable as any other statement.

39 George Santayana, *Materialism and Idealism in American Life: Character & Opinion in the United States* (London, 1920), pp. 168, 170.

40 Robert N. Bellah, *The Broken Covenant: American civil religion in a time of trial* (New York, 1975).

41 See chapter 3 below.

42 Key texts in the rhetorical denunciation of that process include Allan Bloom, *The Closing of the American Mind* (New York, 1987); Roger Kimball, *Tenured Radicals* (New York, 1990); Dinesh D'Souza, *Illiberal Education* (New York, 1991). Such works relate specifically to academic idioms in the USA.

43 For the way in which the already prevailing (and so historically generated) preoccupations of American literary scholarship created a setting highly receptive to postmodernism, see Ellis, *Against Deconstruction*, p. 157.

44 Ceaser, *Reconstructing America*, p. 14.

45 See chapter 7 below.

46 Eagleton, *Illusions of Postmodernism*, p. 5 and *passim*; 'It is as though, having mislaid the breadknife, one declares the loaf to be already sliced', p. 9. Eagleton's most basic concern is not just the collapse of Marxism but, more generally, 'the apparent collapse of some classical epistemological models', p. 12.

47 Ibid., p. 51.

48 E.g. John Vincent, *An Intelligent Person's Guide to History* (London, 1995), pp. 35–44 for 'the normality of awfulness' (p. 41), easily overlooked in England.

49 What early-modern categories of explanation were, if not those established by modernist ideas of stadial development, revolution, organic evolution and so forth is the subject of my current research, to appear in a book provisionally entitled *Providence, Chance and Destiny*.

50   Hugh Trevor-Roper, 'The Invention of Tradition: The Highland Tradition of Scotland', in *The Invention of Tradition*, pp. 15–41.

51   In its first published form, within a volume of essays on counterfactual analysis, this was the essay which attracted most hostile comment within the USA.

NOTES TO CHAPTER 1

1   J. G. A. Pocock, 'Virtue and Commerce in the Eighteenth Century', *Journal of Interdisciplinary History*, 3 (1972–3), pp. 119–34, at 122.

2   Jean Marie Goulemot, 'Le mot *révolution* et la formation du concept de révolution politique (fin de XVIIe siècle)', *Annales historiques de la révolution française*, 39 (1967), pp. 417–44; idem, *Discours, révolutions et histoire. Représentations de l'histoire et discours sur les révolutions de l'Age Classique aux Lumières* (Paris, 1975); Reinhard Koselleck, 'Revolution', in Otto Brunner, Werner Conze and Reinhard Koselleck (eds.), *Geschichtliche Grundbegriffe. Historisches Lexicon zur politisch-sozialen Sprache in Deutschland* (Stuttgart, 1972–), V (1984), pp. 653–788; idem, 'Historical Criteria of the Modern Concept of Revolution' (1969), reprinted in Koselleck, *Futures Past: On the Semantics of Historical Time*, trans. Keith Tribe (Cambridge, Mass., 1985), pp. 39–54; Keith Michael Baker, '"Revolution"' in Colin Lucas (ed.), *The French Revolution and the Creation of Modern Political Culture*, II, *The Political Culture of the French Revolution* (Oxford, 1988), pp. 41–62; Mona Ozouf, 'Revolution' in François Furet and Mona Ozouf (eds.), *A Critical Dictionary of the French Revolution* (Cambridge, Mass., 1989), pp. 806–17; Alain Rey, *'Révolution': histoire d'un mot* (Paris, 1989). Such work is considerably in advance of, for example, George Woodcock, 'The Meaning of Revolution in Britain 1770–1800', in Ceri Crossley and Ian Small (eds.), *The French Revolution and British Culture* (Oxford, 1989), pp. 1–30.

3   Lawrence Stone, 'Theories of Revolution', *World Politics*, 18 (1965–6), pp. 159–76, at 176; cf. Isaac Kramnick, 'Reflections on Revolution: Definition and Explanation in Recent Scholarship', *History and Theory*, 11 (1972), pp. 26–63; Perez Zagorin, 'Theories of Revolution in Contemporary Historiography', *Political Science Quarterly*, 88 (1973), pp. 23–52. Importantly, historians no longer write such articles.

4   The pattern of argument is clear from Stone, 'Theories of Revolution', p. 164: 'Given this classification and definition of revolution, what are its root causes?'; cf. Zagorin, 'Theories of Revolution', p. 28. Such a strategy traps its adherents within a circular argument and reveals nothing that the initial definition did not contain.

5   Stone, 'Theories of Revolution', p. 159; Kramnick, 'Reflections on Revolution', p. 30.

6   Robert Forster and Jack P. Greene (eds.), *Preconditions of Revolution in Early Modern Europe* (Baltimore, 1970), pp. 1–2.

7   Stone, 'Theories of Revolution', p. 164. The monograph which did most to establish this perspective in the English-speaking world was Crane Brinton, *The Anatomy of Revolution* (New York, 1938; revised edns., 1952, 1965). This happened despite Brinton's disclaimer (1965 edn., p. 7) that he was not 'attempting to find an ideal type for revolution'.

8   These flawed hypotheses have been rejected for the nineteenth century and the

seventeenth; in this respect, scholarship on the eighteenth century lags some way behind these adjacent fields.

9 'There might be arguments over "earlier" versus "later", or "retardation" versus "acceleration", but the actual direction appeared to have been established once and for all': Koselleck, 'Historical Criteria of the Modern Concept of Revolution', p. 48.

10 In 1956, Laslett still accepted that 'The name Revolution, in the sense in which we use it, was born in England in 1688–9': Peter Laslett, 'The English Revolution and Locke's "Two Treatises of Government"', *Cambridge Historical Journal*, 12 (1956), pp. 40–55, at 55. In *The World We Have Lost* (London, 1965), especially chapter 8, 'Social Change and Revolution in the Traditional World', Laslett went on to reinterpret the so-called 'English Revolution' of *c.* 1640–60 and to remove it from the typologies apparently appropriate to the revolutions of 1776, 1789 and 1917. He did, however, somewhat blur the significance of 1688 by extending 'the English Revolution' to cover both the execution of Charles I and the deposition of James II (p. 168). By the 1983 edition (p. 206), Laslett had extended his scepticism forwards to doubt the appropriateness of the phrase 'the French Revolution' for the events of 1789.

11 Vernon F. Snow, 'The Concept of Revolution in Seventeenth-Century England', *Historical Journal*, 5 (1962), pp. 167–90.

12 Especially J. G. A. Pocock, *Politics, Language and Time: Essays on Political Thought and History* (London, 1972); *The Machiavellian Moment: Florentine Political Thought and the Atlantic Republican Tradition* (Princeton, 1975); (ed.), *The Political Works of James Harrington* (Cambridge, 1977); *Virtue, Commerce and History: Essays on Political Thought and History, Chiefly in the Eighteenth Century* (Cambridge, 1985).

13 J. R. Jones, *The Revolution of 1688 in England* (London, 1972), p. 331, for the claim that the Glorious Revolution was 'far more conclusive and decisive in its results' than the events of 1640–60.

14 Christopher Hill, 'The Word "Revolution" in Seventeenth-Century England', in Richard Ollard and Pamela Tudor-Craig (eds.), *For Veronica Wedgewood These: Studies in Seventeenth-Century History* (London, 1986), pp. 134–51, at 134–5.

15 I shall present this evidence at length in a book provisionally entitled *Providence, Chance and Destiny*.

16 For analogous developments in the young American republic, see Lester H. Cohen, *The Revolutionary Histories: Contemporary Narratives of the American Revolution* (Ithaca: Cornell University Press, 1980).

17 Hill, 'The Word "Revolution"', p. 139.

18 Koselleck, 'Historical Criteria of the Modern Concept of Revolution', p. 44.

19 For an attempt to place this episode in a wholly different modern explanatory framework, see Rosario Villari, *The Revolt of Naples*, trans. James Newell and John A. Marino (Cambridge, 1993).

20 Goulemot, 'Le mot *révolution*', *passim*; 'personne ne lui donne explicitement une signification sociale: les formes politiques peuvent changer, mais les structures sociales demeurent. Enfin, par rapport au concept moderne de révolution politique, le concept de révolution tel qu'il semble exister à la fin du XVIIe siècle, présente des différences profondes'.

21 In Gabriel Bonnot, abbé de Mably, *Oeuvres complètes*, IX (London, 1789).

22 Ozouf, 'Revolution', p. 806.

23   Baker, "'Revolution'", pp. 41–2.

24   Ibid., pp. 42–3.

25   Laslett had been led to a similar conclusion: 'revolution' in seventeenth-century England 'denoted the political vicissitudes so woefully familiar to the people of the time, when those vicissitudes did indeed take the form of bewildering reversals... In this sense there were revolutions in the 1600s in England; in 1642, in 1646–9, in 1660, in 1688–90, and on other occasions as well... But the word would have to be used in the plural, not the singular, and a query placed against any interpretation which would see them as teleological in their tendency': *The World We Have Lost further explored* (London, 1983), pp. 207–8. My evidence to be presented in *Providence, Chance and Destiny* confirms and extends this insight.

26   Goulemot, *Discours, révolutions et histoire*, pp. 175–221; Baker, "'Revolution'", p. 45; cf. Baker's interpretation of Mably, p. 46.

27   Few major episodes have been as clearly linked as these, though remarkably without much sense in France that the French were re-enacting an American scenario, performing 'a revolution'.

28   Classically explored in Gordon S. Wood, 'Conspiracy and the Paranoid Style: Causality and Deceit in the Eighteenth Century', *William and Mary Quarterly*, 3rd series, 39 (1982), pp. 401–41.

29   The absence of the image of the new American republic from the material very fully presented in E. P. Thompson, *The Making of the English Working Class*, is an important negative evidence.

30   Most directly in Henry Steele Commager, *The Empire of Reason: How Europe Imagined and America Realized the Enlightenment* (London, 1978).

31   J. Hector St John de Crèvecoeur, *Letters from an American Farmer*, ed. Albert E. Stone (Harmondsworth, 1981).

32   See the contemporary reactions cited by Gordon S. Wood, *The Creation of the American Republic 1776–1787* (Chapel Hill, NC, 1969), pp. 3–4.

33   For a systematic appreciation of this, see Gordon S. Wood, *The Radicalism of the American Revolution* (New York, 1992).

34   Cohen, *The Revolutionary Histories*.

35   See J. C. D. Clark (ed.), Edmund Burke, *Reflections on the Revolution in France* (Stanford, 2001), Introduction.

36   Franco Venturi, *The End of the Old Regime in Europe*, trans. R. Burr Litchfield (2 vols., Princeton, 1989, 1991).

37   Ozouf, 'Revolution'.

38   Lawrence Stone, 'The Bourgeois Revolution of Seventeenth-Century England Revisited', *Past & Present*, 109 (1985), pp. 44–54, at 52.

39   Notably in a series of essays by John Morrill, including 'The Church in England 1642–1649' (1982), 'The Religious Context of the English Civil War' (1984), 'The Attack on the Church of England in the Long Parliament' (1985), 'The Ecology of Allegiance in the English Civil Wars' (1987), and 'England's Wars of Religion' (1990), reprinted in Morrill, *The Nature of the English Revolution* (London, 1993).

40   Stone, 'Bourgeois Revolution', p. 53.

41   For a general explanation of prevalent, indeed endemic, political violence in this period in terms which owe nothing to modern theories of revolution, see Yves-Marie Bercé,

Revolt and revolution in early modern Europe: An essay on the history of political violence, trans. Joseph Bergin (Manchester, 1987).

42 For a review of these episodes which assembles them to call in question Whig assumptions about the inherent stability of Britain and its possessions, see J. C. D. Clark, *The Language of Liberty 1660–1832: Political discourse and social dynamics in the Anglo-American world* (Cambridge, 1994), pp. 218–95, a work which argues (p. 218) against the possibility of an explanation of revolutions 'as such'. In claiming (p. 295) that the events of 1776–83 should be viewed as 'a civil war but not a revolution', I implied the extension: 'in the modern sense'.

43 These conclusions are not, of course, universally accepted. For an attempted resuscitation of old arguments see, for example, Robert Brenner, 'Bourgeois revolution and transition to capitalism' in A. L. Beier, David Cannadine and James M. Rosenheim (eds.), *The First Modern Society: Essays in Honour of Lawrence Stone* (Cambridge, 1989), pp. 271–304; idem, *Merchants and Revolution: commercial change, political conflict, and London's overseas traders, 1550–1653* (Princeton, 1993).

44 Forster and Greene, in *Preconditions of Revolution in Early Modern Europe,* p. 14.

45 Cf. Laslett, *The World We Have Lost further explored,* pp. 198, 335: 'Conflict... is a common enough form of social interaction... It has been complained that this suggestion reduces everything to the status of an improbable misfortune, but there is no point in denying the contingency even of epoch-making historical occurrences.'

46 Stone, 'Theories of Revolution', p. 164: 'This effectively disposes of the objections of those historians whose antipathy to conceptual schematization takes the naive form of asserting the uniqueness of each event.' Stone's article reappeared as a chapter in his much acclaimed overview, *The Causes of the English Revolution 1529–1642* (London, 1972), where the argument against great events having small causes is repeatedly advanced (e.g. p. 37). A provocative case so memorably stated meant that it was this book which 'sparked off the revisionist revolt from the mid 1970s': Morrill, *The Nature of the English Revolution,* p. 4 n.

47 The latest and most confident exercises in this idiom are Mark Gould, *Revolution in the Development of Capitalism: The Coming of the English Revolution* (Berkeley, 1987) and Jack Goldstone, *Revolution and Rebellion in the Early Modern World* (Berkeley, 1991). Such works seem not to engage with the developments in historiography discussed in this essay.

48 J. H. Elliott, 'Revolution and Continuity in Early Modern Europe', *Past & Present,* 42 (1969), pp. 35–56, citing, on linguistic usage, Karl Griewank, *Der Neuzeitliche Revolutionsbegriff* (Weimar, 1955).

49 H. G. Koenigsberger, 'Early Modern Revolutions: An Exchange', *Journal of Modern History,* 46 (1974), pp. 99–106.

50 Koenigsberger, 'Early Modern Revolutions'.

51 For an extended exploration of this theme, see Clark, *Providence, Chance and Destiny.*

52 This claim may seem at odds with the unexamined positivist reductionism which underpins much of history conducted as a craft skill. It finds support in the now-prevalent Anglophone methodologies in the history of ideas associated especially with J. G. A. Pocock and Quentin Skinner, and also in Reinhart Koselleck's argument that '*Begriffsgeschichte* reminds us – even when it becomes involved with ideologies – that in politics, words and their usage are more important than any other weapon':

'Historical Criteria of the Modern Concept of Revolution', p. 54.

53 Crane Brinton justified his verdict that 'the doctrine of the absolute uniqueness of events in history seems nonsense' with the profound insight: 'you have only to look at a page of Theophrastus or of Chaucer to realize that Greeks of more than two thousand years ago and Englishmen of six centuries ago seem in some ways extraordinarily like Americans of today': Brinton, *Anatomy of Revolution* (1965 edn.), p. 19.

54 Hedva Ben-Israel, *English Historians on the French Revolution* (Cambridge, 1968); Ian Small, in Crossley and Small (eds.), *The French Revolution and British Culture*, pp. ix–xviii, at xiv–xv; for earlier comparisons, M. S. Anderson, *Historians and Eighteenth-Century Europe 1715–1789* (Oxford, 1979).

55 J. W. Burrow, *A Liberal Descent: Victorians and the English Past* (Cambridge, 1981).

56 François Furet, *Revolutionary France 1770–1880* (Oxford, 1992).

57 Laslett, *The World We Have Lost further explored*, pp. 182, 185.

58 There is one apparent exception: theorists over many decades had predicted eventual independence when Europe's colonies 'came of age', and assembled such predictions after 1776 as apparent proof of the operation of a natural process. It is more remarkable therefore that even those who had voiced such predictions were astonished by what occurred, and wholly unprepared for it to occur when it did. This applied equally to activists, from Benjamin Franklin obtaining Stamp Act commissionerships for his friends to George Washington denying any intention of independence in the colonial governments as late as 1774.

NOTES TO CHAPTER 2

1 For surveys, see Margot Finn, 'An elect nation? Nation, state and class in modern British history', *Journal of British Studies*, 28 (1989), pp. 181–91; Gerald Newman, 'Nationalism revisited', ibid., 35 (1996), pp. 118–27.

2 Susan Reynolds, *Kingdoms and Communities in Western Europe 900–1300* (Oxford, 1984); R. R. Davies (ed.), *The British Isles 1100–1500: comparisons, contrasts and connections* (Edinburgh, 1989); idem, *Domination and Conquest: the experience of Ireland, Scotland and Wales 1100–1300* (Cambridge, 1990); Robin Frame, *The Political Development of the British Isles 1100–1400* (Oxford, 1990); Mark Greengrass (ed.), *Conquest and Coalescence: the shaping of the state in early modern Europe* (London, 1991); Richard Bonney, *The European Dynastic States, 1494–1660* (Oxford, 1991); J. H. Elliott, 'A Europe of composite monarchies', *Past & Present*, 137 (1992), pp. 48–71.

3 Brian Levack, *The Formation of the British state: England, Scotland and the Union, 1603–1707* (Oxford, 1987); Jenny Wormald, 'The creation of Britain: multiple kingdoms or core and colonies?', *Transactions of the Royal Historical Society*, 6th ser., 2 (1992), pp. 175–94. This argument is developed, with reference to state formation in the British Isles since 1536, in J. C. D. Clark, *The Language of Liberty 1660–1832: political discourse and social dynamics in the Anglo-American world* (Cambridge, 1994). The nation state (a polity congruent with what is generally accepted to be a single people) is not the only viable state form: the UK's survival since that time is evidence of the strength of an alternative model.

4 'Nations, we now know... are not, as Bagehot thought, "as old as history". The modern

sense of the word is no older than the eighteenth century': E. J. Hobsbawm, *Nations and Nationalism since 1780: programme, myth, reality* (Cambridge, 1990), p. 3. Gellner saw a role for religion in promoting nationalism only via Weber's thesis that Protestantism was the midwife of capitalism: Ernest Gellner, *Nations and Nationalism* (Oxford, 1983), p. 41. Such works at best propose analytical distinctions within 'nationalism' posited as a single teleological phenomenon. For an important reaction against 'a materialist conception of social reality' in historical sociology in favour of the view that 'identity is perception', see Liah Greenfeld, *Nationalism: five roads to modernity* (Cambridge, Mass., 1992), pp. 13, 496. This work nevertheless continues to use a single term, 'nationalism', to cover a variety of phenomena, contending that nationalism has 'a conceptually evasive, Protean nature' (p. 7). Historians see a series of different phenomena rather than a mysteriously united and Protean one.

5   Gellner, *Nations and Nationalism*, pp. 138–9 and Hobsbawm, *Nations and Nationalism*, pp. 87–9, did so in order to disparage patriotism. This was not the object of Maurizio Viroli, *For Love of Country: an essay on patriotism and nationalism* (Oxford, 1995). This work rightly begins with an argument that patriotism and nationalism 'must be distinguished'; but although it seeks to historicize nationalism by finding for it a precise chronological genesis, it treats patriotism imprecisely as a language that 'has been used over the centuries' (p. 1).

6   *The Oxford English Dictionary* gives the first usage of 'nation' in 1300, 'national' in 1597; both were current long before its first example of 'nationalism', with a political meaning, in 1844. The same work traces 'patriot' to 1596, but finds a source for 'patriotism' only in 1726: for a fuller discussion, see chapter 3 below. The third edition of the *OED* may uncover earlier usages for 'patriotism', but it seems unlikely that general currency will be discovered before the 1720s.

7   Clark, *Language of Liberty*, pp. 46–140.

8   Cf. Finn, 'An elect nation?', p. 181.

9   The recovery of this phenomenon began with Bonamy Dobrée, 'The theme of patriotism in the poetry of the early eighteenth century', *Proceedings of the British Academy*, 35 (1949), pp. 49–65; Betty Kemp, 'Patriotism, pledges and the people' in Martin Gilbert (ed.), *A Century of Conflict* (London, 1966), pp. 37–46; Quentin Skinner, 'The principles and practice of opposition: the case of Bolingbroke versus Walpole' in Neil McKendrick (ed.), *Historical Perspectives* (London, 1974), pp. 93–128: 'By the concept of patriotism both Bolingbroke and his opponents understood the ideal of acting in such a way as to defend and preserve the political liberties which their fellow-countrymen enjoyed under, and owed to, the constitution', p. 99.

10 This idea can be traced at least from Richard Price's *A Discourse on the Love of our Country* (London, 1789); cf. Johan Huizinga, 'Patriotism and nationalism in European history' (1940), in Huizinga, *Men and Ideas* (London, 1960), pp. 97–155. It is present in Michael Ignatieff, *Blood and Belonging: journeys into the new nationalism* (New York, 1993) as 'civic nationalism', which 'maintains that the nation should be composed of all those – regardless of race, colour, creed, gender, language or ethnicity – who subscribe to the nation's political creed'. Ignatieff contrasts this 'rational attachment' with an unacceptable 'ethnic nationalism' (pp. 5–9).

11 'Patriotism' preceded Bolingbroke; the concept appears in the titles of polemical writings from 1731 at the latest. By contrast, the first title in the catalogue of the

Bodleian Library to apply the word 'nationalism' to a contemporary political situation in the British Isles is John Kingsley, *Irish Nationalism* (London, 1887).

12   This assumption was subsequently dispelled by Geoffrey Elton, *The English* (Oxford, 1992), which stressed Anglo-Saxon state formation and the importance of a religious matrix. On this book, see the discussion by Patrick Wormald, John Gillingham and Colin Richmond, in *Transactions of the Royal Historical Society*, 6th ser., 7 (1997), pp. 317–36.

13   Still current with, for example, Ernest Barker, *National Character and the Factors in its Formation* (London, 1928). Chapter 2, 'The genetic factor: race' continued the demolition of Victorian concepts of race even before the political events of the 1930s.

14   H. M. Drucker and Gordon Brown, *The Politics of Nationalism and Devolution* (London, 1980). This phase of academic analysis was not marked by postmodern hostility to national identities; Drucker and Brown indeed accepted as a premise (pp. 2–3) the Kilbrandon Commission's insistence on the reality of national identities in Scotland and Wales.

15   Charles Tilly (ed.), *The Formation of National States in Western Europe* (Princeton, 1975) was a sociological work which lacked the comparisons between many different historical track records that its title seemed to promise. Geoffrey Elton, in his review, lamented: 'Three topics in particular ruin the investigation by their absence: the law, the Church and the ideology of nationalism... The only reason why [law] was left out would seem to be the authors' decision to treat states simply as engines of exploitation; bewildered by their concentration on the "extraction of resources" (mobilization of men and money), they entirely overlooked the fact that among the formative influences were other purposes quite as important to the inhabitants as to the rulers... Leaving out the Church would come naturally to this group of social scientists and historians anxious to be at home in the social sciences, but it tends to make nonsense of the whole enquiry': Elton, *Studies in Tudor and Stuart Politics and Government*, III (Cambridge, 1983), pp. 489–90. Tilly had not learned these lessons in *Coercion, Capital and European States, AD 990–1990* (Oxford, 1990). For a critique of Tilly's neglect of political culture, political theory and religion, see Siep Stuurman, 'A millenium of European state formation', *International Review of Social History*, 40 (1995), pp. 425–41.

16   E.g. Anthony D. Smith, *Theories of Nationalism* (London, 1971).

17   Anthony D. Smith, *The Ethnic Revival* (Cambridge, 1981); idem, *The Ethnic Origins of Nations* (Oxford, 1986). Smith argued (p. 1) against 'the new wave of social scientists and historians', naming Seton-Watson, Tilly, Breuilly, Nairn, Benedict Anderson and Gellner, who 'pronounced the nation a wholly modern creation with few, if any, roots in earlier epochs'.

18   John A. Armstrong, *Nations before Nationalism* (Chapel Hill, 1982); Theda Skocpol (ed.), *Bringing the State back in* (Cambridge, 1985); Michael Mann, *The Sources of Social Power* (2 vols., Cambridge, 1986); Philip Corrigan and Derek Sayer, *The Great Arch: English state formation and cultural revolution* (Oxford, 1986).

19   J. G. A. Pocock, 'British history: a plea for a new subject', *New Zealand Historical Journal*, 8 (1974), reprinted in *Journal of Modern History*, 47 (1975), pp. 601–21, and 'The limits and divisions of British history: in search of the unknown subject' *American Historical Review*, 87 (1982), pp. 311–36.

20   Jeremy Black, *Convergence or Divergence? Britain and the continent* (London, 1994); cf.

the Euro-enthusiast Stephen Haseler, *The English Tribe: identity, nation and Europe* (London, 1996). Haseler, a professor of government, there adopts the erroneous interpretation that 'A serious idea of Englishness... did not begin to cohere until the eighteenth century' (p. 11). The danger of uncritical borrowings by political science from flawed history is now apparent.

21   Wim Blockmans and Jean-Philippe Genet, general eds.: Richard Bonney (ed.), *Economic Systems and State Finance* (Oxford, 1995); Wolfgang Reinhard (ed.), *Power Elites and State Building (13th–18th Centuries)* (Oxford, 1996); Janet Coleman (ed.), *The Individual in Political Theory and Practice* (Oxford, 1996); Antonio Padoa-Schioppa (ed.), *Legislation and Justice: legal instruments of power* (Oxford, 1997); Peter Blickle (ed.), *Resistance, Representation and Community* (Oxford, 1997); Allan Ellenius (ed.), *Iconography, Propaganda, and Legitimation* (Oxford, 1998); Philippe Contamine (ed.), *War and Competition between States* (Oxford, 2000). Patrick Wormald, '*Enga Lond*: the making of an allegiance', *Journal of Historical Sociology*, 7 (1994), pp. 1–24, at 19, questions whether Genet's structural priorities – finding the 'modern' state in the France of Philip the Fair (1285–1314) – like another student of French history, J. R. Strayer, *On the Medieval Origins of the Modern State* (Princeton, 1970), were not 'indulging the French historian's usual habit of confusing the history of France with that of Europe. Englishmen familiar with the vigour of English government on either side of the Norman conquest would be tempted to take their story at least three centuries further back'. The implications of this argument are explored below.

22   J. G. A. Pocock (ed.), *The Varieties of British Political Thought 1500–1800* (Cambridge, 1993); Roger A. Mason (ed.), *Scots and Britons: Scottish political thought and the Union of 1603* (Cambridge, 1994); and John Robertson (ed.), *A Union for Empire: political thought and the Union of 1707* (Cambridge, 1995).

23   Quentin Skinner, *The Foundations of Modern Political Thought* (2 vols., Cambridge, 1978); idem, 'The state' in Terence Ball, James Farr and Russell L. Hanson (eds.), *Political Innovation and Conceptual Change* (Cambridge, 1988), pp. 90–131.

24   Richard S. Tompson, *The Atlantic Archipelago: a political history of the British Isles* (Lewiston, 1986); Hugh Kearney, *The British Isles: a history of four nations* (Cambridge, 1989); J. C. D. Clark, 'English history's forgotten context: Scotland, Ireland, Wales', *Historical Journal*, 32 (1989), pp. 211–28.

25   Michael Hechter, *Internal Colonialism: the Celtic fringe in British national development, 1536–1966* (Berkeley, 1975).

26   Tom Nairn, *The Break-up of Britain: crisis and neo-nationalism* (London, 1977). For the astonishment of a Kenyan literary scholar studying Scotland, at this self-destructive historiography, used as he was to the more self-confident projection of metropolitan culture overseas, see Simon Gikandi, *Maps of Englishness: writing identity in the culture of colonialism* (New York, 1996), p. ix.

27   Conrad Russell, *The Causes of the English Civil War* (Oxford, 1990); idem, *The Fall of the British Monarchies, 1637–1642* (Oxford, 1991) were mature statements of an analysis worked out by Russell earlier, e.g. 'The British problem and the English civil war', *History*, 72 (1987), pp. 395–415.

28   It was given influential expression by the establishment at Cambridge in 1988 of a paper in the Historical Tripos on the 'British problem' from the Union with Wales in 1536 to

the Union with Scotland in 1707, taught chiefly by a civil war scholar, John Morrill, and an historian reasserting a 'nationalist' perspective in an Irish debate, Brendan Bradshaw. A record of the partly programmatic work inspired by this course is now published as Brendan Bradshaw and John Morrill (eds.), *The British Problem, c. 1534–1707: state formation in the Atlantic archipelago* (London, 1996): it stressed, for example, that for nine centuries before 1922, Ireland was 'semi-detached' (p. 3). Addressing similar issues were Steven G. Ellis and Sarah Barber, *Conquest and Union: fashioning a British state, 1485–1725* (London 1995) and Alexander Grant and Keith Stringer (eds.), *Uniting the Kingdom? The making of British history* (London, 1995), the latter justifiably summed up by J. G. A. Pocock (p. 292) as bringing to fruition the new approach to the subject for which he had called in articles published in 1974–5 and 1982 (above).

29   'English nationalism never existed, since there was no need for either a doctrine or an independence struggle': Hugh Seton-Watson, *Nations and States: an enquiry into the origins of nations and the politics of nationalism* (London, 1977), p. 34; John Breuilly, *Nationalism and the State* (Manchester, 1982; 2nd edn. 1993), pp. 5, 75–88; Michael Hurst, *States, Countries, Provinces* (Bourne End, 1986); Hagen Schulze (ed.), *Nation-building in Central Europe* (Leamington Spa, 1987); Peter Alter, *Nationalismus*, translated as *Nationalism* (London, 1989); Bernhard Giesen, *Nationale und kulturelle Identität: Studien zur Entwicklung des kollektiven Bewusstseins in der Neuzeit* (Frankfurt, 1991); Mary Fulbrook, *National Histories and European History* (London, 1993); Mikulás Teich and Roy Porter (eds.), *The National Question in Europe in Historical Context* (Cambridge, 1993); Hagen Schulze, *States, Nations and Nationalisms: from the middle ages to the present* (Oxford, 1996).

30   In England, the crucial works were Hugh Cunningham, 'The language of patriotism 1750–1914', *History Workshop*, 12 (1981), pp. 8–33, which adopted the insistence on patriotism as essentially constitutionalist and libertarian propounded by Skinner, 'The principles and practice of opposition' (1974); E. J. Hobsbawm and T. O. Ranger (eds.), *The Invention of Tradition* (Cambridge, 1983); and Raphael Samuel's edited collection of essays, *Patriotism: the making and unmaking of British national identity* (3 vols., London, 1989).

31   Perry Anderson, *Lineages of the Absolutist State* (London, 1974; 2nd edn., 1979); Benedict Anderson, *Imagined Communities: reflections on the origin and spread of nationalism* (London, revised edn., 1991).

32   Notably, but not exclusively, in Roy Porter (ed.), *Myths of the English* (Cambridge, 1992): 'The past thus seems to be up for grabs, a chest of props and togs ready-to-wear in almost any costume drama, available to fulfil all manner of fantasies' (p. 1).

33   Finn, 'An elect nation?', p. 182. This process evidently preceded the breakup of multinational polities, especially in the former communist bloc after 1989. This last was a development generally welcomed by the Left as an extension of pluralism, and less often deplored as an effect of populist nationalism.

34   The papers of the nineteenth and twentieth meetings of the Ecclesiastical History Society were published in *Studies in Church History*, 18, as Stuart Mews (ed.), *Religion and National Identity* (Oxford, 1982); but despite highly relevant contributions, this research initially had little impact on some of the historians writing on 1660–1832.

35   For its earliest dating, to the England of Bede, see Wormald, '*Enga Lond*'.

36 E.g. Orest Ranum (ed.), *National Consciousness, History and Political Culture in Early-Modern Europe* (Baltimore, 1975), especially John Pocock's discussion of the 'elect nation' in England and Michael Cherniavsky's of the role of the Orthodox Church in Russia.

37 T. C. W. Blanning, 'The role of religion in European counter-revolution 1789–1815', in Derek Beales and Geoffrey Best (eds.), *History, Society and the Churches: essays in honour of Owen Chadwick* (Cambridge, 1985), pp. 195–214. For a reassertion of the role of religious issues in the revolution itself, see Dale Van Kley, *The Religious Origins of the French Revolution: from Calvin to the Civil Constitution, 1560–1791* (New Haven, Conn., 1996).

38 Samuel E. Finer, 'State- and nation-building in Europe: the role of the military', in Tilly (ed.), *Formation of National States in Western Europe* (1975); Smith, *The Ethnic Origins of Nations* (1986), pp. 38–41, 73–6. To some degree, however, this may be a distorting effect on our perspective produced by the world wars of the twentieth century: see Kenneth O. Morgan, 'England, Britain and the audit of war', *Transactions of the Royal Historical Society*, 6th ser., 7 (1997), pp. 131–53.

39 P. G. M. Dickson, *The Financial Revolution in England: a study in the development of public credit 1688–1756* (London, 1967); Peter Mathias and Patrick O'Brien, 'Taxation in Great Britain and France, 1715–1810', *Journal of European Economic History*, 5 (1976), pp. 601–50; Patrick O'Brien, 'The political economy of British taxation, 1660–1815', *Economic History Review*, 2nd ser., 41 (1988), pp. 1–32; idem, 'Public finance in the wars with France 1793–1815', in H. T. Dickinson (ed.), *Britain and the French Revolution, 1789–1815* (Basingstoke, 1990), pp. 165–87.

40 Robert W. Tucker and David C. Hendrickson, *The Fall of the First British Empire: origins of the war of American independence* (Baltimore, 1982), p. 109.

41 John Brewer, *The Sinews of Power: war, money and the English state 1688–1783* (London, 1989). For this theme now see, more comprehensively, Bonney (ed.), *Economic Systems and State Finance*, a survey which spans the period from the Middle Ages to the end of the eighteenth century, covering the themes of taxation, fiscal institutions, the Church, sovereignty, currency, economic theory, the financial relations of centre and periphery, rebellions against taxation, the financing of war, and national debts. For a consideration of this argument in a later time-frame, see Philip Harling and Peter Mandler, 'From "fiscal-military" state to laissez-faire state, 1760–1850', *Journal of British Studies*, 32 (1993), pp. 44–70.

42 Lawrence Stone (ed.), *An Imperial State at War: Britain from 1689 to 1815* (London, 1994), pp. 2, 4, 6. Hobsbawm's dismissal of the perceptions of ordinary men and women is characteristic of one school of thought. The legitimacy of this approach as history is open to doubt.

43 Stone (ed.), *Imperial State at War*, pp. 2, 5, 20.

44 For a more developed functional analysis by an author represented in Stone's volume, see Thomas Ertman, *Birth of the Leviathan: building states and regimes in medieval and early modern Europe* (Cambridge, 1997). Ertman places states in a typology determined by two polarities: absolutist v. constitutionalist, and patrimonial v. bureaucratic.

45 Stone (ed.), *Imperial State at War*, p. 11.

46 'Too little attention has been paid to the fact that Britain in the eighteenth century was little more than a somewhat precarious and recently formed federal political unit. A

viable state is not necessarily coincidental with a nation, the latter being defined by a sense of community in a common culture and patriotic feeling shared by both rulers and ruled': ibid., p. 4. This assumption of the weakness of the eighteenth-century dynastic state depended on an implied comparison with an ideal type, the nineteenth-century ethnically grounded nation state. The inappropriateness of the latter as a general yardstick is one theme of the present chapter.

47   Ibid., p. 17.

48   Clark, *Language of Liberty*.

49   Gerald Newman, *The Rise of English Nationalism: a cultural history, 1740–1830* (London, 1987), pp. 53, 63, 67. Newman denied the applicability of 'nationalism' to the England of the seventeenth century, but treated the mid eighteenth-century phenomenon as continuous with nineteenth-century 'nationalism'. He also argued for 'nationalism' as an essentially secular idea, an offshoot of the Enlightenment.

50   Linda Colley, *Britons: forging the nation 1707–1837* (New Haven, Conn., 1992).

51   Ibid., pp. 367–8.

52   For more sophisticated analyses of the impact of war in shaping societies, often distorting or reversing processes of social evolution or state formation deemed to be linear, see for example Bartholomew H. Sparrow, *From the Outside In: World War II and the American state* (Princeton, 1996); Arnold D. Harvey, *Collision of Empires: Britain in three world wars, 1793–1945* (London, 1992); Clive Emsley, *British Society and the French Wars, 1793–1815* (London, 1979).

53   Colley, *Britons*, pp. 5–6.

54   It seems likely that this concept was borrowed from another discipline and used without a clear sense of its limitations. This echoing of a concept was doubtless encouraged by the literary scholar Edward W. Said's *Orientalism* (New York, 1978), where the Orient was presented as providing Europe's 'deepest and most recurring images of the Other' (p. 1). Here as elsewhere, it took time for a fashionable term to percolate into the historiography.

55   Claude Nordmann, 'Choiseul and the last Jacobite attempt of 1759', in Eveline Cruickshanks (ed.), *Ideology and Conspiracy: aspects of Jacobitism, 1689–1759* (Edinburgh, 1982), pp. 201–17.

56   Jack P. Greene, 'The Seven Years' War and the American Revolution: the causal relationship reconsidered', *Journal of Imperial and Commonwealth History*, 8 (1980), pp. 85–105.

57   For this thesis, see especially Clark, *Language of Liberty*, pp. 296–381.

58   Marianne Elliott, *Partners in Revolution: the United Irishmen and France* (New Haven Conn., 1982); idem, *Wolfe Tone: prophet of Irish independence* (New Haven, Conn., 1989).

59   For the much more complex role of religion see, for example, Tony Claydon and Ian McBride (eds.), *Protestantism and National Identity: Britain and Ireland, c. 1650–c. 1850* (Cambridge, 1998).

60   'It has recently been argued that empire was an instrument of national consolidation, unifying the British against the French, the nation's primary "other". Yet the discourses of imperialism produced as many contradictions as unities, championing libertarianism and chauvinism, celebrating the birthrights of white English men while denying those rights to Britons, and vindicating the libertarian reading of English

constitutional development while also embedding hierarchies of difference in English political culture. The "others" identified or subdued through the imperial project were internal as well as external, domestic as well as foreign, within as well as without': Kathleen Wilson, *The Sense of the People: politics, culture and imperialism in England, 1715–1785* (Cambridge, 1995), pp. 24–5.

61   For the divisions of identity created by the Hanoverian accession, see Wilson, *Sense of the People*, pp. 101–17.

62   Ibid., p. 368.

63   Even that most militantly anti-Catholic part of the British Empire, the Thirteen Colonies, found it possible without substantial controversy to accept France as an ally in 1778.

64   Steven C. A. Pincus, *Protestantism and Patriotism: ideologies and the making of English foreign policy, 1650–1668* (Cambridge, 1996).

65   Colley, *Britons*, p. 18.

66   Ibid., pp. 1, 5, 369.

67   Hobsbawm and Ranger (eds.), *Invention of Tradition*.

68   Colley, *Britons*, p. 36.

69   Ibid., p. 20.

70   Ibid., p. 55.

71   For ambiguities over 'Scottish' and 'British' identities even into the nineteenth century, see Marjorie Morgan, 'The terminology of national identity in Victorian Britain', paper presented to a conference of the North American Conference on British Studies, 5–8 October 1995, and *National Identities and Travel in Victorian Britain* (London, 2001).

72   Keith Robbins, *Nineteenth-century Britain: integration and diversity* (Oxford, 1988), pp. 1–28.

73   Morgan, *National Identities and Travel in Victorian Britain*, discusses other usages in addition to these.

74   For a new interpretation of this theme, see chapter 4 below.

75   Ian F. W. Beckett, *The Amateur Military Tradition 1558–1945* (Manchester, 1991); J. R. Western, *The English Militia in the Eighteenth Century: the story of a political issue, 1660–1802* (London, 1965).

76   William Stafford, 'Religion and the doctrine of nationalism in England at the time of the French Revolution and Napoleonic wars', *Studies in Church History*, 18 (1982), pp. 381–95, at 381; for the complex relationship of militia service to 'patriotism', see J. E. Cookson, 'The English volunteer movement of the French wars, 1793–1815: some contexts', *Historical Journal*, 32 (1989), pp. 867–91. For challenges to and defences of the asserted providentialism of Church and nation in the 1830s, see Sheridan Gilley, 'Nationality and liberty, Protestant and Catholic: Robert Southey's Book of the Church', *Studies in Church History*, 18 (1982), pp. 409–32.

77   Koppel S. Pinson, *Pietism as a Factor in the Rise of German Nationalism* (New York, 1934).

78   The Conclusion quoted with approval a remark by the journalist Peter Scott: 'Britain is an invented nation, not so much older than the United States': Colley, *Britons*, pp. 1, 373.

79   Mona Ozouf, *Festivals and the French Revolution* (1976; trans. Alan Sheridan, Cambridge, Mass., 1988); Eugen Weber, *Peasants into Frenchmen: the modernization of rural France 1870–1914* (London, 1977); Maurice Agulhon, *Marianne into Battle:*

republican imagery and symbolism in France, 1789–1880 (1979; trans. Janet Lloyd, Cambridge, 1981); Lynn Hunt, *Politics, Culture and Class in the French Revolution* (Los Angeles, 1984).

80   Katherine R. Penovich, 'From "Revolution principles" to Union: Daniel Defoe's intervention in the Scottish debate', in Robertson (ed.), *A Union for Empire*, pp. 228–42, shows that Defoe, like Bede, sought to express the Union and British identity in terms of Providential mission.

81   Colley, *Britons*, p. 6. For this political programme adopted as an historical framework, see John Kendle, *Federal Britain: a history* (London, 1997).

82   Anderson, *Imagined Communities*; Nairn and Anderson are acknowledged in *Britons*, pp. 386, 413. As with the work of Clifford Geertz, it may be that these belated borrowings from social anthropology have not been made with sufficient discretion.

83   Colley, *Britons*, pp. 9, 16.

84   Ibid., p. 9. Haseler states the same political agenda more candidly: '"Englishness" was the identity of a small caste which ran the "tribe" and, more importantly, the state... the end of the UK, and the demise of this uniform identity, provides a chance to express finally the diversity of the peoples of the British Isles. This book is dedicated to a rediscovery of that diversity': *The English Tribe*, p. viii. An equally historically flawed component of this analysis is its treatment of the UK as an attempted 'nation state', the claim of which to identity with a nation is compromised by internal diversities (p. 7). The unhistorical programme to *promote* the demise of these things was most cogently expressed in Hobsbawm, *Nations and Nationalism*, esp. pp. 182–3.

85   Colley, *Britons*, esp. pp. 5, 8, 370–2.

86   Clark, *Language of Liberty*, pp. 46–51, 62–71.

87   James Campbell, *The Anglo-Saxons* (Oxford, 1982); idem, *Essays in Anglo-Saxon History* (London, 1986); 'The united kingdom of England: the Anglo-Saxon achievement' in Grant and Skinner (eds)., *Uniting the Kingdom?* (1995), pp. 31–47, at 35; 'The late Anglo-Saxon state: a maximum view', *Proceedings of the British Academy*, 87 (1994), pp. 39–65.

88   Patrick Wormald, 'Bede, the *Bretwaldas* and the Origins of the *Gens Anglorum*' in Patrick Wormald, Donald Bullogh and Roger Collins (eds.), *Ideal and Reality in Frankish and Anglo-Saxon Society: studies presented to J. M. Wallace-Hadrill* (Oxford, 1983), pp. 99–129; idem, 'The Venerable Bede and the "Church of the English"', in Geoffrey Rowell (ed.), *The English Religious Tradition and the Genius of Anglicanism* (Wantage, 1992), pp. 13–32; idem, 'Frederic William Maitland and the earliest English law', *Law and History Review*, 16 (1998), pp. 1–25; idem, *The Making of English Law: King Alfred to the Norman Conquest* (Oxford, 2000).

89   Elton, *The English* (1992), pp. 1–2, citing Wormald, 'Bede, the *Bretwaldas*' (1983).

90   Wormald, '*Enga Lond*', p. 2, correcting Strayer, *On the Medieval Origins of the Modern State*.

91   Ibid., p. 3.

92   Smith, *The Ethnic Origins of Nations*, p. 4 and chapter 5 *passim*.

93   Wormald, '*Enga Lond*', p. 3.

94   Ibid., pp. 9–10.

95   Sarah Foot, 'The making of *Angelcynn*: English identity before the Norman Conquest', *Transactions of the Royal Historical Society*, 6th ser., 6 (1996), pp. 25–49.

96   John Gillingham, 'The beginnings of English imperialism', *Journal of Historical*

Sociology, 5 (1992), pp. 392–409.

97 Wormald, '*Enga Lond*', pp. 10–11, 13.

98 Ibid., p. 14.

99 Ibid., pp. 15, 17.

100 John Gillingham, 'The context and purposes of Geoffrey of Monmouth's *History of the Kings of Britain*', *Anglo-Norman Studies*, 13 (1990), pp. 99–118, for an interpretation of that work as a contribution to 'the politics of cultural nationalism'.

101 This chapter does not concern itself directly with the forms of 'national' identity to be found in Wales, Scotland and Ireland from the Middle Ages to the present. On this theme, see especially Frame, *Political Development of the British Isles 1100–1400*; Davies, *Domination and Conquest*; Murray G. H. Pittock, *Inventing and Resisting Britain: Cultural Identities in Britain and Ireland, 1685–1789* (London, 1997); Alexander Murdoch, *British History 1660–1832: national identity and local culture* (London, 1998); Brendan Bradshaw and Peter Roberts (eds.), *British Consciousness and Identity: the making of Britain, 1533–1707* (Cambridge, 1998); Murray G. H. Pittock, *Celtic Identity and the British Image* (Manchester, 1999). In general, such research has emphasized the degree to which England's neighbours did not subsume their identities in a new British identity after 1707.

102 John Gillingham, 'The beginnings of English imperialism', *Journal of Historical Sociology*, 5 (1992), pp. 392–409.

103 Robert Bartlett, *The Making of Europe: conquest, colonization and cultural change 950–1350* (London, 1993).

104 Barnaby C. Keeney, 'Military service and the development of nationalism in England, 1272–1327', *Speculum*, 22 (1947), pp. 534–49, at 543.

105 John Gillingham emphasizes the importance in this respect of Henry II's partial conquest of Ireland in 1170–71: 'The English invasion of Ireland', in Brendan Bradshaw, Andrew Hadfield and Willy Maley (eds.), *Representing Ireland: literature and the origins of conflict, 1534–1660* (Cambridge, 1993), p. 24.

106 Davies, *Domination and Conquest*, pp. 12, 14, 114–15 and *passim*. The theme is extended in Davies's Presidential Address, 'The peoples of Britain and Ireland, 1100–1400', *Transactions of the Royal Historical Society*, 6th ser., 4 (1994), pp. 1–20; 5 (1995), pp. 1–20; 6 (1996), pp. 1–24; 7 (1997), pp. 1–24, and idem, *The First English Empire: Power and identities in the British Isles, 1093–1343* (Oxford, 2000).

107 Georges Grosjean, *Le Sentiment National dans la Guerre de Cent Ans* (Paris, 1927); Halvdan Koht, 'The dawn of nationalism in Europe', *American Historical Review*, 52 (1947), pp. 265–80; Ernst H. Kantorowicz, '*Pro patria mori* in medieval political thought', *American Historical Review*, 56 (1951), pp. 472–92; John Barnie, *War in Medieval Society: social values and the Hundred Years War 1337–99* (London, 1974); A. K. McHardy, 'Liturgy and propaganda in the diocese of Lincoln during the Hundred Years War', *Studies in Church History*, 18 (1982), pp. 215–27; John Gillingham, 'The English invasion of Ireland', pp. 24–42; idem, 'Conquering the barbarians: war and chivalry in twelfth-century Britain', *Haskins Society Journal*, 4 (1992), pp. 67–84; idem, 'Foundations of a disunited kingdom', in Grant and Stringer (eds.), *Uniting the Kingdom?*, pp. 48–64.

108 'English national self-consciousness', in Elton, *Studies*, IV, p. 132.

109 For studies of national consciousness in the sixteenth century, see Richard Helgerson, *Forms of Nationhood: the Elizabethan writing of England* (Chicago, 1992); Claire

McEachern, *The Poetics of English Nationhood, 1590–1612* (Cambridge, 1996); John M. Richardson, 'The barbarians: humanism and nationalism in early Tudor England' (Oxford Univ. M. Phil. thesis, 1993).

110 William S. Maltby, *The Black Legend in England: the development of anti-Spanish sentiment, 1558–1660* (Durham, NC, 1971).

111 Peter Furtado, 'National pride in seventeenth-century England' in Samuel (ed.), *Patriotism*, I, pp. 44–56, emphasizes the themes of 'national honour and national sin', p. 54.

112 Fletcher, 'The first century of English Protestantism', p. 316; Fletcher, *The Outbreak of the English Civil War* (London, 1981), pp. 191–207.

113 John Wolffe (ed.), *Christianity and National Consciousness* (Leicester, 1987); idem, *God and Greater Britain: religion and national life in Britain and Ireland 1843–1945* (London, 1994); Alan Wilkinson, *The Church of England and the First World War* (London, 1978); idem, *Dissent or Conform: war, peace and the English churches 1900–1945* (London, 1986); W. J. Sheils (ed.), *The Church and War* (Oxford, 1983).

114 Robert Colls and Philip Dodd (eds.), *Englishness: politics and culture 1880–1920* (London, 1986) focused on similar pressures for redefinition within England.

115 Gaines Post, 'Two notes on nationalism in the middle ages', *Traditio*, 9 (1953), pp. 281–320, at 320.

116 Paul Brand, 'Ireland and the early literature of the common law', *Irish Jurist* (1981), reprinted in Brand, *The Making of the Common Law* (London, 1992), pp. 445–63, at 446; cf. Davies, *Domination and Conquest*, pp. 114–15.

117 V. H. Galbraith, 'Nationality and language in medieval England', *Transactions of the Royal Historical Society*, 4th ser., 23 (1941), pp. 113–28, acknowledged that 'There can of course be no doubt about the existence of some sort of a national consciousness in pre-Conquest England' (p. 118), but emphasized the ardent national consciousness of fifteenth-century chroniclers writing in English in the face of military challenge. H. J. Chaytor, *From Script to Print: an introduction to medieval literature* (Cambridge, 1945), chapter 3, 'Language and nationality', traced the beginning of 'a national movement' to the mid thirteenth century (p. 35); V. J. Scattergood, *Politics and Poetry in the Fifteenth Century* (London, 1971).

118 Thorlac Turville-Petre, *England the Nation: language, literature and national identity, 1290–1340* (Oxford, 1996), pp. v–vi, 10. This was the case however much a monarch such as like Henry III, 'not reconciled to the loss piece by piece of the Angevin empire which had in the 1170s stretched from Scotland to the Pyrenees, projected himself as a European monarch in a European court' (p. 5).

119 *Rotuli Parliamentorum* (London, 1783), I, p. 362, quoted in Barnie, *War in Medieval Society*, pp. 102–3.

120 Davies, *Domination and Conquest*, pp. 4–5.

121 Wormald, '*Enga Lond*', pp. 3, 18.

122 For Foxe's *Book of Martyrs* as exemplifying the perspective of international Calvinism, only later absorbed into the national myth, see Clark, *Language of Liberty*, pp. 47–8. For reassertions of prior national self-awareness in the context of the debate over Foxe, see Patrick Collinson, 'Biblical rhetoric: the English nation and national sentiment in the prophetic mode' and Jesse Lander, 'Foxe's *Book of Martyrs*: printing and popularizing the Acts and Monuments', in Claire McEachern and Debora Shuger (eds.), *Religion and*

Culture in Renaissance England (Cambridge, 1997), pp. 15–45, 69–92. For cautions about the means and extent of Foxe's later reception, see Eirwen Nicholson, 'Eighteenth-Century Foxe: Evidence for the Impact of the *Acts and Monuments* in the "Long" Eighteenth Century', in David Loades (ed.), *John Foxe and the English Reformation* (Aldershot, 1997), pp. 143–77.

123 Menna Prestwich, *International Calvinism, 1541–1715* (Oxford, 1985).

124 David Loades, 'The origins of English Protestant nationalism', *Studies in Church History*, 18 (1982), pp. 297–307, at 298, 302.

125 For tensions between the national and the international in early Protestantism, see, for example, Anthony Fletcher, 'The first century of English Protestantism and the growth of national identity', *Studies in Church History*, 18 (1982), pp. 309–17; John McKenna, 'How God became an Englishman', in DeLloyd Guth and John McKenna (eds.), *Tudor Rule and Revolution: essays for G. R. Elton from his American friends* (Cambridge, 1982), pp. 25–43; Michael McGiffert, 'God's controversy with Jacobean England', *American Historical Review*, 88 (1983), pp. 1151–76; Peter Lake and Maria Dowling (eds.), *Protestantism and the National Church in Sixteenth Century England* (London, 1987).

126 It was a scholar well versed in both Reformation history and sixteenth-century state formation who emphasized the function in this respect of a key English institution: G. R. Elton, 'English national self-consciousness and the Parliament in the sixteenth century', in Otto Dann (ed.), *Nationalismus in Vorindustrieller Zeit* (Munich, 1986), pp. 73–81, reprinted in Elton, *Studies in Tudor and Stuart Politics and Government*, IV (Cambridge, 1992), pp. 131–43. Elton there rightly avoided the anachronistic terms 'patriotism' and 'nationalism'.

127 Hans Kohn, 'The genesis and character of English nationalism', *Journal of the History of Ideas*, 1 (1940), pp. 69–94; David Loades, 'The origins of English Protestant nationalism', *Studies in Church History*, 18 (1982), pp. 297–307 ('Such a situation had not been created overnight by the war with Spain'); Anthony Fletcher, 'The first century of English nationalism', Ibid., pp. 309–17; Greenfeld, *Nationalism*, chapter 1, 'God's firstborn: England'. Greenfeld's argument that a semantic shift in the use of the term 'nation' from the elite to the people in early sixteenth-century England 'signaled the emergence of the first nation in the world, in the sense in which the word is understood today, and launched the era of nationalism' (p. 6) cannot however be sustained in the light of the evidence for earlier centuries.

128 Wormald, '*Enga Lond*', p. 18.

129 Ibid.

130 The Authorized Version employs 'nation' 454 times, where the Vulgate used 'natio' on only 100 occasions, and with different meanings: Greenfeld, *Nationalism*, pp. 52–3; Gillian Brennan, 'Patriotism, language and power: English translations of the Bible, 1520–1580', *History Workshop Journal*, 27 (1989), pp. 18–36.

131 For this argument, see Clark, *Language of Liberty*, pp. 19–20, 46–62.

132 Ibid., pp. 1–45, 303–81.

133 Colley, *Britons*, p. 18.

134 From a large literature, see the articles collected in *Studies on Voltaire and the Eighteenth Century* 335, Michael O'Dea and Kevin Whelan (eds.), *Nations and Nationalisms: France, Britain, Ireland and the Eighteenth-Century Context* (Oxford, 1995), especially Thomas Bartlett, 'Protestant nationalism in eighteenth-century Ireland', pp. 79–88, and

Kevin Whelan, 'United and disunited Irishmen: the discourse of sectarianism in the 1790s', pp. 231–47.

135 John Vincent, *Pollbooks: How Victorians Voted* (Cambridge, 1967) revealed denominational patterns not explored for an earlier century until John A. Phillips, *Electoral Behavior in Unreformed England* (Princeton, 1982); idem, *The Great Reform Bill in the Boroughs: English electoral behaviour, 1818–1841* (Oxford, 1992); Frank O'Gorman, *Voters, Patrons and Parties: the unreformed electoral system of Hanoverian England 1734–1832* (Oxford, 1989).

136 P. M. H. Bell, *Disestablishment in Ireland and Wales* (London, 1969); William H. Mackintosh, *Disestablishment and Liberation: the movement for the separation of the Anglican Church from state control* (London, 1972).

137 Keith Robbins, 'Religion and identity in modern British history (presidential address)', *Studies in Church History*, 18 (1982), pp. 465–87, at 465; idem, 'An imperial and multinational polity: the scene from the centre, 1832–1922' in Grant and Stringer (eds.), *Uniting the Kingdom?*, pp. 244–54.

138 Robbins, *Nineteenth Century Britain*, pp. 63–96.

139 For the variety of identities within the empire, rather than a simple polarity between Catholic and Protestant, see Nicholas Canny and Anthony Pagden (eds.), *Colonial Identity in the Atlantic world, 1500–1800* (Princeton, 1987); Bernard Bailyn and Philip D. Morgan (eds.), *Strangers Within the Realm: cultural margins of the first British empire* (Chapel Hill, NC, 1991).

140 It is relevant that the nationalism of 1848 was confined by no religious boundaries and was present in Roman Catholic states as well as in countries with different balances between Protestant denominations to England's.

141 Bruce Galloway, *The Union of England and Scotland 1603–1608* (Edinburgh, 1986). Only an historiographical neglect of law and religion could divert attention away from the Union of 1603 and that seminal legal elucidation of it, *Calvin's Case*, towards the Union of 1707. Galloway's study made clear that James I intended to secure a measure of religious uniformity between his two kingdoms (p. 144): the Union of 1603 had from the outset ecclesiological implications which the Union of 1707 lacked, a feature of 1603 which the failure of the policies of Charles I and Laud later obscured. For the vagueness of the idea of Britain in 1603 (as in 1707), see Jenny Wormald, 'James VI, James I and the identity of Britain', in Bradshaw and Morrill (eds.), *The British Problem* c. *1534–1707*, pp. 148–71.

142 Burke to Adrien Duport [post 29 March 1790], in T. W. Copeland et al. (eds.), The *Correspondence of Edmund Burke* (10 vols., Cambridge, 1958–78), VI, p. 106.

143 Morgan, *National Identities and Travel in Victorian Britain*.

144 For this argument, see Newman, *Rise of English Nationalism*. It is nowhere addressed in *Britons*.

145 James Meadowcroft, *Conceptualising the State: innovation and dispute in British political thought, 1880–1914* (Oxford, 1995), p. 8.

146 For an overview of identities within the British Isles to the eighteenth century, expressed as a deliberate challenge to Hobsbawm's *Nations and Nationalism since 1780*, see Adrian Hastings, *The Construction of Nationhood: ethnicity, religion and nationalism* (Cambridge, 1997), pp. 1–95.

147 As was argued, for example, in Colls and Dodd (eds.), *Englishness* (1986).

148 In that sense, any 'Britishness' built around the Union of 1707 was very different from American identity built around the events of 1776 or 1787.

149 For a survey which gives due weight to these themes, see Keith Robbins, *Great Britain: ideas, institutions and the idea of Britishness* (London, 1998).

150 The term 'race' was still found in English discourse in the late nineteenth and early twentieth centuries, but chiefly as synonymous with the older sense of historically conditioned identity: see chapter 3 below. England was distinguished from twentieth-century Germany, Italy, France and Spain by its lack of formal racialist doctrine or consciousness. In that sense, England enjoyed an important legacy of its *ancien régime*. How the idea of 'race' functioned within Irish and Scots nationalism is not a question examined here. Nor is the question of whether postmodernists neglected to extend their analysis to such phenomena.

NOTES TO CHAPTER 3

1 Sociologists and political scientists (and historians influenced by them) tended within modernism to adopt a functional, typological analysis of 'nationalism' which allowed the term to be applied across centuries apparently to reveal various *forms of* nationalism: this obscured the significance of early nineteenth-century European innovations in general, and the formation of this concept in particular. Cf. Anthony D. Smith, 'Nationalism and the Historians', in Smith (ed.), *Ethnicity and Nationalism* (Leiden, 1992), pp. 58–80. Later they tended to the opposite postmodern extreme in which all national identities were depicted as 'constructed' (implying 'invented') or 'imagined' (implying 'imaginary').

2 For an anticipation of this enquiry, see John A. Armstrong, *Nations before Nationalism* (Chapel Hill, NC, 1982), a study that casts doubt on the quest for 'permanent "essences" of national character' (p. 4), stresses changing conceptions of ethnicity, and ends with an appreciation of the role of 'the universal religions' (pp. 283–7). John Breuilly by contrast analyses nationalism as 'an intellectual response to a crisis of political modernisation': 'Nationalism and the History of Ideas', *Proceedings of the British Academy*, 105 (2000), pp. 187–223, an approach that illuminates many aspects of collective self-awareness in Germany before the conceptualization of 'nationalism' as such.

3 So to pose the alternatives is not only teleological; it constructs ideal types. For the variety of the premises appealed to by nineteenth-century nationalists, see Michael Biddiss, 'Nationalism and the Moulding of Modern Europe', *History*, 79 (1994), pp. 412–32.

4 For an argument that 'organic conceptions of race and nationality' were slow to develop in England because of the prior 'vitality of the social–evolutionary tradition', see Peter Mandler, '"Race" and "Nation" in mid-Victorian thought', in Stefan Collini, Richard Whatmore and Brian Young (eds.), *History, Religion and Culture: British Intellectual History 1750–1950* (Cambridge, 2000), pp. 224–44.

5 See, most recently, Seymour Martin Lipset and Gary Marks, *It Didn't Happen Here: Why Socialism Failed in the United States* (New York, 2000). For the English case, Ross

McKibbin, 'Why was there no Marxism in Great Britain?', *English Historical Review*, 99 (1984), pp. 297–331.

6   Such studies, when English-centred, have often been drawn to focus instead on constitutional, cultural and religious themes, e.g. Robert Colls and Philip Dodd (eds.), *Englishness: Politics and Culture 1880–1920* (London, 1986); John Kendle, *Federal Britain: A history* (London, 1997); Keith Robbins, *Great Britain: Identities, institutions and the idea of Britishness* (London, 1998), p. 27, for scepticism about the ethnic coherence of Celts, Saxons, Danes and Normans; Tony Claydon and Ian McBride (eds.), *Protestantism and National Identity: Britain and Ireland, c. 1650–c. 1850* (Cambridge, 1998).

7   See chapter 2 above.

8   James A. H. Murray (ed.), *A New English Dictionary on Historical Principles* (10 vols. in 20, Oxford, 1888–1928). Volume VI part II, M and N, was published in 1908, edited by W. A. Craigie and sub-edited by the Rev. A. P. Fayers of Leeds. The second edition of the *OED* adds, for example, usages like 'two nations', 'nation building', 'National Assistance', 'National Trust' and 'national grid', but does not modify the inadequate basic definitions of the first edition.

9   See chapter 2 above.

10   The *OED*'s first example of the latter meaning is dated 1851, and in the form of the adjective 'ethnical' is dated 1846.

11   Quentin Skinner, 'The principles and practice of opposition: the case of Bolingbroke versus Walpole', in Neil McKendrick (ed.), *Historical Perspectives* (London, 1974), pp. 93–128; Hugh Cunningham, 'The Language of Patriotism 1750–1914', *History Workshop*, 12 (1981), pp. 8–33.

12   Visual evidence does not suggest a prominent racial basis to xenophobia, although it does consistently emphasize religious antipathies: Michael Duffy, *The English Satirical Print 1660–1832: The Englishman and the Foreigner* (Cambridge, 1986).

13   James Boswell, *Life of Johnson*, sub 7 April 1775.

14   John Cannon, *The Fox–North Coalition: Crisis of the Constitution, 1782–4* (Cambridge, 1969) provides a high-political account.

15   Some examples are given by Cunningham, 'The Language of Patriotism, 1750–1914' and John Dinwiddy, 'England', in Otto Dann and John Dinwiddy (eds.), *Nationalism in the Age of the French Revolution* (London, 1988), pp. 53–70.

16   J. H. Grainger, *Patriotisms: Britain 1900–1939* (London, 1986); Julia Stapleton, 'Political thought and national identity in Britain, 1850-1950', in Collini, Whatmore and Young (eds.), *History, Religion and Culture*, pp. 245–69.

17   Hugh MacNeile, *Nationalism in Religion. A speech delivered at the annual meeting of the Protestant Association... May 8, 1839* [1839].

18   E.g. John Kingsley, *Irish Nationalism; its origin, growth and destiny* (London, [1887]); George Douglas Campbell, Duke of Argyll, *Irish Nationalism: an appeal to history* (London, 1893); Richard Jebb, *Studies in Colonial Nationalism* (London, 1905); Hilda M. Howsin, *The Significance of Indian Nationalism* (London, 1909); Olivar Asselin, *A Quebec View of Canadian nationalism* (Montreal, 1909); Hamid Al-'alaili, *The Future of Egypt. The moral and intellectual aspects of Egyptian nationalism* (Paris, 1910); Edwyn Robert Bryan, *Indian Nationalism. An independent Estimate* (London, 1913); *German Nationalism and the Catholic Church* (London, 1917). English applications were rare, e.g. [F. J. B. Hooper], *Commercial Nationalism v. Anti-Nationalism: or the relative*

desireableness and values of imports and exports (Leeds, [1881]); Cecil Forsyth, *Music and Nationalism. A study of English opera* (London, 1911), perhaps a book on a non-existent subject.

19 E.g. *The Indian War of Independence of 1857. By an Indian nationalist* ([n.p., ?1909]); *The Faith of a Nationalist. A memorandum addressed to Young Wales* (Carnarvon, [1911]); *Is the Irish Party Nationalist? Our policy on the Parliamentary question* (Dublin, [?1918]); rare are specific usages like Hugh Clements, *A Nationalist Party necessary to save the Country from Ruin* ([Dulwich], 1905).

20 E.g. *Foreshadowings of the political tendencies of European nationalities: by a man of no party* (London, 1860); Robert Gordon Latham, *The Nationalities of Europe* (London, 1863); *Scripture Nationalities; or, Ancient peoples spoken of in the Bible* (twelve picture cards; London, [1866]); William Gabriel Davies, *Welsh Nationality, and how alone it is to be saved* (London, 1871); Henry Stuart Fagan, *Irish Nationality. An appeal to educated Englishmen* (London, [1886]); John Ker, *Scottish Nationality, and other papers* (Edinburgh, 1887); David Jones, *The Welsh Church and Welsh Nationality* (London, [1893]); Thomas Darlington, *Welsh Nationality and its Critics* (Wrexham, 1895); Charles Edward Breese, *Welsh Nationality* (Carnarvon, 1895); *The facts and principles of Irish nationality* (Dublin, 1907); Alice Stopford Green, *Irish Nationality* (London, [1911]); Stephen James Meredith Brown, *The Question of Irish Nationality* (Dublin, 1913); Arthur James Balfour, *Nationality and Home Rule* (London, 1913).

21 K. O. Morgan, 'Gladstone and Wales', *Welsh History Review*, 1 (1960–63), pp. 65–82, at 82.

22 Sir John Lubbock et al., *Mr. Gladstone and the Nationalities of the United Kingdom* (London, 1887), p. 15.

23 Richard Bonney, *The European Dynastic States, 1494–1660* (Oxford, 1991); J. C. D. Clark, *The Language of Liberty 1660–1832* (Cambridge, 1994), pp. 46–75. Studies of 'the' modern meaning of the term 'race' tend to draw no distinctions between European cultures: e.g. Nicholas Hudson, 'From "Nation" to "Race": The Origin of Racial Classification in Eighteenth-Century Thought', *Eighteenth-Century Studies*, 29 (1996), pp. 247–64. Yet few of the examples cited by Hudson are English.

24 E.g. Hamon L'Estrange, *Americans no Iewes, or improbabilities that the Americans are of that race* (London, 1652 [i.e. 1651]); [Anthony Hutchins et al.], *Caines bloudy race known by their fruits* (London, 1657); *Some considerations on the naturalizations of the Jews; and how far the publick will benefit from this hopeful race of Israelites. By J. E.* (London, 1753).

25 E.g. *Limitations for the next foreign successor, or new Saxon race* (London, 1701); *Ballad on a Knight of the Bath losing the badge of the order. To the tune of, Noble race was Shenkin, &c* [?London, ?1726]; *Four new songs, and a prophecy. I. A song for joy of our ancient race of Stewarts...* [?Edinburgh, ?1750]; M. Young, *Ancient Gaelic poems respecting the race of the Fians, collected in the Highlands of Scotland in the year M.DCC.LXXXIV* (Dublin, 1787).

26 Margaret T. Hodgen, *Early Anthropology in the Sixteenth and Seventeenth Centuries* (Philadelphia, 1964). For monogenesis, see pp. 207–53. Cultural difference was ascribed to the breach of divine commands by Cain and the descendants of Noah, and by man's presumption at Babel. For a few dissenting voices, including polygenists, pp. 269–90.

27 Quoted in Christine Bolt, *Victorian Attitudes to Race* (London, 1971), pp. 18–19. For continuing monogenist teaching by nineteenth-century 'Liberal Anglicans' like Thomas Arnold and H. H. Milman see Mandler, '"Race" and "nation"'.

28   E.g. *Letters on a variety of subjects. Dedicated, with submission, to the whole human race. By Palemon* (London, 1783); *The mutual obligations to the exercise of benevolent affections, as they respect the conduct of all the human race to each other, proved, and applied to the state of the suffering Africans. By Philadelphos* (London, 1788); George Burges, *A discourse on the necessity and duty of enlightening the human race* (London, 1797). The correlation between monogenist ideas and anti-slavery was strong but not complete: Charles White, anti-slavery campaigner and Manchester physician, was a polygenist.

29   E.g. John Jacobus Flournoy, *An Essay on the Origin, Habits &c. of the African Race: incidental to the propriety of having nothing to do with Negroes: addressed to the good people of the United States* (New York, 1835); Julien Joseph Virey, *The Natural History of the Negro Race. Extracted from the French* (Charleston, 1837); Samuel George Morton, *Crania Americana: Or a comparative view of the skulls of various aboriginal nations of North and South America, to which is prefixed an essay on the varieties of the human species* (Philadelphia, 1839); idem, *An Inquiry into the Distinctive Characteristics of the Aboriginal Race of America* (Boston, 1842); Josiah Priest, *Slavery, as it relates to the Negro or African Race, Examined in the Light of Circumstances, History, and the Holy Scriptures* (Albany, NY, 1842); Samuel Forry, *The Mosaic Account of the Unity of the Human Race, Confirmed by the Natural History of the American Aborigines* (New York, 1843); Robert Jefferson Breckinridge, *The Black Race; its position and destiny as connected with our American dispensation* (Frankfort, Ky., 1851); John Campbell, *'Negro-Mania': Being an Examination of the Falsely Assumed Equality between the Various Races of Men* (Philadelphia, 1851); Mary Howard Schoolcraft, *Letters of the Condition of the African Race in the United States. By a southern lady* (Philadelphia, 1852); William Benjamin Hayden, *Is the Human Race One or Many? A lecture delivered at a social meeting in Boston* (Boston, 1855); John Bachman, *An Examination of the Characteristics of Genera and Species as Applicable to the Doctrine of the Unity of the Human Race* (Charleston, 1855); George M. Weston, *The Progress of Slavery in the United States* (Washington, 1857); James Theodore Holly, *A Vindication of the Capacity of the Negro Race for Self-Government, and Civilized Progress* (New Haven, 1857); Samuel Adolphus Cartwright, *Ethnology of the Negro or Prognathous Race* (New Orleans, 1857); [Sidney George Fisher], *The Laws of Race, as connected with Slavery* (Philadelphia, 1860); Jonathan Baldwin Turner, *The Three Great Races of Men; their Origin, Character, History and Destiny, with special regard to the present condition of the black race in the United States* (Springfield, Ill., 1861); James Ashton Bayard, *The African Race in America, North and South... with an appendix... on the antagonism of the Caucasian and African races* (n.p., 1861); William Aikman, *The Future of the Colored Race in America* (Philadelphia, 1862); John H. Van Evrie, *Negroes and Negro 'Slavery': The first an inferior race: The latter its normal condition* (New York, 1863); Josiah C. Nott, *The Negro Race: its ethnology and history* (Mobile, 1866); [Buckner H. Payne], *The Negro: what is his ethnological status? Is he the progeny of Ham? Is he a descendant of Adam and Eve? What is his relation to the white race? By Ariel* (Cincinnati, 1867). For an early study, see John C. Greene, 'The American Debate on the Negro's Place in Nature, 1780–1815', *Journal of the History of Ideas*, 15 (1954), pp. 384–96.

30   For old usages, see Anna Wheeler, *Appeal of one half of the human race, women, against the pretensions of the other half, men, to retain them in political and thence in civil and*

domestic slavery; in reply to a paragraph of Mr Mill's celebrated 'Article on Government',
by William Thompson (London, 1825); J. H. Whiffen, *Historical memoirs of the first race*
of ancestry whence the House of Russell had its origin (London, 1833); Arthur James
Johnes, *Philological proofs of the original unity and recent origin of the Human Race.*
Derived from a comparison of the languages of Asia, Europe, Africa and America
(London, 1846); William Brock, *The Common Origin of the Human Race* (London,
1849); Robert Gordon Latham, *Varieties of the Human Race* (London, 1854); [R. M. W.],
Vindication of the Mosaic Ethnology of Europe. Primitive or Japhetic Europe; its race,
language and topography (London, 1863); George Sexton, *The Antiquity of the Human*
Race (London, 1864).

31   E.g. [John Crawfurd], *On the So-called Celtic Languages in reference to the Question of*
Race (London, 1863); Isaac Butt, *Land Tenure in Ireland; a plea for the Celtic race*
(London, 1866); Martin A. O'Brennan, *The Celtic Race: their descent, the country whence*
they migrated, their route... (London, [1867]); James Higgin, *The Irish Government*
Difficulty considered as a Race Question (Manchester, 1867). For new usages, see the
Scotsman Robert Knox's *The Races of Men: A Fragment* (London, 1850), the second
edition of 1862 subtitled *A philosophical enquiry into the influence of race over the*
destinies of nations.

32   George M. Fredrickson, *The Black Image in the American Mind: The debate on Afro-*
American character and destiny, 1817–1914 (New York, 1971), p. 135.

33   For US polygenism, see William R. Stanton, *The Leopard's Spots: scientific attitudes*
towards race in America, 1815–1859 (Chicago, 1960); Fredrickson, *The Black Image in the*
White Mind, pp. 71–96. Fredrickson argues that American pluralist ethnology was
'propagated under the banner of anticlericalism', p. 76.

34   E.g. L. P. Curtis, Jr., *Anglo-Saxons and Celts: A Study of Anti-Irish Prejudice in Victorian*
England (Bridgeport, Conn., 1968), which blamed racial 'prejudice in Victorian
England' alone for the failure to resolve the Irish problem, pp. 2–3; Nancy Stepan, *The*
Idea of Race in Science: Great Britain 1800–1960 (London, 1982), driven by an American
critique of Victorian imperialism and 'the British ruling class', p. x; George W. Stocking,
Jr., *Victorian Anthropology* (New York, 1987), a reaction by a self-consciously 'American'
ex-Marxist scholar to 'Anglo-Saxon imperialism', pp. xvii, 81.

35   'By the eighteenth century Europeans were decidedly ethnocentrist and racist': Stepan,
Idea of Race, p. xi; 'To some degree Englishmen, Frenchmen, Poles, as well as Germans
and Hungarians, used the word "race" in their daily lives without thinking...
Eighteenth-century Europe was the cradle of modern racism': George L. Mosse, *Toward*
the Final Solution: a history of European racism (London, 1978), pp. xi, 1; cf. pp. 48, 67,
72, 192, 234. As the title indicates, the work ignores North America and treats 'Europe'
as a homogeneous unit, although saying little about England. For the author's career as
a Jewish refugee from Nazi Germany, chiefly in the USA, see George L. Mosse,
Confronting History: A Memoir (Madison, Wis., 2000). See also Philip D. Curtin, *The*
Image of Africa: British Ideas and Action, 1780–1850 (Madison, Wis., 1964), p. 29 and
passim, for the view that 'full-blown pseudo-scientific racism... dominated... much of
European thought between the 1840s and the 1940s. Curtin argues for the full
emergence in England of a 'racialist' idea of the African within the period of his study.
Even if this were true (and it must now be in doubt) it would be remarkable that it did
not promote the equally early adoption of 'nationalism' in England. Curtin's able study

does not differentiate British from European thought on this question, though for unexamined evidence of Scots differences, see pp. 42–5, 62, 246, 250–51, 368–9, 377–80.

36 So wide ranging and scholarly a study as Stocking, *Victorian Anthropology*, is not drawn to consider an English or British nationalism.

37 Reginald Horsman, 'Origins of Racial Anglo-Saxonism in Great Britain before 1850', *Journal of the History of Ideas*, 37 (1976), pp. 387–410, at 396–7; idem, *Race and Manifest Destiny: The origins of American racial Anglo-Saxonism* (Cambridge, Mass., 1981), pp. 9–17, 62–77; Stocking, *Victorian Anthropology*, pp. 48–53.

38 Ronald Rainger, 'Race, Politics and Science: the Anthropological Society of London in the 1860s', *Victorian Studies*, 22 (1978–9), pp. 51–70. Even then, Hunt stopped short of formal polygenism and 'was careful to dissociate himself from American racists'; in Britain there were 'more opponents than supporters of the views of Hunt': Bolt, *Victorian Attitudes to Race*, pp. 6, 19.

39 Stepan, *Idea of Race*, claims a transition from monogenism to polygenism in 'British' science by the 1860s, but has few examples apart from the Scot Robert Knox (pp. 29–35, 40). English figures were usually monogenistic, from Thomas Henry Huxley and Charles Darwin (pp. 44, 49–66, 77–82) to Alfred Haddon and A. H. Keane (pp. 89–90) in the 1890s and 1900s. Even within the eugenics movement, Francis Galton and others made no attempt to define 'race' precisely, and often used it synonymously with 'descent' (pp. 128–30). It was American eugenists who were 'incautious' about the racial lessons they drew from their study (pp. 126, 133). How different English understandings of race were from German ones was made clear in the years before 1939, when English anthropologists and biologists openly criticized Nazi doctrines (pp. 140–69). Stocking, *Victorian Anthropology*, p. 63 and *passim*, is imprecise about dating the alleged 'process by which "race" took on a clearly biological meaning'. On the contrary, it seems likely that the term retained many meanings, and that what Stocking terms 'a rigidly deterministic biological approach' was uncommon in England. Like Stepan, Stocking's argument relies heavily on Robert Knox (pp. 65–9). Countervailing evidence includes the revolution in man's understanding of time produced by geology and archaeology, which made monogenesis more plausible (pp. 75–6). Outside ethnology and anthropology, older meanings might flourish: Friedrich Engels called the working classes 'a race apart'; Henry Mayhew called the street people of London 'a nomad race' (p. 213). Curtis, *Anglo-Saxons and Celts*, pp. 66–73, similarly relies on Knox and Mackintosh. Since the historians Curtis discusses shared the same stereotypes (pp. 74–89), it is unlikely that these were derived from the private study of the ethnologists.

40 Mandler, '"Race" and "nation"', pp. 233–4 and *passim*; Greta Jones, *Social Darwinism and English Thought: The Interaction between Biological and Social Theory* (Brighton, 1980), pp. 142–59.

41 Babington reviewed the formation of the population of the British Isles and concluded: 'The result of these various changes has been a mixed race of Celtic, Scandinavian, Saxon, and French elements, in proportion varying in different districts in England, as is also the case in Ireland... in England we find a people whose unity is the result of historic causes, not identity of race': *Fallacies of Race Theories*, p. 235. Denying racial essentialism, his phrase 'a mixed race' was an example of the older usage.

42 Chapter 2 above.

43 See *An Answer to a Late Abusive Pamphlet, intitled, The true-born Englishman, &c.*

Together with the true character of a true Englishman (London, 1700 [i.e. 1701]); *The English Gentleman Justified. A poem. Written on the occasion of a late scurrilous satyr, intituled, The true-born Englishman* (London, 1701); *English men no bastards: or, a satyr against the author of The true-born English-man* (London, 1701); [William Pittis], *The true-born Englishman: a satyr, answer'd, paragraph by paragraph* (London, 1701); *The picture of a true born English-man* (London, [?1705]).

44 Edward D. Snyder, 'The Wild Irish: A Study of some English Satires against the Irish, Scots, and Welsh', *Modern Philology*, 17 (1919–20), pp. 147–85; J. O. Bartley, *Teague, Shenkin and Sawney: being an historical study of the earliest Irish, Welsh and Scottish Characters in English plays* (Cork, 1954).

45 E.g. A *Declaration to the Free-Born People of England, now in arms against the tyrannie and oppression of Oliver Cromwell Esq.* ([?London, 1655]); *The Free-Born Subject; or, The Englishman's Birthright: asserted against all tyrannical usurpations either in church or state* (London, 1679); *Vox Patriae; or The resentments & indignation of the free-born subjects of England, against popery, arbitrary government, the Duke of York, or any popish successor* (London, 1681); Henry Care, *English Liberties; or, The free-born subject's inheritance* (London, 1682); *The declaration and admonitory letter of such of the nobility, gentry, and free-born subjects of his Majesty, as under the auspicious conduct of His Royal Highness Charles, Prince of Wales, Steward of Scotland, &c. have taken up arms in support of the cause of their King and country...* [?Edinburgh, 1745].

46 Peter Nockles, *The Oxford Movement in Context: Anglican High Churchmanship, 1760–1857* (Cambridge, 1994).

47 The Rev. Charles Kingsley (1819–75). Influenced by Carlyle, Maurice and Arnold, Kingsley's career was that of a parish priest; even when a professor of history at Cambridge he did not seek a public platform to advocate nationalism.

48 E. R. Norman, *Anti-Catholicism in Victorian England* (London, 1968).

49 Hereward (for unknown reasons termed 'the Wake') led armed resistance to the invasion of William I and became a folk hero, but his resonance was decidedly muted compared to the folk heroes of nineteenth-century continental European literature. For transatlantic comparisons, see Peter Karsten, *Patriot Heroes in England and America: political symbolism and changing values over three centuries* (Madison, Wis., 1978).

50 John Burrow, *Evolution and Society: a study in Victorian social theory* (Cambridge, 1966); idem, *The Crisis of Reason: European Thought, 1848–1914* (New Haven, 2000).

51 Ernest Barker, *National Character and the Factors in its Formation* (London, 1928).

52 Geoffrey G. Field, *Evangelist of Race: the Germanic Vision of Houston Stewart Chamberlain* (New York, 1981). Even then, Chamberlain included Irish Celts as Teutons in *The Foundations of the Nineteenth Century* (London, 1911), I, pp. 499–505.

53 Albert C. Baugh and Thomas Cable, *A History of the English Language* (4th edn., London, 1993), pp. 248–89; Charles Barber, *The English Language: An historical introduction* (Cambridge, 1993), pp. 199–233; Dick Leith, *A Social History of English* (2nd edn., London, 1997), pp. 237–49, at 243, shows how the *OED* viewed the English language as 'intimately bound up with the notion of English national identity'; but this identity was linguistically inclusive and plural. Suzanne Romaine (ed.), *The Cambridge History of the English Language. Volume IV 1776–1997* (Cambridge, 1998), pp. 48–54, assimilates England to Europe and condemns its distinctiveness by appealing to US practice as a yardstick.

54   Pioneered by Sir James Murray (1837–1915), for whom, see Elisabeth K. M. Murray, *Caught in the Web of Words: James A. H. Murray and the 'Oxford English Dictionary'* (New Haven, 1977).

55   Victor Durkacz, *The Decline of the Celtic Languages: a study of linguistic and cultural conflict in Scotland, Ireland and Wales from the Reformation to the twentieth century* (Edinburgh, 1983); Leith, *Social History of English*, pp. 149–79.

56   The situation in the British Isles, although it had an element of linguistic politics, therefore contrasted greatly with that witnessed in many areas of Europe in the nineteenth and twentieth centuries.

57   See chapter 2 above. For the alternative argument (rejected here), placing the key development in the nineteenth century, see Hudson, 'From "Nation" to "Race"', p. 256: 'The emergent concept of the "nation" as a linguistic and cultural community was of considerable importance to the concurrent rise of a racial worldview.'

58   Jacques Barzun, *The French Race: theories of its origin and their social and political implications prior to the Revolution* (Port Washington, NY, 1966); Michael Biddiss, *Father of Racist Ideology: the social and political thought of Count Gobineau* (London, 1970); Claude Blanckaert, 'On the Origins of French Ethnology. William Edwards and the Doctrine of Race', in George W. Stocking, Jr. (ed.), *Bones, Bodies, Behavior: essays on biological anthropology* (Madison, Wis., 1988), pp. 18–55, shows that Edwards responded to a French, not an English, debate on national identity and origins (he wrote also on Celtic languages); Tzevetan Todorov, *On Human Diversity: Nationalism, racism, and exoticism in French thought*, trans. Catherine Porter (Cambridge, Mass., 1993).

59   Stocking, *Victorian Anthropology*, pp 20–25; Hannah Franziska Augstein, *Race: the origins of an idea, 1760–1850* (Bristol, 1996), pp. xxix–xxx.

60   Richard Brent, *Liberal Anglican Politics: Whiggery, Religion and Reform 1830–1841* (Oxford, 1987).

61   J. P. Parry, *Democracy and Religion: Gladstone and the Liberal Party, 1867–1875* (Cambridge, 1986).

62   J. M. Golby and A. W. Purdue, *The Civilization of the Crowd: Popular Culture in England 1750–1900* (London, 1984).

63   Michael Biddiss, 'Dr Robert Knox and Victorian Racism', *Proceedings of the Royal Society of Medicine*, 69 (1976), pp. 245–50.

64   'Mazzini equated English radicalism with Benthamite utilitarianism, criticizing it for its preoccupation with individual rights, self-interest, and unfettered commercial progress, and its failure to recognize the collective life, duties, and destinies of nations': Miles Taylor, *The Decline of British Radicalism, 1847–1860* (Oxford, 1995), pp. 191–3.

65   Rosemary Ashton, *The German Idea: Four English writers and the reception of German thought 1800–1860* (Cambridge, 1980), pp. 1–3.

66   Charles E. McClelland, *The German Historians and England: a study in nineteenth-century views* (Cambridge, 1971).

67   Peter Mandler, '"In the Olden Time": Romantic history and English national identity, 1820–50', in Laurence Brockliss and David Eastwood (eds.), *A Union of Multiple Identities: The British Isles, c. 1750–c. 1850* (Manchester, 1997), pp. 78–92.

68   This interpretation of Kipling suggests a similar one for the verse of Sir Henry Newbolt (1862–1938). For the former's anti-racism, see Edward Shanks, *Rudyard Kipling: A Study in Literature and Political Ideas* (London, 1940).

69 Horsman, 'Origins of Racial Anglo-Saxonism', pp. 387, 399; Stocking, *Victorian Anthropology*, pp. 62–3. Yet Horsman includes much evidence to the contrary: Sharon Turner's *History of the Anglo-Saxons* (1799–1805), for long an influential work in England, 'stressed the love of liberty among the Anglo-Saxons' and 'specifically defended the idea of a single human species' (p. 394). Many of Horsman's examples of the use of 'race' are open to an older reading and do not demand newer ones. Markedly different are the Scots Thomas Carlyle and Robert Knox, and the (in his early novels) militantly Jewish Benjamin Disraeli. Anglican English examples offer a contrast: Thomas Arnold 'expressed uncertainty on the question of the inherent superiority of some races of men over others' (p. 401); John M. Kemble 'was cautious in his racial judgments compared to many of his contemporaries' (p. 403).

70 John Mitchell Kemble, *The Saxons in England* (2 vols., London, 1849), I, pp. v–vi; quoted in Mandler, '"Race" and "nation"', p. 239.

71 E. A. Freeman, *Comparative Politics* (London, 1873), p. 333, and 'Race and Language' [1877], in Michael Biddiss (ed.), *Images of Race* (Leicester, 1979), p. 222, cited in Mandler, '"Race" and "nation"', p. 240.

72 James Hunt, *Introductory Address on the Study of Anthropology Delivered Before the Anthropological Society of London, February 24th, 1863* (London, 1863), p. 13, quoted in Bolt, *Victorian Attitudes to Race*, p. ix.

73 Bolt, *Victorian Attitudes to Race*, p. 16.

74 Lord Milner, *The Nation and the Empire* (London, 1913), pp. xxxv–xxxvi: 'But what do I mean by the British race? I mean all the peoples of the United Kingdom and their descendants in other countries under the British flag. The expression may not be ethnologically accurate. The inhabitants of England, Scotland and Ireland are of various stocks, and in spite of constant intermixture, strongly-marked differences of type persist, even when they are not, as in the case of the Irish, emphasised and nourished by political dissidence. And yet to speak of them collectively as the British race is not only convenient, but is in accordance with broad political facts. Community of language and institutions, and centuries of life together under one sovereignty, have not indeed obliterated differences, but have superadded bonds, which are more than artificial, which make them in the eyes of the world, if not always in their own, a single nation, and which it will be found impossible to destroy.'

75 Quoted in Robbins, *Great Britain*, p. 252.

76 *The Times*, 16 January 1896, quoted in Charles S. Campbell, *From Revolution to Rapprochement: The United States and Great Britain, 1783–1900* (London, 1974), p. 204.

77 Keith Robbins, *Protestant Germany through British Eyes: A Complex Victorian Encounter* (London, 1993), quoted in Robbins, *Great Britain*, p. 225.

78 E. H. H. Green, *The Crisis of Conservatism: The politics, economics and ideology of the British Conservative party, 1880–1914* (London, 1995), pp. 159–83, 199–201.

79 G. K. Chesterton, 'The Secret People' (1915).

80 'Introduction', in Brockliss and Eastwood (eds.), *Union of Multiple Identities*, p. 2. For the relative absence of the theme of ethnicity in Scots and Irish thought before the nineteenth century see, for example, S. J. Connelly, *Religion, Law and Power: The Making of Protestant Ireland 1650–1760* (Oxford, 1992); Murray G. H. Pittock, *Inventing and Resisting Britain: Cultural Identities in Britain and Ireland, 1685–1789* (Basingstoke, 1997); idem, *Celtic Identity and the British Image* (Manchester, 1999). Ethnicity was

absent despite the prominence in Ireland and Scotland of ideas of descent as premises of group identity: see for example John O'Hart, *Irish Pedigrees; or, the Origin and Stem of the Irish Nation* (Dublin, 1876).

81   From a large literature, see for example Sir Reginald Coupland, *Welsh and Scottish Nationalism: A Study* (London, 1954); Jeanne Sheehy, *The Rediscovery of Ireland's Past: the Celtic revival, 1830–1930* (London, 1980); Sean Cronin, *Irish Nationalism: A History of its Roots and Ideology* (Dublin, 1980); D. G. Boyce, *Nationalism in Ireland* (London, 1982; 3rd edn., 1995); Gwyn A. Williams, *When Was Wales? a history of the Welsh* (London, 1985); John Hutchinson, *The Dynamics of Cultural Nationalism: The Gaelic revival and the creation of the Irish nation state* (London, 1987); Maurice Goldring, *Faith of our Fathers: The formation of Irish nationalist ideology 1890–1920* (Dublin, 1987); Charlotte Aull Davies, *Welsh Nationalism in the Twentieth Century: the ethnic option and the modern state* (New York, 1989); Christopher Harvie, 'The Folk and the Gwerin: The Myth and the Reality of Popular Culture in 19th-Century Scotland and Wales', *Proceedings of the British Academy*, 80 (1993), pp. 19–48; idem, *Scotland and Nationalism: Scottish Society and Politics 1707–1994* (2nd edn, London, 1994); Damien Murray, *Romanticism, Nationalism and Irish Antiquarian Societies, 1840–80* (Maynooth, 2000).

82   For Celticism as 'an ethnocentric form of nationalism', see Curtis, *Anglo-Saxons and Celts*, pp. 108–16, at 109. Curtis, however, explained it as a defensive Irish response to prior English determinist racialism (an interpretation questioned here), and defended Irish racial myths as 'innocuous' (p. 115). See also Malcolm Chapman, *The Celts: The Construction of a Myth* (London, 1992). The racialist vision embodied in such texts as Seumas MacManus, *The Story of the Irish Race* (New York, 1921) and *A Short History of the Irish Race* (2 vols., Dublin, [1928]) is now published on a variety of internet sites.

83   William Gladstone, Lord Rosebery, Lord Haldane, Andrew Bonar Law, James Ramsay MacDonald, Arthur Henderson, Sir Henry Campbell-Bannerman, A. J. Balfour, Douglas Haig, David Lloyd George.

84   Robbins, *Great Britain*, pp. 274–5.

85   Davies, *Welsh Nationalism*, p. 39.

86   Prys Morgan, *Iolo Morgannwg* (Cardiff, 1975); idem, 'The hunt for the Welsh past in the Romantic period', in Eric Hobsbawm and Terence Ranger (eds.), *The Invention of Tradition* (Cambridge, 1983), pp. 43–100.

87   D. George Boyce, Robert Eccleshall and Vincent Geoghan (eds.), *Political Thought in Ireland since the Seventeenth Century* (London, 1993).

88   Hutchinson, *Dynamics of Cultural Nationalism*, p. 1 and *passim*.

89   Cronin, *Irish Nationalism*, p. 99.

90   The simianized image of the Irishman which was adopted by some Victorian caricatures after the outbreak of Fenian violence in the 1860s is explicable in much older terms as a visual notation of inferior civilization; it failed to generate any substantial body of English racialist thought on the Irish Question that would bear comparison with continental European phenomena: L. Perry Curtis, Jr., *Apes and Angels: the Irishman in Victorian caricature* (Newton Abbot, 1971), pp. ix, 5–6 traces physiognomy to the humoural divisions of Hippocrates and Aristotle. For a critique of Curtis, see Sheridan Gilley, 'English Attitudes to the Irish in England, 1789–1900' in Colin Holmes (ed.), *Immigrants and Minorities in British Society* (London, 1978), pp.

81–110: 'even bitter prose satire on "the wild Irish" before 1800 expressed a dislike which was national, not racial' (p. 85). English caricatures had developed an equally unflattering image of the Scot in the eighteenth century without resort to racial doctrines. See also Roger Swift and Sheridan Gilley (eds.), *The Irish in Britain 1815–1939* (London, 1989); Lynn Lees, *Exiles of Erin: Irish Migrants in Victorian London* (Manchester, 1979); M. A. G. O'Tuathaigh, 'The Irish in Nineteenth-Century Britain: Problems of integration', *Transactions of the Royal Historical Society*, fifth ser., 31 (1981), pp. 149–73; B. Collins, 'The Irish in Britain, 1780–1921', in Brian J. Graham and L. J. Proudfoot (eds.), *An Historical Geography of Ireland* (London, 1993), pp. 338–98.

91   Sir Robert Anderson, *Sidelights on the Home Rule Movement* (London, 1906), p. 189.

92   Lubbock, in *Mr. Gladstone and the Nationalities of the United Kingdom*, pp. 7–13. Bryce replied (p. 23): 'You may have different nationalities of a race practically the same. You may have a nationality composed of several races.' The Duke of Argyll wrote, less abstractly (pp. 30–32): 'We are all mongrels, and not only are we all equally mongrels, but we are the result of the intermixture of precisely the same breeds all over the United Kingdom... It is now the barbarous work of the Parnellite Liberals to undo the work of union all over the three kingdoms'; there was an 'absence of any dividing line between us and the Irish people in respect to race'. T. H. Huxley agreed (p. 43): 'the same elements have entered into the composition of the population in England, Scotland and Ireland... the ethnic differences between the three lie simply in the general and local proportions of these elements in each region'.

93   A. J. Balfour, 'A Note on Home Rule', in Balfour et al., *Against Home Rule: The case for the Union* (London, 1912), pp. 41–6, at 43.

94   To some degree, of course, they did register; but as an anti-racialist English commentator wrote in 1895, 'The Celtic race theory is acceptable alike to the Irish patriot and to the English apologist for English rule, the latter using it to explain the innate inability of the Irish for self-government': Babington, *Fallacies of Race Theories*, p. 239.

95   Stewart J. Brown, 'Presbyterians and Catholics in Twentieth-Century Scotland', in S. J. Brown and G. Newlands (eds.), *Scottish Christianity in the Modern World: Studies in honour of A. C. Cheyne* (Edinburgh, 2000), pp. 255–82; Joseph M. Bradley, *Football, Religion and Ethnicity: Irish identity in Scotland* (London, 1996); Tom Gallagher, *Glasgow, The Uneasy Peace: Religious tension in modern Scotland, 1819–1914* (Manchester, 1987); James Edmund Handley, *The Irish in Modern Scotland* (Cork, 1947), pp. 93–121, 'Religious and Racial Discord'.

96   A similar conclusion may apply to the new meanings given to the term 'race'.

NOTES TO CHAPTER 4

1   For nineteenth-century radicals' later construction of a tradition extending back to Hampden, Pym and Cromwell, see Günther Lottes, 'Radicalism, Revolution and Popular Culture: An Anglo-French Comparison', in Mark Philp (ed.), *The French Revolution and British Popular Politics* (Cambridge, 1991), pp. 78–98; Margot C. Finn, *After Chartism: Class and nation in English radical politics, 1848–1874* (Cambridge, 1993),

pp. 35–7. By contrast, the actual 'influence of Levellerism on subsequent radical–democratic movements' was only 'subtle and somewhat oblique': F. K. Donnelly, 'Levellerism in Eighteenth and Early Nineteenth-Century Britain', *Albion*, 20 (1988), pp. 261–9, at 261. In recent scholarship, older assumptions of the secular, functional continuities of seventeenth- and eighteenth-century reform movements have everywhere broken down.

2   Alexander Gray, *The Socialist Tradition: Moses to Lenin* (London, 1946; 4th impression, 1963) was a careful and critical study of 523 pages. Gray (1882–1968) had been a civil servant for sixteen years before taking the chair of political economy at Aberdeen in 1921; he held a chair at Edinburgh from 1935 to his retirement in 1956, and also wrote *The Development of Economic Doctrine* (1931). For service on many government boards and commissions, he was knighted in 1947. In the preface to *The Socialist Tradition* (p. v) he recorded his personal dislike of Marx, Lassalle and Rousseau.

3   See Adolf Laube, 'Radicalism as a Research Problem in the History of Early Reformation' in Hans J. Hillerbrand (ed.), *Radical Tendencies in the Reformation*, special issue of *Sixteenth Century Essays & Studies*, 9 (1988), pp. 9–23. Laube cautioned: 'A more detailed analysis of the problem of radicalism indicates that "radical" does not so much refer to a substantive content as to an adjectival quality' (pp. 10–11). More extensive cautions are expressed by Hans J. Hillerbrand, 'Radicalism in the Early Reformation: Varieties of Reformation in Church and Society', ibid., pp. 25–41.

4   George H. Williams, *The Radical Reformation* (Philadelphia, 1962).

5   Michael G. Baylor (ed.), *The Radical Reformation* (Cambridge, 1991), p. xi. For the persistence of this methodological vice of anachronism in some quarters see, for example, Eric Heffer (ed.), *Cromwell and Communism: Socialism and Democracy in the Great English Revolution* (London, 1980); Isaac Kramnick, *Republicanism and Bourgeois Radicalism: Political Ideology in late Eighteenth-Century England and America* (Ithaca, New York, 1990); Gordon S. Wood, *The Radicalism of the American Revolution* (New York, 1992). Cf. George L. Cherry, *Early English Liberalism: its emergence through Parliamentary action, 1660–1702* (New York, 1962); Martin Seliger, *The Liberal Politics of John Locke* (London, 1968); Ruth Grant, *John Locke's Liberalism* (Chicago, 1987).

6   J. C. D. Clark, *The Language of Liberty 1660–1832* (Cambridge, 1994).

7   Paine's remedy for political ills was what he described as 'the representative system', not universal suffrage. Although he was well aware that 'not one person in seven is represented', his remarks on the franchise were few and perfunctory, referring to taxpayers' practical involvement with government and the collective role of 'the people' rather than to the ontological status of individuals: Thomas Paine, *Letter Addressed to the Addressers, on the Late Proclamation* (London, 1792), pp. 27, 39, 48, 57–8, 67–8. In *Rights of Man*, Paine was content with the property qualification in the proposed French constitution; by *Dissertation on the First Principles of Government* (1795) he argued to reduce the property qualification to zero; in neither case did he begin with the individual, as Price and Priestley had done, but rather with the principle of equality. For the origin of the doctrine of universal suffrage, see J. C. D. Clark, *English Society 1660–1832* (Cambridge, 2000), chapter 4.

8   For a recent attempt to invent a long genealogy for class formation, see P. J. Corfield (ed.), *Language, History and Class* (Oxford, 1991). For a later chronology and different analysis, see Clark, *English Society 1660–1832*, chapter 2. The evidence presented here

does not bear out claims that radicalism was intrinsically related to class formation: David Nicholls, 'The English Middle Classes and the Ideological Significance of Radicalism, 1760–1886', *Journal of British Studies*, 24 (1985), pp. 415–33; Edward Royle, 'The language of class and radicalism', *History Review*, no. 29 (December 1997), pp. 38–42.

9 For the process as a whole, see Clark, *English Society 1660–1832*, 'Keywords'. This essay is not an attempt to construct an ideal type but to explain the degree of coherence in a newly coined doctrine. A prosopographical study would be needed to determine how many reformers subscribed to 'radicalism'. Clearly, too, political terms like this are no sooner propounded than they begin to be claimed, or repudiated, for tactical reasons. As we shall see, that was the case with the older term 'radical reformer'. It should be emphasized at the outset that it is not being argued here that all, or even most, reformers were atheists.

10 E.g. John Ward, *Four Essays upon the English Language... To these is subjoined A Catalogue of the English Verbs, formed thro their Radical Tenses* (London, 1758); [John Murdoch], *A Radical Vocabulary of the French Language* (London, 1782); John Jamieson, *Hermes Scythius: or, The Radical Affinities of the Greek and Latin Languages to the Gothic* (Edinburgh, 1814); *A. Thibaudin's Proposed Original System for a Radical, Universal & Philosophical Reform in the Spelling of Languages* (London, [1842]).

11 John Mudge, *A Radical and Expeditious Cure for a recent Catarrhous Cough* (London, 1778).

12 E.g. J. F. Dieffenbach, *Memoir on the Radical Cure of Stuttering, by a surgical operation*, trans. Joseph Travers (London, 1841).

13 E.g. William Spence, *The Radical Cause of the Present Distresses of the West-India Planters Pointed Out* (London, 1807).

14 [Samuel Johnson], *Taxation no Tyranny; an Answer to the Resolutions and Address of the American Congress* (London, 1775), p. 23.

15 Paine, *Letter Addressed to the Addressers*, pp. 8, 33.

16 William Wilberforce, *A Practical View of the Prevailing Religious System of Professed Christians... contrasted with Real Christianity* (London, 1797), pp. 26–7.

17 *Sir Robert Peel the Greatest Radical of the Age, and the Best Friend of O'Connell* (London, 1845).

18 Clark, *English Society 1660–1832*, chapter 4; Derek Beales, 'The Idea of Reform in British Politics, 1829–1850', *Proceedings of the British Academy*, 100 (1999), pp. 159–74, for the general restriction of the term 'reform' to parliamentary reform. Joanna Innes kindly showed me the text of her unpublished paper, 'The Idea of Reform in English Public Life, to 1830'.

19 John Disney (ed.), *The Works... of John Jebb* (3 vols., London, 1787), I, p. 194; Christopher Wyvill, *Political Papers* (5 vols., York, 1794–1804), I, p. 341.

20 [Christopher Wyvill], *A Letter to John Cartwright, Esq.* (York, 1801), pp. 4–5.

21 Sir Walter Scott to Thomas Scott, 16 October 1819, in H. J. C. Grierson (ed.), *The Letters of Sir Walter Scott* (12 vols., London, 1931–7), VI, p. 2.

22 Jonas Dennis, *Church reform, by a Church radical, comprising a Review of the Thirty-nine Articles* (London, 1835), pp. iii–v.

23 *Thoughts on a Radical Remedy for the Present Distresses of the Country* (London, 1820), pp. 8, 21.

24   *The Truth. A Weekly Radical Christian, and Family Newspaper*, vol. 1, no. 1 (10 February, 1833), pp. 1–2.

25   In this chapter I offer an account of the emergence of a coherently defined doctrine out of diverse earlier usages, and its subsequent re-diversification. For a study which adopts a loose definition of radicalism and which consequently focuses on the diverse practical commitments of the individuals involved, see Eileen Groth Lyon, *Politicians in the Pulpit: Christian Radicalism in Britain from the Fall of the Bastille to the Disintegration of Chartism* (Aldershot, 1999). This work seeks to make a case for the salience of religion in reforming movements, and so neglects the role of irreligion in the conceptualization of that particular variety of reform that came to be called 'radicalism'.

26   Its imprecision in current scholarship is often acknowledged. Writing a survey of the subject before the recent reinterpretation of the long eighteenth century, two historians had been compelled to preface their study with the warning: 'The word "radicalism" has so many meanings that as a concept in historical analysis it is practically useless... To impose coherence on this evidently vague topic is misleading. There is no clear picture of tributaries feeding into a main stream which can then be followed to the estuary and the sea': Edward Royle and James Walvin, *English Radicals and Reformers 1760–1848* (Brighton, 1982), pp. 9–10. Cf. Richard L. Greaves and Robert Zaller (eds.), *Biographical Dictionary of British Radicals in the Seventeenth Century* (3 vols., Brighton, 1982–4): 'The term "radical" as we use it is confessedly an anachronism for the seventeenth century' (I, p. vii). No more adequate definition of the term was offered in Joseph O. Baylen and Norbert J. Gossman (eds.), *Biographical Dictionary of Modern British Radicals* [1770–1914] (4 vols., Hassocks, 1979–88).

27   It will therefore be clear that the twentieth-century hybrid, 'bourgeois radicalism', is a double solecism.

28   [George Huddesford], *Bubble and Squeak, a Galli-maufry of British Beef with the Chopp'd Cabbage of Gallic Philosophy and Radical Reform* (London, 1799), pp. 41, 43. Timotheus, statesman and general, incited the Athenians in 358 or 357 BC to expel the Thebans from Euboea. Huddesford quoted Dryden's *Alexander's Feast*, Act II: 'Revenge, revenge, Timotheus cries, / See the furies arise, / See the snakes that they rear, / How they hiss in their hair, / And the sparkles that flash from their eyes!'

29   *The Radical-House which Jack would build* (2nd edn., Exeter [1820]). This was a reply to the pamphlets of William Hone; for whom, see below.

30   Electoral malpractice in the borough of Grampound had reached such a level in the 1818 election that the ministry was finally shamed into legislation to remove its right to return two Members. The ministry wished to transfer that right to Yorkshire.

31   *An Address to The Ministerial Radicals, and a call upon all who love the constitution, and are anxious for its preservation in that state in which it was delivered by our forefathers to the House of Brunswick, by one of the middle class of the people* (London, 1820), pp. 1, 17–18, 27. The author was evidently an Evangelical who objected to the ministers for swearing, blaspheming, and breaches of Sabbath observance (p. 22).

32   *Hints for Radical Reform, on Principles of Equity. By Amor Patriae* (London, 1821), pp. 1–3, 46, 51–2.

33   *The Radical Reformists. A Narrative, adapted to the Present Times* (London, n.d. [? 1816]), p. 4.

34 *Radical Reform, the Only Remedy for the Disorders of our Country; or, Observations on the Changes Necessary both in Church and State. By Britannicus* (London, 1819), pp. 4, 6.

35 Ibid., pp. 8–10, 15.

36 E.g. *Radical Reform: or a Better Cure for Poverty and Distress, than Burning Corn Stacks and Destroying Thrashing Machines. A Dialogue* (Doncaster, 1831).

37 John S. Harford, *Some Account of the Life, Death and Principles of Thomas Paine, together with Remarks on his Writings, and on their intimate connection with the avowed objects of the Revolutionists of 1793, and of the Radicals in 1819* (Bristol, 1819), pp. v–vi, 17.

38 Ibid., pp. 17–19.

39 Ibid., p. 73.

40 Ibid., p. 81.

41 John Scandrett Harford (1785–1866). Son of a Quaker banker, he converted to the Church of England after the death of his brother in 1804. He became a zealous supporter of the Church Missionary Society and the Bible Society, and was a close friend of Hannah More and William Wilberforce. He succeeded to his father's estates in 1815, and acted as JP, deputy lieutenant and high sheriff for his county.

42 Harford, *Principles of Thomas Paine*, pp. 22, 82. Part of his tract was taken up with a defence of the veracity of Scripture.

43 See above, n. 8.

44 *Hints to Radical Reformers, and Materials for True* (London, 1817), p. 3.

45 For primarily social and economic studies of the tithe question, which nevertheless capture its virulence and wide extent, see Eric J. Evans, 'Some Reasons for the Growth of English Rural Anti-Clericalism *c.* 1750–*c.* 1830', *Past & Present*, 66 (1975), pp. 84–109, and idem, *The Contentious Tithe: the Tithe Problem and English Agriculture, 1750–1850* (London, 1976). Resentment against tithes had, of course, been evident earlier without alone engendering 'radicalism': cf. Margaret James, 'The Political Importance of the Tithes Controversy in the English Revolution 1640–60', *History* 26 (1941), pp. 1–18.

46 *A Letter from a Manufacturer to his Son, upon Radical Reform* (London, [?1815]), pp. 1–3, 13.

47 John Galt (1779–1839), a Scot who pursued a career in England. Unsuccessful in a series of business ventures, he turned to writing and can in some ways be compared with that other ministerial supporter, Sir Walter Scott.

48 [John Galt], *The Radical. An Autobiography* (London, 1832), pp. iii, 5, 16.

49 Ibid., pp. 17, 25, 55, 61.

50 Ibid., pp. 75, 79, 92.

51 Ibid., pp. 93, 98, 106–7, 109.

52 Ibid., pp. 111–12, 121.

53 Ibid., p. 132.

54 Ibid., pp. 132–3, 193–4.

55 Ibid., pp. 99–104.

56 Ibid., pp. 111–12.

57 Ibid., pp. 133–4.

58 J. S. Mill, *Autobiography and Literary Essays*, ed. John M. Robson and Jack Stillinger (Toronto, 1981), p. 81; Thomas, *Philosophic Radicals*, p. 1.

59 George William Downing, *An Address to the Independent Livery of London, on the Advantages to be Derived from a Radical Reform in the Commons House of Parliament*

(2nd edn., London, n.d. [?1818]), p. 4.

60 Samuel Bamford (1788–1872). Son of a Methodist who was converted away from Christianity by Paine in the 1790s. Himself a weaver, poet and political organizer, he opposed violent means and became a special constable during the Chartist disturbances. Present at the Peterloo incident, he was convicted of conspiracy to incite a riot and imprisoned for a year; he then withdrew from politics. Martin Hewitt argues that Bamford's 'religious beliefs were a crucial source of his radicalism... his anti-clericalism was deep-rooted' and virulent as late as 1859: 'Radicalism and the Victorian Working Class: the Case of Samuel Bamford', *Historical Journal*, 34 (1991), pp. 873–92, at 880, 884.

61 Samuel Bamford, *Passages in the Life of a Radical* (2 vols., Heywood, [1841–2]), I, p. 3.

62 Bamford, *Passages in the Life of a Radical*, I, pp. 10–11.

63 [Louis Simond], *Journal of a Tour and Residence in Great Britain, During the Years 1810 and 1811, by a French Traveller* (2 vols., Edinburgh, 1815), I, p. 36.

64 Vernon F. Storr, *The Development of English Theology in the Nineteenth Century 1800–1860* (London, 1913), pp. 383–94, at 384. Storr, like other theologians, did not establish connections between Bentham's religion and his politics, and Storr's insights were generally overlooked by later historians of religion. They tended to treat the Benthamites' irreligion as a reason for passing them over, preferring to focus on the more congenial John Stuart Mill: cf. Bernard M. G. Reardon, *Religious Thought in the Victorian Age: A Survey from Coleridge to Gore* (2nd edn., London, 1995), pp. 198–200.

65 Elie Halévy, *The Growth of Philosophic Radicalism*, trans. Mary Morris (London, 1928; 2nd edn., 1934), p. 264. Nowhere else in the work did Halévy mention, let alone explore, the emergence of this concept. J. H. Burns, 'Jeremy Bentham: From Radical Enlightenment to Philosophic Radicalism', *The Bentham Newsletter*, 8 (1984), pp. 4–14, sought to place Bentham more exactly in his setting but without defining and locating these key terms.

66 '... it looked as if the Whig government which had passed the Reform Bill would let the reform movement flag unless a united body of radicals goaded it on. A name was needed which would be a rallying point without becoming another sectarian label': William Thomas, *The Philosophic Radicals: Nine Studies in Theory and Practice 1817–1841* (Oxford, 1979), p. 2.

67 Thomas, *Philosophic Radicals*, pp. 1, 4.

68 Professor J. H. Burns reminds me that the edition was left incomplete because of the publisher's financial difficulties, and more research is needed into this question. Nevertheless, it seems fair to say that the next generation of Bentham's followers understood his canon as one hardly concerned with religion.

69 The fullest and most perceptive investigation of Bentham's religious views is now James E. Crimmins, *Secular Utilitarianism: Social Science and the Critique of Religion in the Thought of Jeremy Bentham* (Oxford, 1990). This able study does not, however, examine the nature of 'radicalism' or draw the connections between religion and politics proposed here. In arguing for the chronological and conceptual priority of men's religion in explaining their politics, I am retaining a model first developed in my *English Society 1688–1832* (Cambridge, 1985).

70 For Bentham's Oxford years (1760–4) and the controversy of 1773, see J. E. Crimmins, 'Bentham's Unpublished Manuscripts on Subscription to Articles of Faith', in *British*

Journal for Eighteenth Century Studies, 9 (1986), pp. 33–44 and idem, *Secular Utilitarianism*, pp. 115–28. For this culture at Oxford, and its requirements, see J. C. D. Clark, *Samuel Johnson: Literature, religion and English cultural politics from the Restoration to Romanticism* (Cambridge, 1994) and idem, 'Religion and Political Identity: Samuel Johnson as a Nonjuror' in Jonathan Clark and Howard Erskine-Hill (eds.), *Samuel Johnson in Historical Context* (London, 2002).

71 James Steintrager, 'Morality and Belief: the Origin and Purpose of Bentham's Writings on Religion', *The Mill News Letter*, 6, no. 2 (Spring 1971), pp. 3–15. Steintrager concluded that 'A strong opposition to religion was built into the very fibre of his utilitarian system almost from the very beginning in 1768', p. 7.

72 [Jeremy Bentham], *A Fragment on Government* (London, 1776), p. xvi; Clark, *English Society 1660–1832*, chapter 3.

73 Bentham to Grafton, *c.* 7 September 1790, in Alexander Taylor Milne (ed.), *The Correspondence of Jeremy Bentham*, IV (London, 1981), p. 201.

74 Bentham to Francis Place, 24 April 1831, in Graham Wallas, *The Life of Francis Place, 1771–1854* (London, 1898), p. 82.

75 Halévy, *Philosophic Radicalism*, p. 520. *Traités de législation* was not published in England until 1864, although it began to appear in the USA in 1830. Halévy included this insight in an appendix; his text gave the misleading impression that Bentham's writings on religion were merely opportunistic, provoked by the controversy over rival school systems in the late 1810s: cf. Steintrager, 'Morality and Belief', p. 7; Crimmins, *Secular Utilitarianism*, pp. 165–81.

76 For legal action in such cases, see William H. Wickwar, *The Struggle for the Freedom of the Press 1819–1832* (London, 1928); Joel H. Wiener, *Radicalism and Freethought in Nineteenth-Century Britain: The Life of Richard Carlile* (Westport, Conn., 1983); Olivia Smith, *The Politics of Language 1791–1819* (Oxford, 1984); Clark, *English Society 1660–1832*, chapter 5.

77 Jeremy Bentham, *The Elements of the Art of Packing, as applied to Special Juries, particularly in cases of Libel Law* (London, 1821). 'Libel' included the religious offence of blasphemous libel.

78 Alexander Bain, *James Mill. A Biography* (London 1882), pp. 98, 101–2, 108, 127; Stephen Conway (ed.), *The Correspondence of Jeremy Bentham*, VIII (Oxford, 1988), pp. 26, 37, 60–61, 93–4, 430.

79 *Swear not at All* (1817); *Church-of-Englandism and its Catechism Examined (1818); Analysis of the Influence of Natural Religion on the Temporal Happiness of Mankind* (1822); *Not Paul, but Jesus* (1823).

80 James E. Crimmins, 'Bentham's Metaphysics and the Science of Divinity', *Harvard Theological Review*, 79 (1986), pp. 387–411; idem, 'Bentham on Religion: Atheism and the Secular Society', *Journal of the History of Ideas*, 47 (1986), pp. 95–110; idem, *Secular Utilitarianism*, pp. 161–4 and *passim*.

81 Clark, *English Society 1660–1832*, p. 492.

82 John Henry Newman, *Discourses on the Scope and Nature of University Education* (Dublin, 1852), p. 132.

83 'At bottom, in Bentham and James Mill anticlerical and democratic opinions were confused...': Halévy, *Philosophic Radicalism*, p. 294.

84 Clark, *English Society 1660–1832*, chapter 4.

85 Halévy, *Philosophic Radicalism*, pp. 261–3.

86 Thomas, *Philosophic Radicals*, p. 33.

87 I differ here from the argument of J. R. Dinwiddy, 'Bentham's Transition to Political Radicalism, 1809–10', *Journal of the History of Ideas*, 36 (1975), pp. 683–700. Although learned and illuminating, this article did not examine the category 'radicalism'.

88 Dinwiddy, 'Bentham's Transition', p. 688.

89 Recent scholarship has urged that Bentham's unpublished papers show that he was strongly led in the direction of universal suffrage by the logic of his utilitarianism as early as *c.* 1788–90. For an overview, see James E. Crimmins, 'Bentham's Political Radicalism Examined', *Journal of the History of Ideas*, 55 (1994), pp. 259–81. Yet the evidence so far presented suggests that Bentham's priority in *c.* 1788–90 was to secure good government by procedural means rather than to begin with individual entitlements to the franchise. Nor would such a conversion in *c.* 1788 explain the conceptual innovations in the late 1810s and early 1820s examined here.

90 Halévy, *Philosophic Radicalism*, p. 259; Dinwiddy, 'Bentham's Transition', pp. 690–91.

91 Cf. Crimmins, 'Bentham's Political Radicalism', pp. 274–81. This antedating of Bentham's conversion to democracy to *c.* 1790 appears to neglect the emergence of religious questions to prominence in Bentham's thought in the years *c.* 1808–17.

92 Robert A. Fenn, *James Mill's Political Thought* (New York, 1987), pp. 30–3, argued that Mill's loss of faith owed much to conversations with Bentham.

93 Bain, *Mill*, pp. 22, 32, 88–9. In 1818, Mill was approached to be a candidate for the chair of Greek at Glasgow University: he declined, among other reasons being his unwillingness to subscribe to the Westminster Confession of Faith that the post required: ibid., pp. 166–8. For Mill's atheism, see Crimmins, 'Bentham on Religion', p. 99. 'The Established Church in England was virtually Mill's *bête noire*': Fenn, *Mill's Political Thought*, p. 89. The extent of Mill's determination to transform the Church was only revealed at the end of his life in his article 'The Church, and its Reform', *The London Review*, 1 (July 1835), pp. 264–304: Fenn, loc. cit., pp. 89–93; Bain, *Mill*, pp. 381–8. It was quickly followed by his equally revealing article 'Aristocracy' in *The London Review* for January 1836: Bain, *Mill*, pp. 399–403. For an element in Mill's intellectual formation that may have struck a chord with Bentham, see Clark, *English Society 1660–1832*, pp. 159–60.

94 Thomas, *Philosophic Radicals*, pp. 99–100.

95 Even Bentham, according to Bowring's report, said of James Mill that 'His creed of politics results less from love for the many than from hatred of the few': Bain, *Mill*, p. 461.

96 Thomas, *Philosophic Radicals*, pp. 124–7, 133–4. For Mill's deliberate concealment of his 'profound radicalism' in this area, see Fenn, *Mill's Political Thought*, pp. 108–27.

97 Fenn, *Mill's Political Thought*, p. iv.

98 Cf. Wiener, *Carlile*, pp. 21–2, 24, 26, 63–5, 101–19.

99 Richard W. Davis, *Dissent in Politics: The Political Life of William Smith, MP* (London, 1971), pp. 190–203.

100 Jeremy Bentham, *Plan of Parliamentary Reform, in the Form of a Catechism, with Reasons for each Article, with an Introduction, shewing The Necessity of Radical, and the Inadequacy of Moderate, Reform* (London, 1817). The work consisted of a 337-page introduction to a 'Catechism of Parliamentary Reform' of fifty-two pages. In the

Introduction, Bentham paid tribute to John Cartwright as 'the worthy father of radical reform' and commended the late Duke of Richmond for championing universal suffrage in 1780 and 1783: his pamphlet, urged Bentham, could be bought from William Hone's bookshops (ibid., pp. xxxix, clii). Perhaps Bentham owned a copy of *The Bill of the late Duke of Richmond, for Universal Suffrage, and Annual Parliaments* (London: W. Hone, 1817).

101 Bentham, *Plan of Parliamentary Reform*, pp. ii, vi, xviii–xix.

102 Ibid., pp. xxxvi–xxxvii, lviii, xciii, 9.

103 [Jeremy Bentham], *Bentham's Radical Reform Bill, with extracts from the reasons* (London, 1819), pp. 1, 8–9.

104 Jeremy Bentham, *Church-of-Englandism and its Catechism examined* (London, 'printed, 1817: published, 1818'). This work includes *The Church of England Catechism Examined*, separately paginated. Perhaps the high price, 20s., helped shield it from legal action.

105 Ibid., pp. x–xi.

106 Ibid., pp. xi–xii, xv, xix, xxxv–xxxvi, xliii.

107 Ibid., 'Church of England Catechism', pp. 194–5.

108 Thomas, *Philosophic Radicals*, p. 36.

109 In the 'Advertisement' to this work, Bentham explained that he was induced to publish by 'the addition so lately made of the scourge of religious persecution to the yoke of despotism': Crimmins, *Secular Utilitarianism*, p. 151.

110 Thomas, *Philosophic Radicals*, pp. 31, 42. Hone's works included *The Late John Wilkes's Catechism of a Ministerial Member* (1817); *The Political Litany* (1817); *The Sinecurist's Creed* (1817); *The Political House that Jack Built* (1819); *The Right Divine of Kings to Govern Wrong!* (1821), etc. Unusually, Hone's journey led in the opposite direction. He converted to Christianity in 1832, and was received into the Church in 1834: Smith, *Politics of Language*, pp. 154–201, at 174–5. For Hone's trials as a formative influence on 'Carlile's evolution as a radical Freethinker', see Wiener, *Carlile*, p. 24.

111 For his republications of freethinking classics, see Wiener, *Carlile*, pp. 35–6. Bentham tried to persuade Carlile to accept free legal representation, but he refused: ibid., p. 45.

112 George Grote (1794–1871), heir to a banking firm. A Freethinker, he was introduced by Ricardo to Mill and by Mill to Bentham. Grote's first pamphlet, published anonymously, was *Statement of the Question of Parliamentary Reform* (London, 1821), which argued for virtually universal suffrage.

113 Crimmins, *Secular Utilitarianism*, pp. 207–26.

114 [Jeremy Bentham, ed. George Grote], 'Philip Beauchamp', *Analysis of the Influence of Natural Religion, on the Temporal Happiness of Mankind* (London: R. Carlile, 1822), pp. iv–v, 16, 35, 128–137.

115 James Steintrager, 'Language and Politics: Bentham on Religion', *The Bentham Newsletter*, 4 (1980), pp. 4–20, at 10–11. Grote evidently omitted this material from the published version.

116 Place claimed editorship in a note on his copy, now in the British Library: Halévy, *Philosophic Radicalism*, p. 544; Crimmins, *Secular Utilitarianism*, pp. 227–53.

117 [Jeremy Bentham, ed. Francis Place], 'Gamaliel Smith', *Not Paul, But Jesus* (London: John Hunt, 1823), pp. v–vi, xiv, 366, 372.

118 Steintrager, 'Morality and Belief', p. 11.

119 Jeremy Bentham, *Radicalism not Dangerous*, in John Bowring (ed.), *The Works of Jeremy*

Bentham (11 vols., Edinburgh, 1838–43), III, pp. 599–622, at 600, 609. This was the work's first publication.

120   Bentham, *Radicalism not Dangerous*, pp. 612–13, 616.

121   [John Locke], *Two Treatises of Government*, ed. Peter Laslett (Cambridge, 1988), I, s. 6; II, ss. 25–6, 34, 36, 50.

122   Thomas Paine, *Rights of Man: Being an Answer to Mr. Burke's Attack on the French Revolution* (London: J. S. Jordan, 1791), pp. 46–7.

123   Thomas Paine, *Agrarian Justice opposed to Agrarian Law* (2nd edn., London [1797]), pp. v–vi, 12, 16, 29: 'Land... is the free gift of the Creator in common to the human race.'

124   T. M. Parsinnen, 'Thomas Spence and the Origins of English Land Nationalization', *Journal of the History of Ideas*, 34 (1973), pp. 135–41.

125   John Dunn, 'The politics of Locke in England and America in the eighteenth century', in John W. Yolton (ed.), *John Locke: Problems and Perspectives* (Cambridge, 1969), pp. 45–80, at 68–9, quoting Thomas Spence, *The Rights of Man as Exhibited in a Lecture* (4th edn., London, 1793), pp. 23–4.

126   Thomas R. Knox, 'Thomas Spence: The Trumpet of Jubilee', *Past & Present*, 76 (1977), pp. 74–98. For Murray, see Clark, *Language of Liberty*, pp. 31, 124–5, 267, 329–31.

127   Thomas Spence, *The Rights of Infants* (London, 1797), p. 3.

128   Dunn, 'The politics of Locke in England and America', pp. 68–9, quoting *The Important Trial of Thomas Spence* (London, 1803), pp. 59–60.

129   Knox, 'Spence', p. 98.

130   Thomas A. Horne, *Property Rights and Property: Political Argument in Britain, 1605–1834* (Chapel Hill, NC, 1990), p. 235.

131   Gregory Claeys, *Machinery, Money and the Millennium: From Moral Economy to Socialism, 1815–1860* (Princeton, 1987), pp. 8–9. The most clearly secular critique of landownership in the 1790s was that of William Godwin. Yet Godwin's atheism, like James Mill's, took its intellectual shape as a result of their abandonment of their careers as Nonconformist ministers: Clark, *English Society 1660–1832*, pp. 404–6. It is suggested here that Bentham and Mill were more influential in formulating a new doctrine in the 1820s than Godwin had been in the 1790s. Godwin's problem was that his doctrine undercut all private property; Ricardo's strength was that his was directed against the landlord.

132   For the role of Ricardian economics in negating the Anglican model of the social order, see Clark, *English Society 1660–1832*, chapter 2.

133   For a rehabilitation of the Whigs and of Whiggism from the perspectives imposed on them by students of utilitarianism, especially Halévy, see William Thomas, 'L'utilitarisme et le libéralisme anglais au début du XIXe siècle', in Kevin Mulligan and Robert Roth, 'Regards sur Bentham et l'utilitarisme', *Recherches et Rencontres*, 4 (Geneva, 1993), pp. 39–58.

134   Constraints of space prevent anything more than a brief consideration of the relation of radicalism to socialism: this deserves a study in itself.

135   For Richard Carlile invoking the 'Norman Yoke', Wat Tyler and Oliver Cromwell in these years, see Wiener, *Carlile*, pp. 30 n. 10, 31 n. 23, 116 n. 11.

136   *The Radical Reformer, or People's Advocate*, vol. 1, no. 1 (15 Sept. 1819), pp. 1–2.

137   'Carlile's radicalism, as it developed from the pressure of events in the early 1820s, was essentially preindustrial. It was not directed against the inequalities of the new

economic system... nor did it consciously appeal to the class feelings of poor people... Carlile... blamed the "traditional" enemies of the poor... kings, lords, taxgatherers, fundholders, magistrates, and, above all, clergymen. They were the appropriators of the soil and of common property'; as Carlile wrote, "'Property holding tempered by the elective principle" would be allowed to flourish': Wiener, *Carlile*, pp. 101, 104–5. Wiener identifies Bentham's collaborator Francis Place as one man who encouraged Carlile towards full atheism in these years (ibid., p. 111).

138 Horne, *Property Rights and Poverty*, p. 227.

139 Henry Hunt (1773–1835). A parliamentary reformer since at least 1806, he lost money in a series of farming ventures and gravitated to the circle of extremists by the time of the Spa Fields meeting in 1816. In 1818 he stood for election at Westminster on a platform of universal suffrage, the secret ballot and annual parliaments. For his role in organizing the mass meeting at St Peter's Fields, Manchester, he was sentenced to two years' imprisonment in 1820. John Belchem's *'Orator' Hunt: Henry Hunt and English Working-Class Radicalism* (Oxford, 1985), explains Hunt's politics chiefly as 'democratic constitutionalism' via mass political mobilization.

140 Henry Hunt, *To The Radical Reformers, Male and Female, of England, Ireland and Scotland* (1 July 1820; '40th day of the 2nd year after the Manchester Massacre', pp. 3–4; '23d Day, 2d Month, 2d Year...', p. 7). Hunt distanced himself from Carlile's atheism, but Hunt's diverse reforming enthusiasms lacked unity, and he was not a leader in the formulation of radicalism.

141 *Will Waver, or Radical Principles. A Tale* (Oxford, 1821), pp. 3–7, 22.

142 Although a distinction between 'productive' and 'un-productive' workers can be traced back at least to Adam Smith, it became polemical, and lost its technical meaning, after Ricardo.

143 Harford, *Principles of Thomas Paine*, p. 73. Denunciations of the national debt led some radicals like Cobbett into openly anti-semitic remarks about financiers: W. D. Rubinstein, 'British Radicalism and the "Dark Side" of Populism', in Rubinstein, *Elites and the Wealthy in Modern British History* (Brighton, 1987), pp. 339–73, at 350–55. The degree to which xenophobia and racialism were integral to early English radicalism, or part of racially unspecific denigration of groups outside Cobbett's ideal rural society, deserves further study.

144 *The Radical*, no. 1 (20 August 1831), p. 1.

145 Henry Hunt, *To The Radical Reformers* ('1st Day, 3rd month, 2nd year...'), p. 20.

146 Clark, *English Society 1660–1832*, chapter 6.

147 *The Radical*, no. 1 (20 August 1831), pp. 1–3.

148 *The Truth. A Weekly Radical Christian, and Family Newspaper*, I, no. 1 (10 February, 1833), pp. 1–2.

149 [Thomas Peronnet Thompson], *The Article on Radical Reform. From the Westminster Review, no. XXII, For January 1830* (London, 1830), pp. 2–3, 8, 10. Thompson (1783–1869), an army officer, took up politics on his return from India in 1822 and soon associated himself with the circle of Bentham. In 1829 he became the owner of *The Westminster Review*, and wrote for it prolifically over the next seven years.

150 E.g. Thomas Doubleday, *A Letter to the Radical Reformers of Newcastle upon Tyne, on the Late Election and its Attendant Circumstances* (Newcastle, 1835), p. 10.

151 Arthur E. Bestor, Jr., 'The Evolution of the Socialist Vocabulary', *Journal of the History*

of Ideas, 9 (1984), pp. 259–302; G. de Bertier de Sauvigny, 'Liberalism, Nationalism and Socialism: The Birth of Three Words', *Review of Politics*, 32 (1970), pp. 147–66, at 163–4; Gregory Claeys, '"Individualism", "Socialism", and "Social Science": Further Notes on a Process of Conceptual Formation, 1800–1850', *Journal of the History of Ideas*, 45 (1986), pp. 81–93.

152 For the relations between socialism and radicalism in this period, see especially Gregory Claeys, *Citizens and Saints: Politics and anti-politics in early British socialism* (Cambridge, 1989), chapters 1–4.

153 *The New Moral World*, no. 50 (10 October 1835), pp. 396–7.

154 Samuel Bower, *The Peopling of Utopia; or, the Sufficiency of Socialism for Human Happiness: being a Comparison of the Social and Radical Schemes* (Bradford, 1838), pp. 3–4.

155 Bower, *Peopling of Utopia*, p. 4.

156 Ibid.

157 Ibid., p. 5.

158 Francis W. Newman, *An Appeal to the Middle Classes on the Urgent Necessity of Numerous Radical Reforms, Financial and Organic* (London, 1848), pp. 4–5, 13. Not everything was immediately referred to economics. In 1832 Thomas Hodgskin invoked Lockeian natural rights arguments to contest the Benthamite case for inequalities of private property: Dunn, 'The Politics of Locke in England and America', p. 69; Horne, *Property, Rights and Poverty*, pp. 237–43. Hodgskin was chiefly concerned with land.

159 Horne, *Property Rights and Poverty*, p. 234.

160 'Carlile, the prophet of a counter-hegemonic ideology of infidel-republicanism, was also the harbinger of the mid-Victorian *rapprochement* between radicalism and liberalism': Belchem, *Hunt*, p. 7. For the later evolution of the position, see especially Miles Taylor, *The Decline of British Radicalism, 1847–1860* (Oxford, 1995).

161 'Are Radicals Socialists?' in Arnold Toynbee, *Lectures on the Industrial Revolution in England* (London, 1884), p. 204.

NOTES TO CHAPTER 5

1 For the present author's attempted response to what is perhaps the largest of historical problems in the English-speaking world, see J. C. D. Clark, *The Language of Liberty 1660–1832: Political Discourse and Social Dynamics in the Anglo-American World* (Cambridge, 1994).

2 A handful have posed the question, but not seriously. See Roger Thompson, 'If I had been the Earl of Shelbourne in 1762–5', in Daniel Snowman (ed.), *If I Had Been...* (London, 1979), pp. 11–29 and Esmond Wright, 'If I had been Benjamin Franklin in the early 1770s', in ibid., pp. 33–54. For a recent attempt, see Richard Dreyfuss and Harry Turtledove, *The Two Georges* (London, 1995).

3 For another approach to this question, see chapter 1 above.

4 Geoffrey Parker, 'If the Armada had Landed', *History*, 61 (1976), pp. 358–68.

5 Conrad Russell, 'The Catholic Wind', reprinted in Russell, *Unrevolutionary England, 1603–1642* (London, 1990), pp. 305–8.

6   'But from the moment of using the conditional tense, we have begun to consider counterfactuals. There are obvious objections to doing so. History entails an infinite number of contingent variables, and for this reason our selection of counter-suppositions is necessarily undisciplined. But counter-history is not the study of what would have happened, so much as of what might have happened; and the case for considering outcomes which did not occur, but which those engaged in the happenings knew might occur – or we with the benefit of hindsight see might have occurred – is that it enables us to understand better the problematics in which the actors were entangled. Any event in history is both what did occur and the non-occurrence of what might have happened; nobody knows this better than we who spend our lives within the thinking distance of unthinkable possibilities, some of which happen from time to time': J. G. A. Pocock, 'The Fourth English Civil War: Dissolution, Desertion and Alternative Histories in the Glorious Revolution', *Government and Opposition*, 23 (1988), pp. 151–66, esp. p. 157.

7   Robert C. Ritchie, *The Duke's Province: A Study of New York Politics and Society, 1664–1691* (Chapel Hill, NC, 1977).

8   Viola Florence Barnes, *The Dominion of New England: A Study in British Colonial Policy* (New Haven, 1923), pp. 35–6, 44.

9   David Lovejoy, *The Glorious Revolution in America* (2nd edn., Middletown, Conn., 1987).

10   The option of an America in which military governors and bureaucrats rather than representative assemblies were central is reconstructed in the works of Stephen Saunders Webb: *The Governors-General: The English Army and the Definition of the Empire, 1569–1681* (Chapel Hill, NC, 1979); idem, *1676: The End of American Independence* (New York, 1984); idem, *Charles Churchill* (New York, 1996). This thesis runs counter to prevailing assumptions and has not received its due.

11   Geoffrey Holmes and Daniel Szechi, *The Age of Oligarchy: Pre-industrial Britain 1722–1783* (London, 1993), p. 97.

12   E.g. 'His Majestie's Most Gracious Declaration to all his Loving Subjects', 17 April 1693, in Daniel Szechi, *The Jacobites: Britain and Europe 1688–1788* (Manchester, 1994), pp. 143–5.

13   Belatedly, Charles Edward Stuart's note of points to be included in his next declaration, of 1753, included: '7th. An union between the three kingdoms to be proposed to a free Parliament': Szechi, *The Jacobites*, pp. 150–51. But this was an unrealistic counter-factual, and French plans for the invasion attempt of 1759 still envisaged a dissolution of the Union of 1707: Claude Nordmann, 'Choiseul and the Last Jacobite Attempt of 1759' in Eveline Cruickshanks (ed.), *Ideology and Conspiracy: Aspects of Jacobitism, 1689–1759* (Edinburgh, 1982), pp. 201–17.

14   Richard Price, *Observations on the Nature of Civil Liberty, the Principles of Government, and the Justice and Policy of the War with America* (London, 1776), p. 28: 'An *Empire* is a collection of states or communities united by some common bond or tye. If these states have each of them free constitutions of government, and, with respect to taxation and internal legislation, are independent of the other states, but united by compacts, or alliances, or subjection to a Great *Council*, representing the whole, or to one monarch entrusted with the supreme executive power: In these circumstances, the Empire will be an Empire of Freemen.'

15   John Adams, 6 February 1775, in John Adams and Jonathan Sewall [sc. Daniel Leonard], *Novanglus and Massachusettensis; or Political Essays, published in the Years 1774 and 1775, on the Principal Points of Controversy, between Great Britain and her Colonies* (Boston, 1819), p. 30.

16   Gaillard Hunt (ed.), *The Writings of James Madison* (9 vols., New York, 1900–10), VI, p. 373.

17   James Otis, *The Rights of the British Colonies Asserted and proved* (Boston, 1764), p. 23.

18   Richard Bland, *An Enquiry into the Rights of the British Colonies; intended as an Answer to "The Regulations lately made concerning the Colonies, and the Taxes imposed upon them considered." In a Letter addressed to the Author of that Pamphlet* (Williamsburg, 1766; reprinted London, 1769), p. 12.

19   Even Thomas Jefferson's *A Summary View of the Rights of British America* (Williamsburg, 1774), which echoed Bland's and Otis's doctrine on people's right to establish new societies (p. 6), was expressed in the old idiom of petitioning the Crown for a redress of grievances as well as the new idiom of natural rights.

20   Barnes, *Dominion of New England*, p. 178; Charles M. Andrews, *The Colonial Period of American History* (4 vols., New York, 1934–8), I, p. 86n.

21   [Franklin], 'On the Tenure of the Manor of East Greenwich', *The Gazetteer*, 11 January 1766, in Leonard W. Labaree *et al.* (eds.), *The Papers of Benjamin Franklin* (New Haven, 1959–), XIII, pp. 18–22.

22   *Novanglus and Massachusettensis*, p. 94.

23   [William Cobbett and T. C. Hansard], *The Parliamentary History of England from the Earliest Period to the Year 1803* (36 vols., London, 1806–20), XVIII, cols. 957–8.

24   For recent versions of the claim that the causes of the revolution were essentially internal to the colonies, see Gordon Wood, *The Radicalism of the American Revolution* (New York, 1992) and Clark, *The Language of Liberty 1660–1832*.

25   Drew R. McCoy, *The Elusive Republic: Political Economy in Jeffersonian America* (Chapel Hill, 1980); Doron S. Ben-Atar, *The Origins of Jeffersonian Commercial Policy and Diplomacy* (London, 1993).

26   Carl Bridenbaugh, *Mitre and Sceptre: Transatlantic Faiths, Ideas, Personalities, and Politics, 1689–1775* (New York, 1962); William H. Nelson, *The American Tory* (Oxford, 1961).

27   T. H. Breen, 'An Empire of Goods: the Anglicization of Colonial America, 1690–1776', *Journal of British Studies*, 25 (1986), pp. 467–99; '"Baubles of Britain": The American and Consumer Revolutions of the Eighteenth Century', *Past & Present*, 119 (1988), pp. 73–104.

28   Durand Echeverria, *Mirage in the West: a History of the French Image of American Society to 1815* (Princeton, 1957); François Furet, 'De l'homme sauvage à l'homme historique: l'expérience américaine dans la culture française', in *La Révolution Américaine et L'Europe* (Colloques Internationaux du Centre National de la Recherche Scientifique, Paris, 1979), pp. 91–105.

29   J. Hector St John de Crèvecoeur, *Letters from an American Farmer* (London, 1782); trans., Paris, 1787; Leipzig, 1788–9.

30   In Franklin, *Papers*, XIII, pp. 124–59, at 135.

31   [Thomas Pownall], *The Administration of the Colonies* (London, 1764), p. 25.

32   Thomas Pownall, *The Administration of the Colonies* (2nd edn., London, 1765),

Dedication, sigs. A2v–A3r.

33   Ms. history of Virginia, Virginia Historical Society, quoted in Kate Mason Rowland, *The Life of George Mason 1725–1792* (2 vols., New York, 1892), I, pp. 123–4.

34   George Washington to Captain Robert Mackenzie, 9 October 1774, in John C. Fitzpatrick (ed.), *The Writings of George Washington* (39 vols., Washington, 1931–44), III, pp. 244–7.

35   [Joseph Galloway], *Letters to a Nobleman, on the Conduct of the War in the Middle Colonies* (London, 1779), pp. 8–10.

36   Douglass Adair and John A. Schutz (eds.), *Peter Oliver's Origin & Progress of the American Rebellion: A Tory View* (San Marino, 1961), pp. 3, 145.

37   Edward H. Tatum, Jr. (ed.), *The American Journal of Ambrose Serle Secretary to Lord Howe 1776–1778* (San Marino, 1940), pp. 46–7.

38   [Daniel Leonard], *The Origin of the American Contest with Great-Britain, or The present political State of the Massachusetts-Bay, in general, and The Town of Boston in particular* (New York, 1775), p. 12; for these sources, see Gordon S. Wood, *The Creation of the American Republic 1776–1787* (Chapel Hill, NC, 1969), esp. pp. 3–4 for the 'strangely unaccountable' causality of the Revolution.

39   Within this older agenda, doubts began to be cast on the inevitability of a breakdown in such works as Ian R. Christie and Benjamin W. Labaree, *Empire or Independence 1760–1776* (Oxford, 1976). Still within this agenda, a powerful counterfactual analysis was provided by Robert W. Tucker and David C. Hendrickson, *The Fall of the First British Empire: Origins of the War of American Independence* (Baltimore, 1982), a work whose counterfactual novelty was often obscured by its pragmatic conclusions that British policy could hardly have been other than it was.

40   The myth can still be aggressively and indignantly restated as an historical explanation: Jack P. Greene, 'Why Did the Colonists Rebel?', *The Times Literary Supplement*, 10 June 1994.

41   An early attempt was made to diversify the secular litany of 'ostensible causes' of the Revolution by framing arguments about the effect of the Great Awakening in political mobilization; but this was denied by a counterfactual claim that even without the Awakening, 'colonial resistance would have taken very much the same forms it did and within the same chronology': John M. Murrin, 'No Awakening, No Revolution? More Counterfactual Speculations', *Reviews in American History*, 11 (1983), pp. 161–71, at 164.

42   Especially Bernard Bailyn, *The Ideological Origins of the American Revolution* (Cambridge, Mass., 1967) and *The Origins of American Politics* (New York, 1968).

43   Especially Jack P. Greene, *Peripheries and Center: Constitutional Development in the Extended Polities of the British Empire and the United States, 1607–1788* (New York, 1986), but anticipated in many of Greene's writings since the 1960s.

44   Tucker and Hendrickson, *Fall of the First British Empire*, p. 71.

45   Christie and Labaree, *Empire or Independence*, pp. 277–8.

46   John Shy, 'Thomas Pownall, Henry Ellis, and the Spectrum of Possibilities, 1763–1775', in Alison Gilbert Olson and Richard Maxwell Brown (eds.), *Anglo-American Political Relations, 1675–1775* (New Brunswick, 1970), pp. 155–86.

47   This interpretation was stressed by Jack P. Greene, 'The Seven Years' War and the American Revolution: The Causal Relationship Reconsidered', *Journal of Imperial and Commonwealth History*, 8 (1980), pp. 85–105.

48   For a bibliography of the pamphlets, see Clarence W. Alvord, *The Mississippi Valley in British Politics* (2 vols., Cleveland, 1917), II, pp. 253–64; for the debate, William L. Grant, 'Canada versus Guadeloupe, an Episode of the Seven Years' War', *American Historical Review*, 17 (1911–12), pp. 735–53.

49   [Cobbett, ed.], *Parliamentary History*, XV, col. 1265.

50   William Burke, *Remarks on the Letter Address'd to Two Great Men. In a Letter to the Author of that Piece* (London, 1760), pp. 50–51.

51   [Benjamin Franklin], *The Interest of Great Britain considered, With Regard to her Colonies, And the Acquisitions of Canada and Guadaloupe* (London, 1760), in Franklin, Papers, IX, pp. 47–100, at 73, 77, 90.

52   Gerald S. Graham, *The Politics of Naval Supremacy: Studies in British Maritime Ascendancy* (Cambridge, 1965), p. 27.

53   Tucker and Hendrickson, *Fall of the First British Empire*, pp. 50–53.

54   Richard Price, *Observations on the Nature of Civil Liberty, the Principles of Government, and the Justice and Policy of the War with America* (London, 1776), pp. 43–4.

55   Richard Price to Benjamin Franklin, 3 April 1769, in W. Bernard Peach and D. O. Thomas (eds.), *The Correspondence of Richard Price* (3 vols., Cardiff, 1983-94), I, pp. 58–79, at 76–7. When this was read to the Royal Society, the words 'by an unjust and fatal policy' were omitted.

56   Richard Price to Ezra Stiles, 2 November 1773, in Price, *Correspondence*, I, p. 165; in response to Stiles to Price, 20 November 1772, ibid., p. 149.

57   Quoted in Lawrence Henry Gipson, 'The American Revolution as an Aftermath of the Great War for the Empire, 1754–1763', *Political Science Quarterly*, 65 (1950), pp. 86–104, at 104.

58   John M. Murrin, 'The French and Indian War, the American Revolution, and the Counterfactual Hypothesis: Reflections on Lawrence Henry Gipson and John Shy', *Reviews in American History*, 1 (1973), pp. 307–18, at 309.

59   Alison Gilbert Olson, 'The British Government and Colonial Union, 1754', *William and Mary Quarterly*, 17 (1960), pp. 22–34.

60   Quoted in Sir Lewis Namier and John Brooke, *Charles Townshend* (London, 1964), pp. 39–40.

61   [Thomas Paine], *Common Sense; Addressed to the Inhabitants of America* (Philadelphia: R. Bell, 1776), p. 31.

62   Jack P. Greene, 'An Uneasy Connection: An Analysis of the Preconditions of the American Revolution' in Stephen G. Kurtz and James H. Hutson (eds.), *Essays on the American Revolution* (Chapel Hill, NC, 1973), pp. 32–80, at 64. Greene argued (pp. 65, 72) that the 'salient condition' of the Revolution was 'the decision by colonial authorities in Britain [specifically, Lord Halifax, President of the Board of Trade from 1748 to 1761] to abandon Walpole's policy of accommodation' in favour of 'a dependence upon coercion', a thesis now difficult to sustain against the evidence presented in Tucker and Hendrickson, *Fall of the First British Empire*.

63   Wood, *Making of the American Republic*, pp. 12–13.

64   [John Dickinson], *Letters from a Farmer in Pennsylvania, to the Inhabitants of the British Colonies* (Philadelphia, 1768), pp. 7–13, 16.

65   Franklin to Joseph Galloway, 9 January 1769, in Franklin, *Papers*, XVI, p. 17.

66   Worthington Chauncey Ford (ed.), *Journals of the Continental Congress 1774–1789* (34

vols., Washington, 1904–37), I, pp. 84, 89.

67   Tucker and Hendrickson, *Fall of the First British Empire*, pp. 114–17.

68   Ibid., pp. 117–27.

69   Jack P. Greene and Richard M. Jellison, 'The Currency Act of 1764 in Imperial–Colonial Relations, 1764–1776', *William and Mary Quarterly*, 18 (1961), pp. 485–518; Joseph Albert Ernst, *Money and Politics in America 1755–1775: A Study in the Currency Act of 1764 and the Political Economy of Revolution* (Chapel Hill, NC, 1973).

70   J. Wright (ed.), *Sir Henry Cavendish's Debates of the House of Commons during the Thirteenth Parliament of Great Britain* (2 vols., London, 1841–3), I, pp. 494–5, cited in Tucker and Hendrickson, *Fall of the First British Empire*, p. 217.

71   Ibid, p. 226 n.

72   Ibid., p. 238.

73   Franklin, *Papers*, XIV, pp. 110–16, at 114–15.

74   Peter D. G. Thomas, *Revolution in America: Britain and the Colonies, 1763–1776* (Cardiff, 1992), pp. 29, 37.

75   [Thomas Whately], *The Regulations Lately Made concerning the Colonies, and the Taxes Imposed upon Them, considered* (London, 1765), p. 109.

76   For an important study which deals with divine-right monarchy and representative democracy as equally 'fictions', see Edmund S. Morgan, *Inventing the People: The Rise of Popular Sovereignty in England and America* (New York, 1988).

77   [Cobbett, ed.], *Parliamentary History*, XVI, col. 100.

78   Sir Lewis Namier and John Brooke (eds.), *The History of Parliament: The House of Commons 1754–1790* (3 vols., London, 1964), I, pp. 366, 419.

79   [Paine], *Common Sense*, p. 30.

80   Tucker and Hendrickson, *Fall of the First British Empire*, pp. 335–41.

81   Julian P. Boyd, *Anglo-American Union: Joseph Galloway's Plans to Preserve the British Empire 1774–1788* (Philadelphia, 1941), pp. 34–8.

82   Galloway, in Edmund C. Burnett (ed.), *Letters of Members of the Continental Congress* (8 vols., Washington, 1921–36), I, p. 59.

83   For the Commons' debate on North's proposal on 20 February 1775, see [Cobbett, ed.], *Parliamentary History*, XVIII, col. 320.

84   Tucker and Hendrickson, *Fall of the First British Empire*, pp. 367–78.

85   Josiah Tucker, *The true Interest of Great Britain set forth in regard to the Colonies* in Tucker, *Four Tracts, together with Two Sermons, On Political and Commercial Subjects* (Gloucester, 1774), p. 195.

86   W. Paul Adams, 'Republicanism in Political Rhetoric Before 1776', *Political Science Quarterly*, 85 (1970), pp. 397–421. In *Rights of Man: part the second* (1792), Paine was to record an astonishing vagueness about just what republicanism meant.

87   Tucker and Hendrickson, *Fall of the First British Empire*, pp. 160–61. Such measures may have formed part of Charles Townshend's programme in the late 1760s (ibid., pp. 241–8); by then it was, perhaps, too little and too late.

88   Ibid., p. 304; Bernard Bailyn, *The Ordeal of Thomas Hutchinson* (Cambridge, Mass., 1974), pp. 212–20.

89   Tony Hayter, *The Army and the Crowd in Mid-Georgian England* (London, 1978); Tucker and Hendrickson, *Fall of the First British Empire*, p. 322.

90   Ibid., pp. 261–3, 322.

91 Ibid., pp. 265–6.

92 Ibid., p. 289.

93 John Shy, *Toward Lexington: The Role of the British Army in the Coming of the American Revolution* (Princeton, 1965), pp. 52–68, 82–3.

94 Tucker and Hendrickson, *Fall of the First British Empire*, p. 88.

95 Shy, *Toward Lexington*, pp. 142–3.

96 Tucker and Hendrickson, *Fall of the First British Empire*, p. 359.

97 Jeremy Black, *War for America: The Fight for Independence 1775–1783* (London, 1991), pp. 24–7.

98 Ibid., pp. 14–15 and *passim*.

99 Ibid., p. 23.

100 Shy, *Toward Lexington*, p. viii.

101 [Galloway], *Letters to a Nobleman*, p. 36.

102 Black, *War for America*, p. 249.

103 William Gordon, *The History of the Rise, Progress, and Establishment of the Independence of the United States of America* (4 vols., London, 1788), II, pp. 568–9.

104 Lester H. Cohen, T*he Revolutionary Histories: Contemporary Narratives of the American Revolution* (Ithaca, NY, 1980), pp. 58–60, 67, 71–85. 'The historians thus preserved the ideological and cultural values traditionally associated with providence even as they rejected providence as an explanatory concept', p. 82.

105 Ibid., p. 83.

106 Ibid., p. 185.

107 Ibid., p. 119.

108 For the Indian question, see Tucker and Hendrickson, *Fall of the First British Empire*, pp. 87–95.

109 Benjamin Quarles, 'Lord Dunmore as Liberator', *William and Mary Quarterly*, 15 (1958), pp. 494–507.

110 Sidney Kaplan, 'The "Domestic Insurrections" of the Declaration of Independence', *Journal of Negro History*, 61 (1976), pp. 243–55; Sidney Kaplan and Emma Nogrady Kaplan, *The Black Presence in the Era of the American Revolution* (revised edn., Amherst, Mass., 1989).

111 Anne-Robert Jacques Turgot, *Mémoire sur les colonies américaines* (Paris, 1791), quoted in Anthony Pagden, *Lords of all the World: Ideologies of Empire in Spain, Britain and France c. 1500 – c. 1800* (New Haven, 1995), p. 192.

NOTES TO CHAPTER 6

1 'Even though many American historians today eschew exceptionalism, in the absence of an alternative organizing framework the vast bulk of US history is still written in terms that accept the primacy of the national focus... In popular culture, exceptionalism remains strong': Ian Tyrrell, 'American Exceptionalism in an Age of International History', *American Historical Review*, 96 (1991), pp. 1031–55, at 1032; Byron Shafer (ed.), *Is American Different? A New Look at American Exceptionalism* (Oxford, 1991); Michael Kammen, 'The Problem of American Exceptionalism: A

Reconsideration', *American Quarterly*, 45 (March, 1993), pp. 1–43. British historians and political scientists have not recently been prominent in producing such studies of the United Kingdom. They have been more active in dismantling British exceptionalism than in finding academic explanations for an exceptionalism the survival of which they were willing to acknowledge.

2   For the still greater problems of presenting French culture to a modern American audience, see Antoine Compagnon, 'The Diminishing Canon of French Literature in the United States', in *France-Amérique: Dialogue and Misreadings*, special issue of *Stanford French Review*, 15 (1991), pp. 103–15. Although the linguistic barriers against French culture are higher, it may be that the intellectual consequences of Anglo-American dissociation are more extensive.

3   Daniel Walker Howe, *American History in an Atlantic Context: An Inaugural Lecture delivered before the University of Oxford on 3 June 1993* (Oxford, 1993), pp. 4–5, optimistically reviewed some monographs which indeed deal with the transatlantic dimension; but (most notably with David Hackett Fischer's provocatively anti-exceptionalist *Albion's Seed* (Oxford, 1989)) they were often resented in the USA rather than welcomed, and they are small in number compared with the works that deal separately with domestic British and domestic American history.

4   J. G. A. Pocock, 'British History: A Plea for a New Subject', *Journal of Modern History*, 47 (1975), pp. 601–21; idem, 'The Limits and Divisions of British History: In Search of an Unknown Subject', *American Historical Review*, 87 (1982), pp. 311–36.

5   John H. Elliott, *National and Comparative History: An Inaugural Lecture delivered before the University of Oxford on 10 May 1991* (Oxford, 1991) highlighted the appropriateness of attention to the Anglo-European dimension in anticipation of the European Union's Maastricht Treaty of 1992.

6   The possible disengagement, in some areas, periods and respects, of the historiographies of England, Wales, Ireland and Scotland is a valid question, not examined here. The use of 'British' has a conventional currency in an international context and is not intended to pre-empt answers to this issue.

7   This has emerged as a common argument in a series of collections edited by Roy Porter and Mikuláš Teich and published by Cambridge University Press: *The Enlightenment in National Context* (1981); *Revolution in History* (1986); *Romanticism in National Context* (1988); *The Renaissance in National Context* (1992); *The National Question in Europe in Historical Context* (1993); and, with Bob Scribner as an additional editor, *The Reformation in National Context* (1994).

8   Most recently and most notably, the controversies in the US historical profession surrounding Peter Novick's *That Noble Dream: The 'Objectivity Question' and the American Historical Profession* (Cambridge, 1988) and Joyce Appleby, Lynn Hunt and Margaret Jacob, *Telling the Truth about History* (New York, 1994) evoked little response in Britain.

9   'There is no doubt that our century has witnessed a widespread rebellion against historical consciousness': Allan Megill, 'Foucault, Structuralism and the Ends of History', *Journal of Modern History*, 51 (1979–80), pp. 451–503. For this theme, see Introduction above.

10   Francis Fukuyama, *The End of History and the Last Man* (New York, 1992): see Introduction above.

11   Geoffrey Elton, delivering his inaugural lecture at Cambridge on 15 February 1968, dismissed the warning that 'the world will no longer concern itself with its history'. On the contrary, he argued robustly, 'the world is dominated by its history', revolutionaries being especially historically aware: Geoffrey Elton, *The Future of the Past* (Cambridge, 1968), p. 6. After postmodernism, I do not think that we can be so sure of this.

12   J. M. Bourne, 'History at the Universities', *History*, 71 (1986), pp. 54–9, at 57. The process has of course continued since.

13   Reba N. Soffer, *Discipline and Power: The University, History and the Making of an English Elite, 1870–1930* (Stanford, 1994).

14   John Searle has argued that, in the USA, 'both sides tend to think of education as a matter of acquiring a certain body of knowledge, together with the appropriate attitudes'. Searle drew a sharp distinction between these shared American assumptions and the essentially English attitude to education of Michael Oakeshott, who regarded it as the acquisition of 'judgement' rather than of 'a set of beliefs or attitudes': 'The Storm Over the University', *New York Review of Books*, 6 December 1990, pp. 34–42, at 41.

15   Lester H. Cohen, *The Revolutionary Histories: Contemporary Narratives of the American Revolution* (Ithaca, NY, 1980).

16   For the elimination of Providence in Hume's *History of England* (1754–62), see especially Nicholas Phillipson, *Hume* (London, 1989).

17   Classically countered by Michael Oakeshott, 'The Activity of Being an Historian' in *Rationalism in Politics and Other Essays* (London, 1962); idem, *On History and Other Essays* (Oxford, 1983); G. R. Elton, *The Practice of History* (Sydney, 1966); for an overview, see Christopher Parker, *The English Historical Tradition since 1850* (Edinburgh, 1990).

18   Theodore S. Hamerow, 'The Bureaucratisation of History', *American Historical Review*, 94 (1989), pp. 654–60.

19   J. G. A. Pocock, 'History and Sovereignty: The Historiographical Response to Europeanisation in Two British Cultures', *Journal of British Studies*, 31 (1992), pp. 358–89.

20   E.g. Conrad Russell, 'John Bull's other nations', *The Times Literary Supplement*, 12 March 1993, pp. 3–4: 'To attempt to explain an event [the English Civil War] so deep in England's sense of identity, in terms which are not merely English, is to create one's own opposition. English undergraduates, and some English scholars, resist this attempt, both because it threatens their identity, and because it demands a vast body of knowledge which is frightening because unfamiliar... This reluctance is reinforced by the need of American historians of the Whig persuasion to see seventeenth-century England in terms which validate the American Declaration of Independence.'

21   'Labour history has been characterised as institutionally based, Eurocentric, prioritising the experiences of male workers, theoretically naive and verging on and sometimes collapsing into antiquarianism. Such a neanderthal is appropriately dismissed by devotees of post-modernism, feminist and cultural historians and many others': David Howell, 'Editorial', *Labour History Review*, 60, pt. 1 (1995), p. 2. For the ensuing debate, ibid. 60, pt. 3 (1995), pp. 46–53.

22   Patrick Joyce, 'The end of social history?', *Social History*, 20 (1995), pp. 73–91, at 73–4. It is regrettable that these debates have not hitherto involved wider bands of the historiographical spectrum.

23 William E. Leuchtenburg, 'The Historian and the Public Realm', *American Historical Review*, 97 (1992), pp. 1–18. By contrast, an attempt to discern the shape of and major currents within the British historical profession largely in terms of social function was not plausible: David Cannadine, 'British History: Past, Present – and Future?', *Past & Present*, 116 (1987), pp. 169–91. To do so was to impose American priorities on British experience.

24 The problem may be worse in anthropology, political science, sociology or psychology, indeed terminal in some of those disciplines, but this question is not addressed here. The present assumption is only that disciplines might helpfully be more mutually self-critical, instead of engaging in an inexpert mutual borrowing. For one such appraisal, see Reba N. Soffer, 'Why Do Disciplines Fail? The Strange Case of British Sociology', *English Historical Review*, 97 (1982), pp. 767–802.

25 Diane Ravitch and Arthur Schlesinger, 'Remaking New York's History Curriculum', *New York Times*, 12 August 1990, quoted by J. H. Hexter, *American Historical Review*, 96 (1991), p. 681.

26 Leszek Kolakowski, *The Alienation of Reason: a History of Positivist Thought* (New York, 1968); for a naturalized English example, see M. M. Postan, *Fact and Relevance: Essays on Historical Method* (Cambridge, 1971).

27 Charles M. Andrews, 'These Forty Years', *American Historical Review*, 30 (1924–5), pp. 225–50.

28 Joyce, 'The end of social history?', p. 75.

29 Nathan Tarcov and Thomas Pangle, 'Leo Strauss and the History of Political Philosophy', in Leo Strauss and Joseph Cropsey (eds.), *History of Political Philosophy* (3rd edn., Chicago, 1986), pp. 907–38, at 908, 928.

30 Allan Bloom, *The Closing of the American Mind* (New York, 1987); Fred Matthews, 'The Attack on "Historicism": Allan Bloom's Indictment of Contemporary American Historical Scholarship', *American Historical Review*, 95 (1990), pp. 429–47; Sidney Hook, 'The Closing of the American Mind: An Intellectual Best-Seller Revisited', *The American Scholar*, 58 (1989), pp. 123–35; Gordon Wood, 'The Fundamentalists and the Constitution', *New York Review of Books* (18 February 1989), pp. 33–40.

31 Matthews, 'The Attack on "Historicism"', pp. 429–30.

32 Hook, 'The Closing of the American Mind', pp. 127, 130.

33 J. H. Hexter, 'Carl Becker, Professor Novick, and Me; or, Cheer Up, Professor N!'; Linda Gordon, 'Comments on *That Noble Dream*'; David A. Hollinger, 'Postmodernist Theory and *Wissenschaftliche* Practice'; Allan Megill, 'Fragmentation and the Future of Historiography'; Peter Novick, 'My Correct Views on Everything'; Dorothy Ross, 'Afterword': *American Historical Review*, 96 (1991), pp. 683–708.

34 Novick, in *American Historical Review*, 96 (1991), p. 702.

35 Novick, in *American Historical Review*, 96 (1991), pp. 699–700.

36 Gordon, in *American Historical Review*, 96 (1991), p. 686; cf. Amanda Vickery, 'Golden Age to Separate Spheres? A Review of the Categories and Chronology of English Women's History', *Historical Journal*, 36 (1993), pp. 383–414, at 414: 'even those who assert that nothing exists outside language usually have non-linguistic phenomena and convenient supporting "facts" lurking in their footnotes – most popular in my experience being capitalism, the Industrial Revolution, the consumer society, international trade, the rising middle class, the companionate marriage, rural poverty and ruling class hegemony'.

37   Gertrude Himmelfarb, reviewing *Telling the Truth about History* by Joyce Appleby, Lynn Hunt and Margaret Jacob (*The Times Literary Supplement*, 10 June 1994, pp. 8–9) characterized the book as a defence of the 'multiculturalism, pluralism and "inclusiveness"' of the new social history of the 1960s against 'the kind of relativism and scepticism espoused by postmodernists', which would, according to its three authors, turn history into 'an ideological construction that serves particular interests, making history a series of myths establishing or reinforcing group identities'. Professor Himmelfarb asked ironically how the relativism practised by 1960s' social historians might be distinguished from the relativism of the deconstructionists; but the intention of Professors Appleby, Hunt and Jacob was evidently to do just that.

38   Especially Daniel J. Boorstin, *The Americans: the colonial experience* (New York, 1958); idem, *The Americans: the national experience* (New York, 1967); idem, *The Americans: the democratic experience* (New York, 1973); Henry Steele Commager (ed.), *Britain Through American Eyes* (New York, 1974); idem, *The Empire of Reason: how Europe imagined and America realized the Enlightenment* (New York, 1977). In Britain, by contrast, G. M. Trevelyan's scenario of national history now occupies no such place in the public mind.

39   Wood, 'The Founders and the Constitution', p. 33.

40   This was not necessarily the real aim. Eve Tavor Bannet, *Structuralism and the Logic of Dissent: Barthes, Derrida, Foucault, Lacan* (London, 1989), pp. 263–4, confessed that these deconstructionists' 'apparent nihilism' was 'offset' by their deliberate 'advocacy of plurality, difference and decentralization... They have taught us that theoretical languages and structures are always informed by positions taken on ideological, educational, social and political issues, and that university intellectuals therefore have more social, political and ideological power than they used to think'. Deconstructionists have political programmes too.

41   For one New Historicist critic, what he terms 'idealist' literary criticism is that which is 'preoccupied with supposedly universal truths which find their counterpart in "man's" essential nature; the criticism in which history, if acknowledged at all, is seen as inessential or a constraint transcended in the affirmation of a transhistorical human condition': Dollimore, in Jonathan Dollimore and Alan Sinfield (eds.), *Political Shakespeare: New Essays in Cultural Materialism* (Manchester, 1985) p. 4.

42   For these changes applied to Anglo-German relations, see chapter 7, section II below.

43   David Boucher, *The Social and Political Thought of R. G. Collingwood* (Cambridge, 1989).

44   John Stuart Mill, 'Coleridge', in Mill, *Essays on Politics and Culture*, ed. Gertrude Himmelfarb (New York, 1962), p. 133, quoted in Himmelfarb, 'Reflections', p. 669.

45   For the materialist assumptions of the 'old' social history, now challenged by a 'linguistic turn', see Joyce, 'The end of social history', p. 75; for a defence, Geoff Eley and Keith Nield, 'Starting over: the present, the post-modern and the moment of social history', *Social History*, 20 (1995), pp. 355–64.

46   Although one of its most distinguished proponents, J. G. A. Pocock, a pupil of Herbert Butterfield at Cambridge, latterly pursued his career in St Louis and Baltimore, it may be that his considerable influence was even greater in England than in the USA.

47   Glenn Burgess, 'On Revisionism: An Analysis of Early Stuart Historiography in the 1970s and 1980s', *Historical Journal*, 33 (1990), pp. 609–27.

48 For an insightful account of such historians which nevertheless attributes too much coherence to them as a school, see Richard Brent, 'Butterfield's Tories: "High Politics" and the Writing of Modern British Political History', *Historical Journal*, 30 (1987), pp. 943–54.

49 The key critiques in this tradition were Maurice Cowling, *The Nature and Limits of Political Science* (Cambridge, 1963) and *Mill and Liberalism* (Cambridge, 1963). Only a contextual reconstruction reveals the purposes behind these opaque works.

50 The works consciously in this tradition include books such as Edward Norman, *The Catholic Church and Ireland in the Age of Rebellion, 1859–1873* (London, 1965); Maurice Cowling, *1867: Disraeli, Gladstone and Revolution* (Cambridge, 1967) and *The Impact of Labour, 1920–1924* (Cambridge, 1971); Andrew Jones, *The Politics of Reform, 1884* (Cambridge, 1972); and Alistair Cooke and John Vincent, *The Governing Passion: Cabinet Government and Party Politics in Britain, 1885–86* (Brighton, 1974). Lawrence Stone, 'The Revival of Narrative: Reflections on a New Old History', *Past & Present*, 85 (1979), pp. 3–24, strangely neglected to mention such works, the most sophisticated political narrative histories then being written.

51 One sort of controversy over method then largely ceased. The rivalry of the 1960s and 1970s between positivists and idealists ended in a peace treaty: Robert William Fogel and G. R. Elton (eds.), *Which Road to the Past? Two Views of History* (New Haven, Conn., 1983). The authors recorded a 'long period of cultural warfare' between the two schools and argued for future coexistence (pp. 7, 73, 123–9); yet positivism did not long survive the cessation of hostilities. Sir Geoffrey Elton's opposition to postmodernism in historical practice disguised his alignment with (idealist) political historians against the reductionists. It is significant that high-political narrative and the contextualist approach to political thought flourished together in Elton's Cambridge.

52 Conrad Russell, *The Fall of the British Monarchies 1637–1642* (Oxford, 1991); cf. idem, *The Causes of the English Civil War* (Oxford, 1990).

53 Patrick Collinson, in his inaugural lecture as Regius Professor of Modern History at Cambridge on 9 November 1989, observed: 'As to which skills and methods, the "which road to the past" debate seems to have subsided of recent years... Most historians now seem to favour a latitudinarian position: all helpful roads. At least this is the atmosphere prevailing in this as in most other British history faculties and departments. Not for us the fierce methodological and ideological wars which beset some other subjects, which shall be nameless': '*De Republica Anglorum*: Or, History with the Politics Put Back', in Collinson, *Elizabethan Essays* (London, 1994), pp. 1–29, at 4. These 'helpful roads' did not, however, lead to random diversity.

54 E.g. Edward Norman, *Church and Society in England, 1770–1970* (Oxford, 1976); Maurice Cowling, *Religion and Public Doctrine in Modern England* (3 vols., Cambridge, 1980–2001); J. P. Parry, *Democracy and Religion: Gladstone and the Liberal Party, 1867–1875* (Cambridge, 1986); Richard Brent, *Liberal Anglican Politics: Whiggery, Religion and Reform, 1830–1841* (Oxford, 1987); Boyd Hilton, *The Age of Atonement: The Influence of Evangelicalism on Social and Economic Thought, 1795–1865* (Oxford, 1988). For the religious dimension of political economy, formerly explained in wholly secular terms, see A. M. C. Waterman, *Revolution, Economics and Religion: Christian Political Economy, 1798–1833* (Cambridge, 1991).

55 Burgess, 'On Revisionism', pp. 613–14, 621, 624, 627.

56   Lawrence Stone, 'History and the social sciences in the twentieth century' (1976) in Stone, *The Past and the Present* (London, 1981), pp. xi, 3–44.

57   Instead, law had always played a much larger part in US historical consciousness, but normally the sort of essentialist constitutional law sustained by the study of a secular written constitution. For changes in this area see, for example, Stephen B. Presser, *The Original Misunderstanding: the English, the Americans and the Dialectic of Federalist Jurisprudence* (Carolina U.P., 1991); idem, *Recapturing the Constitution* (Chicago, 1994).

58   E.g. Mark Kishlansky, *A Monarchy Transformed: Britain 1603–1714* (London, 1996). By contrast, a British historian's review of this work (Ronald Hutton, in *The Times Literary Supplement*, 15 November 1996, p. 9) contended that the 'collapse' of Marxist historiography had left historians 'facing the frightening fact that the true motor for development consists of ideology', which 'appears more than ever before to have a life of its own'.

59   E.g. Patrick Joyce, *Visions of the People: Industrial England and the Question of Class, 1840–1914* (Cambridge, 1991); James Vernon, *Politics and the People: A Study in English Political Culture c. 1815–1867* (Cambridge, 1993); Margot C. Finn, *After Chartism: Class and Nation in English Radical Politics, 1848–1874* (Cambridge, 1993); James A. Epstein, *Radical Expression: Political Language, Ritual, and Symbol in England, 1790–1850* (Oxford, 1994); Patrick Joyce, *Democratic Subjects: The Self and the Social in Nineteenth-Century England* (Cambridge, 1994); James Vernon (ed.), *Rereading the Constitution* (Cambridge, 1996). For a review essay covering some of these works, see Dror Wahrman, 'The new political history', *Social History*, 21 (1996), pp. 343–54.

60   For a reductionist critique of Vernon's *Politics and the People* as postmodernist, see Neville Kirk in *Labour History Review*, 59 (1994), pp. 71–8: 'According to the author it is language, as opposed to external, experiential reality, which constitutes being and meaning.'

61   This is not the place for a detailed appreciation of either; what is here at issue is how certain elements of each (or of similar scenarios) might contribute to the profoundly simplified image of British history projected in the USA.

62   David Cannadine, *Lords and Landlords: the Aristocracy and the Towns, 1774–1967* (Leicester, 1980); *The Decline and Fall of the British Aristocracy* (New Haven, Conn., 1990); idem, *Aspects of Aristocracy: Grandeur and Decline in Modern Britain* (New Haven, Conn., 1994). Such arguments had been familiar since Harold Wilson's election victory in 1964. Now they were given a catastrophic rather than a triumphalist twist. For an important critique of this scenario, see William M. Kuhn, *Democratic Royalism: The Transformation of the British Monarchy, 1861–1914* (London, 1996); for a study which similarly takes a mixed constitution seriously, see Andrew Adonis, *Making Aristocracy Work: the Peerage and the Political System in Britain, 1884–1914* (Oxford, 1993).

63   The Revolution of 1776 found a natural place in this scenario in works like J. G. A. Pocock (ed.), *Three British Revolutions: 1641, 1688, 1776* (Princeton, 1980) and John Brewer, *Party Ideology and Popular Politics at the Accession of George III* (Cambridge, 1976).

64   Cannadine, 'British History', 169–91, at 180, 188, 191. It was pointed out in the debate which followed (P. R. Coss, in *Past & Present*, 119 (1988), pp. 176–7) that, as to the specific content of this new version, 'Cannadine has nothing to offer'. This appears to overlook the thesis of aristocratic archaism consistently presented elsewhere in his work.

65 Martin J. Wiener, *English Culture and the Decline of the Industrial Spirit 1850–1980* (Cambridge, 1981). For explorations of English ideas of class which show the more complex distribution of pro- and anti-industrial ideals across social groups, see Marjorie Morgan, *Manners, Morals and Class in England, 1774–1858* (London, 1994) and Penelope Corfield, *Power and the Professions in Britain 1700–1850* (London, 1995). For a critique of Wiener, see M. J. Daunton, '"Gentlemanly Capitalism" and British Industry 1820–1914', *Past & Present*, 122 (1989), pp. 119–58; James Raven, 'British History and the Enterprise Culture', *Past & Present*, 123 (1989), pp. 178–204.

66 Between 1951 and 1992, annual log growth rates of GNP per capita per annum, measured in 1985 prices, were: in the UK, 2.04 per cent; in the USA, 1.70 per cent: Robert Summers and Alan Heston, *Penn World Tables*, 1994 version. I am grateful to Professor Gregory Hess for consulting this database for me.

67 Linda Colley, *Britons: Forging the Nation 1707–1837* (New Haven, Conn., 1992). It is debatable whether the present discussion should instead focus on another work written in the USA, Gerald Newman's *The Rise of English Nationalism: A Cultural History, 1740–1830* (New York, 1987), where similar theses had earlier been advanced.

68 E.g. David Cannadine, *The Times Literary Supplement*, 12 March 1993, p. 5.

69 It was a simplified response to methodological change. Joyce, 'The end of social history?', p. 82, noted the impact of post-structuralist ideas in the field of identities, including those of gender: 'It... follows that if identity is composed through the relations of systems of difference, then it is marked by conflict, and is plural, diverse, and volatile.' *Britons* by contrast treated 'Britishness' as a unitary successor to Englishness and Scottishness, not a dual identity; employed a homogenized notion of Protestantism; and largely passed over divisive conflicts such as 1776 and 1798. It may be that dwelling on British survival of these centrifugal forces was a moral less appealing to a US audience than the plasticity of all identities (other than US national ones).

70 Benedict Anderson, *Imagined Communities: reflections on the origins and spread of nationalism* (London, 1983); Eric Hobsbawm and Terence Ranger (eds.), *The Invention of Tradition* (Cambridge, 1983); Celia Kitzinger, *The Social Construction of Lesbianism* (Newbury Park, Calif., 1987); Christopher Shaw and Malcolm Chase (eds.), *The Imagined Past: history and nostalgia* (Manchester, 1989); Judith Lorber and Susan A. Farrell (eds.), *The Social Construction of Gender* (Newbury Park, Calif., 1991); Jack P. Greene, *The Intellectual Construction of America: exceptionalism and identity from 1492 to 1800* (Chapel Hill, NC, 1993). Cf. Himmelfarb, 'Some Reflections', p. 667.

71 The position that language is the only reality can be used to dissolve common-language distinctions between truth and fiction, a strategy consciously exploited in Simon Schama, *Dead Certainties (Unwarranted Speculations)* (New York, 1991). Gordon Wood's critical review (*New York Review of Books*, 27 June 1991, pp. 12–16) may be compared with his criticisms of Straussian historiography: 'The Fundamentalists and the Constitution', ibid. (18 February 1988), pp. 33–40.

72 Cannadine, 'British History', pp. 177, 182.

73 Alan Macfarlane, *The Origins of English Individualism* (Oxford, 1979); *Marriage and Love in England: Modes of Reproduction, 1300–1840* (Oxford, 1986); *The Culture of Capitalism* (Oxford, 1987).

74 See especially a series of essays by John Morrill, including 'The Church in England

1642–1649' (1982), 'The Religious Context of the English Civil War' (1984), 'The Attack on the Church of England in the Long Parliament' (1985), 'The Ecology of Allegiance in the English Civil Wars' (1987), and 'England's Wars of Religion' (1990), reprinted in Morrill, *The Nature of the English Revolution* (London, 1993).

75   E.g. Steven G. Ellis and Sarah Barber, *Conquest and Union: Fashioning a British State, 1485–1725* (London, 1995); Alexander Grant and Keith Stringer (eds.), *Uniting the Kingdom? The Making of British History* (London, 1995); John Morrill and Brendan Bradshaw (eds.), *The British Problem, c. 1534–1707: State Formation in the Atlantic Archipelago* (London, 1996).

76   Gordon S. Wood, *The Radicalism of the American Revolution* (New York, 1992), pp. 3–92 and *passim*, provided a starting point for a revised account of the American Founding which could easily be integrated with British historiography but was very different from that posited by the older, but still dominant, scenarios of Bernard Bailyn and Jack P. Greene. Each of these, in its own way, explained how the causes of the American Revolution were external to an already exceptionalist America; indeed, that the Revolution was provoked by an affront to homogeneous American exceptionalism. For this argument at length, see chapter 5 above.

77   See chapter 4 above.

78   For one such investigation of transatlantic links, see Mark A. Noll, David W. Bebbington and George A. Rawlyk (eds.), *Evangelicalism: Comparative Studies of Popular Protestantism in North America, the British Isles, and Beyond, 1700–1990* (New York, 1994).

79   Louis Hartz, *The Liberal Tradition in America* (New York, 1955). For some consequences of the weakening of this conceptualization, see chapter 7 below.

80   E.g. N. F. R. Crafts, *British Economic Growth during the Industrial Revolution* (Oxford, 1985).

81   E.g. Jeremy Black, *Convergence or Divergence? Britain and the Continent* (London, 1994).

82   E.g. Anthony Pagden, *Lords of All the World: Ideologies of Empire in Spain, Britain and France, c. 1500 – c. 1800* (New Haven, Conn., 1995).

83   For one among many claims that the Founding Fathers, rightly interpreted, had anticipated the correct answers to modern problems, see John G. West, Jr., *The Politics of Revelation and Reason: Religion and Civic Life in the New Nation* (Lawrence, Kansas, 1996).

84   For one historiographical influence, see the particularly American reading of the significance of the work of E. P. Thompson offered by David Montgomery of Yale University in *Labour History Review*, 59 (1994), pp. 4–5.

85   Charlotte Crabtree and Gary B. Nash, project co-directors, *National Standards for World History* (Los Angeles, 1994).

86   Walter A. McDougall, 'Whose History? Whose Standards?', *Commentary* (May 1995), pp. 36–43, at 41.

87   The title of Conrad Russell's volume *Unrevolutionary England, 1603–1642* (London, 1990) is symptomatic.

88   Lawrence Stone, 'The Revolution over the Revolution', *New York Review of Books* (11 June 1992), pp. 47–52.

89   I have offered answers to Stone's questions elsewhere.

90   For a speculation that 'the common anti-positivism of a "leftist" post modernism and

a "rightist" revisionism might make common cause', see Joyce, 'The end of social history?', p. 81. This chapter is a revised version of my then unpublished paper to which Joyce there refers.

NOTES TO CHAPTER 7

1 Cf. Eckart Kehr (1902–33), *Der Primat der Innenpolitik*, ed. Hans-Ulrich Wehler (Berlin, 1965). Charles Maier has pointed to a movement in German historiography which means that 'After twenty years of *Primat der Innenpolitik*, the *Primat der Aussenpolitik* has returned' with a form of geopolitical determinism: Charles Maier, *The Unmasterable Past: History, Holocaust, and German National Identity* (Cambridge, Mass., 1988), p. 116. In this chapter, I am particularly indebted for an account of the recent German debate to Maier and to Richard J. Evans, *In Hitler's Shadow: West German Historians and the Attempt to Escape from the Nazi Past* (London, 1989).

2 As one of the few available surveys observes, 'Systematic study of the history of the social sciences is a relatively recent academic endeavour, and among these disciplines, historical reflection on the field of political science may well be the least developed': David Easton, John G. Gunnell and Luigi Graziano (eds.), *The Development of Political Science: A Comparative Survey* (London, 1991), pp. 1–2. The editors also recognized that a history like theirs of the development of political science in different countries constituted an implicit challenge to the assumption that the subject in countries in which it had experienced a 'vast growth', especially the USA, 'must necessarily provide the basis for a universal body of knowledge and practices' (p. 7). This line of enquiry nevertheless seems to be at an early stage in that discipline. The editors (two Americans and one visiting professor in America) did not, for example, question the homogeneity of the concept of a 'Western political science' embracing the USA and Western Europe, or reject the possibility of 'a truly universal set of standards', which is the point at issue here.

3 William Maltby, *The Black Legend in England: the development of anti-Spanish sentiment, 1558–1660* (Durham, NC, 1971).

4 This concept was, of course, influential to different degrees on other countries also; but the circumstances of Germany's conquest in 1945 and subsequent re-education make the German case by far the most clearly defined.

5 Norman Davies, *Europe: A History* (Oxford, 1996), pp. 22–5.

6 The United States had its own parochial 'West', normally excused by the adjective 'wild', and not easily interpreted as identifying the rest of the republic with a European inheritance.

7 H. J. Mackinder, *Democratic Ideas and Reality* (London, 1919), p. 154.

8 Henri Massis, *Defence of the West*, trans. F. S. Flint (New York, 1928), pp. 66, 160–62, 224, 235.

9 Oswald Spengler, *The Decline of the West*, trans. Charles Francis Atkinson (2 vols., London, [1926–9]), I, pp. 3, 226, 239, 334; II, p. 305.

10 Winston S. Churchill, *A History of the English-Speaking Peoples* (4 vols., London, 1956–8), I, pp. vii, xiii; IV, p. viii.

11   Davies, *Europe*, pp. 37–8.

12   Hanson W. Baldwin, *Defence of the Western World* (London, [1941]), pp. 75–86, 144.

13   The idea of 'Western Civilization' within US academe was derived from the 'Great Books' curriculum devised at Columbia University in 1921 and adopted at Chicago from 1930.

14   James Farr, John S. Dryzek and Stephen T. Leonard (eds.), *Political Science in History: Research Programs and Political Traditions* (Cambridge, 1995), p. vii. The aim of this book was to explore postbehavioural approaches that make 'history, both as subject and method, central to political science inquiry' (p. 6). Nevertheless, this collection of essays by American authors on the American discipline did not analyse US political science as an historical formation contrasting with other national traditions.

15   Davies, *Europe*, pp. 39–45.

16   Harold James, *A German Identity 1770–1990* (London, 1989), pp. 12–13.

17   Ibid., pp. 40–41, 50–51, 57.

18   Gordon A. Craig, *Germany and the West: The Ambivalent Relationship* (London, 1982), pp. 3–4, 6–7. For Craig's implicit anti-British stance, see pp. 11–12. This way of characterizing 'the Enlightenment' has, of course, now collapsed.

19   Wolfgang J. Mommsen, *Two Centuries of Anglo-German Relations: A Reappraisal* (London, 1984), p. 7.

20   'Whatever became of the *Sonderweg*?' in Richard J. Evans, *Rereading German History: From unification to reunification 1800–1996* (London, 1997), pp. 12–22, at 12–13, 15; Hans-Ulrich Wehler, *Das deutsche Kaiserreich 1871–1918* (Göttingen, 1973), and later work.

21   Ernst A. Breisach's *American Progressive History: An Experiment in Modernization* (Chicago, 1993) was the first work to locate this US school of thought from the early 1900s to the 1940s in its relation to comparable developments in Europe. For recent essays on US–German relations, see David E. Barclay and Elizabeth Glaser-Schmidt (eds.), *Transatlantic Images and Perceptions: Germany and America since 1776* (Cambridge, 1997).

22   See chapter 6.

23   V. Norskov Olsen, *John Foxe and the Elizabethan Church* (Berkeley, 1973); Paul Christianson, *Reformers and Babylon: English Apocalyptic Visions from the Reformation to the Eve of the Civil War* (Toronto, 1978); Richard Bauckham (ed.), *Tudor Apocalypse* (Abingdon, 1978); Katherine Firth, *The Apocalyptic Tradition in Reformation Britain, 1530–1645* (Oxford, 1979).

24   Nicholas Phillipson, *Hume* (London, 1989); Philip Hicks, *Neo-classical History and English Culture: from Clarendon to Hume* (London, 1996); Karen O'Brien, *Narratives of Enlightenment: cosmopolitan history from Voltaire to Gibbon* (Cambridge, 1997).

25   Thomas Gordon (trans. and intro.), *The Works of Tacitus* (2 vols., London, 1728); Frank M. Turner, 'British Politics and the Demise of the Roman Republic: 1700–1939', *Historical Journal*, 29 (1986), pp. 577–99; Howard D. Weinbrot, 'Politics, Taste, and National Identity: Some Uses of Tacitism in Eighteenth-Century Britain' in T. J. Luce and A. J. Woodman (eds.), *Tacitus and the Tacitean Tradition* (Princeton, 1993).

26   Anglo-German contacts in this period are under-explored. Studies of eighteenth-century influences largely focus on diplomatic relations, e.g. Adolf M. Birke, *England und Hannover* (Berlin, 1986); Uriel Dann, *Hanover and Great Britain 1740–1760: diplomacy and survival* (1986; trans., Leicester, 1991).

27 For England and Germany as 'natural allies', see, however, Adolf M. Birke, *Britain and Germany: Historical Patterns of a Relationship* (London, 1987).

28 The major contacts were among reformers, but even here the links were not as strong as might have been expected: Henry Pelling, *America and the British Left from Bright to Bevan* (London, 1956); Jon Roper, *Democracy and its Critics: Anglo-American democratic thought in the nineteenth century* (London, 1989).

29 Max Beloff, 'The Special Relationship: an Anglo-American Myth', in Martin Gilbert (ed.), *A Century of Conflict 1850–1950: Essays for A. J. P. Taylor* (London, 1966), pp. 151–71. Beloff stressed residual Anglo-American dissimilarities and made no use of a concept of 'the West', a concept challenged in this chapter.

30 Lionel Morris Gelber, *The Rise of Anglo-American friendship: a study in world politics, 1898–1906* (Oxford, 1938).

31 For studies of points of contact, see Adolf M. Birke and Kurt Kluxen (eds.), *Viktorianisches England in Deutscher Perspektive* (Munich, 1983); Adolf Birke (ed.), *Church, State and Society in the 19th Century: An Anglo-German Comparison*, Prince Albert Studies 2 (Munich, 1984); A. M. Birke and K. Kluxen (eds.), *Deutscher und Britischer Parliamentarismus/British and German Parliamentarism* (Munich, 1985).

32 For German Anglophilia in the nineteenth century, see James, *A German Identity*, pp. 21–5; Paul Kennedy, *The Rise of Anglo-German Antagonism 1860–1914* (London, 1980).

33 Charles E. McClelland, *The German Historians and England: A Study in Nineteenth-Century Views* (Cambridge, 1971); J. W. Burrow, *A Liberal Descent: Victorian Historians and the English Past* (Cambridge, 1981); Benedikt Stuchtey and Peter Wende (eds.), *British and German Historiography 1750–1950: Traditions, Perceptions, and Transfers* (Oxford, 2000), especially the editors' Introduction, 'Towards a Comparative History of Anglo-German Historiographical Traditions and Transfers'.

34 Hedva Ben-Israel, *English Historians on the French Revolution* (Cambridge, 1968); Burrow, *A Liberal Descent*.

35 By contrast, those British historians who sought to build bridges with developments in France faced an uphill struggle, like Peter Laslett, in his alliance with French demography, or Peter Burke, advocating the example of the *Annales* school: see Peter Burke, *The French Historical Revolution: The Annales School, 1929–89* (Cambridge, 1990).

36 For an over-optimistic celebration of similarities, see Douglas Johnson, François Crouzet and François Bédarida (eds.), *Britain and France: ten centuries* (London, 1980). Bédarida's 'Postface' (pp. 361–4), however, more candidly confesses profound differences.

37 It has been established that Jean Monnet, often hailed as the father of European integration, received money from the USA's Central Intelligence Agency to promote that end: see Lord Beloff, *Britain and European Union: Dialogue of the Deaf* (London, 1996), pp. 122–6, citing (p. 123 n. 17) research by Richard J. Aldrich; and Max Beloff, *The United States and the Unity of Europe* (Washington and London, 1963).

38 See chapter 6 above.

39 Wolfgang J. Mommsen, *Britain and Germany 1800 to 1914: Two Developmental Paths Towards Industrial Society* (London, 1985), pp. 3, 7, 20. Mommsen objected to Paul Kennedy's *The Rise of Anglo-German Antagonism, 1860–1914* for making things 'appear worse than they were merely because Anglo-German relations are here treated in relative isolation from developments in the rest of Europe', p. 32.

40   James Joll, *National Histories and National Historians: Some German and English Views of the Past* (London, 1984), pp. 3–6, 14–15.

41   For these innovations interpreted in the light of Anglo-American history, see chapter 6, section IV above.

42   For a theoretical case for the counterfactual, see Niall Ferguson, 'Introduction', in Ferguson (ed.), *Virtual History: Alternatives and Counterfactuals* (London, 1997). Such arguments are almost inconceivable in the USA outside the realm of econometric economic history. Even in this technical area the conclusions of counterfactual analysis were resisted within America with a strange bitterness.

43   Shmuel N. Eisenstadt, *Japanese Civilization: a comparative view* (Chicago, 1996). Eisenstadt observes a source of fascination with Japan in Europe and the USA: 'Japan's distinctiveness or peculiarity was very soon perceived to reside, not in its being totally different from Europe or the United States, but in its combining such great differences with far-reaching similarities to the West.' Eisenstadt rightly observes that the resistance of Japan to analytical assimilation calls for a re-examination of 'some of the most basic assumptions of Western civilization' (pp. 1–4). Similar lessons might have been learned from an examination of German society but for the priority understandably given to moral condemnation after the events of the early twentieth century.

44   See chapter 2 above.

45   This interpretation finds room for a much more corporatist and collectivist reading of the USA, a culture in which the pressure of the community or peer group on the individual is heavy.

46   Byron Shafer (ed.), *Is American Different? A New Look at American Exceptionalism* (Oxford, 1991); Michael Kammen, 'The Problem of American Exceptionalism: A Reconsideration', *American Quarterly*, 45 (March, 1993), pp. 1–43; for a recent exceptionalist restatement, Jon Butler, *Becoming America: the Revolution before 1776* (Cambridge, Mass., 2000).

47   Glenn Burgess, *Absolute Monarchy and the Stuart Constitution* (New Haven, 1996).

48   Michael J. Braddick, *The nerves of state: taxation and the financing of the English state, 1558–1714* (Manchester, 1996).

49   R. R. Palmer, *The Age of the Democratic Revolution* (2 vols., Princeton, 1959–64).

50   Gerhard A. Ritter, *Parlament und Demokratie in Grossbritannien* (Göttingen, 1973).

51   Clark, *English Society 1660–1832*, ch. 5.

52   E. J. Hobsbawm, *Industry and Empire* (Harmondsworth, 1968).

53   See chapter 1 above.

54   E. A. Wrigley, *People, Cities and Wealth: The Transformation of Traditional Society* (Oxford, 1987), chapter 2, 'The Classical Economists and the Industrial Revolution'; M. J. Daunton, *Progress and Poverty: An Economic and Social History of Britain 1700–1850* (Oxford, 1995), pp. 1–10.

55   P. K. O'Brien and Calgar Keyder, *Economic Growth in Britain and France, 1780–1914: two paths to the twentieth century* (London, 1978); N. F. R. Crafts, *British Economic Growth during the Industrial Revolution* (Oxford, 1985).

56   Harold Perkin, *The Origins of Modern English Society 1780–1880* (London, 1969); idem, *The Rise of Professional Society: England since 1880* (London, 1989); idem, *The Third Revolution: professional elites in the modern world* (London, 1996); P. J. Corfield, *Power and the professions in Britain, 1700–1850* (London, 1995).

57 James, *A German Identity*, p. 2.

58 Ibid., p. 3. James argued for the repetition of a similar cycle in German identities after 1945.

59 This development dates especially from Gareth Stedman Jones, *Languages of Class: studies in English working class history, 1832–1982* (Cambridge, 1983).

60 Günther Lottes, 'Hegels Schrift über die Reformbill im Kontext des Deutschen Diskurses über Englands Verfassung im 19. Jahrhundert', in *Politik und Geschichte*, Beiheft 35 (Bonn, 1995), pp. 151–74.

61 This had been partly anticipated. Fichte's programme of a new social elite with a new national sensibility, fostered by state education, was initially set forth in Berlin in 1808 in response to the collapse of Germany's old elites, the military defeat and occupation of Prussia by the armies of revolutionary France: James, *A German Identity*, pp. 42–4. But Prussia, and its elites, survived Napoleon.

62 Perkin, *Origins of Modern British Society*.

63 For a comparative study of social reform in Edwardian Britain and Wilhelmine Germany, see Gerhard A. Ritter, *Sozialversicherung in Deutschland und England* (Munich, 1983).

64 Hagen Schulze, *Germany: A New History*, trans. Deborah Lucas Schneider (Cambridge, Mass., 1998), pp. viii–ix, 1–2, 16–17.

65 David Blackbourn and Geoff Eley, *The Peculiarities of German History: Bourgeois Society and Politics in Nineteenth-Century Germany* (Oxford, 1984), p. 12. This is a revised version of a work originally published as *Mythen Deutscher Geschichtsschreibung. Die gescheiterte bürgerliche Revolution von 1848* (Frankfurt am Main, 1980), and the authors' cautious doubts about the use made of the English model derive from work on English history at a very early stage in the process of reinterpretation discussed here. Blackbourn's and Eley's remarks now need to be carried further than could be appreciated in 1980.

66 Blackbourn and Eley, *Peculiarities of German History*, pp. 52–3, noted revisionist work to 1983 which had constituted a 'direct assault' on the received account of the French Revolution and a 'slow attrition' of the similar model of the 'English Revolution', but inferred only that 'This paradox of... the negative invocation of a concept whose positive uses have fallen into disrepute' should be 'kept in mind'; they did not think through the implications of this revision.

67 A scholarly and important book, Horst Dippel's *Germany and the American Revolution 1770–1800: A sociohistorical investigation of late eighteenth-century political thinking* (Chapel Hill, NC, 1977) argued the opposite, but did not compare the impact of the American Revolution on Germany with its impact on France. It acknowledged the influence of R. R. Palmer's *The Age of the Democratic Revolution*, a work whose presentist and parochially American explanatory framework is now in question (hence post-Revolutionary America appears in Dippel's pages as 'a Bourgeois Utopia', p. 307). Dippel throughout posited an ideal-typical 'bourgeoisie' who were 'bound to welcome any event that seemed to work toward' bourgeois ideology (p. 357). For a different view, see Rodney Atwood, *The Hessians: Mercenaries from Hessen-Kassel in the American Revolution* (Cambridge, 1980); for the French case, Durand Echeverria, *Mirage in the West: A history of the French image of American society to 1815* (Princeton, 1957).

68 Blackbourn and Eley, *Peculiarities of German History*, p. 3.

69 James, *A German Identity*, pp. 91–103.

70 For the substantial absence of ethnic nationalism in nineteenth-century England, see chapter 3 above.

71 J. R. Seeley, *The Expansion of England* (London, 1888), p. 11, quoted in Joll, *National Histories*, p. 18.

72 J. A. Froude, quoted in J. W. Burrow, *A Liberal Descent: Victorian Historians and the English Past* (Cambridge, 1981), p. 238.

73 For a review of these arguments, see Maier, *Unmasterable Past*, pp. 115–20.

74 The Whiggish vision of England as 'our island story' had assumed the opposite, that the English Channel and North Sea were natural defences. Such a story unconsciously assumed English naval supremacy. It also took for granted that the non-intervention of the military in the state's internal affairs was an international norm.

75 Niall Ferguson reminds me that the 'Fischer thesis' could be read in Germany as a condemnation of the alliance between a Junker officer class and reactionary industrialists, and so as a confirmation of a *Sonderweg*.

76 Klaus Hildebrand, *Reich–Nation State–Great Power. Reflections on German Foreign Policy 1871–1945* (London, 1995), p. 11.

77 John M. Hobson, *The Wealth of States: A Comparative Sociology of International Economic and Political Change* (Cambridge, 1997), pp. 171, 202.

78 Margaret Lavinia Anderson and Kenneth Barkin, 'The Myth of the Puttkamer Purge and the Reality of the *Kulturkampf*: Some Reflections on the Historiography of Imperial Germany', *Journal of Modern History*, 54 (1982), pp. 647–86.

79 Maurizio Viroli, *For Love of Country: An Essay on Patriotism and Nationalism* (Oxford, 1995), pp. 111–39. Viroli discerned a 'tendency to disconnect patriotism and liberty' from Herder and Schlegel onwards, but argued that they did not speak for other libertarian nationalists like Fichte. Viroli added: 'Fichte introduced an important change in the language of patriotism: love of country is no longer *caritas* but fondness for one's own uniqueness as a people no longer understood as a community of free citizens, but as a community of individuals who share a culture and are capable of spiritual freedom' (p. 135). His novelty would have seemed less plausible had Fichte been compared with a more representative sample of eighteenth-century Englishmen.

80 P. K. O'Brien and P. A. Hunt, 'The Rise of a Fiscal State in England, 1485–1815', *Historical Research*, 66 (1993), pp. 129–76; Michael J. Braddick, *State Formation in Early Modern England* c. 1550–1700 (Cambridge, 2000).

81 James J. Sheehan, *German History, 1770–1866* (Oxford, 1989); cf. Richard J. Evans's critique of Thomas Nipperdey's *Deutsche Geschichte* [1800–1918] (3 vols., Munich, 1983–92) for implying the natural or inevitable nature of the *kleindeutsch* outcome, and apologetic stance on German foreign policy in 1914: Evans, *Rereading German History*, pp. 23–43, at 27, 29–31.

82 For the repudiation by post-war German historiography of its earlier characteristic methodologies, and for important analogies with the work of Anglophone historians of ideas like J. G. A. Pocock and Quentin Skinner, see Melvin Richter, *The History of Political and Social Concepts: A Critical Introduction* (New York, 1995).

83 For figures, see Kenneth Barkin, 'Germany and England: Economic Inequality', *Tel Aviv Jahrbuch für deutsche Geschichte*, 16 (1987), pp. 200–11. Only in Prussia east of the Elbe were there areas of large estates, but even here concentrations fell well below the norms

in England and Scotland.

84 Blackbourn and Eley, *Peculiarities of German History*, p. 6; Maier, *Unmasterable Past*, pp. 102–20; Richard J. Evans, 'The Myth of Germany's Missing Revolution', in Evans, *Rethinking German History: Nineteenth-Century Germany and the Origins of the Third Reich* (London, 1987), pp. 93–122. Insightful and scholarly works like these still make strikingly little reference to the significance of the discrediting of the idea of transformative revolution in the British case.

85 Anderson and Barkin, 'Myth of the Puttkamer Purge', pp. 674–5. For a survey of the conflict between the ideas of *Agrar-* and *Industriestaat*, see Kenneth D. Barkin, *The Controversy over German Industrialization 1890–1902* (Chicago, 1970).

86 Maier, *Unmasterable Past*, p. 104.

87 Blackbourn and Eley, *Peculiarities of German History*, p. 7. The authors proposed 'a less abject bourgeois role in modern German history' (p. 13) but did not fundamentally challenge the terms of the debate. They merely argued that 'The bourgeoisie characteristically became the dominant class in European countries (which is not the same as the ruling class) through other than heroic means or open political action', and that in the nineteenth century Germany did see something like a bourgeois revolution, understood in a more extensive sense than in traditional Marxist historiography (p. 16; cf. pp. 144, 286–7).

88 James, *A German Identity*, p. 210–18. James has pointed to the surprisingly late emergence in Germany of the claim that Germany had had no bourgeois revolution, and explained it as 'party propaganda' of the 1890s. Until then, he suggests, Germans more usually said that Germany was less aristocratic and more meritocratic than England because the German bureaucracy mattered more.

89 This thesis was set out combatively, at an early stage of the debate, in J. C. D. Clark, *Revolution and Rebellion: state and society in England in the seventeenth and eighteenth centuries* (Cambridge, 1986).

90 Reba Soffer, *Discipline and Power: the university, history and the making of an English elite, 1870–1930* (Stanford, 1994); Peter R. H. Slee, *Learning and a Liberal Education: the study of modern history in the universities of Oxford, Cambridge and Manchester, 1800–1914* (Manchester, 1986); Adrian Wooldridge, *Measuring the Mind: Educational Theory and Psychology in England* c. 1860 – c. 1990 (Cambridge, 1994); Brian Harrison (ed.), *History of the University of Oxford*, VIII, *The Twentieth Century* (Oxford, 1994).

91 Michael Bentley, *Politics without Democracy 1815–1914* (London, 1985).

92 Evans, *In Hitler's Shadow*, p. 115.

93 Maier, *Unmasterable Past*, p. 115. Patrick O'Brien has suggested that the key determinant was not the extent of the franchise but the balance struck between employer and employee by labour legislation: in this respect, Britain industrialized within a legal nexus which greatly favoured the employer.

94 Rohan Butler, *The Roots of National Socialism, 1783–1933* (London, 1941) gave some attention to Luther and princely absolutism but began his detailed account of 'national pantheism' with Herder, and traced the 'exaltation of the heroic leader' to Fichte. Yet even in 1941, Butler recorded Herder's claim in *Ideen zur Philosophie der Geschichte der Menschheit* (1829): 'Compare England with Germany: the English are Germans, and even in the latest times the Germans have led the way for the English in the greatest things' (p. 10). Butler dated German Anglophobia to Treitschke.

95 Alan Bullock, *Hitler: a study in tyranny* (London, 1952).

96 Hagen Schulze, in idem (ed.), *Nation-Building in Central Europe* (Leamington Spa, 1987), pp. 1–2.

97 A. J. P. Taylor, *The Course of German History: A survey of the development of Germany since 1815* (London, 1945); idem, *The Origins of the Second World War* (London, 1961); Sir John Wheeler-Bennett, *Munich: Prologue to Tragedy* (London, 1948); idem, *The Nemesis of Power: The German Army in Politics, 1918–1945* (London, 1953).

98 Evans, *Rereading German History*, pp. 29–31.

99 This was clear from such classic studies as G. A. Craig, *The Politics of the Prussian Army 1640–1945* (Oxford, 1955) and F. L. Carsten, *Princes and Parliaments in Germany, from the 15th to 18th Centuries* (Oxford, 1959).

100 G. E. Aylmer, *The King's Servants: the civil service of Charles I, 1625–1642* (London, 1974); idem, *The State's Servants: the civil service of the English Republic, 1649–1660* (London, 1973). There are few other studies. John Brewer, *The Sinews of Power: War, Money and the English State, 1688–1783* (London, 1989) argued for a strong bureaucracy in England but did not compare it with bureaucracies in other European states.

101 E.g. Hagen Schulze, *The Course of German Nationalism: from Frederick the Great to Bismarck, 1763–1867* (1985; trans. Sarah Hanbury-Tenison, Cambridge, 1991).

102 Sir Geoffrey Elton, 'English National Self-Consciousness and the Parliament in the Sixteenth Century', in Elton, *Studies in Tudor and Stuart Politics and Government*, IV (Cambridge, 1992), pp. 131–43.

103 Butler, *Roots of National Socialism*, p. 287.

104 Arno J. Mayer, *The Persistence of the Old Regime: Europe to the Great War* (London, 1981). When first published, this book seemed an isolated protest and received limited recognition. It now relates to a substantial historiography on the English case.

105 For German admiration of US models in the twentieth century, see James, *A German Identity*, pp. 26–8.

106 Ernst Breisach drew attention to the prominence in his text of the terms 'modernity' and 'modernization', but warned that 'their vagueness can be only partially alleviated': *American Progressive History*, p. 2.

107 The key text was Crane Brinton (1898–1968), *The Anatomy of Revolution* (New York, 1938; revised edns., 1952, 1965). A notable work in the same idiom was Barrington Moore, Jr. (1913–), *Social Origins of Dictatorship and Democracy* (Boston, 1966), which offered three paths of social development from the pre-industrial to the modern: 'the bourgeois revolutions leading to capitalist democracy, the abortive bourgeois revolutions leading to fascism, and the peasant revolutions leading to communism' (1967 edn., p. xvii). If these were indeed the options, it is unsurprising that almost all historians chose to celebrate the first. Blackbourn and Eley, *Peculiarities of German History*, recorded (pp. 65–66 n.): 'One of the most striking features of this theoretical tradition (which probably reached its climax in the mid 1960s) was the self-confident willingness to generalize "scientifically" about the nature of politics and political systems. But with this went a curiously naive belief in the solidity and permanence of the currently existing historical knowledge.' That historical knowledge has, since the early 1980s, been fundamentally revised.

108 For studies of these academic émigrés, see Blackbourn and Eley, *Peculiarities of German History*, p. 67 n.; Donald Fleming and Bernard Bailyn (eds.), *The Intellectual Migration:*

Europe and America, 1930–1960 (Cambridge, Mass., 1969); Robert C. Bannister, 'Principle, politics and profession: American sociologists and fascism 1930–1950', in Stephen Turner and Dirk Käsler (eds.), *Sociology responds to Fascism* (London, 1992); Marcus Lutter, Ernst C. Stiefel and Michael H. Hoeflich (eds.), *Der Einfluss deutscher Emigranten auf die Rechtsentwicklung in den USA und in Deutschland* (Tübingen, 1993). The models favoured by émigrés to the USA contrast with the idealization of the English model of émigrés who made their home in England, such as (earlier) the Pole Lewis Namier, or from the 1930s Geoffrey Elton, Michael Howard, Nikolaus Pevsner, Erwin Panofsky, Karl Popper or Walter Ullmann. This is not a theme that has yet been focused on in scholarly studies like Marion Berghahn, *German-Jewish Refugees in England: the Ambiguities of Assimilation* (London, 1984); Gerhard Hirschfeld (ed.), *Exile in Great Britain: Refugees from Hitler's Germany* (Leamington Spa, 1984). A. J. Sherman, *Island Refuge: Britain and Refugees from the Third Reich 1933–1939* (1973; 2nd edn., London, 1994), noted: 'The generosity of British consular officials [in issuing visas], known to the Foreign Office but never publicised, contrasts vividly with the rigid, unsympathetic administration by American consuls of their country's immigration regulations' (p. 7).

109 Such projects are effectively normative in so far as they are unthinking. Evidence of their unreflective quality is the paucity and inadequacy of studies like Edward G. McGrath (ed.), *Is American Democracy Exportable?* (Beverly Hills, 1968). In that volume, as so often, 'democratization' and 'modernization' were treated as synonymous terms.

110 For an argument that 'liberal democracy has a special need for political science... Not any kind of political science, however, can answer this need. It must be a political science that is conscious of the intellectual niche potentially open to it in modern society and that is willing to engage in a constructive enterprise in behalf of liberal democracy', see James W. Ceaser, *Liberal Democracy and Political Science* (Baltimore, 1990), p. 2. Ceaser diagnosed a 'renaissance of the study of values and justice in the discipline' of American political science, p. 4.

111 Allan Bloom, in Bloom (ed.), *Confronting the Constitution: the challenge to Locke, Montesquieu, Jefferson and the Federalists from Utilitarianism, Historicism, Marxism, Freudianism, Pragmatism, Essentialism...* (Washington, 1990), p. 1. Bloom paid tribute to Leo Strauss, a refugee from Nazism: 'The American regime was friendly to him as Jew and philosopher, and, of course, the protections of these two aspects of his being were related in the rational universality of liberal principles. He had had experience, both theoretical and practical, of the German critique of those principles, and he unhesitatingly, like many refugees, preferred not the mystifying old cultures, however splendid, but a regime that in its founding faced the issues of reason and revelation' (p. 6). Bloom's reaction compares closely with Peter Gay's celebratory review of Roy Porter's celebratory book *Enlightenment* (London, 2000) in *The Times Literary Supplement* (6 October 2000), pp. 4–6.

112 This purposefulness has survived the fragmentation of positivism recorded in Peter Novick's *That Noble Dream: The 'Objectivity Question' and the American Historical Profession* (Cambridge, 1988).

113 John H. Langbein, 'The Influence of the German Emigrés on American Law: The Curious Case of Civil and Criminal Procedure' in Lutter, Stiefel and Hoeflich (eds.),

Der Einfluss deutscher Emigranten, pp. 321–32, for the extreme difficulty of reforming US legal practice on the basis of European example.

114 Bernard Crick, *The American Science of Politics* (London, 1959), pp. v–vi.

115 Breisach, *American Progressive History*, pp. 3–4. For a general survey, see Ernst Breisach, *Historiography: Ancient, Mediaeval, & Modern* (Chicago, 1983), pp. 386–95, 'Historiography as a Mirror of Postwar America', which nevertheless expresses a more approving interpretation than that advanced here.

116 Jack Hayward, 'Cultural and contextual constraints upon the development of political science in Great Britain', in Easton, Gunnell and Graziano (eds.), *Development of Political Science*, pp. 93–107, at 96. Hayward argued that British amateurism and governmental secrecy ultimately produced 'insularity' in British political science (p. 104).

117 Hans Kastendieck, 'Political development and political science in West Germany', in Easton, Gunnell and Graziano (eds.), *Development of Political Science*, pp. 108–26, contends that 'West German political science was stimulated but not imposed from abroad' (p. 118).

118 Kastendieck, ibid., p. 123.

119 Crick, *American Science of Politics*, p. xiii.

120 For which, see Jennifer Platt, *A History of Sociological Research Methods in America 1920–1960* (Cambridge, 1996). This was 'a period during which American sociology became dominant quantitatively and qualitatively; since then other national sociologies have grown, but the directions in which they have moved cannot be understood without understanding what happened in America, even if they have often reacted against American influence in general, as well as particular American tendencies. Especially important in this has been the flow of migration created by Hitler and the Second World War, which led many European sociologists to the USA... After the war, both the contacts which this established and the American political position in postwar Europe had considerable influence on European developments' (p. 2).

121 Dorothy Ross, *The Origins of American Social Science* (Cambridge, 1991), pp. xiii–xiv. American political science could be positively hostile to the sort of history which it saw as an alternative to itself, e.g. 'Decline into Historicism' in David Easton, *The Political System: An Inquiry into the State of Political Science* (New York, 1953), pp. 234–7. Easton had argued that 'the development of a systematic theory [in political science] will normally be related to the moral views of the theorist' (p. 232); he condemned 'historicism' as the claim that 'all ideas, both moral and causal, are purely relative' (p. 235).

122 Ross, *Origins of American Social Science*, pp. xiii–xvii, 471.

123 Crick, *American Science of Politics*, p. xv. For a critique of the related American tradition of political theory see J. G. A. Pocock, 'Political Theory, History and Myth: A Salute to John Gunnell', in John S. Nelson (ed.), *Tradition, Interpretation and Science: Political Theory in the American Academy* (Albany, NY, 1986), pp. 21–42.

124 For the apparent paradox that 'Japan may become the epitome of a post-modern civilization without ever having been a fully modern one', see Eisenstadt, *Japanese Civilization*, p. 6.

125 Especially with the work of François Furet, e.g. François Furet and Denis Richet, *La Révolution* (Paris, 1965), trans. Stephen Hardman as *The French Revolution* (London, 1970); Furet, *Penser la Révolution Française* (Paris, 1978), trans. Elborg Forster as

Interpreting the French Revolution (Cambridge, 1981).

126 Crick, *American Science of Politics*, p. 236.

127 One American historian explained how the American past nourished a belief 'that an elaborate or outspoken political theory was superfluous for us, on the simple ground that we already possessed a theory. Explicit political philosophy has seemed unnecessary precisely because our history and institutions have seemed to contain an implicit political philosophy adequate to all our needs. We have drawn values out of "facts"': Daniel J. Boorstin, *The Genius of American Politics* (Chicago, 1953), p. 133.

128 Easton, Gunnell and Graziano (eds.), *Development of Political Science*, p. 10.

129 The reluctance of modern English to accord capital letters to nouns indicates the unique significance as transformative events accorded to the Reformation, the Civil War, the Glorious Revolution, the Founding, the Enlightenment and the Industrial Revolution. The capitals are intended to indicate categories that are beyond historical questioning. Such categories are, for that reason, particularly vulnerable.

130 A rare exception, but a preliminary study, was Hans Sperber and Travis Trittschuh, *American Political Terms: an Historical Dictionary* (Detroit, 1962). The neglect of this book, and the absence of others like it, is revealing. Daniel T. Rodgers, *Contested Truths: Keywords in American Politics since Independence* (New York, 1987) shades into a general survey of central aspects of American political thought.

131 Jürgen Habermas, 'Neoconservative Culture Criticism in the United States and West Germany: An Intellectual Movement in Two Political Cultures', trans. Russell A. Berman, *Telos*, 56 (1983), pp. 75–89, reprinted in Richard J. Bernstein, *Habermas and Modernity* (Cambridge, Mass., 1985), pp. 78–94, at 93; quoted in Maier, *Unmasterable Past*, pp. 39–40; Evans, *In Hitler's Shadow*, p. 112.

132 Peter Gay, *The Enlightenment* (2 vols., London, 1967–70); Roy Porter and Mikulás Teich (eds.), *The Enlightenment in National Context* (Cambridge, 1981).

133 'Beyond the *Historikerstreit*' in Evans, *Rethinking German History*, pp. 221–4.

134 In the case of the USA, three episodes have been often alleged by US historians: the treatment of Native Americans, black slavery, and abortion. The merits of these claims are not discussed here.

135 Fritz Fischer, *Griff nach der Weltmacht: Die Kriegszielpolitik des Kaiserlichen Deutschland, 1914/18* (Düsseldorf, 1961), translated as *Germany's Aims in the First World War* (New York, 1967); idem, *Krieg der Illusionen. Die Deutsche Politik von 1911 bis 1914* (Düsseldorf, 1969). For this, see John A. Moses, *The Politics of Illusion: The Fischer Controversy in German Historiography* (London, 1975).

136 Ernst Nolte, *Der Faschismus in seiner Epoche: die Action Française, der Italienische Faschismus, der Nationalsozialismus* (Munich, 1963), translated as *Three Faces of Fascism* (London, 1965); idem, *Der Europäische Bürgerkrieg 1917–1945: Nationalsozialismus und Bolschewismus* (Berlin, 1989). For this controversy, see Maier, *The Unmasterable Past*; Evans, *In Hitler's Shadow*.

137 Daniel Goldhagen, *Hitler's Willing Executioners: Ordinary Germans and the Holocaust* (New York, 1996).

138 See chapter 6 above.

139 For one such comparative study, especially of social-anthropological, economic and demographic evidence, see Alan Macfarlane, *The Savage Wars of Peace: England, Japan and the Malthusian Trap* (Oxford, 1997).

NOTES TO CONCLUSION

1   I take this to be a central theme of a courageously innovative work, Raphael Samuel, *Theatres of Memory* (2 vols., London, 1994–7).
2   George Orwell, *Nineteen Eighty-Four* (Harmondsworth, 1987), pp. 30–31, 126, 35, 62, 76.
3   John Milton, *Paradise Lost* (1667), Book xii, lines 645–9.
4   W. B. Gallie, *Philosophy and the Historical Understanding* (2nd edn., New York, 1964), pp. 40–41, 72, 87–91, 125.
5   The tension between the counterfactual and the contingent is present in much recent historical writing which seeks to dissolve the old teleologies, and it is a tension as yet unresolved either in historical method or in the substance of the historical story.

INDEX

150, 155–6, 167–8, 207–8, 222, 262
revolution, 29, 33–58, 116, 118, 122, 125, 146–8, 154, 191, 254, 264–5
Rhodes, Cecil, 225
Ricardo, David, 119, 137, 139, 232, 300
Robertson, John M., 95
Robbins, Keith, 83
Rome, ancient, 60, 76, 81, 235
Romilly, Sir Samuel, 127
Rosenberg, Hans, 242
Rousseau, Jean Jacques, 8–9
Russell, Conrad, 64, 148, 214
Russia, 11–12, 71, 99, 220, 237
Russian Revolution, 36

S
Samuel, Raphael, 257
Santayana, George, 24
Schochet, Gordon, 64
Schulze, Hagen, 235
Schwoerer, Lois, 64
Scientific Revolution, 16, 36, 205
Scotland, Scots, 23–5, 31, 62–4, 69–70, 72, 77–8, 80, 83–5, 89–93, 98, 100–1, 105–8, 120, 150, 153, 190, 194, 196, 207, 289–90
Scott, Hugh, 92
Scott, Sir Walter, 113
secularization, 4, 6, 8, 11, 13, 26, 62, 66, 100, 125, 183–4, 200
Seeley, J. R., 237–8
Serle, Ambrose, 159
Service of Nine Lessons and Carols, 18
Seven Years' War, 44, 70–1, 158, 164, 170, 179, 184–5
Shy, John, 162
Sidmouth, lord, 132
Sidney, Algernon, 138
Sigerson, George, 101
Simond, Louis, 124–5
Sinn Fein, 107
Six Acts (1819), 130
Skinner, Quentin, 65, 201
slavery, 9, 93–5, 132, 170, 184, 186–8, 283
Smith, Anthony, 66
Snow, Vernon, 36
social reform, 5, 18

social sciences, x, 29, 33–58, 189, 202–3, 221, 236, 323
socialism, 28, 31, 88, 110, 136–45, 209, 233, 250
society, concept of, 231
Socinianism, 145
sociology, 32, 64, 76, 218, 226, 236, 246–7, 251–2, 280, 309, 324
Somersett's Case (1772), 186
Sonderweg, 222, 226–7, 231, 234–6, 241–3, 253–5
Spain, 66, 78–9, 99, 148, 166, 187, 219, 237
'special relationship', 32, 225, 234, 241
Spence, Thomas, 135–6, 138
Spengler, Oswald, 219–20
Sperander, 42
stadial theory, x, 8, 10, 15–17, 20, 26, 29–30, 39, 53, 102, 116, 207, 228–9, 242, 246–7, 251, 260
Stamp Act, 156–7, 160, 162, 169–71, 187
state formation, 60–5, 68–70, 75–8, 80, 93, 148–51, 207, 228–30, 232, 239–41
Stone, Lawrence, x, 34–5, 51–4, 67–9, 203, 207–8, 214
Stormont, lord, 112
Strauss, Leo, 198–201, 214, 324
Stuart, Charles Edward, 302
Stuart, Sir James, 129
symbols, significance of, 8, 18–20, 22
Stürmer, Michael, 252
Synge, J. M., 101

T
Tacitus, 224
Thatcher, Margaret, 234
'Third World', 9, 16
Thirty Years' War, 230
Thomas, William, 125
Thompson, Thomas Peronnet, 300
tithes, 119, 121, 124, 294
Tocqueville, Alexis de, 224
Tooke, Horne, 128
Tories, Toryism, 70, 91, 122, 125, 134, 151, 178, 213
Townshend, Charles, 162–3, 168, 171
tradition, xi, 10, 15, 17–20, 30, 33, 47, 59, 69, 222